*The Defence of Canada*

# THE
# DEFENCE
## OF
# CANADA

*In the Arms of the Empire*

GWYNNE DYER

*and*

TINA VILJOEN

M&S

A Peter Livingston Book
*Canadian Cataloguing in Publication Data*
Dyer, Gwynne
   The defence of Canada

Based on the NFB/CBC television series: Defence of Canada.
Partial contents: v. 1. In the arms of the Empire, 1760-1939.
Includes bibliographical references.
ISBN 0-7710-2975-6

1. Canada – Military policy.   2. Canada – Defenses.
3. Canada – Military relations – United States.
4. United States – Military relations – Canada.
5. Canada – Military relations – Great Britain.
6. Great Britain – Military relations – Canada.
I. Viljoen, Tina, 1947–     . II. Title.

UA600.D8 1989     355'.0335'71     C89-094820-8


Printed and bound in Canada
Text design by Linda Gustafson

McClelland & Stewart Inc.
*The Canadian Publishers*
481 University Avenue
Toronto, Ontario
M5G 2E9

# Contents

|  | Introduction | 7 |
|---|---|---|
|  | Acknowledgements | 17 |
| 1. | "Canada Must Be Demolished!" | 21 |
| 2. | Invasion and Occupation | 37 |
| 3. | A Conditional State | 54 |
| 4. | Unfinished Business | 67 |
| 5. | 1837 | 89 |
| 6. | Fifty-four Forty or Fight | 110 |
| 7. | Drifting Toward Commitment | 135 |
| 8. | Just A Little Precedent | 157 |
| 9. | "This Conclusion Was Not Discussed with Canada . . ." | 174 |
| 10. | A Long Way from Home | 204 |
| 11. | The Great Crusade | 233 |
| 12. | A Country Divided | 263 |
| 13. | The Fireproof House | 294 |
| 14. | Descent into War | 315 |
|  | Picture Credits | 343 |
|  | Bibliography | 346 |
|  | Index | 357 |

*To Evan, Melissa, and Owen*

# *Introduction*

[A neutral state] is a nation beyond others . . . fit and free to do
what is honest and truly serviceable for the peace of the world.
U.S. President Woodrow Wilson, "Appeal for Neutrality"
August 1914

This book has grown out of a television series of the same name that we
made in 1984-86. Even the television series was not our own idea, to be
honest: the CBC suggested it to us as a natural sequel to the National Film
Board series *War* – a sort of case study applying the arguments and perspectives of that series to the particular case of Canada. And although we
eventually agreed to do the *Defence of Canada* series as an NFB-CBC co-
production, we were not enormously enthused about it at first, because
Canada seemed a pretty hopeless case: just about the worst place to start
if your interest is in finding ways to stop the next world war.

The confrontation between the superpowers is potentially lethal and
fundamentally frivolous and wrong, we said in our original proposal, but

7

Canada is trapped by its geography and its history. We have to continue in our alliances, and exercise what influence we can at the margin. It was, in fact, the classic Canadian stance of fatalism masquerading as realism. However, in the course of making the *Defence of Canada* series we spoke to hundreds of people, read more Canadian history than we had imagined existed, and spent a great deal of time just thinking and arguing, and gradually we changed our minds. We eventually concluded that it would be possible (though tricky) for Canada to extricate itself from its alliances – and, moreover, that doing so might have beneficial effects on the wider international confrontation whose outcome will eventually decide our fate and everybody else's.

Neutrality, on closer investigation, proved not to be a completely unattainable goal for Canada. Moreover, although neutrality could not save Canada from destruction in a superpower nuclear war – no defence policy could do that, including the present one of membership in the alliances – it seemed to us that Canadian neutrality might provide a useful example of how to avert that war *while peace still lasts*.

The main purpose of neutrality, especially for a country like Canada, would be to subvert the myth that large, "mainstream" industrial countries have no choice but to stay within their nuclear-armed alliances and sleepwalk toward oblivion. If the task we should really be addressing is that of prying the entire northern hemisphere away from nuclear confrontation and starting to dismantle the alliances, then Canadian neutrality could be a useful lever in that task. It was not that we expected other countries to smite their collective foreheads in sudden enlightenment when they saw the highly moral Canadians leading the way. Our reasoning was rather that Canada was better situated than most to make the first move toward non-alignment (in the sense that there can be no plausible Canadian nightmares about enemy tanks rolling in if we leave our alliances), and that what was most sorely needed was a *precedent* for neutrality.

At least half the countries that belong to the North Atlantic Treaty Organization (NATO) would not join it today if they had the choice to make again, but nobody has ever actually left the alliance. If such a precedent were set by Canada, it might ignite a similar domestic political debate in Spain, Greece, Norway, the Netherlands – all the European countries that have really moved beyond the alliance systems in their thinking about the world already. It might also, after some further delay, create a comparable debate even in the Warsaw Pact countries. (That may sound obvious enough now, when the Hungarian media and the Lithuanian parliament openly discuss neutrality and the Soviet government officially espouses the dismantling of the alliances, but we must confess that in 1985 it felt like one of the shakier bits of the argument.)

We were, of course, aware that in Canada, where "defence debates" traditionally focus on burning issues like the colour of uniforms, any argument based on the proposition that nuclear-armed alliances are bad for your health was bound to sound naïve, flying as it does in the face of forty years of rhetoric about the need for strong alliances and the reliability of "nuclear deterrence." But the true naiveté is to imagine that nuclear deterrence, which works by threatening nuclear war, can forever stop short of delivering it. *Coitus interruptus* is a rotten basis for a defence strategy.

Even after we were convinced that Canadian neutrality was politically desirable and strategically possible, for a time we remained reluctant to push the argument. We simply doubted whether Canadians, given their alliance-oriented military traditions, would ever consider adopting a neutral policy. There is no point in discussing the desirability of fish riding bicycles, because they just aren't equipped to do it.

> You can change your defence budget up, down or sideways . . . There are all kinds of options within what I consider to be the limits of our manoeuvrability. But I don't think there is an option of having a quite different kind of foreign policy. We're not non-aligned. There's no point in trying to force upon the population of a country a tradition which it just doesn't have.
>
> Geoffrey Pearson, Director, Canadian Institute for International Peace and Security, 1985-88

The ancestral wisdom is that Canadians don't know how to be neutral, but as we got deeper into the project our original assumptions about what Canadians really think began to evaporate. The Second World War and its attendant mythology killed the idea of non-alignment for a long time, but there *was* a nascent neutralist movement in this country – most significantly, in the English-speaking elite of this country – in the years between the two world wars. And although the post-1945 context discouraged any renewed consideration of neutrality, it gradually became evident to us, as we spoke to the retired Canadian politicians and senior officials who had helped to create the existing defence orthodoxy in the early post-war years, that many of them had the gravest reservations at the time about sliding back into just one more military alliance.

So with considerable trepidation and rather a lot of effort (changing the direction of a television series in mid-production is rather like trying to turn a supertanker in a bath-tub), we set out to explore the feasibility and desirability of Canadian neutrality. As a result, the series almost did not make it onto the air: our producer quit (twice), and the CBC threatened not to broadcast it if we did not tone down the "advocacy" of our conclusion. After the statutory mock-apocalyptic confrontation in an airport hotel room a compromise ending was agreed, and the series was broadcast in early 1986 (preceded by a public mental health warning about the views expressed in it, from which the CBC explicitly dissociated itself). Even so, the rebuttals and rebukes from official sources that rained down on us afterwards rather surprised us.

> Moderation is a means, not an end. Our purpose is to enlarge freedom. . . . Geography is not the paramount reason we belong in NATO or NORAD. Freedom is. Those alliances, with all their imperfections, defend a system of free societies and – by maintaining strength in the face of Soviet strength – help keep the peace.
>
> Joe Clark, Secretary of State for External Affairs,
> *The Gazette*, Montreal, 3 April 1986

The Secretary of State for External Affairs does not normally write unsolicited articles for newspapers to dispute the policy suggestions of a television series, nor does the CBC usually succumb to political pressure from Ottawa and refrain from giving an expensive and high-rating series a second broadcast. (CBC representatives must, of course, deny in public that government displeasure had anything to do with the decision not to rebroadcast *Defence of Canada*, but several senior Corporation executives have admitted it to us in private.) Only in retrospect, and knowing what we now know about the hidden crisis that sprang up between Ottawa and

NATO in the months immediately preceding the broadcast of the series (in which the Minister of National Defence, Erik Nielsen, made a secret and unsuccessful attempt to pull Canadian troops out of Germany), does the vigour of the government's assault on our modest proposal become understandable. Ottawa was seeking to re-establish "credibility" with its NATO allies after the Nielsen debacle, and the very last thing it needed was for the National Film Board and the CBC, two government-funded corporations, to make and broadcast a television series about Canadian neutrality.

That was merely a fluke of timing, but what really struck us about the heated condemnations that our proposal attracted was how little attention they paid to the practical consequences of Canada's going neutral: would we be any safer, would we save money, would the Americans let us get away with it, would it do the world any good? The first line of defence for the *status quo* was rather to question the morality of neutrality. "Moral equivalence" was the name of our crime: we had failed to realize that modern history is a crusade of Good against Evil and that Canada's place is in the ranks of the Righteous.

> The history of the 20th century is the story of Western democracies fighting Prussian militarism, Nazi totalitarianism, and the gulag.
>
> Barbara Amiel, *Maclean's*, 31 March 1986

Well, that was three years ago, when the assumptions and the rhetoric of the Cold War still reigned largely unchallenged in public debate in Canada. Far fewer people would wish to be identified publicly with such crudely ideological and historically distorted arguments today; the times have changed.

Nor, for that matter, do we see a Canadian initiative for non-alignment as such an urgent requirement today. Canadian neutrality will probably come anyway, in the medium-term future. As we all fumble our way slowly towards a non-aligned international system that genuinely operates on collective security principles, there is the strong possibility that we will pass through a lengthy interim stage in which smaller countries from both alliances – and especially those which occupy strategic territory between the greater powers – will adopt 'Finlandized' defence policies as their contribution to the process of defusing the confrontation. But that is a process which, even with luck, will take up most of the 1990s, and meanwhile circumstances do alter cases: the case for 'premature' Canadian neutrality as a means of kick-starting the process of dismantling the alliances is hardly as compelling when that process is already underway.

But even if Canada's role in the lengthy and difficult task of dismantling the alliances now seems likely to be that of an intelligent supporting player rather than that of an initiator, the value of its contribution will still depend on Canadians' understanding of the international system that they must help to change. And in that respect, the national understanding is woefully defective: we inhabit an almost entirely mythologized historical landscape, with only the vaguest comprehension of what has happened to us in the past and hardly any idea of why.

❖

Canada's present defence policy commits it to fighting in Europe (as it has already done twice in this century) should a war break out between the alliances. We are also committed to "fighting" a nuclear war in North America, should a European war escalate in the manner that is virtually guaranteed by present NATO doctrine. This would be an absurd situation even if we had no choice in the matter – yet Canadians often appear to be enthusiastic volunteers in this game. In fact, however, we are not so much a nation of volunteers as a nation that has lost its bearings.

If you had to justify Canadian defence policy to an inquisitive visitor from Mars, the major difficulty would be to explain why we, almost alone among the countries of the Western Hemisphere, act as if we had a vital security frontier somewhere in central Europe. It is an extraordinary misapprehension, but it arises quite naturally from the history of Canadian defence policy.

Until the beginning of this century, Canada behaved like any other small or medium-sized nation in the Western Hemisphere: it restricted its defence efforts to its immediate vicinity. Canada's sole land frontier is with the United States, so like Mexico our military history was mainly concerned with avoiding absorption by the American republic. But there was one over-riding difference between Canada and Mexico: Canada depended on a *European* power to protect it. Our strategy worked very well (in the sense that there is a lot more left of Canada than of Mexico), but it ultimately landed us with some quite peculiar ideas about exactly where our important borders lie.

The *real* Canadian border is right here in North America, and the most important fact about that border is that the wealth and population south of it have always been many times greater than to the north of it. The border itself has survived down the centuries only because there was always a major European imperial power committed to maintaining itself in the lands to the north: first France, later Britain. It is no coincidence (and no cause for embarrassment) that Canada was, by more than half a century, the last major country in the Western Hemisphere to achieve independence. It would probably not have escaped absorption by the United States if it had become independent earlier.

However, the ultimate and quite unforeseen result of our dependence on Britain for defence was that Canada also became the first country in the Western Hemisphere to send a large army overseas to fight in a European war. To be fair, Canada did not start sending its troops abroad to fight in great-power wars simply out of colonial subservience. It seemed politically necessary to many Canadians at the end of the nineteenth century, because they still feared that Canada would be taken over by the Americans unless it had the might of the British Empire behind it. Canadians thus felt poorly placed to refuse British requests for military help elsewhere, and so we began to "pay our dues" to the British Empire by sending troops abroad to fight in British imperial wars, first in South Africa, then in Europe.

In this century, a hundred thousand young Canadians have been killed, all of them far from home, in wars that can now be seen to have benefitted neither Canada's particular interests nor the general cause of peace in the world. But the losses Canada suffered in these wars were so grievous that Canadians *had* to believe they were about something important to our own interests. To think otherwise, we instinctively felt, would be somehow to betray the dead – and so we became psychologically committed to playing a permanent (if subordinate) role in the great-power struggle.

Canadian troops have been in Europe for well over half of this century. Since many of us have known nothing else all our lives, we do not see this as odd. *Of course* we send troops abroad; *of course* we belong to alliances. What would our friends think of us if we didn't? What would our dead of past wars say if they knew we had let down the side? Yet ours are the only military forces in Europe (except for the Americans, who at least have the excuse of being a superpower) that are not native to that continent.

All the rest of the countries in our own hemisphere (again, except the Americans) see Canada's behaviour as evidence that we are still psychologically a European dependency. It is rather more complicated than that, but although we may dismiss the opinions of Latin Americans because we are richer than they, there is much truth in what they say.

Canadians are particularly prone to think in simplistic terms about international affairs because the country has spent its entire history as a military appendage of either Britain or the United States. As the dominant superpowers of the nineteenth and twentieth centuries respectively, those countries have been involved in a fair number of wars – but since Canada shares their heritage of democratic government, it has been possible for us to rationalize the wars we have fought by their side as struggles for democracy and human rights. So long as Canadians remain in thrall to these myths, we will not be able to consider our present options sensibly.

In fact, it is even more complicated than that, for we are really dealing with two sets of myths. We have been dealing here mostly with the myths of the English-speaking majority, which have usually driven the country's foreign policy, but French Canada has its own, very different myths. On the international spectrum of heterogeneity Canada falls near the middle for most purposes, being far more diverse than states like Japan or Sweden but not nearly so divided by language, race, and religion as countries like the Soviet Union or India. Canada is virtually unique, however, in that the country's two dominant cultures have highly coherent but almost always conflicting views of the meaning and even the content of their shared history.

English Canadians, including that near-majority who are not of British descent, have largely traded in the memory of their own past experience of the world for a homogenized and internationalized version of Anglo-American historical orthodoxy, modified only to give Canada a somewhat larger role in the twentieth century's great events than anyone else would easily recognize. Even the basic historical compromise on which the modern Canadian state was founded in the mid-nineteenth century (the violation of which would still promptly result in Canada's disintegration) is largely ignored or denied west of Ontario, where the very concept of two "founding peoples" is often questioned. And if English Canadians remember too little history, French Canadians remember too much.

French Canadians inhabit a moral and mythological territory in which they are the perennial victims of history, forever poised on the brink of extinction, rather than seeing themselves as one of the most extraordinary cultural success stories of modern history. They buttress their conviction of being under constant siege by tenaciously recalling deplorable episodes of English Canadian tyranny from the past like the Riel rebellion, the Manitoba and Ontario schools questions, and the conscription crises, and they have a profound mistrust of the English-speaking majority's reflexes in international affairs.

The bi-national, almost schizophrenic character of Canada has been rather obscured in the past few decades, so far as Canada's international relations are concerned, by the unusual (we almost wrote "unnatural") accord between the two Canadian groups on foreign and defence policy that arose from the peculiar circumstances of the early Cold War years. Once we had lost our old American adversary, the one potential enemy in the world whom Anglo-Saxon alliance supporters and deeply Catholic and conservative French Canadians could hope to unite against was the Godless Russian Commies – and lo! that was exactly who took on the role of enemy after 1945.

But as we near the end of the twentieth century French Canadians are no longer particularly Catholic or conservative, and English Canada is rapidly ceasing to be Anglo-Saxon, so the domestic basis for this consensus is as deeply eroded as the international confrontation that called it into being. In fact, the post-1949 consensus would probably vanish almost instantly if Canada were required to make any major sacrifices in support of its existing commitments. In any case, the changed international context now demands a new foreign policy consensus.

It will be difficult to achieve, for if Canada is to play the useful role that it could, French Canadians will have to give up their instinctive isolationism and English Canadians will have to abandon their habit of clinging to the skirts of whatever alliance is patronized by the largest English-speaking countries. And of course it all depends, as ever, on the country contriving for a while longer not to fall apart into petty successor states defined solely by language.

We have a lot of past to sort through, understand, and then finally put behind us, but it might be worth it. Who knows? Enough mutual comprehension (let us not talk ambitiously of trust, or love), and Canada might even be spared the anger, tears, and general waste of time involved in sub-dividing the existing Canadian state, when the long-term trend and objective is so obviously not to surrender to the principle of the almighty state but rather to get beyond it.

One other thing: there are bound to be times in this book when what we say makes us sound like Canadian nationalists, and perhaps anti-American to boot. We are neither of those things. Nationalism is always a regrettable phenomenon, and we are under no illusions that Canadians would collectively behave any better than Americans if exposed to similar temptations. However, Canada is not, and has never been, a great power, and Canadians have thus been largely spared the excesses of national megalomania and paranoia to which the citizens of great powers usually fall victim.

It is therefore possible for Canadians to behave internationally in ways that are not imaginable south of the border. On the whole we don't, but we *could*, and we might be of some use to the world if we took that trouble. In particular, we are better placed than Americans to take a tough, clear look at just what kind of game we have got caught up in internationally and what our role in it has been, to draw the correct conclusions, and to act on them in the common interest–which, when it comes to averting future war, is our own supreme national interest as well.

Gwynne Dyer and Tina Viljoen,
*Montreal and London*

# Acknowledgements

In finishing this book we have had much help and encouragement from Doug Gibson of McClelland and Stewart who, confronted with a manuscript that was very long for a single book, amazed us by suggesting that, rather than cutting and gutting it, we publish in two volumes, and from Dinah Forbes, who has edited it and shepherded it through every stage of production with unflappable competence. Our agent, Peter Livingston, efficiently assumed the duty of appearing greedy on our behalf, thus allowing us to represent ourselves as being above all that.

But our debts extend a good deal further back than that, for this project has had a long and chequered history. At one point a considerable portion of the book was destroyed, and during the subsequent alarums and delays the original publisher had to pull out, but we owe thanks to Malcolm Lester and Louise Dennys for their support to that earlier incarnation of the book, and the large proportion of the manuscript that survives from that time still shows the benefit of Betty Corson's careful editing.

Before it even started to be a book, it was a series of films, and film-making is a collective endeavour. So we want to acknowledge the influence that Cathy Mullins, Michael Bryans, Steven Steinhouse, Kent Nason, Mike Mahoney, and Savas Kalogeras had on our approach to the topic, and the encouragement they gave even at the worst times. Paul Wright at the CBC was always a gentleman, as was Paul LaRose at Radio-Canada. Tina's mother, Madeleine Viljoen, provided a twenty-four-hour long-distance emergency service for checking French translations whenever we were filming somewhere at the back of beyond, and Rose-Aimée Todd of the National Film Board library and her staff were extremely resourceful in exploiting the inter-library loan system. Floyd Elliott of Studio 'G' also allowed us to raid his extensive private library; we have finally returned all the books that the rabbit didn't eat.

Peter Langille, now at Bradford University in England, has given us some very valuable material for the second volume. Ian Cowman, now at Macquarie University in Australia, brought the San Juan Island incident to our attention and did most of the research in the Public Record Office in London. Mac Johnston, the editor of *Legion Magazine*, was remarkably quick and helpful in finding and sending us material from his archives on the Canadian intervention in Russia. Nancy Grenville of the Centre for Newfoundland Studies at Memorial University did much of the research on Sir Edward Morris. Dr. Jim Boutilier of Royal Roads Military College, Manon Lamontagne of Prince Albert and Montreal, and Professor Peter Neary of the University of Western Ontario were all kind enough to read the manuscript and offer their comments (and Peter also steered us towards that invaluable record of small-town Ontario life, *At the Forks of the Grand*).

The many retired officers, politicians, and civil servants whom we interviewed were generous with their time and remarkably open in their comments; even if they do not agree with our conclusions, we hope that they do not feel we have abused their trust. Many serving members of the Canadian armed forces were also extremely kind and helpful to us; we know that some of them felt burned immediately afterwards, when the series was broadcast, but we hope that they will now accept that there was no deceit in what we did, and that our change of mind was both belated and genuine. In particular we want to thank Major Ray Windsor for his patience and good humour (hoping that it did not harm his career to have been associated with us in the line of duty).

Above all we want to thank Jim Lee, who has been with us on the project almost from the start. He did much of the text research and most of the photographic research for this book, but even more importantly he has been a constant support, an excellent source of advice, and a very good friend.

About sources and quotations: we have avoided footnotes not only because they are distracting, but also because the assurance of historical accuracy they convey is almost entirely spurious. In skilled and unscrupulous hands, the *apparatus criticus* can be made to sit up and beg in the service of any kind of special pleading that you care to name. Unless you have hundreds of hours available to chase down every reference, you still end up having to trust in the integrity of the writers and their ability to interpret evidence intelligently. So we have restricted ourselves to brief and fairly general bibliographical notes on sources for each chapter, except in the case of a few particularly controversial or little-known episodes where we have tried to give fuller information about the evidence. There may also be one or two items missing, since our bibliographical notes were destroyed at one point, but we think we have managed to fill almost all the gaps. Quotes in the text from living individuals, if given without further attribution, are almost invariably from personal interviews.

### CHAPTER ONE

# *"Canada Must Be Demolished!"*

Canada did not have a virgin birth. It came into being as a result of war, and it may well perish as a result of war. If that final war were to happen tomorrow, Canadians would bear proportionately just as much responsibility as Russians and Americans for its occurrence: We are an integral part of the system. We always have been.

North Americans, both Canadian and American, often cherish the illusion that they are more virtuous than the Europeans, whose senseless quarrels have so often dragged the world into war. A dominant theme in the domestic propaganda of both countries during the two world wars of this century, and even more prominently in the Cold War era, was that of "the New World stepping forth to the rescue of the Old" – as though we inhabited two different worlds. We do not, of course. The struggles of the major continental powers were duplicated in the New World from the start, with the enthusiastic participation of the settlers in New England and New France.

Q. *Are the United States and Canada natural allies?*
A. In a way, we're historic enemies. We've been living side by side for four centuries, people forget, and for at least three centuries we were exceedingly hostile, ideologically and every other way. I would say that the alliance, which has only lasted some fifty years, is a kind of triumph of reason and sense over natural antipathy.

> John Holmes, former director general, Canadian
> Institute of International Affairs

It *is* a triumph of reason over emotion, or at least over habit, and it is certainly preferable to the old relationship. No rational Canadian government now would ever choose to be an enemy of the United States. But is the only alternative to be a close military ally? What has been lost from the Canadian popular memory as a result of this half-century alliance is any recollection of what Canada's real strategic concerns used to be, and, therefore, any understanding of the real roots of our own international behaviour. Only by starting out from that forgotten reality can we understand how we have gradually drifted into our present preposterous position.

❖

Permanent European settlement in the temperate parts of North America began around the time that the modern international system came into being, with a half-dozen great powers and a dozen or so minor ones jostling for position in a continuous competition that periodically broke down into general war not only in Europe, but also in their empires overseas. Britain and France, the two major colonial powers in North America, were invariably on opposite sides in these conflicts, so the fighting usually spread to the western side of the Atlantic, too. Canada and the United States were both born out of this intense rivalry: the bastard twin offspring of two empires each determined to destroy the other:

"Canada must be demolished – *Delenda est Carthago* – or we are undone!"

> William Livingston, 1756, later first Revolutionary
> Governor of New Jersey

The English colonists in North America often had their own names for the imperial wars that repeatedly devastated the little colonies of "New England" and "New France" – the War of the Spanish Succession (1702-14) became "Queen Anne's War" in the American colonies, for example, and the Seven Years' War (1756-63) was known as the "French and Indian War" – but their origins all lay in European rivalries. By the end of the latter war, however, peace seemed about to descend on the New World at last. After the capture of Quebec in 1759 and the fall of Montreal in the following year, all of New France was under British control and there was nobody left to fight. From Georgia all the way up to Hudson's Bay, North America paid allegiance to King George III.

But the peace actually lasted scarcely a decade, for then the American colonists revolted against the British crown. Canada exists, in essence, because the newly conquered French-speaking inhabitants of "Canada" (a territory roughly corresponding to the present-day province of Quebec) decided that their religion, language, and culture would be safer under British rule than immersed in the Protestant, English-speaking sea of the new American republic.

It was undoubtedly the right decision for the long-term future for their society, for there were fewer than ninety thousand French Canadians. Even at the time of the American Revolution, the French-speaking population in North America was outnumbered about twenty-five-to-one by English speakers. The English-French ratio is now more like forty-five-to-one, and the fate of French Canadians as part of the United States would probably have been little different from that of the Louisiana French or the California Spanish. But it would be ludicrous to pretend that the battered little society along the banks of the St. Lawrence that fell into British hands in 1760 – an overwhelmingly illiterate society with a century-long heritage of pitiless warfare against the hated English Protestants – consciously took a far-sighted decision about its best strategy for cultural survival. On the contrary, the British conquerors deliberately set out to lure it into collaboration with them for strategic reasons of a very different order. Right from the start, British policy in the newly conquered province of Canada was dominated by fear of the impending American rebellion.

That was what impelled the first British governor of Canada, General James Murray, systematically to evade his instructions to anglicize the colony's laws and institutions. He justified his behaviour to his superiors in England by arguing that the French Canadians, "who are perhaps the bravest and the best race on the globe . . . would soon get the better of every National Antipathy to their Conquerors and become the most faithful and most useful set of Men in this American Empire," if only they were granted "a few priveledges which the Laws of England deny to Roman Catholicks at home." Murray's behaviour towards French Canadians after the Conquest was not part of some general British policy of tolerance towards conquered peoples, however. In 1755 the British government had ruthlessly deported most of the French-speaking Acadians from Nova Scotia on the grounds that their continuing loyalty to France made them a strategic danger, and in different circumstances the same fate might have befallen the Quebec French.

*L'Acadie* (Nova Scotia) had passed into British hands in 1713, but few Acadians had been forced to take an oath of allegiance to the British crown. While Britain and France were at peace the question of allegiance did not really arise, and so the Acadians came to see the British neglect to impose an oath of allegiance on them as a licence to behave in ways that would actually prove quite unacceptable to London in a crisis. The tragedy of the Acadians happened essentially because Britain largely ignored Nova Scotia for a generation after acquiring it.

For decades the British turned a blind eye to the French priests travelling through Nova Scotia, who served as agents in maintaining links between the Acadians and the French authorities in Île Royale (Cape Breton Island), which remained a possession of France for another half-century after 1713. Despite their attempts to represent themselves as "neutral French," the Acadians were not really "neutral"; they were still basically "French" in their loyalties, and living in what was then part of the British Empire exposed them to terrible temptations and risks when the Anglo-French wars resumed after a pause of three decades. Most Acadians had the sense not to get directly involved, but the complicity of some local hotheads in the French army's attacks on Annapolis Royal in 1744 and 1745 and in the massacre of British troops at Grand Pré in 1747 tried British patience severely. When war broke out again between Britain and France in 1755, and some three hundred Acadians were found helping the French at the siege of Fort Beauséjour, the British acted.

Empires have a variety of methods for dealing with recalcitrant ethnic or religious minorities: if there are relatively few of them, the traditional solutions are massacre or deportation. From the great "resettlements" carried out by the Roman and Ottoman empires down to the expulsion of the Huguenots from France, deportation was generally considered the more civilized method – and deporting six thousand Acadians who refused to take the oath of allegiance from Nova Scotia in 1755 was no challenge for the British Empire, whose ships were annually carrying much larger numbers of unwilling West Africans all the way across the Atlantic Ocean as slaves.

Deporting over ten times as many French Canadians from what is now Quebec after the British conquest in 1759-60 would have been a much bigger undertaking, but it could and would have been done if Britain had seen it as a vital interest. However, London's initial law for the new "Fourteenth Colony," the Proclamation of 1763, merely assumed that the French Canadians would rapidly be overwhelmed by more numerous English-speaking immigrants to the province, and decreed a framework of English law and institutions into which these anomalous former French subjects would just have to assimilate. But General James Murray, a cultured, bilingual soldier from Scotland, took a longer view than his political superiors (as soldiers sometimes do).

Murray had survived the decisive battle on the Plains of Abraham in 1759, in which his commander, James Wolfe, was killed. He had shared his army's rations with starving French Canadian refugees from the devastated countryside around Quebec City during the succeeding winter (when the Ursuline nuns took pity and knitted long stockings for his bare-legged Highland troops). He had kept his hold on the city through a far bloodier battle at Sainte-Foy and a subsequent siege the following spring when what was left of the French army in North America marched down from Montreal to recapture Quebec City, until at last the ice broke up on the St. Lawrence and a British (rather than a French) fleet appeared below Quebec City in May 1760 to seal the colony's fate. Murray knew and liked the French Canadians, and as a Scot whose own country had spent centuries at war with England but had ended up in a mutually advantageous union with the English, he was open to the idea that the defeated French Canadians could also be turned into England's allies.

So he stalled on applying the Proclamation of 1763, especially its promise of an elected assembly – from which French Canadians would automatically be excluded, since English law still denied Roman Catholics full political rights. "An assembly so constituted might pretend to be a representative of the people there," wrote a British official, "but it would be a representative of only the 600 new English settlers, and an instrument in their hands of dominating over the 90,000 French."

Religion had become virtually irrelevant in international politics by the late eighteenth century, but it was still important in domestic politics. In 1555 the principle of *cuius regio, eius religio* ("your region determines your religion," or more loosely, "you must have the same religion as your king") had been instituted at the Peace of Augsburg in an attempt to end the bloody wars between Catholics and Protestants in Europe. By 1763 Europe's religious wars were long past, and a smidgin of tolerance was beginning to creep in – people professing a different religion from their ruler were seldom compelled to renounce their faith – but old suspicions die hard, and having the right religion remained an important badge of allegiance to the state. It was still thought that a Catholic could not be a loyal British subject, rather in the same way that it continues to be seen as impossible for a loyal American to be a Communist, or a loyal Russian a liberal democrat, long after the passion has gone out of those particular confrontations.

But such ideological considerations have never carried much weight in *international* politics. Just as the Soviet Union made a tactical alliance with Nazi Germany in 1939 and as the United States ended up supporting Khmer Rouge guerrillas in Cambodia after the Vietnamese invasion in 1978, so Protestant England in the eighteeenth century was quite ready to make alliances with Catholic Austria. Governor Murray's task was to convince London that the same non-ideological rules about who could be an ally should be applied *within* the British empire, in order to turn the French Canadians into allies.

The most convincing argument for this was the fact that Britain would soon desperately need allies in North America, for the "British-Americans" to the south were rapidly becoming Britain's enemies. In fact, it was the British conquest of Canada that made the American Revolution inevitable. In the Thirteen Colonies, revolutionary agitators like John Adams (later the second president of the United States) were quick to note that the end of the old French military threat from the north meant the American colonists no longer needed British soldiers to protect them, and so could afford to think of independence.

The French government also foresaw the possibility of an American revolt; indeed, it was the main reason why Paris had not tried harder to get New France back in the peace negotiations at the end of the war, preferring to recover the rich sugar island of Martinique instead. Defending New France had cost the French treasury vast sums for little return during a century of intermittent warfare, and King Louis XV's government was increasingly disinclined to go on pouring out its limited resources for "a few acres of snow" (as Voltaire dismissively described Canada). More importantly, the French government was beginning to realise that there could be positive strategic advantages in losing its North American colony. At the peace negotiations in 1763 the Duc de Choiseul, the King's chief minister, let New France go without much argument, explaining that it was only the French military threat in North America that had held Britain and its colonies together. With New France in British hands and that danger removed, the British and Americans would soon be at each other's throats.

In Canada, they were already virtual enemies. The Yankee traders (*les Bostonnais*) who flocked into Montreal and Quebec after the Conquest to make their fortunes bitterly resented General Murray's attempt to protect French Canadian rights, and eventually their protests to London got him recalled. He was replaced in 1766 by General Guy Carleton, who had instructions to enforce the Proclamation of 1763. But Carleton, an Anglo-Irish professional soldier, was also deeply concerned about the impending rebellion in the American colonies. He soon became as determined as Murray to win the loyalty of French Canadians and to build up the military strength of the province.

Carleton was a tall, erect, slightly balding man, still a bachelor in his mid-forties, whose entire life had been spent in military service. He had been wounded in the head outside Quebec's walls in 1759 (and was wounded again in an attack on the west coast of France in 1761, and once more at Havana in 1762). His admirers called him "grave," while a lieutenant who served under him described him more sourly as "one of the most distant, reserved men in the world. He has a rigid strictness in his manner which is very unpleasant and which he observes even to his most particular friends and acquaintances." His policy towards the French Canadians was founded on the cold strategic calculation that the province could be turned into a secure military base for the suppression of any revolutionary outbreak in the English-speaking colonies – and his autocratic manner and aristocratic prejudices led him to try to achieve his goal by preserving and strengthening the existing semi-feudal society of New France.

Carleton reckoned that the great majority of the French Canadian population, the simple *habitants*, would remain impervious to the egalitarian ideas of the American revolutionaries: most were illiterate subsistence farmers, deeply attached to their traditional ways and knowing little of the outside world (there had been hardly any immigration from France to "New France" for many decades). They seemed content enough, and there was almost no real poverty, but the habitants lived in what appeared to be a perfectly preserved feudal society, controlled by only a few hundred people of rank. About one hundred feudal land-owners (the *seigneurs*) and one hundred and fifty parish priests, plus about the same number of doctors, lawyers, and merchants, seemed to be in a position to make all the decisions for the French Canadians, so Carleton set out to win them over.

Six years before the American Revolution broke out, he wrote to the British secretary of state, Lord Hillsborough, that it would be particularly wise to win the support of the French Canadians in case France itself decided to back the thirteen American colonies "in their independent notions." Quebec must be made the bulwark of British power, for it was "the principal scene where the fate of America may be determined." The whole population had been more or less disarmed (so far as military-style weapons were concerned) at the same time as the oath of allegiance was administered in the parishes in 1763, and the old French militia organization had fallen into disuse, but Carleton believed that if French Canada's "natural leaders" sided with the British, then the habitants could be counted on to provide eighteen thousand soldiers for the coming war, "of which Number above one-half have already served with as much Valor, with more zeal, and more military knowledge for America than the regular Troops of France, that were joined with them."

In 1774, after almost four years in England arguing his case, Carleton finally saw the Quebec Act passed by Parliament. It abandoned all the assimilationist goals of the Proclamation of 1763 and enshrined the French civil law, the authority of the Roman Catholic Church, and the traditional social order as the pillars of British rule in Quebec. The government tried to pass the bill with the least possible publicity, since it gave rights to French Canadian Catholics that would have caused a social revolution if they were also granted to Catholics in Ireland. Even so, when the King went to Westminster to give formal assent to the Quebec Act, he was greeted by an angry mob shouting "No Popery."

It seemed an extraordinarily far-sighted measure by the standards of the time, for it would be another half-century before Roman Catholics enjoyed full civil rights in England itself – but perhaps the more appropriate adjective is "cynical." The Quebec Act was later hailed as the cornerstone of the "second British Empire," embodying the revolutionary notion that you didn't have to be English to be "British," but at the time it was just an *ad hoc* bribe to buy the loyalty of influential French Canadians. As Dr Samuel Johnson observed, a tolerance that might be mischievous nearer home (i.e., Ireland) did not matter at Quebec.

By the time Carleton returned to Quebec (having married the eighteen-year-old Lady Maria Effingham and acquired two infant sons during his stay in England), the Thirteen Colonies were on the brink of rebellion. The Quebec Act itself played a large role in goading the Americans into open revolt, for it extended Quebec's boundaries to take in most of what is now the U.S. Midwest. This action was mainly intended to block the westward expansion of the American colonists into new lands where their settlements would cause trouble with the Indians and eventually ruin the fur trade, but it was also quite obviously an attempt to win Quebec's support in the anticipated war. Americans were outraged, and stories circulated in the Thirteen Colonies of a secret Anglo-French treaty by which Canada was to be returned to France in order to recreate the French military threat in the north and bring the revolting Americans to heel:

> Harried again by Frenchmen and Indians, the wretched Colonists would have to grovel at the foot of the throne, and supplicate a papist, perhaps a Stuart, or at any rate a hereditary tyrant, for scanty and grudging aid on any terms he pleased!
> *Essex Gazette* (Massachusetts), 10 January 1775

❖

The American revolutionaries were optimists, and they believed that they could win French Canadians over even in the face of the shameless bribery the British were employing. Only months before the fighting began, the Continental Congress, meeting in Philadelphia, invited the French Canadians to join their budding revolution. But it was a rather ambiguous invitation, with undertones of menace:

> You are a small people compared to those who with open arms invite you into fellowship. A moment's reflection should convince you which will be most for your interest and happiness, to have all the rest of North America your unalterable friends, or your inveterate enemies. The injuries of Boston [the Tea Party, etc.] have roused and associated every colony, from Nova Scotia to Georgia. Your province is the only link that is wanting to complete the bright strong chain of union.
>
> Address of the Continental Congress to the Inhabitants
> of Quebec, 26 October 1774

Although agents of the American revolutionary cause were active in Canada throughout the winter of 1774-75, their arguments were severely undermined by the fact that the same Continental Congress, only five days before it invited French Canadians to join the Americans in rebellion, had condemned the Quebec Act as "this worst of laws" for its generosity toward the Catholic church, a "religion which has . . . dispersed impiety, bigotry, persecution, murder and rebellion throughout every part of the world." The average American Protestant in 1775 regarded Catholicism with the same horror that his descendant would hold for Communism two centuries later, so there was never much chance for a happy political union between Americans and French Canadians. And it was no coincidence at all that the first open instances of revolt in the American colonies, the clashes at Lexington and Concord, happened only a few days after the Quebec Act came into effect on 1 May 1775.

The American Revolutionary War began as a civil war within the Anglo-Saxon world. Its ostensible cause was petty – a clumsy attempt by the British parliament to tax the American colonies in order to recover some of the cost of defending them – and even the political principles in dispute were equally hotly debated on either side of the Atlantic. The opposition party in England supported the American case against the King's party, and many Americans put loyalty to the King above every other consideration. Even the most radical opponents of British policy in the American colonies, although prepared to use armed force, hesitated to talk openly of independence. But what really infuriated them, and won them much popular support, was the fact that the British government was planning to employ Papist foreigners – French Canadians – against its own people in this family quarrel.

> We have received certain intelligence that General Carleton, the Governor of Canada, is instigating the people of that province and the Indians to fall upon us. . . . We are reduced to the alternative of chusing an unconditional submission to the tyranny of irritated ministers, or resistance by force. The latter is our choice.
>
> "Declaration of the Causes and Necessity of Taking Up Arms," Second Continental Congress, Philadelphia, May 1775

In fact, Britain was preparing to do more than mobilize the French Canadians against the Americans. With too few soldiers of its own, the British government was also trying to hire mercenaries from the German states and from Russia. The American rebels, meanwhile, were planning a pre-emptive invasion of Quebec. But when Carleton summoned the militia of Canada on 9 June 1775, the weapon he had been counting on turned out to be a fantasy.

❖

> By his Excellency Guy Carleton, Captain-General and Governour-in-Chief in and over the Province of Quebec . . .
>
> To the end, therefore, that so treasonable an invasion may be soon defeated; that all such traitors, with their said abetters, may be speedily brought to justice, and the publick peace and tranquillity of this Province again restored . . . I shall . . . execute martial law . . . and to that end, I shall order the Militia within the same to be forthwith raised. . . . Given under my hand and seal of arms at Montreal, this 9th day of June, 1775.

At Carleton's urging, Parliament in London had already taken the unprecedented step of agreeing to arm Roman Catholics in Canada, but in fact the Quebec Act had not won over the loyalty of the mass of French Canadians, for Carleton had misunderstood the social structure of French Canada. As early as February 1775, with the habitants showing great reluctance to turn out for militia training, Carleton was warning London that they "have in a manner emancipated themselves, and it will require Time, and discreet management likewise, to recall them to their ancestral Habits of obedience and Discipline."

However much the average habitant loved his religion, he was far from delighted at the Quebec Act, which made the tithes that he should theoretically be paying to the church a legally enforceable obligation once again. And as for the seigneurs whom Carleton assumed to be the "natural leaders" of a feudal society, in New France this class of men were in fact mostly of humble origin and relatively poor, a pale reflection of the powerful *noblesse* of France – and they were neither loved nor feared by the average habitant, whose habits of mind were not submissively feudal at all.

Indeed, the seigneurs were not even the traditional military leadership class of New France; the captains of militia (who also provided much of the local administration) had been drawn mostly from the habitants. So when the Quebec Act gave seigneurs the legal right to exact feudal dues and obligations that had long fallen into abeyance, the general reaction of an unwilling peasantry was precisely the opposite of what Carleton had intended. Paradoxically, he created a fairly receptive audience among ordinary French Canadians for the American revolutionaries' subversive talk of liberty and equality.

When the American rebels began mustering their forces in mid-1775 to strike at Quebec (which they fully realized was the key British strategic base in North America), Carleton called out the French Canadian militia and distributed arms to them, but he was beginning to wonder which way their muskets would end up pointing. "I have proclaimed Martial law, and ordered the Militia to be enrolled; what I shall make of them, or of the Savages [Indians], I cannot positively say, but I am sure it is become highly necessary to try." At least the priests and seigneurs whose loyalty Carleton had bought by underwriting their authority stayed bought.

The Roman Catholic Church in Canada kept its part of the bargain with its British benefactors and urged its flock to fight. Even though most of the hierarchy in Canada were French-born and educated, their ultimate loyalty was not to the French crown but to their version of the Kingdom of God. And if the strategic fluctuations of the secular world meant that the freedom of their flock to practise their religion was now better served by collaboration with a Protestant government, well, then, that was what they would recommend to French Canadians.

> *Une troupe de sujets révoltés contre leur légitime Souverain, qui est en même temps le nôtre, vient de faire irruption dans cette Province . . . dans la vue de vous entraîner dans leur révolte. . . .*
>
> Monseigneur Jean-Olivier Briand, Bishop of Quebec,
> *Mandement,* 22 May 1775
> (*Mandements des Evêques de Québec, tome II*)

[A troop of subjects in revolt against their lawful Sovereign, who is at the same time ours, have just made irruption into this Province . . . with a view to dragging you into their revolt. . . . The remarkable goodness and gentleness with which we have been governed by His Very Gracious Majesty King George the Third since the fortune of war subjected us to his rule; the recent favours with which he has loaded us . . . would no doubt be enough to excite your gratitude and zeal in the support of the interests of the British Crown. . . . Your oaths and your religion lay upon you the unavoidable duty of defending your Country and your King with all the strength you possess.]

It was probably a greater surprise to Bishop Briand than to Carleton when this thunderous proclamation had virtually no effect except to stimulate the circulation of dozens of scurrilous verses mocking the bishop's promises of indulgences to those who fought for Britain and his threats of excommunication against those who did not – and suggesting that it was all due to the large pension that he had recently been granted by the British government.

> *Bernard n'étoit qu'une bête*
> *Auprès de nôtre Briand.*
> *Grand Dieu! quelle bonne tête!*
> *C'est du ciel un vrai présent.*

*Au mandat de sa croisade*
  *Armons nous, mes chers amis.*
*Boston n'est qu'une promenade:*
  *Ces mutins seront soûmis. . . .*

Anonymous (to the tune of
*Belle brune, que j'adore*)

Francis Maseres, *Additional Papers Concerning
the Province of Quebeck*, London, 1776

[St. Bernard was a blockhead
  Next to our Briand.
What a clever man he is!
  Heaven's gift to our poor land.

Friends, to arms! The Bishop calls;
  Let us do his pious job!
Boston, – just a promenade!
  'T won't take long to quell that mob.

Plenary indulgences
  Will ensure our seats on high,
If we back his politics
  And as good fanatics die.

Then let's die, so dear Briand –
  Clever head he wears – may get
From our courage and our blood
  Bigger gifts and pensions yet.]

The average habitant, alienated by the Quebec Act and distracted by wild stories that seven thousand Russians were coming up the St. Lawrence (and quite accurate reports that comparable numbers of Americans were on the way), did not take his bishop's advice, nor was he inclined to fight for his feudal superiors. Some militia units rather grudgingly turned out, especially in the Quebec area, but in most other areas there was not even superficial compliance. Rather, there were several local revolts against seigneurs who were too zealous in their attempts to mobilize the militia in the service of their British benefactors.

Nobody felt an urge to die for the British, and the mass of the population took up a neutral position, waiting to see who was likely to win before they committed themselves. Their caution was understandable, for they had no real stake in the incomprehensible quarrel between the English and the Americans, nor did they have privileges and power to lose as did the Church and the great land-owners. What they knew for certain was that if they backed the wrong side, they might lose their lands and face the same mass deportations that the Acadians had suffered only twenty years earlier. Moreover, a good many people (particularly women, who were more often able to read than their husbands) were intrigued by the radical ideas of the Americans, and would support them if it seemed safe:

> *La veuve Gabourie, à Saint-Vallier, a fait plus de mal dans cette paroisse qu'aucun autre; elle tenait souvent chez elle des assemblées où elle présidait tandant à soulever les esprits contre le gouvernement et à les animer en faveur des rebelles. Pour mieux parvenir à son but détestable, elle leur faisait boire des liqueurs fortes.*
> François Baby, Gabriel Taschereau *et* Jenkin Williams,
> *Journal . . . de la tournée qu'ils ont faite . . . par ordre*
> *du général Carleton . . . pour l'examen des personnes qui*
> *ont assisté ou aidé les rebelles. . . .*

[At Saint-Vallier the widow Gabourie did more harm in this parish than anyone else. She held meetings at her house, where she presided, trying to turn people against the government so they would support the rebels. To help her achieve her detestable goal she made them drink strong spirits . . . ]

*La femme d'Augustin Chabot, à Saint-Pierre de l'Île d'Orléans a perverti par ses discours séditieux (en courant les maisons d'un bout à l'autre) presque tous les habitants; il parait que cette femme a beaucoup de langue et a fait, suivant les rapports de plusieurs habitants, beaucoup de sensations dans leurs esprits.*

[At Saint-Pierre de l'Île d'Orléans the wife of Augustin Chabot perverted by her seditious speeches almost all the inhabitants by going to every house from one end of the island to the other. It appears that this woman had a ready tongue, and according to the reports of a number of people, made a great impression.]

Mme. Chabot did her work so well that when three agents of the government crossed over to the Île d'Orléans to organize the militia, two hundred and fifty men gathered in Saint-Pierre and beat them almost senseless. So in the autumn of 1775 Carleton, with virtually no militia support, was obliged to commit three-quarters of his tiny garrison of British regulars to the ramshackle little fort at Saint-Jean (St. John's), south of Montreal, to block the American army that was gradually working its way north along the traditional Richelieu River invasion route – and the American invaders were able to raise two French Canadian regiments from the district south of Montreal.

Hardly a Canadian will take up arms to oppose them. Everything seems to be desperate and I cannot but fear that before this reaches your Lordship Canada will be as fully in the Possession of the Rebels as any other Province upon the Continent. I shall stay till every hope is gone, which will I fear be but a short time. . . . Many of the Canadians [near Saint-Jean] are in arms against the King's Troops and not one hundred in the Towns of Montreal and Quebec are with us. St. John's and Montreal must soon fall into their hands – and I doubt Quebec will follow too soon. In this situation I hold myself in readiness to embark for England.

Chief Justice William Hey to Lord Chancellor Apsley,
from Quebec, 18 September 1775

### CHAPTER TWO

# *Invasion and Occupation*

Guy Carleton's adversary in the struggle for Canada was General Richard Montgomery, a competent ex-British officer who had once been his neighbour in Ireland. Montgomery had been present at the capture of Montreal in 1760 and had been wounded alongside Carleton in Cuba in 1762, but then he had sold his commission and quit the army. The story was that he had been passed over for promotion, and perhaps that played a part in his decision, but in 1772 he took passage to New York, bought an estate at Kingsbridge, and shortly after married Janet Livingston, whom he had first met a dozen years before on his way up to the attack on Montreal in 1760. They had fallen in love (although one must be careful, when describing the relationship between an upper-class man and woman of the eighteenth century, not to impose twentieth-century definitions too cavalierly) and eventually, after all the delays inherent in a world of harsh rules, slow communications, and limited resources, Richard Montgomery had abandoned his military career and rearranged his life so that they could be together.

Janet Livingston was a daughter of the most prominent New York family that supported the Revolution, and such marriages carry their obligations. So in 1775, at the age of thirty-eight, Montgomery found himself in command of the American troops invading Canada. In London he had known the leaders of the Opposition in the House of Commons – men like Burke and Fox – and there was no doubt that he was in sympathy with the rebels' cause, but he did not want to command their army. He just happened to be the most experienced professional officer around who had the right family connections and political sympathies, and so it was expected of him. As he took leave of his wife to try to capture Montreal for the second time, he remarked after a long silence: " ' 'Tis a strange world, my masters. I once thought so, now I know it.' "

"He is a genteel appearing man, tall and slender of make, bald on the Top of his head," said a fellow officer of Montgomery, and the amateur soldiers he commanded were much impressed by his martial bearing. "General Montgomery was born to command," wrote Private George Morrison. "His easy and affable condescension to both officers and men, while it forbids an improper familiarity, creates love and esteem; and exhibits him the gentleman and the soldier." Montgomery was not equally impressed with the discipline and training of his volunteer American troops – "If Job had been a general in my situation, his memory had not been so famous for patience" – but they were a lot more numerous than Carleton's soldiers.

Montreal was a city second in importance only to Quebec, but when Montgomery's troops captured the key fort at Saint-Jean that guarded the southern approach to the city on 3 November, Carleton did not have enough British regular troops left to defend Montreal itself. As Montgomery's army closed in, the British commander abandoned Montreal on 12 November. But it was hard to leave. First his vessels were trapped in the port for several days by an unfavourable wind, and then, as the flotilla of eleven little ships dropped downstream, it was discovered that the delay had given the Americans time to set up an artillery battery at Sorel, forty-five miles below Montreal, to prevent Carleton from reaching Quebec. There was no chance of escaping by land, as the habitants were going over to the Americans all the way down the river on both sides – and the commander of the battery at Sorel was summoning Carleton to surrender:

Sir: . . . You are very sensible that I am in Possession at this Place, and that, from the strength of the United Colonies on both sides your own situation is Rendered Very disagreeable. . . . If you will Resign your Fleet to me Immediately, without destroying the Effects on Board, You and Your men shall be used with due civility, together with women & Children on Board. To this I shall expect Your direct and Immediate answer. Should you Neglect You will Cherefully take the Consequences which will follow.

Colonel James Easton, Sorel, 15 November 1775

Carleton ordered the officer commanding the little fleet of British ships trapped in the narrow channel above Sorel not to surrender before the last possible moment. Then he and two soldiers dressed themselves as habitants—grey homespun clothes, tasselled red cap, red sash and *bottes sauvages* – and entrusted themselves to Captain Bouchette, one of the ships' captains who knew the river well. They rowed quietly past the American guns in a whale-boat at the dead of night, at one point passing so close to the American sentries that they shipped their oars and lay in the bottom of the boat, paddling the icy water with cupped hands to muffle the noise. In the morning, at Three Rivers, they found a British ship which took them the rest of the way to Quebec:

On the 19th [of November 1775] . . . to the unspeakable joy of the friends of the Government, and to the utter Dismay of the abettors of Sedition and Rebellion, General Carleton arrived in the *Fell*, arm'd ship, accompanied by an arm'd schooner. We saw our Salvation in his Presence.

Thomas Ainslie, Collector of Customs, Quebec

Meanwhile, on 13 November, the American army had marched into Montreal. A delegation of merchants tried to dissuade General Montgomery from allowing his troops into the city, but he pointed out that they were suffering from the cold–and reminded the merchants of the "dreadful consequences of a bombardment." Twelve prominent Montrealers (six French and six English) signed the terms of capitulation, by which Montgomery granted the citizens of the city religious freedom and promised

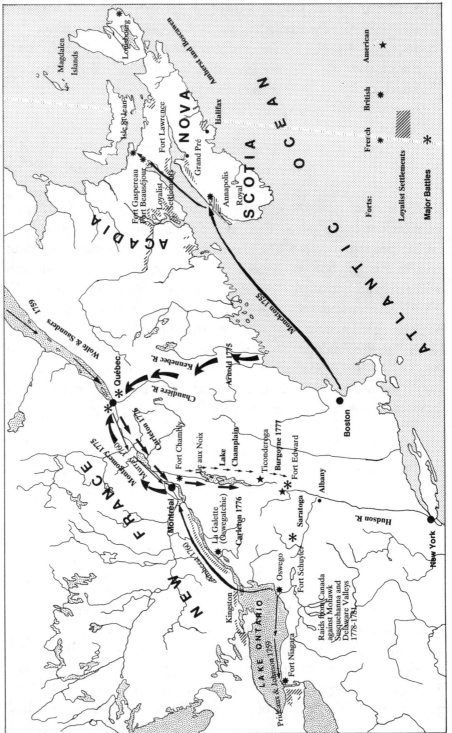

THE STRUGGLE FOR NORTH AMERICA – 1750-1790

that they would not be required to contribute to the cost of the American invasion, nor would they be expected to fight against the British crown. It was an attempt to win over the hearts and minds of the Montrealers. As General George Washington had warned in his orders to the American expeditionary force, "You will be particularly careful to pay the full value for all provisions, or other accomodations, which the Canadians may provide for you on your march."

General Montgomery's father-in-law, Robert R. Livingston, now came north as far as Fort Ticonderoga at the head of a Congressional committee sent to assess the progress of the Canadian campaign, but Montgomery was otherwise engaged and could not meet him. On 28 November, leaving a garrison behind him in Montreal under the command of General David Wooster, he sailed down to Quebec City with what was left of his army. (Many had gone home after the surrender of Montreal, and others had to be left to garrison the city.) But he wrote to Janet: "I live in hopes to see you in six weeks," and he had some reason for his optimism. Virtually all of the settled part of the province – a cleared strip of land extending about three miles inland on either side of the river along a two-hundred-mile stretch between Montreal and Quebec, almost like a northern Nile valley hemmed in by forests, not deserts – was now under American occupation. Less than one square mile of Canada, the area within the walls of Quebec City, remained under British control, and that was already besieged by another force of Americans, commanded by Benedict Arnold, which had marched straight north through the wilderness from New England.

But so long as the British held Quebec, Canada was not really conquered, for there was every chance that a British fleet would arrive in the spring, land a fresh army at the fortified city, and set out to reconquer the province. Everybody knew that – there were several recent historical precedents for it – so there was no point in expecting the majority of French Canadians to come down off the fence until Quebec fell. Moreover, most of General Arnold's soldiers were almost certain to go home after their term of enlistment expired at the end of the year, and Richard Montgomery's volunteers were equally impatient to get the job finished and get home, as he was himself: "The instant I can with decency slip my neck out of this yoke," he had written to Janet, "I will return to my family and farm, and that peace of mind which I can't have in my present situation."

So Montgomery decided that the American revolutionary forces had to make a direct assault on Quebec on the first dark and stormy night.

Since the Americans had hardly any siege equipment except ladders, they decided to avoid the walled city on the heights, and instead to attack along the shore against both ends of the Lower Town, a narrow strip of land between the base of the cliff and the St. Lawrence given over mainly to commercial properties. It was an easier target, since its streets were merely closed off with barricades, but even if the Americans succeeded, that would still leave the walled city uncaptured. However, Montgomery hoped that the merchants of the city would then insist on surrender to protect their warehouses in the Lower Town.

> If you receive this it will be the last this hand will ever write you. Orders are given for a general storm of Quebec this night; and Heaven only knows what may be my fate; but whatever it be, I cannot resist the inclination I feel to assure you that I experience no reluctance in this cause, to venture a life which I consider is only lent to be used when my country demands it.
>
> Captain John Macpherson of Philadelphia, aide-de-camp
> to General Montgomery, to his father,
> 31 December 1775

Montgomery and Arnold had around two thousand New Englanders and Virginians outside Quebec City. The five thousand people inside the walls included about eighteen hundred men of military age, but only ninety were British regular soldiers: the rest of Carleton's force was composed of over five hundred French-speaking militia (whose devotion to the British crown was doubtful); three hundred English-speaking militia (mostly of American origin, and even more doubtful); around five hundred seamen and marines from the ships in port; two hundred Royal Highland Emigrants (mostly Scottish veterans of the army that had taken Quebec in the previous war, who had subsequently settled on the St. Lawrence below Quebec); and about one hundred and fifty volunteers from Newfoundland who had arrived just before the siege began. Carleton could hardly be sure that even half of them would actually fight – but at four in the morning on New Year's Eve, Montgomery and Arnold began their assault on the city under the cover of a blinding snowstorm. Since many of the Americans were wearing British uniforms captured at Saint-Jean, they had pinned little paper streamers to their caps on which were printed the words "Liberty or Death." Montgomery's men were to attack the western end of the Lower Town, while Arnold's force worked its way along the shore from the east.

It now began to grow a little light, the Garrison had discover'd us and Sent out Two hundred men who took possession of Some houses which we had to pass. . . . They Sallied down in a lane from the wall. . . . I order'd . . . my men . . . to follow me, and we pushed on as fast as possible. . . .

I heard a shout in Town, which made me think that our people had got possession of the Same, the men were so thick within the Picketts, . . . I was Just about to Hail them, when one of them hail'd me, he asked who I was (I was now within Six rods of the Picketts) I answer'd a friend, he asked me who I was a friend to, I answered to liberty, he then reply'd God-damn you, and then rais'd himself partly above the Picketts, I Clapt up my Piece which was Charged with a ball and Ten Buck shott Certainly to give him his due, But to my great mortification my Gun did not go off, I new prim'd her, and flushed and Try'd her again, but neither I, nor one in Ten of my men could get off our Guns they being so exceeding wet . . .

I order'd my men to go into a lower room of an house, and new Prime their Guns, and prick dry Powder into the Touch-holes, we Now found ourselves Surrounded by Six to one, I now finding no possibility of getting away, my Company were divided, and our arms being in such bad order, I thought it best to Surrender after being promis'd good quarters and Tender usuage.

Captain Henry Dearborn, Quebec, 1775

The assault was a total failure. General Arnold's column struggled along the narrow shore road leading to the Sault au Matelot (Sailor's Leap) promontory in knee-deep snow drifts, under constant fire from the British troops on the walls fifty to a hundred feet above them, and took the first barricade ("Pickett") by storm – but Arnold was wounded in that attack, and his men were forced to abandon the single cannon they had been towing on a sleigh. So when they rounded the point and faced the main barricade across the end of Sault au Matelot and St. Peter streets, stretching a hundred yards from the cliff to the river, they hesitated. Eventually, they tried to storm the twelve-foot barricade with scaling ladders, but by then it was fully manned by the British defenders, and no American got over the top alive. Many of Arnold's men now sought cover from the deadly British fire in the houses on either side of the narrow street leading up to the barricade – and then a British force poured out from the Palace gate behind them and trapped them between two fires.

> Captain Lawes of the Royal Engineers and Captain M'Dougall of the Royal Emigrants with a hundred and twenty men . . . had hardly reached the advanced barricade before they fell in with the enemy's rearguard [Dearborn's men], which they took by complete surprise and captured to a man. Leaving M'Dougall to secure these prisoners before following on, Lawes pushed eagerly forward, round the corner of the Sault au Matelot cliff, and running in among the Americans facing the main barricade, called out, "You are all my prisoners."
>
> "No, we're not, you're ours!" they answered. "No, no," replied Lawes, as coolly as if on parade, "don't mistake yourself, I vow to God you're mine!"
>
> "But where are your men?" asked the astonished Americans; and then Lawes suddenly found that he was utterly alone. The roar of the storm and the work of securing the prisoners on the far side of the advanced barricade had prevented the men who should have followed him from understanding that only a few were needed with M'Dougall.
>
> But Lawes put a bold face on it and answered, "O, Ho, make yourselves easy! My men are all around here and they'll be with you in a twinkling." He was then seized and disarmed. Some of the Americans called out, "Kill him! Kill him!" But a Major Meigs protected him. The whole parley had lasted about ten minutes when M'Dougall came running up with the missing men, released Lawes, and made prisoners of the nearest Americans. Lawes at once stepped forward and called on the rest to surrender. . . . A few men ran round by wharf and escaped on the tidal flats . . .

but after a hurried consultation the main body . . . laid down their arms.

William Wood, *The Father of British Canada:*
*A Chronicle of Carleton*

The column that attacked the western end of the Lower Town didn't even get as far as Arnold's. General Montgomery rose at two – having written to Janet earlier in the evening: "I wish it were well over with all my heart, and sigh for home like a New Englander" – and led his New Yorkers east along the narrow path between the cliff and the river. It was heaped with slabs and chunks of ice heaved up out of the river. "The worst Path I ever travelled," recalled Colonel Donald Campbell, Montgomery's Deputy Quartermaster-General, "being obliged in several places to scramble up the slant of the Rocks (with 2 foot snow on them & a precipice to our right) & then descending by pulling the Skirt of our Coats under us & sliding down 15 or 20 foot, & this repeated several times before we got to the first Barrier."

Around five in the morning, Montgomery's troops reached the Près-de-Ville barricade, only fifty feet wide between cliff and river, sealing off the western access to the Lower Town. With axes and saws they cut narrow gaps in the two lines of thick posts that barred the path. When they stepped through the second barrier, Montgomery and his officers were just dimly visible in the swirling snow and pre-dawn murk to the fifty French Canadian militia and British gunners crouching silently in a fortified two-storey log building another hundred yards on. A lone American came cautiously forward, the storm in his face, to examine it. Then Montgomery waved his sword, shouted "Come on, brave boys, Quebec is ours," and led the charge. Seconds later, the four guns in the building fired a lethal hail of grapeshot into the Americans, while the French Canadians simultaneously poured in a musket volley. The whole front of the American column went down together, and the survivors retreated back into the blizzard. When the light came, Richard Montgomery's frozen body was found a couple of dozen yards from the barricade, with one arm stiffly protruding from the snow that covered everything else. Nearby was the body of John Macpherson, the twenty-year-old idealist who had been lent his life by his country.

The command of the Army, by the death of my truly great and good friend, General Montgomery, devolved on me, a task, I find, too heavy under my present circumstances. I received a wound by a ball through my left leg, at the time I gained the first battery, at the lower town, which, by the loss of blood, rendered me very weak. As soon as the main body came up, with some assistance I returned to the hospital, near a mile, on foot, being obliged to draw one leg after me, and a great part of the way under continual fire of the enemy from the walls, at no greater distance than fifty yards. I providentially escaped, though several were shot down at my side. . . .

About three hundred . . . were taken prisoners, and as near as I judge, about sixty killed and wounded. . . . The prisoners are treated politely, and supplied with every thing the garrison affords. Governour Carleton sent to let me know that the soldiers' baggage, if I pleased, might be sent to them, which I shall immediately send. . . .

I have no thoughts of leaving this proud town, until I first enter it in triumph. My wound has been exceeding painful, but it is now easy, and the surgeons assure me will be well in eight weeks. I know you will be anxious for me . . .

General Benedict Arnold to his sister Hannah,
Camp before Quebec, 6 January 1776

❖

In a desperate effort to maintain an image of irresistible success for the increasingly doubtful French Canadians, the Americans pretended at first that their attack had not been a total failure. (To explain Montgomery's absence they concocted a story saying that he had gone to Boston through the woods to bring new forces north.) A few French Canadians believed this, and on 1 January 1776 a group of them appeared at Saint-Roch, just outside Quebec City, expecting to join Montgomery's soldiers in the pillage of the Lower Town. They were disappointed, and the story of Montgomery's defeat quickly spread about the country all the way up to Montreal.

There is little confidence to be placed in the Canadians. . . . The
Clergy almost universally refuse absolution to those who are our
friends, and preach to the people that it is not now too late to
take arms against us; that the Bostonians are but a handful of
men; which, you know, is too true.

> Brigadier-General David Wooster, commanding the
> Congressional forces in Montreal, January 1776

The nuns of Quebec were compassionate to the enemy's troops, as
they had been in 1759. The Mother Superior of the Ursuline convent in
the city sent Arnold's men outside the walls "coverlets and linen for
bandages, and the nuns, although relieved that an enemy had failed, went
about [the hospital containing the wounded American prisoners] repeat-
ing sympathetically, 'Poor Montgomery is dead!' ." But while General
Arnold still clung to the belief that he could raise a new Canadian regiment of three to four hundred men for another attack, his surgeon, Dr.
Senter, was less hopeful: "The peasants, however friendly disposed,
thought it too precarious a juncture to show themselves in that capacity
[i.e., join up and fight the British], and those nigh rather retreated back
into the country than gave any assistance."

The French Canadians could scarcely be blamed for their caution.
Even those who dreamt of independence knew that it could be fatal for
an outsider to take sides in a family quarrel that might still be reconciled,
and in the winter of 1775-76 the breach between the Americans and
the British was not yet permanent. Carleton's gentle behaviour toward
captured rebels and disaffected local English speakers clearly showed
his belief that these were merely deluded people who might yet be
brought back to their proper loyalty, and indeed there were few Americans who were yet ready to go all the way to independence. They preferred rather to define their dispute as being with the King's evil ministers,
not with the King himself (and so habitually referred to British troops as
"Ministerials").

Matters were sliding rapidly out of control in the Thirteen Colonies
now that the shooting had started, and forbidden thoughts were being
expressed in public–Tom Paine's *Common Sense*, a pamphlet attacking the
very principle of monarchy, was published early in 1776, and sold

120,000 copies in three months – but there would be no American declaration of independence until the following July. In the circumstances,
French Canadians were bound to be cautious: the Americans themselves
were still on the fence politically, and Quebec City had not fallen. When
the news of the disaster there on New Year's Eve reached General Washington, he urgently wrote to Benedict Arnold (now commanding all
American forces around Quebec despite his incapacitating wound):

> I need not mention to you the great importance of this place, and
> the consequent possession of all Canada in the scale of American
> affairs; you are well apprized of it. To whomsoever it belongs, in
> their favour, probably, will the balance turn. If it is ours, success,
> I think, will most certainly crown our virtuous struggles; if it is
> theirs, the contest, at least, will be doubtful, hazardous and
> bloody. The glorious work must be accomplished this Winter,
> otherwise it will become difficult, most probably impracticable.
> For [the British] Administration knowing that it will be impos-
> sible ever to reduce us to a state of slavery and arbitrary rule
> without it, will certainly send a large reinforcement there in the
> Spring. . . .
>     Wishing you a speedy recovery, and the possession of those
> laurels which your bravery and perseverance justly merit, I am,
> dear sir, etc.,
>
>                                             George Washington

Congress even managed to scrape up some fresh troops to send to
Arnold outside Quebec – but by now disease had become rife in the American camp, as it often did during eighteenth-century sieges because of
poor sanitation and crowded conditions. The worst problem was smallpox. It was potentially a fatal illness, but most American soldiers were
well aware that you could inoculate yourself against it by rubbing smallpox discharge into an open cut, and so escape with a relatively mild case
of the disease. With a number of real cases of smallpox in the camp, it
proved impossible to prevent the American troops from inoculating themselves, even though it would put them out of action for up to a month,
and so "from the 1st of January to the 1st of March, we never had more
than seven hundred effective men on the ground, and frequently not more

than five hundred." Arnold was never able to launch another assault against Quebec – and meanwhile Carleton's numerically superior forces, safe and relatively warm inside the walls of the city, had only to wait patiently for British reinforcements to arrive when the ice melted on the river.

Throughout the winter of 1775-76, however, almost all French Canadians lived under American military occupation. Probably no more than five hundred French Canadians fought openly for the Americans, although in the fifty parishes affected by the invasion almost all the captains of militia compromised themselves to some extent by cooperating with the American military occupation. There was certainly little hostility to the Americans in the early stage of the occupation, but five months was long enough to make the American presence thoroughly unpopular, especially in Montreal, where the man whom Montgomery had left in charge, Brigadier-General David Wooster, was a Protestant bigot and a petty tyrant. "When Wooster was appointed, I washed my hands of the consequences, by declaring him in my Opinion, totally unequal to the Service," wrote Silas Deane, an American Congressman. And when Wooster grew nervous about the state of public opinion in Montreal, he arrested "forty sledloads" of suspected British sympathisers and sent them into exile in Albany, New York – which made everybody else who was not an outright American partisan very nervous.

There was also the usual quota of misbehaviour by undisciplined volunteer troops in a strange country (there is no shame a hundred miles from home), and by early spring an American officer was reporting: "The peasantry in general have been ill-used; they have in some instances been dragooned, with the point of the bayonet, to furnish wood for the garrison . . . It is true, they have been promised payment, from time to time; yet they look upon such promises as vague, their labour and property lost, and the Congress and the United Colonies as bankrupts." And the peasants were not entirely wrong: like all revolutionaries, the Americans were desperately short of money, and when Congress tried the expedient of printing paper money the Canadians found their patience with the occupiers wearing very thin.

To the Inhabitants of the District of Quebec. . . . We have seen fit to give Circulation among the Public to a necessary Amount of the Paper money issued by Order of the honourable Congress, upon the general credit of the united Colonies of the Continent. . . . Whoever shall accept the said Money of the Congress, shall receive the Amount of it in Gold and Silver within the space of three or four Months from the date of this Present; while on the contrary Every Person who shall refuse to accept it at Par and without Discount, shall be considered an Enemy of the united Colonies and treated As Such.

Decree by General Arnold, 6 March 1776

"About fifteen thousand Dollars have been paid away," wrote one of his officers at the end of the month, "and with it is gone the affections of the people in general." The French Canadians distrusted paper money from bitter experience, and the "Continental" dollar was even worse than the paper money that had been forced on them in wartime by the old French regime. Continental dollars went into a steep decline on the day they were issued, and by 1779 they were worth only three cents. "Not worth a Continental" was already becoming a catch-phrase, and being forced to accept this paper in payment for American purchases totally alienated the French Canadians from their would-be liberators. Arnold's army was subsequently reduced to handing out handwritten IOUs ("certificates") for the supplies it requisitioned.

When Benjamin Franklin and a group of commissioners were sent to Montreal by Congress in April 1776 to try to improve matters, Franklin ended up lending the army of occupation £353 in gold of his own money. "If money cannot be had to support your Army here with honour, so as to be respected, instead of hated by the people, we report it as our firm and unanimous opinion that it is better immediately to withdraw it," the Commissioners wrote back to Congress – and added: "Till the arrival of money, it seems improper to propose the Federal union of this Province with the others." The amount that was needed was £20,000. "With this supply, and a little success," the Commissioners wrote, "it may be possible to regain the affections of the people, to attach them firmly to our cause, and induce them to accept a free Government, perhaps to enter into the Union." The Congress immediately sent all the hard currency in the treasury to Canada – but it amounted to only £1,600, less than one-twelfth of the amount required.

The signs of disaffection multiplied, and in the early spring some hundreds of habitants responded to the summons of the seigneur of l'Île-aux-Grues, Louis Liénard de Beaujeu, and the local *curé*, and marched to attack the American outpost at Pointe-Lévis. But other French Canadians warned the Americans, and helped them stop Beaujeu. Fifty of his advance guard were intercepted at Saint-Pierre-de-Montmagny on 25 March.

> *Ces éclaireurs rencontrèrent les Américains auxquels s'étaient joints une centaine des Canadiens, amis du Congrès. Dans l'escarmouche qui s'ensuivit, deux frères, Joseph et François Morin, de Saint-Roch des Aulnaies, et un petit garçon de Saint-Thomas, appartenant au corps des éclaireurs de M. de Beaujeu, furent tués. Sur trente-deux soldats du même parti qui s'étaient barricadés dans la maison de Michel Blais, dix furent blessés et faits prisonniers avec les autres enfermés dans la maison.*
>
> Abbé Ivanhoë Caron, *Les Canadiens Français et l'invasion américaine de 1774-1775*

[These scouts encountered the Americans and about a hundred Canadians who were supporters of Congress. In the skirmish that followed two brothers, Joseph and François Morin, from Saint-Roch-des-Aulnaies, and a young boy from Saint-Thomas, who was serving as a scout for M. de Beaujeu, were killed. Out of thirty-two soldiers of the same party who had barricaded themselves in Michel Blais' house, ten were wounded and taken prisoner along with the others.]

It was really a kind of mini-civil war among French Canadians, of the sort that very often happens among occupied peoples, but it did mark a substantial shift in opinion. By spring many, perhaps most, ordinary people had decided that the British devil they knew was preferable to the newer American one (especially since the American devil had no money and stole a lot). So when the British navy arrived in the river below Quebec City carrying regular army troops on 6 May 1776 and the great American retreat began, most French Canadians did not grieve to see them go. There were no battles, but the occupation of Montreal ended on 15 June, six months after it began, and the Americans fled south up the Richelieu

River by boat back to Île aux Noix, a swampy, malarial island on the present Quebec-Vermont border that lay "scarcely above the surface of the water."

By then, their army was in a truly dreadful state, "broken and dis-heartened, half of it under inoculation, or under other diseases; soldiers without pay, without discipline, and altogether reduced to live from hand to mouth," reported the Congressional commissioners. Near the end a new commander, General John Thomas, had tried to forbid the rage for inoculation in the army, and set an example by refusing to do it himself – but he was soon dead of smallpox in its virulent, uninoculated form, after having lain blind and comatose for weeks.

> All day long the dead-pits were open; and this poor body after that, lying mute and still in its rags on a dirty blanket, passed down to an unknown grave "without a sie [sigh] from a Friend or relative, or a single morner to follow it." Unable to bear such "scenes of horror" longer without a respite, several excellent officers deliberately sat down together "in good Earnest," and calmly drank themselves insensible.
>
> *Our Struggle for the Fourteenth Colony*

By the end of June 1776, all of Canada was clear of Americans. Over ten thousand had come across the frontier, and almost half never saw their homes again. Three years later, Benedict Arnold changed sides, becoming the most celebrated traitor in American history, and in the winter of 1782, when Brigadier-General Benedict Arnold of the British army made his first appearance at court in London, he "was ushered into the Royal presence on the arm of Sir Guy Carleton." One should not judge him too harshly: it was, after all, a kind of Anglo-Saxon civil war.

In the meantime, Carleton was already a hero, both in Quebec and at home in England, even though his hope of being able to raise a large army of French Canadian volunteers had been disappointed. In September 1776 he wrote to the Colonial Secretary in London: "I think there is nothing to fear from them while we are in a state of prosperity, and nothing to hope for while in distress." However, the influence of the Catholic Church, and in particular the refusal of almost all priests to administer the Sacraments to anybody fighting for the Americans, had at least been enough to stop the mass of the population from defecting to the other side.

Nor did the efforts of the Church on behalf of the British slacken after the American retreat. On the first anniversary of Montgomery's assault against Quebec, a solemn High Mass with a sung *Te Deum* was held in the cathedral, with Bishop Briand on the throne. Twelve French Canadians who had assisted the Americans were obliged to present themselves with ropes round their necks, do penance before the congregation, and humbly "crave pardon of their God, Church and King." But many years later there were still isolated gravestones in some parishes where French Canadians who had fought for the Revolution, and refused to crawl before the Bishop afterward, were buried, at the last, in unconsecrated ground.

### CHAPTER THREE

# *A Conditional State*

Once British reinforcements had arrived in Quebec in May 1776 (including a garrison force of four thousand German mercenary troops who were quartered on the French Canadian population as if to punish them for their lack of enthusiasm for the British cause), Canada provided a secure base from which the British army could operate against the American rebels, just as Carleton had foreseen. But the one time Carleton's strategy was actually tried, when General "Gentleman Johnny" Burgoyne tried to cut the Thirteen Colonies in two in 1777 by marching down to the Hudson river and linking up with another British force coming up from New York, the enterprise ended in disaster and Burgoyne's surrender at Saratoga. And it was that American victory which persuaded France to enter the war on the American side.

The French alliance with the Thirteen Colonies was motivated by France's global power struggle with Britain, not by any desire to regain "New France," but the question of a renewed attack on Canada naturally arose very quickly, for the French fleet under Admiral d'Estaing was soon at Boston awaiting orders. By October 1778 the young Marquis de Lafayette, a French nobleman who had taken service in the Continental army, had concocted a vast scheme whereby he would lead five thousand American troops north in the spring of 1779 and seize Montreal. Then, when almost all the British troops in the province had been drawn westwards to meet that invasion, "a Body of from 2,000 to 5,000 French Troops" convoyed by four ships of the line and as many frigates would pass up the St. Lawrence and seize Quebec. "By the latter End of July or about the Middle of August the Reduction of *Canada* might be so far compleated that the Ships might proceed to the Investiture of Halifax," with the assistance of militia from Massachusetts and New Hampshire. By October, with luck, the Franco-American forces would occupy Newfoundland, the last piece of British territory in North America.

The entry of France into the war transformed French Canadian opinion. "There is scarcely a Rebel, or Canadian, or Indian, in, or near the Province but believe [the French fleet is coming], & I fear most even expect it with Pleasure," reported the new Governor of Canada, Frederick Haldimand, a French-speaking Swiss Protestant by origin, in October 1779. "[Not much] would be required to raise the whole Country in Arms against England." Even the Church was getting shaky in its loyalty to the British:

> However sensible I am of the good conduct of the clergy in general during the invasion of the Province of the year 1775, I am well aware that since France was known to take part in the contest, and since the address of Count d'Estaing and a letter of M. de la Fayette . . . have been circulated in the Province, many of the Priests have changed their opinions, and in the case of another Invasion would, I am afraid, adopt another system of conduct.
>
> Governor Haldimand, 1779

Haldimand and Canada were spared another invasion because the Americans and the French did not trust each other – and both were quite right. France had absolutely no intention of helping to evict the British from Canada, since it was their presence there that made the Americans dependent on France. In March 1778 the Comte de Vergennes, the

French Foreign Minister, sent secret instructions to Conrad-Alexandre Gérard, France's representative to the American Congress:

*La défaite du general Bourgoyne ayant précipité les evenemens au de là de toute attente, Le Roi Sentit la nécessité de prendre enfin un parti décisif à l'égard de l'Amérique: cette nécessité devint d'autant plus urgente que l'Ang^re de son côté commença à cette époque, à ouvrir les yeux sur ses fautes et son impuissance, et qu'elle songea sérieusement aux moyens de se réconcilier promptement avec ses Colonies. . . .*

[General Burgoyne's defeat having accelerated events beyond all expectation, the King felt the need to take decisive action at last with regard to America. The need became all the more urgent since England, at this time, began to realize its errors and its weakness, and to consider seriously ways of achieving a prompt reconciliation with its Colonies. . . . Therefore the King had talks opened with the Deputies of the Congress, and on 6 February of this year a treaty of friendship and trade and a conditional alliance were concluded with Them. . . .

The Independence of North America and its permanent association with France have been the King's principal goal. . . .

The deputies of Congress have proposed that the King commit himself to supporting the conquest *by the Americans* of Canada, Nova Scotia, and the Floridas . . . but the King considers that the retention of these three countries, or at least of Canada, by England would make the Americans anxious and vigilant, *and make them feel all the more that they need the King's friendship and alliance*, and that it is not in his interest to destroy that. Therefore, His Majesty thinks that he should not undertake any commitment regarding the proposed Conquest.

This is the King's guiding principle in the matter, and he wishes M. Gérard to adopt it as the basis of his diplomatic conversations. If, however, the Congress becomes too pressing and M. Gérard judges that the King cannot refuse to cooperate without creating suspicion about his good will and the rectitude of his intentions, he can, in that case, accede to their wishes; but he must make them understand nevertheless that [keeping] the conquest that they have in mind, if it comes to pass, must not be made an essential condition of the next peace settlement. M. Gérard will be well aware that this last reservation will have to be made with enough skill not to upset the Congress.]

As it turned out, the French came under no serious pressure from the Continental Congress to help in the conquest of Canada, because the Americans, after a little thought, concluded that the re-emergence of a permanent French military presence in Canada would be just as unwelcome as a continuation of the British military presence there. Quite apart from the practical military defects in Lafayette's invasion proposal, General Washington informed Congress, there was another objection "which is, in my estimation, insurmountable, and alarms all my feelings for the true and permanent interests of my country. This is the introduction of a large body of French troops into Canada, and putting them in possession of the Capital of that Province, attached to them by ties of blood, habit, manners, religion, and former connexion of government." Washington was afraid that once France regained Canada, the French government might find it "impracticable to withdraw." So Congress agreed to cancel the whole plan in January 1779, and it was never discussed again.

There was no further attempt to invade the colony before the war ended in defeat for Britain and in London's recognition of American independence in 1783. The Treaty of Paris confirmed the fact that even in victory France had no interest in regaining "New France." The North American colony would be practically impossible for the French to hold in the long run. British seapower generally dominated the North Atlantic crossing and would probably cut Quebec off from France once more as soon as the next Anglo-French war came along, while the Americans had a rapidly expanding population (about three million people at independence) and were right next door to Canada. By the 1780s it was absolutely clear that control of Canada could fall only to Britain or the United States in the coming decades, and the Comte de Vergennes' preference was clear.

While Canada rightfully belonged to France, the French Foreign Minister said, she would waive her claim: Great Britain should stay in Canada, in order to ensure that the United States would remain Britain's enemy and France's ally. So although the French were on the winning side at the peace negotiations in 1783, in the end the defeated British were allowed to keep their remaining North American possessions, while the French settled for the return of their West Indian islands that had been occupied by the British during the war, plus the acquisition of Tobago. At one point in the peace negotiations, when the chief American negotiator, Benjamin Franklin, demanded that the United States be given Quebec and Nova Scotia, it was the French negotiators who persuaded the demoralized British to resist the demand and maintain their presence in North America. It made perfectly good sense in terms of the great-power game, but this second and more callous act of abandonment stretched the emotional ties between France and its former Canadian colony very thin.

That, in a nutshell, is why Canada exists. All the apparatus of the Canadian state and all the convolutions of the Canadian identity grace the world with their presence only because in a long-forgotten strategic context, when Britain and France were mortal enemies and the United States was a struggling new nation, it suited everybody's tactics of the moment to leave Canada under British control. That outcome was not even a vital aim of any of the major players, in the sense that they would have died in a ditch rather than abandon it. It simply suited their purposes rather better than any alternative arrangement, and required less effort since it merely perpetuated the *status quo*. (But if the Americans had captured Quebec in 1775 and held on to it throughout the war, it is to be doubted that anybody would have cared enough to try to reverse that new *status quo* either.) Like most countries, the Canadian state is an accident, not the realization of some immortal destiny. Nor had the accident yet become an irrevocable fact in 1783: it remained only a *conditional* fact for quite a long time afterward.

❖

Tories with their brats and wives
Should fly to save their wretched lives
                              Popular rhyme during the American Revolution

Before 1759, the British had ruled south of a line more or less corresponding to the present eastern Canadian border, and the French had ruled north of it. After 1783, Britain ruled *north* of the line, and the Americans (allied to the French, whose fleet had played a major role in their victory) ruled south of it. The irony was even richer because, for at least half a century afterwards, most of the people over whom the British ruled were French-speaking. But the French Canadians did not remain all alone in "British North America" for long: the British defeat in the Revolutionary War caused a northward flood of English-speaking refugees ("Tories" to the revolutionaries, "Loyalists" in their own estimation) who had backed the losing side in what was, after all, partly a civil war among Americans. (The traditional estimate is that at the outset of the war one-third of Americans wanted independence, one-third supported the British crown, and one-third were neutral.)

> Kind husband, I am sorry to aquant you that our farme is sold. . . . they said if I did not quitt posesion that they had aright to . . . imprisen me – I have sufered most every thing but death it self in your long absens pray grant me spedy releaf or God only knows what will become of me and my frendles children. . . .
>
> Thay say my posesion was nothing, youre husband has forfeted his estate by joining the British Enemy with a free and vollentary will and thereby was forfeted to the Stat and sold. All at present from your cind and loveing wife.
>
> Letter from Phebe Ward of New Jersey to her husband
> serving with the King's forces, 6 June 1783

> Your memorialist was indicted for High Treason as it was then termed by usurped power of the rebels of the province of Connecticut for his attachment to the British government and was found guilty and condemned in Simsbury Mines a cavern seventy feet underground for two years. After lying in that dreadful situation four months and better and then with the greatest risk of his life attended with hunger and fatigue, escaped and got within the British lines at New York.
>
> "Memorial" (testimony) of Alexander Fairchild,
> Loyalist claimant to the British government

In the triumphant and vengeful atmosphere prevailing in the new United States after the victory, there could be no safety for the many Americans who had fought for the British, or even for their relatives.

When the British evacuation got underway in 1783 Sir Guy Carleton, now commanding all British forces in North America, held New York City, the last British foothold in the United States, while thousands of terrified Loyalists crammed into British ships in the harbour. Every empire gets its turn sooner or later. It was not quite the fall of Saigon in 1975, but it was close.

The largest proportion of the Loyalist refugees – an estimated thirty-two thousand – went to New Brunswick and Nova Scotia, tripling their previous populations. Thirteen disbanded Loyalist regiments were settled in a vast military colony extending up the St. John river valley:

> Our people went on shore and brought on board spruce and gooseberries and grass and pea vines with the blossoms on them, all of which grow wild here . . . Our land is five and twenty miles up the river. It is, I think, the roughest land I ever saw; but this is to be *the city*, they say!
>
> Sarah Frost, 28 June 1783, on her arrival at Saint John,
> New Brunswick

One obvious place to settle the rest of the refugees was along the border with New England in what was now becoming known as "Lower Canada" (Quebec), but that was barred to the Loyalists by Governor Haldimand. For the moment, at least, he preferred to leave that area (eventually to be called the "Eastern Townships") as an untouched forest barrier against any future American invasion. He also saw it as an area that should eventually be inhabited by French Canadians, on the grounds that "the frontiers should be settled by people professing a different language, and accustomed to other laws and government from those of our restless and enterprising neighbours of New England." Instead, Haldimand laid out sixteen townships west of Montreal along the upper St. Lawrence river and the northern shore of Lake Ontario for some eight thousand officially assisted Loyalists who, together with others making their own way west through New York state and back into British territory west of Lake Ontario, created the nucleus of "Upper Canada" (Ontario).

> [Lower Canada] is governed by the laws of France, and Popery is the established religion; [Upper Canada] by the laws of England, both in Church and State. . . .

Niagara is the present seat of government in Upper Canada. . . . This is a poor wretched straggling village, with a few
scattered cottages erected here and there as chance, convenience
or caprice dictated. . . .

The inhabitants of this country are very hospitable. Soon after
the entrance of a visitor, spirituous liquors, and madeira are
almost always introduced. . . . Among a people, where the cold is
extreme a considerable part of the year, where covered carriages
are unknown, and the roads indifferent, with few houses of
accomodation, it may be presumed that such refreshments are
not unacceptable. Indeed, if there is occasion to employ any of
the lower ranks, there is small progress to be made, without the
aid of liquors. Pay what you will to them for any small service
performed, the compact is never acknowledged as a just one,
unless there is an appeal to the rum bottle.

> "A Traveller's Impression in 1792-93"
>
> (author unknown)

Even after the Loyalist influx, francophones were at least a two-to-
one majority in British North America, but the anglophone settlements
in Ontario were the beginning of a process that was to cut French Canadians off from the westward expansion of the country and ultimately
reduce them to minority status even in the British-ruled part of the continent. Had the French Canadians realized that, the delicate balance of
their allegiance might have tipped the other way, for it was *their* ancestral
west – *le pays d'en haut* – that was being lost. But of course they didn't.

❖

There could be no doubt about the determination of the English-speaking
Loyalists to live under British rule, but even after the American Revolution
it was difficult to be as certain about the French Canadians. Being a
conquered people is a miserable experience even if the conquerors behave
tolerably well, and although the Americans seemed a less attractive proposition after French Canadians had experienced a winter's occupation by
them, the possibility of re-annexation to France – or even a kind of independence with French support – continued to tempt some sectors of
French Canadian society. It became even more tempting after the French

Revolution broke out in 1789, for the dilemma that had previously paralysed many French Canadians who were attracted to the ideas of liberty and equality – the fact that those ideas were only available in English, through the United States – seemed to be resolved.

> Imitate the examples of the peoples of America and of France. . . . Fear nothing from George III, or from his soldiers, whose numbers are too small to oppose your valor. The moment is favorable, and insurrection is the holiest of duties for you. Remember that being born French, you will always be suspected and persecuted by the English kings . . . Canadians, arm yourselves; call the Indians to your aid. Count on the support of your neighbours and on that of the French.
>
> *The Free French to their Brothers in Canada*,
> pamphlet issued in 1793 by Citoyen Edmond Genêt,
> representative of the French Republic in the
> United States

If French troops had actually appeared in force in the St. Lawrence valley at any time during the next twenty years of war between revolutionary France and Great Britain, they would probably have received a tumultuous welcome from much of the population. But the forces of the French Revolution were very unlikely to appear in the flesh, given British control of the sea, and their spiritual influence was greatly diminished, as time went on, by the revulsion that even sympathisers felt at the excesses of the Terror – and, far more importantly, by the resolute opposition of the Church. For the French revolutionaries had attacked every pillar of the *ancien régime* in France – including, very prominently, the Roman Catholic church. When a regime in Paris that elevated "reason" over religion appealed to French Canadians for support, the Catholic hierarchy in Quebec clung even more tightly to the skirts of the British.

> Our conquerors . . . inspired only horror and a foreboding chill. We could not persuade ourselves that men strange to our land, to our language, to our laws, to our usages and to our belief would ever be able to give to Canada that which she had just lost in changing masters. Generous nation, which has proved with so

much evidence how false were these prejudices; . . . kind nation, which gives each day new proofs to Canada of your liberality; no, no, you are not our enemies, nor those of our Holy Religion, which you respect. . . .

And if, after having learned of the overturn of the State and of the destruction of the true Faith in France . . . some amongst us are still found so blind or so evil-intentioned as to . . . inspire in the people criminal desires to return to their ancient masters, blame not on the whole what is only the vice of a small number.

Abbé Joseph-Octave Plessis, funeral oration for<br>Monseigneur Briand, former Bishop of Quebec, June 1794

The Catholic Church had become the dominant social and intellectual influence on the population of Quebec – far more powerful than it had been under French rule, for it was now the only major institution in the colony that remained under exclusively French Canadian control – and its horror of the free-thinking French revolutionaries bound it ever more closely to the conservative British rulers of Quebec. In November 1793 Monseigneur Charles-François Hubert, who had replaced Briand as the Bishop of Quebec on the latter's retirement in 1784, issued a circular letter to the clergy of the entire colony declaring that "the bonds which attached them to France had been entirely broken, and that all the loyalty and obedience which they formerly owed to the King of France, they now owed to His Britannic Majesty."

It would be many decades before the authority of the Church made the ideas of the French Revolution completely unmentionable in respectable French Canadian circles, however, and there might have been quite serious outbreaks of resistance to British rule if the regime Carleton had created with the Quebec Act had continued unchanged. He had got the importance of the Church right, and the position of that indispensable ally of British rule was not undermined by any subsequent legislation, but his ill-advised attempt to use the seigneurs as an instrument of British political control, by turning them into a North American equivalent of the English landed gentry, had been an unmitigated failure. Most French Canadians saw them simply as self-seeking collaborators. In 1788, one of the prominent French Canadian merchants of Montreal publicly protested that they had no right to claim to be "protectors of the people," as they had taken "very good care not to join their voices to those of the oppressed when the Germans, sent to defend the colony, came into it as if it were a conquered country."

But many of the potential causes of strife between French Canadians and their British rulers were removed by the Constitutional Act of 1791. It divided the province into Lower and Upper Canada (Quebec and Ontario), which meant that the French Canadians would remain comfortably in the majority in a province governed under French law, while almost all the new settlements of the English-speaking Loyalists would be in a separate province with English law and institutions. And both provinces were given elected legislatures, as a necessary concession to the spirit of the times. It was a far cry from the egalitarian democracy south of the border or in revolutionary France, but the legislatures were an important safety valve for political discontent – and in Quebec the existence of an elected Assembly created a new class of democratic politicians who rapidly eclipsed the seigneurs as spokesmen for popular grievances (a role which the seigneurs had filled extraordinarily badly). The French Canadians' struggle to hold their own against the commercially dominant English-speaking minority in Montreal and Quebec was to become a permanent, never fully resolved theme in the politics of Lower Canada, but the introduction of a kind of democratic politics allowed it to be waged mostly without violence.

As it happened, Carleton himself (now Lord Dorchester) was governor of Canada again by the time all this came about – but he applied the new arrangements with perfect grace and aplomb, while his wife held court in the manner she had learned as a girl at the court of Versailles. That sort of thing has always gone down well in Quebec City.

❖

It is easy to envisage plausible scenarios, from a sleepy sentry at the Près-de-Ville barricade in 1775 to a somewhat less competent British negotiator at the peace talks in 1783, that would have resulted in the loss of most or all of Britain's remaining North American territories to the United States. The French Canadians would have been assimilated, submerged by newcomers, or if necessary coerced, and the Loyalist refugees would all have been sent to the West Indies or England. The one constant factor which created even the *possibility* of a different outcome was the attitude of the French Canadians. They were certainly not enthusiastic about British rule, but their reluctance to leap out of the British frying pan into the American fire meant that the Americans actually needed an overwhelming military victory on the ground to foreclose the question of Canada's future. They never got that.

French Canada was hardly more than a collection of villages when, in the last third of the eighteenth century, it was cast adrift to survive as best it could in a continent overrun by English-speaking Protestants. And it is a considerable simplification to say that the French Canadians "chose" loyalty to Britain as the only strategy holding any hope of success. They were not free agents but a conquered people, and there was no public debate or public opinion in the society in any sense that we would recognize today. At the time of the Conquest, after the French officials had been repatriated, there were probably not five thousand people in Canada who could even read and write in French. Nevertheless, in some sense a choice *was* made, even if it was a perpetually conditional choice until something better turned up. There was little or no sentiment in French Canadian loyalty to Britain, but it held, largely unshaken, for more than a century.

On the face of it, there was not a lot of common ground between the French Canadians who occupied Canada at the close of the American Revolution and the Loyalist refugees who joined them there; both could be called conservative, but there was little in common between the traditional peasant conservatism of the French Canadians and the angry ideological conservatism of the dispossessed Loyalists. In any case, French Canadian political views modernized with breathtaking speed after 1791, while English Canadian politics would acquire a reformist tinge within a generation or so. But the fact that British North America never had a successful revolution was crucial to its political style, and from the beginning that meant that both the founding "races" (as they were then called) were quite distinct in attitude and sensibility from the Americans. It seems a slight distinction, but it was enough.

The American Revolution was not just an early example of decolonisation. It was a genuine revolution, and the turbulent, egalitarian nation it created was just as much a product of the intellectual currents of the Age of Enlightenment as the revolutionary republic that erupted in bloody fury in France fifteen years later. Moreover, in the United States, unlike France, there was never a restoration of the ancien régime.

British North America, by contrast, *was* the ancien régime. Canada, in a quite specific sense, is founded on the idea of not being American. Time and evolutionary change have now brought about a large degree of convergence between Canada and the United States, but their very different heritages are still discernible today. In the first half of the nineteenth century, the contrasts between their political and social attitudes were huge, and these acute differences served as a focus for patriotic emotions whenever other factors brought the two countries into confrontation.

In the early decades of the Republic, Americans still quite rightly saw Britain as their main enemy, and they realized that Carleton's concept of Canada as a British strategic base flanking the United States still held true. As the United States grew rapidly in population and confidence, it also acquired the national ambition later dignified by the phrase *manifest destiny*: the conviction that the entire continent was America's birthright and that the absorption of anomalies like the British colonies to the north was just a matter of time. About thirty years after America's own independence had been confirmed by the Treaty of Paris, President James Madison signed a declaration of war against Great Britain, and the project for the invasion of Canada lumbered into motion.

CHAPTER FOUR

# *Unfinished Business*

An infatuated enemy has declared an unjust war against us; a war not founded upon the broad basis of real injuries sustained, but whose foundation is discovered to have been delineated by the contaminating finger of the arch-usurper, Napoleon.

*The Montreal Gazette*, 13 July 1812

The madness which has for many years pervaded the European continent has at length reached this hemisphere, which is now to be visited by war and all its horrors.

*Nova Scotia Royal Gazette*, 1 July 1812

It is certainly not true that the evil genius of Napoleon lay behind President Madison's decision to launch the United States into war with the British Empire, as the *Montreal Gazette* alleged (although Madison later admitted that if he had known Napoleon would be defeated, he would have stayed out). However, all the pressures and temptations that brought the American president to his decision arose in the context of the great European war then raging.

Americans now like to remember the War of 1812 as a "Second War of Independence," and are taken aback by the suggestion that it was really just an attempt to conquer Canada. Nationalist Canadian historians have tried to inflate it into the war of independence that Canada has never actually had (and to give the Canadian militia a leading role in the "winning" of the war). But there is more truth in the contemporary view, held both in Canada and in London, that the war in North America was essentially a part of the long world war that was then nearing its climax.

It had begun in 1792, soon after the French Revolution, and by two decades later fighting was going on all over the European-inhabited world: the French burned Moscow in 1812, the Americans burned Toronto (then called York) in 1813, and the British burned Washington in 1814. But the War of 1812 was never much more than a side-show for the great powers, and by 1815, when British, Russian, and German troops marched through the streets of Paris in triumph after thwarting Napoleon's come-back attempt at the Battle of Waterloo, the fighting on the western side of the Atlantic had sputtered out in a draw.

Nevertheless, the war in Europe almost caused the extinction of British North America, for great convulsions like the Napoleonic Wars eventually drag in not only all the great powers, but most of the smaller powers as well. Some of the smaller powers just get invaded, and others are forced to fight when the strain of maintaining their neutrality, under enormous pressure from both sides, grows too great. And still others seize the opportunity to do a little smash and grab amid the general chaos.

The United States was not yet a great power in 1812, and it had remained neutral for fully two decades of global war. Its stated reason for entering the war at that time suggested that a proud nation's patience had finally snapped in the face of intolerably high-handed British actions against neutral American shipping. But in fact the New England states, whose large shipping interests bore the brunt of British harassment as the Royal Navy tried to enforce an economic blockade of continental Europe, were almost unanimously opposed to going to war with Britain. Indeed, the New Englanders effectively sat the war out on the sidelines, and even held a convention in 1814 to consider a "separate peace" with Britain.

The real American motive for entering the war was that of a looter at a riot.

> Agrarian cupidity, not maritime rights, directs the war.
> John Randolph (U.S. House of Representatives,
> 1799-1829)

The bulk of Congressional support for the war came from the more recently settled "western" states along the southern shores of the Great Lakes (where every act of resistance by the Indians along the expanding frontier of settlement was blamed on British intrigue), and from the South, where the desire to strike a blow against the old British enemy was combined with a safe distance from the likely theatre of operations along the Canadian border. More powerful than these particular motives, however, was the general belief among Americans that the Almighty had ordained the North American continent as their exclusive domain, and that it was high time to conclude the unfinished business of the Revolutionary War and expel Britain from its remaining North American possessions. Thomas Jefferson felt sure that "the acquisition of Canada this year, as far as the neighbourhood of Quebec, will be a mere matter of marching," thus beginning the fulfilment of the prophecy he had made a dozen years earlier:

> However our present interests may restrain us within our limits, it is impossible not to look forward to distant times when our rapid multiplication will expand itself beyond those limits, and cover the whole northern, if not the southern, continent, with a people speaking the same language, governed in similar forms and by similar laws.
> President Thomas Jefferson, Inaugural Address,
> March 1801

❖

Jefferson's ambition was by no means unrealistic, given the state of British North America in 1812. What are now the Atlantic Provinces would certainly have been able to hold out for a long time; they were protected from American attack by the strength of the Royal Navy, and New Brunswick and Nova Scotia contained large majorities of Loyalists who would probably have fought very hard for Britain. But farther west, along the St. Lawrence River and north of the Great Lakes, the bulk of the population of British North America was strung out along a long, porous frontier, and most of them were not Loyalists or even English-speakers.

Two-thirds of British North America's total population of about half a million lived in Lower Canada (Quebec). There had been some recent immigration of English-speakers, mostly Americans, to Montreal and the Eastern Townships, but at least ninety per cent of the population in Lower Canada were descendents of the original French-speaking inhabitants. They had shown considerable interest in the ideas of the American and French revolutions, despite the Catholic church's steadfast loyalty to the British crown. The British governors of the 1780s and 1790s found the French Canadians "much tinged with Yankey politics," and there were serious riots against British authority in 1794 and 1796. Moreover, the tolerant approach that the British had taken in the first thirty years after the Conquest did not last.

The breadth of vision of Britain's first three governors in Canada had made it possible for French-speaking Catholics to give their loyalty (however conditionally) to an English-speaking Protestant empire. Significantly, all three were men with an inborn understanding for the dilemma of small religious and ethnic groups trying to survive in a world run by giants: a Scot, an Irish Protestant, and a French Swiss. But under their successors after 1796 that vision became blurred. Subsequent British governors of Lower Canada cooperated more or less openly with the English-speaking minority – who were already much richer than the population they lived among, thanks partly to blatant government favouritism toward English speakers – and even came to share their assumption that the French language and even the Catholic religion should and eventually would be extinguished in the province.

> What remains to be done? Withdraw these privileges . . . in which the conquered rejoice too freely; and order matters so that the administration of public affairs will be carried on in English, by Englishmen, or men of English principles. This will be the first

step, and the most efficacious one, towards the anglicization of the province.

"Anglicanus," *Mercury*, Quebec, 24 November 1806

You say that the [French] Canadians use their privileges too freely for a conquered people, and you threaten them with the loss of those privileges. . . . [F]rom what right dare you derive this odious distinction of conquerors and conquered, when [the British parliament] wished to efface it forever? You ask absurdly whether the Canadians have the right to exercise these privileges in their own language. In what other tongue could they exercise them? Did not the parliament of Great Britain know what their language was?

*Le Canadien*, 6 December 1806

The conflict reached a peak under the profoundly prejudiced British governor who took office in 1805, Sir James Craig. In 1810 he seized the presses of *Le Canadien*, jailed three of its founders, Pierre Bédard, Jean-Thomas Taschereau, and François Blanchet (all elected members of the Legislative Assembly) without charge or trial, and filled the streets of Quebec City with military patrols. It was only at virtually the last minute, in 1812, that Lower Canada received a new governor, Sir George Prevost (another French Swiss in Britain's service), who understood the nature of the original unwritten bargain between the French Canadians and the British.

It was Prevost who gave Pierre Bédard back the militia commission that had been withdrawn as a punishment for his role in publishing *Le Canadien*. A few months later Prevost appointed Bédard a judge – and a few months after that, when the United States declared war on Britain, it was Bédard who persuaded a secret meeting of key French Canadian members of the Legislative Assembly that French Canadians should not remain neutral and leave it entirely to the British to defend the country from an American invasion. But it was certainly true that in 1812 most French Canadians had no good reason to die for British rule.

What may have tipped the balance of French Canadian loyalties, in the end, is simply inertia. Quite unlike the situation in 1775, there was now no French Canadian under the age of about sixty who could personally recall French rule. British rule might be alien and irritating, but by 1812 most French Canadians had known nothing else all their lives – and so it was tolerated within quite broad limits. But if the Americans had actually occupied Lower Canada again, they would have found plenty of people there to welcome them.

As for Upper Canada (Ontario), which had been separated from the French-settled territories in 1791, it was entirely possible that it would defect wholesale to the United States. The first settlers in Upper Canada had been Loyalist refugees, but they were virtually submerged numerically by later waves of American settlers, part of the general westward migration in the United States, who had been drawn north of the Great Lakes by Ontario's plentiful cheap land. Of Upper Canada's 77,000 people in 1812, an estimated four-fifths were of American origin, and three-quarters of those had arrived *after* the Loyalists. American immigrants were required to swear an oath of allegiance to the British crown, but in practice many never did, and it was considered doubtful that the more recent American arrivals would fight against their former countrymen in a war with the United States. The danger, indeed, was that they would return to their former allegiance and fight alongside them.

❖

The army under my command has now invaded your country. Separated by an immense ocean and an extensive wilderness from Great Britain, you have no participation in her councils, nor interest in her conduct. You have felt her tyranny, you have seen her injustice. . . .

Many of your fathers fought for the freedom and independence we now enjoy. Being children, therefore, of the same family with us, the arrival of an army of friends must be hailed by you with a cordial welcome. . . . If, contrary to your own interest and the just expectation of my country, you should take part in the approaching contest, you will be considered and treated as enemies and the horrors and calamities of war will stalk before you.

Brigadier-General William Hull (Governor of Michigan Territory), *Appeal to the Inhabitants of Canada,* issued at Sandwich (Windsor), Ontario, 13 July 1812

Our enemies have indeed said that they can subdue the country
by a proclamation, but it is our part to prove to them that they
are sadly mistaken, that the population is determinedly hostile,
and that the few who might be otherwise inclined will find it to
their safety to be faithful.

> Major-General Isaac Brock, Commander-in-Chief and
> Lieutenant-Governor of Upper Canada, 27 July 1812

Isaac Brock was a big, blunt, handsome man, starting to run a bit to fat
at forty-two but still "hard as nails" in his own estimation, who had been
in Canada ten years and was more than ready to leave. "You, who have
passed all your days in the bustle of London, can scarcely conceive the
uninteresting and insipid life I am doomed to lead in this retirement," he
remarked to his brother Irving in a letter in 1811.

As a professional soldier, Brock longed to be with the Duke of Wellington in Spain, where other British officers of his age and rank were
winning high reputations for themselves in the Peninsular campaign
against Napoleon's armies. Instead, by 1812, he found himself stuck in
the backwater of Upper Canada, where there were not even the conso-
lations of good food and wine, a moderately sophisticated society, and
good books that he had previously enjoyed at Quebec and Montreal. But
he was reasonably well connected in England, and the great irony of his
life was that he finally got leave to depart from Upper Canada just as war
with the United States became imminent. At that point, whether from
ambition or a sense of duty, he felt that he could not go.

Most of the people have lost all confidence. I, however, speak
loud and look big.

> Isaac Brock, July 1812

General Brock was a good deal less optimistic in private. Although
every fit adult male was legally liable for militia service in 1812, most of
them, whether English or French-speaking, would not actually fight for
the British crown – so Brock decided to depend almost entirely on volunteers. Early in 1812, as war loomed, he instructed the militia regiments
of Upper Canada to select one-third of their men for special "flank companies" that would receive extra training. He made it clear that these

units, the first to be mobilized in wartime, should be composed of politically reliable men, and he warned London that "it might not be prudent to arm more than 4,000" of the eleven thousand militiamen in the province. (And in Lower Canada, Sir George Prevost similarly "embodied" some two thousand picked militia in 1812, leaving the great majority of the indifferent safely unarmed at home.)

In May, scarcely a month before the United States declared war, Brock wrote: "My situation is most critical, not from anything the enemy can do, but from the disposition of the people. . . . The population, believe me, is essentially bad. . . . A full belief possesses them all that this Province must inevitably succumb." It was not that there were really many settlers in Upper Canada who longed for "freedom" in an American rather than a British version, but they were waiting to see how things went. "These cool calculators are numerous in all societies," Brock noted – and given that the American army was expected to arrive momentarily, they were not going to tie themselves too closely to the British. In fact, many of Brock's own officials, including magistrates and militia officers, were reluctant to do anything that would compromise their position if and when the American occupation troops arrived. "They dread the vengeance of the democratic party," he explained.

Brock's bleak realism about the shaky loyalty of Upper Canada drove him to take the offensive at the outbreak of the war. In July 1812 his scanty forces captured the American fort at Michilimackinac which controlled access to Lake Michigan, thus placing the western fur trade in Canadian hands for the duration of the war and bringing the Indians in to fight on the British side. In August he seized Detroit and forced the surrender of the bombastic General Hull and his command. And in October, Brock stopped a numerically far superior American force from invading the Niagara frontier.

Queenston Heights was the one battle of the war whose loss could have meant the collapse of resistance in Upper Canada, but the British won it. The American invaders managed to get about sixteen hundred men across the Niagara River below the falls and to seize the heights overlooking Queenston, but then, as the British forces from up and down the river converged on the scene, the thousands of other American militiamen waiting to cross grew unruly and refused to enter the boats. And on Queenston Heights, the young American regular army officer who

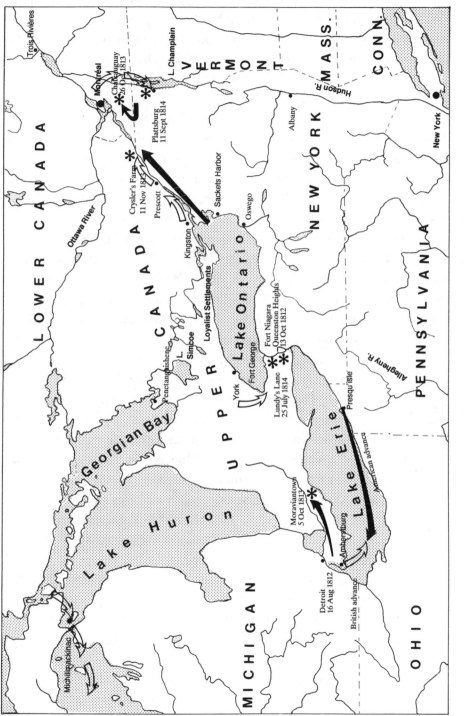

## THE WAR OF 1812

assumed command of the troops that did get across, Lieutenant-Colonel Winfield Scott, was not able to keep his ill-trained men steady when they were faced with the relentless, disciplined advance of British regiments and the terrifying tactics of their Indian allies. The British brought their bayonets down and charged; the Americans fired a single, straggling volley, then broke and fled.

There were no boats left on the Canadian side of the river to carry Scott's men back to the American shore; deserters had already taken them all. Some of the Americans clambered down the cliffs and tried to swim across. A few, panic-stricken, just leaped off the cliffs into the Niagara gorge in their desperate desire to get back to the American side. "The river presented a horrible spectacle," wrote one officer who was there, "filled with poor wretches who plunged into the stream from the impulse of fear, with scarcely the prospect of being saved." Most of the Americans, however, clustered under the trees at the edge of the cliff in utter confusion. Winfield Scott mounted a fallen log and tried to rally them with a dramatic harangue about avenging the dishonour of Hull's surrender at Detroit; he was imposingly tall and splendid in his uniform, but he might as well have been reciting nursery rhymes for all the good it did.

Scott eventually decided to surrender so that his men would at least be taken prisoner by the British regulars instead of being massacred by their Indian allies, but it wasn't easy: two couriers carrying white flags were killed by Indians while trying to get to the British lines. Finally Scott himself borrowed a white cravat from a fellow officer, tied it to the tip of his sword and went forward. He too was seized by Indians almost immediately, but he was saved at the last moment by a twenty-one-year-old law student in the York Volunteers, John Beverley Robinson, and taken through to the British lines where his surrender was accepted. (Robinson was immediately named acting attorney-general of Upper Canada to replace the mortally wounded incumbent, Colonel John Macdonell, who had been acting as Brock's aide-de-camp.)

Sir Isaac Brock himself never knew that he won the battle of Queenston Heights, nor indeed that he had been knighted in London three days previously for his capture of Detroit. He died in the early part of the battle, shot down leading a reckless charge when it looked as if the American crossing had succeeded: an American stepped out from behind a tree and shot him square in the chest at thirty yards' range. But Brock's bold, even desperate policy of attack at any cost convinced the wavering population of Upper Canada that they had to back the British. An American immigrant in Upper Canada described the psychological effect produced by Brock's string of early victories:

> None of the people in this district [Newcastle] bear arms, except twelve at Presquile harbour. They are universally in favour of the United States. . . . In August, the inhabitants were called together, in order that all who had not taken the oath of allegiance, might take it without exception. However, some refused, some were put in the cells, and . . . many took the oath rather than suffer thus.
>
> The inhabitants at large would be extremely glad to get out of their present miserable situation, at almost any rate; but they dare not venture a rebellion, without being sure of protection. And as they now do not expect that the American government will ever send in a sufficiently large army to afford them a security, they feel it their duty to kill all they can while they are coming over, that they may discourage any more from invading the province, that the [American] government may give up the idea of conquering it.
>
> Michael Smith (who left Upper Canada rather than take the oath of allegiance to the Crown), 1812

❖

The Battle of Queenston Heights was the starting point for the English Canadian belief that it was the sturdy militiamen of Ontario who fought off the Yankee hordes and saved British North America in the War of 1812, but in reality there were few occasions when the presence of the part-time Canadian militia, called from their fields for a week or two, was indispensable. London had learned the lesson of its unfortunate attempt to tax the American colonists for the costs of their own defence (which had been one of the main sources of discontent leading to the Revolution), and had sensibly concluded that he who owns the empire must pay the piper. While the British North American colonies were expected to maintain a militia, the rest of the defence burden, in both peace and war, was borne by the British taxpayer. And even in southern Ontario, British regular soldiers were the mainstay of the defences.

> The growing discontent & undissembled dissatisfaction of the Mass of the people of Upper Canada, have compelled me for the preservation of that Province to bring forward my best and reserved Soldiers to enable me to support the positions we hold on the Niagara and Detroit Frontier. I have been also induced to adopt this measure from the further consideration that the Militia have been considerably weakened by the frequent desertion of even the well disposed part of them to their farms, for the purpose of getting seed into the ground before the short summer of this Country has too far advanced.
>
> Lieutenant-General Sir George Prevost, Governor-in-Chief, 26 May 1813

In the second summer of the war, the Americans made repeated incursions into Upper Canada and even captured and burned York, the capital, but they were unable to maintain occupation forces very deep inside the province for long without naval control of Lake Ontario. In any case, although Sir George Prevost had reinforced the upper province, his main concern was to hold Lower Canada. If the Americans were to take Montreal, it would doom all the British forces on the tenuous supply line stretching a thousand miles west from there that sustained Upper Canada. Quebec City would be the next target: if that fell, it would be difficult for Britain even to attempt the reconquest of Canada. And in the autumn of 1813, the Americans finally moved to attack Montreal.

> The ensuing week settles the fall of Upper Canada forever. The fall of Quebec in the ensuing spring will give our youth experience to ward against the evils of thirty years' neglect of military knowledge. . . . Canada once ours, we shall have no enemy but a few domestic traitors and foreign emissaries on our soil.
>
> *National Intelligencer*, Washington, October 1813

One of the attacking American armies, commanded by Major-General Wade Hampton, began to move north down the Châteauguay River toward Montreal in October 1813, planning to link up near the city with another army commanded by Major-General James Wilkinson that was advancing down the St. Lawrence from the west. The militia units of Montreal and the surrounding area were called out to stop Hampton's army – and this time, unlike during the invasion of 1775, the French Canadians turned out in large numbers.

> We came up with several regiments of [French Canadian] militia on their line of march. They had all a serviceable, effective appearance – had been pretty well drilled, and their arms, being direct from the Tower [of London, brought over by ship], were in perfectly good order, nor had they the mobbish appearance that such a levy in any other country would have had. Their *capots* and trowsers of home-spun stuff, and their blue *tuques* were all of the same cut and colour, which gave them an air of uniformity that added much to their military look.
>
> Dr William "Tiger" Dunlop describing the Beauharnois militia, 1813

But the troops who actually stopped Hampton's advance on Montreal, although almost all French Canadian, included very few ordinary militia. As General Hampton and his four thousand American regular troops moved slowly down the Châteauguay River toward Montreal, Lieutenant-Colonel Charles-Michel de Salaberry, a French Canadian professional soldier who had seen service in the British army in many parts of the world, was building entrenchments along several little streams that ran into the river one behind the other near La Fourche. Most of the troops in his position, about thirty-five miles southwest of Montreal where the road was squeezed between dense forest and the river, were French Canadian regulars or near-regulars: his own regiment, the Provincial Corps of Light Infantry (popularly known as the "Voltigeurs"), and units of the so-called "Select Militia" who had already spent eighteen continuous months in the field.

When the main body of Americans advanced at around ten in the morning of 26 October 1813, only one-fifth of the 460 men in de Salaberry's firing line, sheltered behind the first line of breastworks, were not regular soldiers. De Salaberry promptly started the battle by shooting down a mounted American officer, and then climbed on a huge tree-stump to get a better view of the battlefield. "I have won a victory mounted on a wooden horse," he wrote to his father afterward (and indeed the pictures of the time show him standing on a log waving his sword, gesturing in grand style towards the enemy). He had chosen his ground well. His men in the firing line were outnumbered four-to-one by the Americans who were thrown against them, but it would have taken a very determined force to drive them out of their position, and that was not what they were facing.

> *Le colonel avait l'oeil partout. En voyant un soldat qui épaulit son arme, il se plaça derrière celui-ci pour juger du tir. Le coup partit. L'homme visé restait debout.*
>
> *"C'est-y pour ça que tu es venu ici, Jérôme?" lui dit le colonel d'un air bourru.*
>
> *Il savait nos noms par coeur. Lorsque [le général américain] Izard monta par le chemin pour nous prendre en flanc, le colonel passa tranquillement derrière notre compagnie, on l'entendit dire tout haut, comme s'il était agacé: "Bravez, mes damnés! bravez! si vous ne bravez pas, vous n'êtes pas des hommes!"*
>
> Sergent Charles Burke, quoted in Benjamin Sulte,
> *La Bataille de Châteauguay*, Quebec, 1899

[The colonel kept his eye on everything. Seeing a soldier raise his musket, he stood behind him to check his aim. The shot went off, but the man he had aimed at remained standing.

"Is *that* what you came here for, Jérôme?" asked the colonel gruffly.

He knew our names by heart. When (U.S. Brigadier-General George) Izard advanced up the road to attack us on our flank, the colonel moved quietly behind our company. Then we heard him say loudly, as if annoyed: "Show them what you're made of, my old rascals. If you can't face them down, you're not men at all."]

After losing about fifty men General Hampton withdrew. (De Sala-berry's losses were only two killed and sixteen wounded.) The next day Hampton and his officers decided that "it is necessary for the preservation of this army . . . that we immediately return by orderly marches to such a position as will secure our communications with the United States" – which turned out to be Plattsburg, New York, safely back across the border. But meanwhile, the other American army doggedly continued down the St. Lawrence toward Montreal. About half the American troops were aboard the huge fleet of barges and flatboats slowly working its way down the river and through the rapids; the rest of them were marching down on the Canadian side.

> Wherever [the Americans] encamped there was great destruction of cattle, grain, fences and every species of property within their reach. . . . The weather was cold and as they were not well pro-vided with camp equipage and still worse with clothes, they fell upon an easy expedient of keeping themselves warm at night, that of setting fire to the fences as they stood and lying down by them. . . . The sky was so illuminated as if the whole country was in a blaze.
>
> Rev. John Bethune, Williamstown, Ontario, 1813

Enchanting though the image of hundreds of recumbent Americans toasting themselves beneath burning fences may be (one presumes that they had to move to a new line of fence every couple of hours through the night – "Right! Everybody up! Next fence!"), General Wilkinson's army of seven thousand men posed a serious threat to Montreal even after Hampton's defeat. But two weeks after Hampton's army was turned back at Châteauguay, Wilkinson's army was also defeated – or acutely discour-aged, to be more precise.

A small British force of eight hundred men had been shadowing Wilk-inson's progress downstream, and on 11 November he ordered his troops to turn around and drive them off. But the American brigade contrived to lose four hundred men in a half-hearted attack at Crysler's Farm, and that was enough for Wilkinson. The grand invasion was abandoned "[for] want of bread, want of meat, want of Hampton's division, and a belief that the enemy's force was equal [to] if not greater than our own," and Wilkinson's army gratefully headed south for winter quarters on the other side of the frontier.

Montreal was never threatened again; and east of Montreal, given the virtual neutrality of the New England states, there was no land fighting at all except a successful British operation in 1814 that temporarily placed half the state of Maine under British control. American strategy was fatally distorted by the fact that it was mainly the western states that were enthusiastic about the war: that was why the Americans mostly attacked Upper Canada. And even there, once the inhabitants had opted for loyalty to Britain, the war settled into a much more predictable pattern.

Along the sparsely settled western parts of the frontier – there were fewer than ten thousand white men west of Lake Erie at the time – the war was mostly an affair of ambushes and raids, with Indians playing a large part on the British side. Despite several deep incursions into the settled parts of Ontario, the Americans never managed to establish a sufficient naval superiority on the Great Lakes to hold their gains, or even to prevent British counter-attacks into Michigan, Ohio, and New York.

In the peninsula of southern Ontario, between the Detroit frontier and Hamilton, the repeated American invasions eventually tempted many of their sympathizers to come out of the woodwork – and gave their neighbours every opportunity to take vengeance on them after the Americans had retreated again. Eight collaborators were eventually hanged at the "bloody assize" of Ancaster, but hundreds of people in southern Ontario fought for the Americans. It was a renegade member of the Provincial Assembly, Abraham Marcle, who guided the American raid that hit the village of Dover on the shore of Lake Erie in May 1814.

> As my mother and myself were sitting at breakfast, the dogs kept up a very unusual barking. I went to the door to discover the cause; when I looked up, I saw the hill-side and fields, as far as the eye could reach, covered with American soldiers. . . . Two men stepped from the ranks, selected some large chips, and came into the room where we were standing, and took coals from the hearth without speaking a word. My mother knew instinctively what they were going to do. She went out and asked to see the commanding officer.
>
> A gentleman rode up to her and said he was the person she asked for. She entreated him to spare her property, and said she was a widow with a young family. He answered her civilly and respectfully, and expressed his regrets that his orders were to

burn. . . . Very soon we saw columns of dark smoke arise from every building, and of what at early morn had been a prosperous farmstead, at noon there remained only smouldering ruins.

Mrs. John Harris, Dover, Ontario, May 1814

Twenty houses, three flour mills and three distilleries were burned at Port Dover, and raids like that were becoming quite common by the end of the war. But even though the fighting in southern Ontario eventually took on much of the style of a guerilla war and some of the bitterness of a civil war, the actual battles were generally not much more than skirmishes by European standards. In July 1814, however, there was a clash near Niagara Falls that stood comparison with the worst battles of Napoleon or Wellington in its ferocity, if not in its scale.

By 1814 some American officers, like Brigadier-General Winfield Scott (who had been freed in a prisoner exchange the previous year and promoted for his gallantry at Queenston Heights), had convinced their superiors that patriotic fervour was no substitute for military skills. The American militia troops that Scott drilled ten hours a day for several months through the early summer of that year were just as good as his own brigade of American regulars, or the British regulars they had to face when they came marching down the road along the Canadian side of the Niagara River on the stifling hot afternoon of 25 July. It was a renewed American attempt to seize the whole of the Niagara Peninsula – and just after six, along a country road called Lundy's Lane that ran inland from the Falls, they collided with Lieutenant-General Sir Gordon Drummond's British force, which had been marching all day to intercept them.

There were four thousand Americans against three thousand British troops, and the fighting raged through the sunset and into the dusk, at ever closer quarters. "The Yankees was loth to quit their position," recalled a British sergeant who survived the battle, "and being well fortified with whisky made them stand longer than ever they did. Some of them was so drunk as to stagger into our lines, but they suffered for their temerity." However, some of the Americans got close enough to Drummond's battery of seven guns, stationed on a low rise, to kill every British gunner with a sudden bayonet charge, and there followed a series of desperate British and American surges across the battery position, with the silent guns changing hands four times in an hour. It was pitch dark by now, and the lull that ensued seemed like the end of the fight – but then reinforcements arrived for the exhausted British, who had lost nearly a third of their men, and the fighting resumed, though each side could only aim at the flash of the other's muskets.

> In so determined a manner were [the American] attacks directed against our guns that our artillerymen were bayoneted by the enemy in the act of loading, and the muzzles of the enemy's guns were advanced within a few yards of ours. The darkness of the night during this extraordinary conflict occasioned several uncommon incidents. . . . In limbering up our guns at one period one of the enemy's six-pounders was put by mistake upon a limber of ours, and one of our six-pounders on his, by means of which the pieces were exchanged.
>
> Lieutenant-General Sir Gordon Drummond, commanding
> British troops at the Battle of Lundy's Lane,
> 25 July 1814

About midnight the last American assault died away. By now General Drummond himself was wounded, and his second-in-command, Major-General Sir Phineas Riall, was both wounded and a prisoner. On the American side, Winfield Scott was wounded too, and so was the militia officer who was his nominal commander-in-chief, Major-General Jacob Brown. As the sound of the Falls made itself heard again after six hours of incessant musket fire, the surviving American troops turned and felt their way back in the dark to their camp at Chippawa, nine miles upstream; the British troops lay down in their ranks to sleep where they were. The sun rose four hours later.

> The morning light ushered to our view a shocking spectacle, men and horses lying promiscuously together, Americans and English, laid upon one another, occasioned by our advance and retreat. . . . It was found impossible to bury the whole, so we collected a number of old trees together and burned them – which, although it may appear inhuman, was absolutely necessary and consequently justifiable.
>
> Sergeant James Commins, 8th Foot,
> present at Lundy's Lane

Almost a thousand British troops were killed, wounded or captured at Lundy's Lane, and about the same number of Americans. But that was the last major American incursion into Canada, for in April 1814 the great war in Europe had ended with Napoleon's abdication and exile to Elba, freeing large numbers of British troops to fight the United States. However, the Duke of Wellington was under no illusion that even the thirteen thousand battle-hardened veterans of the Peninsular War who were ordered to Canada in June would enable Britain to impose a victor's peace on the Americans:

> That which appears to be wanting in America is . . . naval supe-
> riority on the Lakes. Till that superiority is acquired, it is impos-
> sible, according to my notion, to maintain an army in such a
> situation as to keep the enemy out of the whole frontier, much
> less to make any conquest from the enemy. . . . If we can't, I shall
> do you but little good in America; and I shall go there only to . . .
> sign a peace which might as well be signed now.
>
> The Duke of Wellington to the prime minister,<br>Lord Liverpool, 9 November 1814

Wellington's advice was accepted, and the Treaty of Ghent was signed on Christmas Eve, 1814, leaving the pre-war U.S.-Canadian border entirely unchanged. But although the War of 1812 had shown Britain's willingness to send reinforcements to defend its North American colonies even when it was distracted by the demands of a great war in Europe, the demonstration would have to be repeated at regular intervals. The Rush-Bagot Agreement, negotiated in 1817, resulted in naval disarmament on the Great Lakes (where both sides had been building three-decker men-of-war larger than Nelson's *Victory* by the end of the war), but there was no disarmament on land.

In the following year a convention established the Forty-ninth Parallel as the boundary between British and American possessions from the head of the Great Lakes all the way west to the Rocky Mountains, and provided for the joint occupation of the Oregon country on the Pacific slope, between the Spanish territories to the south and Russian Alaska to the north, for a ten-year period. But only one year later, in 1819, U.S. Secretary of State John Quincy Adams (later president, 1825-29) announced that the world must be "familiarized with the idea of considering our proper dominion to be the continent of North America. From the time when we became an independent people it was as much a law of nature that this should become our pretension as that the Mississippi should flow to the sea. Spain has possessions upon our southern and Great Britain upon our northern borders, [but] it is impossible that centuries should elapse without finding them annexed to the United States."

So the British continued to take the defence of their North American colonies very seriously and kept regular military forces in North America approximately equal in number to the entire United States regular army for more than a generation after the War of 1812. They also spent very large sums, by the standards of the time, in building major fortifications at Halifax, Quebec, and Kingston in the 1820s and 1830s, together with smaller forts in a number of other places. The biggest defence project of all was the 126-mile Rideau Canal: completed in 1832, it involved the construction of forty-seven locks and twenty-four dams in order to provide a water link between Montreal and Lake Ontario via Ottawa and Kingston, thus bypassing the exposed reach of the narrow upper St. Lawrence river (which would be unusable in wartime since its southern bank was United States territory).

However, Britain never had to fight the Americans again. After 1814, the "long peace" descended on the world. It would be a full century before there was another world conflagration on the scale of the Revolutionary and Napoleonic Wars. It was that lull in the cycle of great wars in Europe, far more than any change in local circumstances, that brought peace to North America, which had spent the previous century and a half in almost constant wars arising out of European rivalries. So the United States, which had been prematurely plunged into the European great-power game as an independent player by the circumstances of its birth, was able to withdraw again for a whole century while it nailed down its share of the continent. British North America was also granted a century of peace to sort itself out and decide on its identity: it turned out, of course, to have a split personality.

❖

The security of British institutions depends on the attachment of the [French] Canadian race. Twice have they been sorely tried, and they have not been found wanting. In the contest of 1812 they even "set an example" to those whose loyalty wavered in the Upper Province.

Lieutenant-Colonel B. W. A. Sleigh, a British Army<br>officer serving in Canada, 1853

Mythology is far stronger than mere history. By the mid-nineteenth century it was an article of faith that French Canadians (or simply "Canadians," as Colonel Sleigh called them, in distinction to the "British" who inhabited the English-speaking parts of British North America) had twice rallied to fight for the British crown. The plain fact is that the vast majority of French Canadians had stayed neutral during the American invasion of 1775, with fewer than a thousand actively fighting for the British and perhaps five hundred for the Americans; and only once in the second war, at Châteauguay in 1813, did French Canadians have a decisive role in battle. But the implicit bargain between the British and the French Canadians, which gave Britain its indispensable bases at Quebec and Montreal, was not that French Canadians would die in large numbers to hold off the Americans. It was an agreement (subject to termination without notice) that the French Canadians would obey the British government, and the *British* would do the dying.

In Upper Canada, the myth that the American invasion of 1812 had been repulsed primarily by the Loyalist militia forces was of enormous political importance. It furnished the moral justification for the control of the province by a narrow elite of Loyalist families (the "Family Compact") for a full generation: for example, John Beverley Robinson, who had saved Winfield Scott from the Indians at Queenston Heights, rapidly rose to be Chief Justice of Upper Canada. Although he might well have attained that office anyway, since he had the right family antecedents, it was battlefield exploits like his, suitably embellished in the retelling, and the allegedly crucial political role of the Loyalists in holding Upper Canada for the British crown during the war, that made the privileges of those powerful families so difficult to attack. In the long run, when everybody who had been involved was safely dead (or at least too old to argue back), a tidied-up and romanticized version of the War of 1812 would provide the mythological foundation for an embryonic version of local patriotism in much of English Canada.

However, in the short term, the British authorities were acutely aware of how close the colony had come to defection in the war and took steps to ensure that that would never happen again. After 1814 American immigrants were no longer welcome in Upper Canada: new laws required seven years' residence before Americans could own land there. At the same time, determined measures were taken to encourage immigration from Britain. As early as 1815 an advertisement appeared in the Edinburgh press offering free transportation, one hundred acres of land, and eight months' food to any prospective settler of good character who could deposit £18 as a security that he would remain in Canada for at least two years.

And the immigrants came. Driven by the long depression that followed the Napoleonic Wars, and then even more urgently by the potato famine in Ireland, some eight hundred thousand immigrants, almost all from the British Isles, crossed the Atlantic to the British possessions in North America in the following thirty-five years. Most settled in Ontario, whose population was nearing a million by 1850. This utterly changed the character of British North America: around 1830 the English-speaking population drew even with the French, and by 1865 French Canadians were outnumbered two-to-one by people of British origin. But a rapid and radical social transformation on this scale is always a difficult feat to accomplish peacefully, and once it nearly came off the rails.

### CHAPTER FIVE

# *1837*

Sunday night all the country back of Laprairie presented the frightful spectacle of a vast expanse of livid flames, and it is reported that not a single rebel house has been left standing . . . God knows what will become of the [French] Canadians who have not perished, of their wives and families, during the winter which approaches, since they have in prospect only the horrors of hunger and cold. . . . Nevertheless the supremacy of the laws must be maintained inviolate, the integrity of the Empire respected, and peace and prosperity assured to the English, even at the expense of the whole [French] Canadian people.

*Montreal Herald*, 14 November 1838

They have only one feeling – the French hate the English and would cut all their throats if they could – the English hate the French and only desire to ride rough shod over them.

Baron Sydenham, Governor General of
British North America, 13 March 1840

It would be plausible, in a book which was primarily a military history of Canada, to leap straight from 1814 to around mid-century, when the American threat reappears in a tangible form. But our purpose is to investigate the roots of Canada's behaviour in matters of defence, not just to jog through a history of its foreign wars, and that is a different matter, for some of those roots are domestic. If Canada had been an entirely English-speaking colony like Australia or New Zealand, there might still have been a minor rebellion in Upper Canada in 1837, but there would certainly have been nothing like the events of 1837 in Lower Canada.

A country's behaviour is determined largely by the half-remembered history that becomes part of its national mythology, and for French Canadians the year 1837 is crucial. The ancestral myth of the repression of French Canada by the English is generally supposed to derive from the defeat on the Plains of Abraham in 1759, but that actually has very little to do with modern French Canadian attitudes. What really shapes the basic French Canadian perspective, and makes it so different from that of English Canadians, with consequences that can be felt down to today, is a vague collective memory of the crushing of the Patriotes in 1837.

The slow progression from the (provisionally) loyal French Canada of 1814 to the rebellious and bitter society of 1837 was epitomized in the career of Louis-Joseph Papineau, who became speaker of the elected Assembly of Lower Canada the year after the war ended and held the post for twenty-two years until he found himself leader of an armed revolt against British rule and had to flee into exile. Nobody could have been more surprised by this turn of events than Papineau himself, for although he had long been the dedicated leader of the French Canadian opposition to the anglicizing policies of British rule, he was an extremely unlikely rebel. A seigneur, he was quintessentially a member of the establishment – handsome, intelligent, educated, and rich. His views in 1820 were summed up in his assessment of the benefits of the British connection for French Canadians on the occasion of the death of King George III (the only monarch Canada had known since the Conquest sixty years before).

[Since] George III . . . succeeded Louis XIV [of France] . . . the reign of law has succeeded to that of violence; since that day the treasure, the fleet and the armies of Great Britain have been employed to provide us with an effective protection against all foreign danger; since that day her best laws have become ours, while our faith, our property and the laws by which they were governed have been conserved; soon afterwards the privileges of her free constitution were granted us. . . . All these advantages have become our birthright, and will be, I hope, the lasting heritage of our posterity. In order to conserve them, we should act like British subjects and free men.

*Quebec Gazette*, July 1820

Papineau's family were virtually French Canadian "Loyalists." His father had carried dispatches through the American lines for Carleton at the siege of Quebec in 1775-76, and Papineau himself served in the militia as a staff captain in the second American war and was present at the capture of Detroit. The extraordinary shift in his opinions that eventually turned him into a revolutionary leader reflected a general movement in French Canadian attitudes, rather than led it – and one of the largest influences on that shift was the tide of English-speaking immigrants that now swept over Canada. They not only filled up what is now Ontario and closed off French Canada's old access to the West, but they also began to change the population balance in Lower Canada itself. From less than a tenth of Lower Canada's population in 1812, English speakers soared to a quarter by the late 1830s: 263,000 immigrants (about half of them Irish) settled in the province between 1830 and 1838 alone.

The penniless, often disease-ridden migrants who ended up as a new urban proletariat in Montreal and Quebec (often the poorest of the poor, who lacked the resources to move further westwards) had little in common with the wealthy anglophone merchants of those cities except their language, but their constantly growing numbers worried French Canadians as much as they emboldened the English-speaking masters of the province. Both groups, with very different emotions, were contemplating the day when French Canadians would be reduced to a politically helpless minority even in Lower Canada. And if that were the prospect, then for French Canadians their bargain with the British was no longer worth keeping: there was no point in a deal that saved you from absorption by the Americans if it led to your being submerged at home by other foreigners.

"It was not enough to send among us avaricious egotists . . . to enrich themselves at the expense of the [French] Canadians, and then to enslave them," wrote Edouard Rodier, a spokesman of the increasingly frustrated and extremist group in the Assembly who had made Papineau their leader. "They must also rid themselves of their beggars and cast them by the thousands on our shores; . . . they must send us in their train pestilence and death." Rodier was writing in 1832, when an epidemic of cholera brought by the immigrants was decimating the population of the St. Law-rence valley, and by then there were French Canadians who were prepared to see immigration as a British conspiracy literally to wipe them out.

This fundamental French Canadian anxiety about their survival as a community and culture was sharply focussed on the fact that they had no real political power. French Canadians held a majority of seats in the Legislative Assembly of Lower Canada from the time of the first elections in 1792, but the Assembly had no executive powers – and it was the English-speaking merchants of the "Château clique" who dominated the British governor's councils, virtually monopolized lucrative government appointments, and brazenly exploited their positions to make themselves still richer. Every attempt by Papineau and his followers to make the government of the province more responsive to its elected assembly was seen by this ruling minority as proof of the French majority's disaffection and treachery, and of the urgent need to reduce it to a minority by further immigration.

The blank refusal of the Château clique to share its political power even with the French Canadian elite, let alone to surrender it to the popular majority, gradually convinced even privileged French Canadians like Papineau that no compromise was possible. After three French Cana-dians were killed by British troops in an election riot in 1832, the dead-lock between the Assembly and the government became total, and in February 1834 the Assembly passed the "Ninety-Two Resolutions," a catalogue of French Canadian grievances and demands. Papineau, whose followers were becoming known as "Patriotes," virtually claimed the right to revolution in his speech introducing the Resolutions: "It is certain that before long all [North] America is to be republican. Meanwhile, ought a change in our constitution, if necessary, be guided by this consideration; and is it criminal to raise the question?" The 1834 election was a sham-bles, with the Patriotes encouraging runs on English-owned banks and the anglophone merchants importing strong-arm squads of Irish canal-build-ers to control the outcome in a number of ridings. By the end of the year "Committees of Correspondence," quite deliberately named after the precursors of the American Revolution, were active in all the major cities of Lower Canada.

> We are so poor, so little organized to repel by force of arms a domination which has become so burdensome to us. Are we ready; are the people ready; are you ready? Should we take so great a responsibility upon ourselves? . . . Here are questions to which you, like us, must soon reply.
>
> Montreal Committee of Correspondence to the Quebec
> Committee, 20 November 1834

Although the Patriote leadership included numbers of English-speak-ing radicals (especially immigrants from Ireland, whose experience of British rule had been far longer and far more bitter than French Canada's), and even despite the large element of class conflict in the confrontation in Lower Canada, it ended up being essentially a French-English clash, which made a compromise very difficult. In the last couple of years before the shooting started, a new British governor, Lord Gosford, began to take his distance from the "ultra-Tories" of the Château clique and to seek compromise with Papineau and the other French Canadian leaders in the Assembly, but it was too late.

> *Résolu:*
>
> *[Que nous reconnaissons] enfin combien le pays a été abusé par les promesses mensongères qui l'ont porté à combattre contre un peu-ple qui lui offrait la liberté, des droits égaux, pour un peuple qui lui préparait l'esclavage. Une triste expérience nous oblige à reconnaître que de l'autre côté de la ligne 45 étaient nos amis et alliés naturels. . . .*
>
> Declaration of Saint-Ours (twelve resolutions of the
> Patriotes' Permanent Central Committee), adopted
> by an assembly of 1,200 people, Saint-Ours (Richelieu),
> 7 May 1837

[Resolved:

That . . . we recognize at last how much this country has been misled by the lying promises which persuaded it to fight against a people who offered it liberty and equal rights on behalf of a people who planned to enslave it. Sad experience forces us to recognize that our true friends and natural allies were on the other side of the 45th parallel [in the United States].

That we deny to the English parliament the right to legislate on the internal affairs of this colony without our consent. . . .

That we shall abstain . . . from consuming imported goods . . . such as tea, tobacco, wine, rum, etc. . . . that we shall regard as deserving well of the homeland whoever establishes the manufacture of silk, cloth, linen, sugar, spirits, etc. . . . We shall regard as wholly lawful the commerce known as contraband.]

It is evident that Papineau's party will not be satisfied with any concession that [does not serve] its ultimate intentions, that is to say, the separation of this country from England and the establishment of a republican government. . . . The violent and unjustifiable attacks which have been made by the ultra-Tories against the French Canadians in general have created an animosity of which M. Papineau has not failed to take advantage. . . . The government needs to be invested with the fullest power, and . . . you may be under the necessity of suspending the constitution.

Lord Gosford to the Colonial Secretary,
2 September 1837

By 1837, the dominant French Canadian political grouping and its Irish allies were moving beyond constitutional methods in the struggle for self-government. Most of the leaders shied away from violence, but they were advocating a total boycott of imported goods (except those smuggled in from the United States) to deprive the government of customs revenues, its principal source of income. Buying only smuggled imports became a patriotic duty, which meant, given the deficiencies in the smuggling organization, that the patriote deputies at the opening of the Assembly in August 1837 were rather unusually dressed:

Mr. Rodier's dress excited the greatest attention, being *unique*, with the exception of a pair of Berlin gloves, viz.: frock coat of granite coloured *étoffe du pays* [homespun]; inexpressibles and vest of the same material, striped blue and white; straw hat and beef shoes, with a pair of home-made socks, completed the *outré* attire. Mr. Rodier, it was remarked, had no shirt on, having doubtless been unable to smuggle or manufacture one. Dr. O'Callaghan's 'rig-out' was second only to that of Mr. Rodier, being complete with the exception of hat, boots, gloves, and shirt and spectacles.

*Mercury*, Quebec, (government controlled), August 1837

It was a sartorial version of the Boston Tea Party, and it was soon followed by open revolt, for much the same reason: the moderate leaders who thought mere economic boycotts would eventually sway the British government could not control their fiercer followers. In Montreal, young men began drilling (with sticks and brooms, since they lacked weapons) as *les Fils de la Liberté*, named after the Sons of Liberty of the American Revolution. They started calling each other *citoyen* in the style of the French Revolution, and took oaths, hand upon the Liberty Pole, to be faithful to the fatherland and to conquer or to die. The Catholic hierarchy inveighed strongly against revolt–"Do not let yourself be seduced if someone wishes to engage you in rebellion against the established government, under the pretext that you form part of the 'Sovereign People'," warned sickly old Bishop Jean-Jacques Lartigue of Montreal – but in the region around Montreal and the Richelieu valley two crop failures in a row had made the peasants in the crowded seigneurial lands desperate enough for almost any adventure.

On November 6, the "Doric Club," a gang of young upper-class English Canadian toughs, deliberately attacked *les Fils de la Liberté* in an attempt to precipitate an open confrontation before the patriote organization was ready to move. Street fighting raged through Old Montreal all day, axe handles and leaded whips being the favourite weapons; ten days later, the government yielded to anglophone pressure and issued twenty-six arrest warrants for patriote leaders on charges of treason. Most of the prominent leaders escaped to the Richelieu valley south-east of Montreal, however, and the first clash between volunteer cavalry patrols of English-speaking Montrealers and a force of Patriotes occurred near Longueuil on 16 November 1837.

The only faint hope for an independent French-speaking state in North America in 1837 lay in American support – and even then this new state would not have been likely to escape incorporation in the neighbouring republic for very long. As it happened, however, the United States was not prepared to consider fighting the British Empire in 1837, as it was caught up in a severe depression, and the U.S. government promptly declared its neutrality in the struggle. Without American help, the Patriote uprising would have been doomed even if it had spread throughout the province, but in fact only the distressed rural regions of the Richelieu valley and Lac-des-Deux-Montagnes rose in arms. They were systematically crushed by British troops pulled in from all the North American colonies.

The only Patriote victory was the first major fight, at Saint-Denis on the Richelieu, on 23 November 1837, and there the rebels made the mistake of murdering an English prisoner, Lieutenant George Weir, as he tried to escape. Six miles farther up the river, two days later, British troops managed to fight their way into Saint-Charles, the other village on the Richelieu that the Patriotes had turned into an improvised fortress. "On entering the town," recalled George Bell, a young British officer, "there was little quarter given, almost every man was put to death; in fact they fought too long before thinking of flight. Many of them were burned alive in the barns and houses which were fired as they would not surrender." At least one hundred and fifty Patriotes were killed, and after the Weir incident and the Saint-Charles massacre, atrocities became commonplace on both sides.

On 14 December the British commander, Sir John Colborne, attacked the village of Saint-Eustache, just north of the island of Montreal, with two thousand troops, and burned the defenders out of their positions one by one until only the large group in the church, commanded by the local leader of the revolt, Dr. Jean-Olivier Chénier, was still holding out. Some British soldiers broke into the church through a poorly guarded rear door: "The rebels were found stationed in the gallery still defending themselves," wrote a British officer, "and having cut away the staircase, every attempt to dislodge them for a while proved utterly fruitless." So the

1 THE BATTLE OF SAINTE-FOY, 1760.
General James Murray held onto Quebec City through this bloody battle
and a subsequent siege until the British fleet appeared in May 1760.

2 *A View of the Plundering and Burning of the City of Grymross,*
*Capital of the Neutral Settlements on the River St. John's in the Bay of*
*Fundy, Nova Scotia,* 1758. The Acadians were not really "neutral";
they were still basically "French" in their loyalties.

3 GENERAL GUY CARLETON. Carleton believed that Quebec would be "the principal scene where the fate of America may be determined," and he tried to retain the loyalty of the habitants during the American Revolutionary War.

5 A rather stylized depiction of the death of General Montgomery at dawn 1 January 1776. Montgomery's frozen body was found close to the barricade, only an arm protruding from the snow.

4 General Richard Montgomery leading the charge at the
Près-de-Ville barricade. "Come on, brave boys. Quebec is ours."

6 "Most of the people
have lost all confi-
dence. I, however,
speak loud and look
big." Isaac Brock,
July 1812.

7 Lieut.-Col. de Salaberry at Châteauguay: "I have won a victory
mounted on a wooden horse." 26 October 1813.

8 Execution of deserters at Laprairie, 1812-1813.

9   The Battle of Lundy's Lane, 25 July 1814. "In so
determined a manner were [the American] attacks directed
against our guns that our artillery men were bayoneted by
the enemy in the act of loading."

10   The capture of the city of Washington, as retaliation for the
burning of York (Toronto), 1814.

QUEBEC LIGHT INFANTRY
N°4 Company     N°2,3 N°5 Companies
Co. of 4th Battalion 2nd L. Infy. N.S.
1859

11 "An officer is useful to his regiment because he has the means to spend and the will to spend it . . . "

12 ". . . the regiment is useful to him because the paths towards social distinction are smoothed for the militia officer."

LINE CLAIMED BY THE UNITED STATES.
LINE CLAIMED BY GREAT BRITAIN.
PROPOSED MIDDLE CHANNEL.

13  SAN JUAN ISLAND.
"We must defend ourselves, a militia must be formed. San Juan is
the key to British Columbia." (Speaker of the B.C. House of
Assembly, 1859.)

14   AMERICAN ARTILLERY ON SAN JUAN ISLAND.
For a dozen years the British and American regular troops sat on
San Juan, glowering at each other.

15   British Officer's Quarters on San Juan Island.

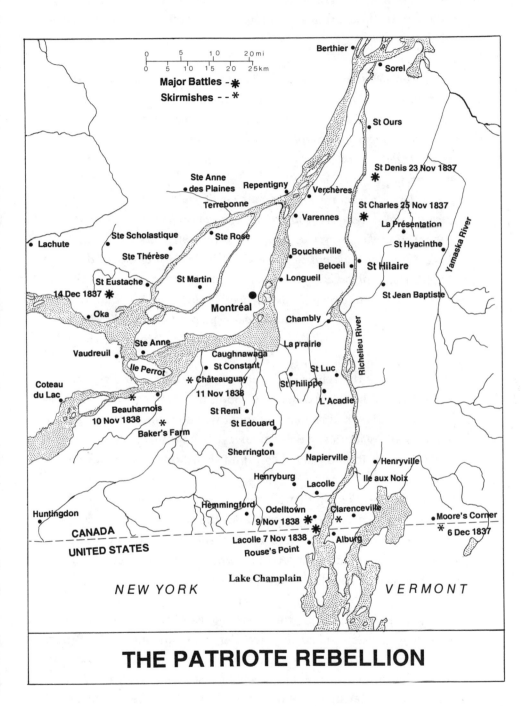

Major Battles - ✳
Skirmishes - - ✳

Berthier
Sorel
St Ours
St Denis 23 Nov 1837 ✳
Ste Anne des Plaines
Repentigny
Verchères
St Charles 25 Nov 1837 ✳
Terrebonne
Varennes
La Présentation
Yamaska River
Ste Scholastique
Ste Rose
St Hyacinthe
Lachute
Ste Thérèse
Boucherville
Beloeil
St Hilaire
St Eustache
St Martin
Longueil
14 Dec 1837 ✳
St Jean Baptiste
Oka
Montréal
Chambly
Ste Anne
La p'rairie
Richelieu River
Vaudreuil
Caughnawaga
Ile Perrot
St Constant
St Luc
Coteau du Lac
✳ Châteauguay
11 Nov 1838
St Philippe
L'Acadie
✳
Beauharnois
10 Nov 1838
St Remi
St Edouard
✳
Baker's Farm
Sherrington
Napierville
Henryville
Henryburg
Ile aux Noix
Lacolle
Huntingdon
Hemmingford
Odelltown
Clarenceville
Moore's Corner
9 Nov 1838 ✳
✳
✳ 6 Dec 1837
CANADA
✳
Lacolle 7 Nov 1838
Alburg
UNITED STATES
Rouse's Point
Lake Champlain
*NEW YORK*
*VERMONT*

# THE PATRIOTE REBELLION

British troops who had got into the church, sheltering behind the altar from the fire of the Patriotes in the gallery, set the building alight and then fled.

> *la position des insurgés dans l'église était des plus critiques et de moment en moment devenait plus affreuse. . . . bientôt les flammes vinrent les obliger de fuir; la fuite était difficile pour eux, car les escaliers des jubés était coupés. . . . quelques-uns d'entr'eux même ne purent le faire, et plus tard on trouva leurs corps entièrement brulés et calcinés.*
>
> *Le Dr. Chénier, voyant que tout espoir était perdu . . . réunit quelques-uns de ses gens et sauta avec eux par les fenêtres du côté du couvent. Il voulait essayer de se faire jour au travers des assaillans et de s'enfuir, mais il ne put sortir du cimetière, et bientôt atteint d'un coup de feu, il tomba et expira presque immédiatement.*
>
> "Un Témoin Oculaire," *Journal Historique des Événements*
> *arrivés à Saint-Eustache pendant la Rébellion.*
> (Montreal, 1838)

[the position of the rebels in the church was critical, and getting more dreadful by the moment. . . . Soon the flames reached the point where they had to flee, but flight was difficult, because the stairs to the galleries were cut away . . . Some of them just couldn't make it, and later they found their bodies, burned to a crisp.

Dr. Chénier, seeing that all hope was lost, gathered some of his men together, and they jumped out the windows on the convent side. He wanted to try to break through the attackers and escape, but he couldn't get out of the graveyard, and soon, struck by a shot, he fell and died almost immediately.]

Seeing their leader dead, the surviving Patriotes in the cemetery dropped their arms and tried to surrender, but someone in the British ranks shouted "Remember Jock Weir" and the execution continued until they were almost all killed. And it was not just Saint-Charles and Saint-Eustache that were burned: Colborne was known ever after in Quebec as Vieux Brûlot – "old firebrand":

*Il me serait impossible de vous peindre la désolation que cette marche et les scènes barbares dont elle était accompagnée, répandirent dans les familles. . . . l'on fit rassembler dans ma cour, qui est très large, comme vous savez, un nombre considérable d'habitants; ils y furent mis en rang, et l'on braqua sur eux deux canons par la porte-cochère, en leur disant qu'on allait les exterminer en peu de minutes. Il n'est point d'injures et d'outrages dont on ne les accabla, et de menaces qu'on ne leur fit pour les intimider et les forcer à déclarer la retraite de tous ceux que l'on appellait leurs chefs. Aucun d'eux ne put ou ne voulut donner le moindre indice. . . .*

Joseph Girouard, describing the sack of St-Benoît<br>15 December, 1837 (L.-O. David, *Les Patriotes 1837-38*)

[It would be impossible for me to describe to you the desolation which (Colborne's) march and the barbarous scenes accompanying it spread through our homes. . . . A considerable number of the inhabitants were assembled in my courtyard, which, as you know, is very large; they were lined up, and two cannon placed in the gateway were aimed at them, while they were told they would be exterminated in a few minutes. There were no insults and outrages which were not heaped upon them, no threats which were not made, to frighten them into revealing the hiding places of those whom (the British) called their leaders. Not one of them would give the least hint. . . .

Then began scenes of devastation and destruction more atrocious . . . than any seen in a town taken by storm and given over to pillage after a long, hard siege. After completely pillaging the village, the enemy set fire to it and reduced it from one end to the other to a heap of ashes. Then they went in different directions, ravaging and burning on their way . . . carrying their fire as far as the village of Sainte-Scholastique.]

The worst of the destruction was wrought by English-speaking militia units, who conducted a campaign of systematic terror against the habitants in the areas affected by the revolt. Papineau fled to the U.S.A. at the end of November 1837, but it was several months before the last sparks of resistance were extinguished. It took six thousand British troops to crush the revolt – and there was a further brief flare-up late in the following year, when two or three thousand Patriotes gathered at Napierville near the American border and a prominent English leader of the Patriotes, Robert Nelson (a cousin of the British naval hero Admiral Horatio Nelson), proclaimed himself president of the Provisional Republic of Lower Canada.

His revolt collapsed in five days, but by now racial hatred was certainly the predominant theme of the conflict. Among the plans for raising money for Nelson's provisional republic, apart from nationalizing the banks and the Lachine Canal, was a modest little proposal to strangle all the Jews in Lower Canada (who were anglophone, of course) and confiscate their money. By the time peace finally returned to Lower Canada in late 1838, some hundreds of Patriotes had been killed, twelve of those who were captured had been publicly hanged, fifty-eight had been deported to Australia, and a dozen of those who had fled to the United States, including Papineau, were declared guilty of high treason and condemned to be executed if they returned to British territory. And meantime, there had been a revolt in Upper Canada, too.

❖

I carried my musket in '37. The day was hot, my feet were blistered – I was but a weary boy – and I thought I should have dropped under the weight of the flint musket which galled my shoulder. But I managed to keep up with my companion, a grim old soldier who seemed impervious to fatigue.

John A. Macdonald (later the first prime minister of the Dominion of Canada)

Although it was not the bloody and desperate affair of ethnic hatreds that tore the lower province apart, the revolt in Upper Canada was a serious political event. Indeed, the "Reformers" of Upper Canada, led by a bristling fox-terrier of a journalist called William Lyon Mackenzie, were in close touch with Papineau's Patriotes. The Reformers had even been asked to stage their uprising first, as a signal for revolt in Lower Canada (although in the event the Patriotes were pre-empted by the street fighting in Montreal and the subsequent government actions).

Canadians! The struggle will be of short duration in Lower Canada, for the people are united as one man. . . . If we rise with one consent to overthrow despotism, we will make quick work of it. . . . With governors from England, we will have bribery at elections, corruption, villainy and perpetual discord . . . but independence would give us the means to enjoy many blessings.

William Lyon Mackenzie, Toronto, November 1837

The small, irascible, enormously determined idealist who issued the call to rebellion was an immigrant from Scotland who had arrived in Upper Canada in 1820. Hundreds of thousands of British immigrants had utterly swamped the previous population of Loyalists and ex-Americans by 1837, and many brought with them the radical political ideas that were now circulating in the rapidly growing industrial cities of Britain. When they arrived in Upper Canada, however, they entered a time warp where the "Family Compact" manipulated the transient British governors, controlled the province as completely as any eighteenth-century absolute monarchy, and (though they bore such titles as Chief Justice and Attorney-General) exploited their official powers to their own advantage as blatantly as feudal robber barons. But their cozy game was never likely to survive the influx of so many ambitious and disrespectful newcomers, and Mackenzie's muck-raking, rabble-rousing newspaper, the *Colonial Advocate*, became the focus for popular discontent.

There was no doubt that the social and political order in Upper Canada was going to change under the impact of this immigration sooner or later; the question that mattered was whether the process of change would take it out of the British Empire and into the American republic. So far as William Lyon Mackenzie was concerned, it was an open question, although he preferred to talk in terms of "Independence" rather than of the annexation to the United States that would probably follow in fairly short order. As to method, he was not opposed to force, but he thought in terms of a *coup d'état* at the centre of power, York (Toronto), rather than a general uprising. So when all the regular troops in Upper Canada were sent down to Montreal to deal with the anticipated patriote revolt, Mackenzie decided to move on City Hall, where enough weapons to equip six thousand men were guarded by only two constables. In October he called his leading adherents together at Doel's Brewery near the capital:

> I said that the troops had left; . . . and that my judgment was that
> we should instantly send for Dutcher's foundrymen and Arm-
> strong's axe-makers, all of whom could be depended on, and with
> them go promptly to the Government House, seize Sir Francis
> [Bond Head, the Lieutenant-Governor of Upper Canada], carry
> him to the City Hall, a fortress in itself, seize the arms and ammu-
> nition there and the artillery etc. in the old garrison; rouse our
> innumerable friends in town and country, proclaim a provisional
> government . . . and either induce Sir Francis to give the country
> an executive council responsible to a new and fairly chosen
> assembly . . . or, if he refused to comply, go at once for
> Independence.
>
> William Lyon Mackenzie, October, 1837

His supporters were not ready for such bold action, however, and it
was not until late November, after fighting had already broken out in
Lower Canada, that Mackenzie finally persuaded them to set the date of
7 December for the rising. The rendezvous would be at Montgomery's
Tavern on Yonge Street (a hotel about four miles outside the city). But
after Mackenzie had left the little city by the lakeshore to tour the nearby
towns alerting his supporters, one of his aides advanced the date for the
uprising to 4 December, and the first of the rebels began to gather at
Montgomery's Tavern only a few hours after Mackenzie himself reached
there on the fourth. Neither arms nor food in sufficient quantities were
ready there yet, but all chance of surprise was lost. As the rest of Mackenzie's people trickled in to Montgomery's Tavern over the next couple
of days, all the militia of the province were summoned to defeat him.

> Buried in the obscurity of these woods [near Peterborough, Ont.],
> we knew nothing, heard nothing of the political state of the coun-
> try, and were little aware of the revolution which was about to
> work a great change for us and for Canada. . . . At the landing we
> were met by old Jenny, who had a long story to tell us . . . all
> about the Queen and the Yankees; that there was war between
> Canada and the States; that Toronto had been burnt and the gov-
> ernor killed, and I know not what other strange and monstrous
> statements. After much fatigue, Moodie climbed the hill, [and

found] a copy of the Queen's proclamation, calling upon all loyal
gentlemen to join in putting down the unnatural rebellion.

Susannah Moodie, *Roughing It in the Bush*, 1837

There would be no bloodless *coup d'état*. Mackenzie would have to
fight to take the capital – and he would have to be quick about it, for he
had gone too far in his opposition to the established order to carry the
mass of the population with him voluntarily. There were some radicals
who backed him in the few towns of the province, and some republican
sympathizers among the American-descended farmers of the southern
Ontario peninsula, but the majority of more recent settlers in the "back
townships" away from the lakes were reflexively loyal to Britain.

The honest backwoodsmen, perfectly ignorant of the abuses that
had led to the present position of things, regarded the rebels as a
set of monsters, for whom no punishment was too severe, and
obeyed the call to arms with enthusiasm. The leader of the insur-
gents must have been astonished at the rapidity with which a large
force was collected, as if by magic, to repel his designs. . . . I must
own that my British spirit was fairly aroused, and, as I could not
aid in subduing the enemies of my beloved country with my arm,
I did what little I could to serve the good cause with my pen:

THE OATH OF THE CANADIAN VOLUNTEERS

Huzza for England! – May she claim
    Our fond devotion ever. . . .

In weal or woe, whate'er betide,
    We swear to die, or save
Her honour from the rebel band
Whose crimes pollute our injured land. . . .

The stars for us shall never burn,
    The stripes may frighten slaves,
The Briton's eye will proudly turn
    Where Britain's standard waves.
Beneath its folds, if Heaven requires,
We'll die, as died of old our sires!

Susannah Moodie, 1837

Upon arrival [at De la Rey's Tavern near Port Hope] the more youthful and unsuspicious immediately sought such comforts as might be obtained in the bar and kitchen of rural inns, while the "old and knowing" were looking ahead and reserving the best bedrooms. . . . Fourteen of the thirty-six in the Cobourg Rifles secured the choice beds, the rest having to make the best of the one that remained. It broke down when eight threw themselves upon it, and after a friendly struggle for the bedclothes, it was decided that the mattress should be placed in the centre of the floor, and that no one should lay more than his head upon it.

. . . the circumstances were not conducive to sleep, and at three o'clock they decided to while away the time around a bowl of punch until it should be the hour of marching. A youth of seventeen, who although in the last stages of tuberculosis had bought a pony to enable him to accompany the force, read a poem, "The Time to Die", of his own composition and bearing upon his condition. . . .

Captain Warren ordered his men to get breakfast and fall in, and after they had eaten a large platter of cold fat pork and boiled potatoes the Rifles shouldered arms and with three cheers for the Queen set off westwards. . . . The pale youth on the pony struck the key-note for the whole army as he rode along murmuring the lines of Ossian – "Happy are they who die in their youth while their renown is around them!"

> "With the Newcastle District Militia," *The Lives
> and Times of the Patriots* (Toronto, 1938)

Most of the volunteers from outside the town of York (pop. 12,000) never heard a shot fired in anger, for Mackenzie moved against the capital before they got there. It was one of the few uprisings in modern history where the leading oppressors actually came out and fought in person.

We saw the Lieutenant-Governor in his everyday suit, with one double-barrelled gun in his hand, another leaning against his breast, and a brace of pistols in his leathern belt. Also Chief Justice Robinson, Judges Macaulay, Jones, and McLean, the Attorney-

General, and the Solicitor-General with their muskets, cartridge-boxes and bayonets, all standing in the ranks as private soldiers under the command of Colonel Fitzgibbon.

*Lives and Times of the Patriots*

Early on the morning of Thursday, 7 December, Mackenzie's Reformers, an utterly unmilitary gaggle of fewer than three hundred men, marched down Yonge Street (leaving a couple of hundred others who lacked arms behind at the tavern), and the York militia marched up Yonge Street, some fifteen hundred strong, to the tune of "Yankee Doodle Dandy" played by two bands. There were, according to a contemporary report, "Judges, Crown Officers, and most of the other public functionaries, the Merchants, Mechanics and labourers, the White and Coloured population, mingled in the lines without distinction of rank, station or colour" – and hundreds of unarmed civilians (including Archdeacon Strachan, the patriarch of the Family Compact) trailed behind to watch the fun. The two groups collided just south of what is now St. Clair Avenue. Joseph Gould was with the rebel force:

We had no arms but our rifles, and some had only rude pikes and pitchforks. The troops, besides their muskets and plenty of ammunition, had two small field-pieces – one controlled by a friend of ours, and the other by an enemy. The friend fired grape-shot, and fired over us into the tops of the trees, cutting off the dead and dry limbs of the hemlocks, which, falling thickly amongst us, scared the boys as much as if cannon-balls had been rattling around us. The other gun was fired low, and so *careless* that I did not like it. One of the balls struck a sandbank by my feet and filled my eyes with sand, nearly blinding me . . . Captain Wideman was killed on my left side. . . . But we got to the west of the troops. They then turned and crossed to Yonge Street behind us.

*Lives and Times of the Patriots*

The shooting lasted about twenty minutes, but Captain Ludovick Wideman was the only man killed in action on either side. Then the rebel force broke and fled, while the militiamen torched Montgomery's Tavern.

GOD SAVE THE QUEEN
Thursday, Three o'clock, P.M., 7th December
One Thousand Pounds Reward for the apprehension of W. Lyon
Mackenzie. He is a short man, wears a sandy-coloured wig, has
small twinkling eyes that can look no man in the face – he is about
five feet four or five inches in height.

Despite a major manhunt, William Lyon Mackenzie managed to make
it safely across the American border, from where he directed small-scale
and futile incursions into Canada over the next year. And as for all the
rural militia units that set out so excitedly for the big city and a big battle
– most of them eventually got to the capital, where they passed in review
before the lieutenant-governor, were treated to a banquet and the best
lodgings York could find (which were generally pretty dire, because the
rescuers outnumbered the resident population), and were then sent home
again.

> In a week, Moodie returned. So many volunteers had poured into
> Toronto that the number of friends was likely to prove as disas-
> trous as that of enemies, on account of the want of supplies to
> maintain them all. The companies from the back townships had
> been remanded, and I received with delight my own again.
>
> Susannah Moodie, 1837

❖

The rebellions were failures militarily, but they left a very ugly mood in
both parts of Canada. In Upper Canada, a sort of "Tory terror" prevailed
in the capital and around London, where there had very nearly been a
rising, too. In Lower Canada, as Lord Durham reported after his brief
sojourn as governor in 1838, both the French and the English communities were in a state of shock.

> [The French] brood in sullen silence over the memory of their
> fallen countrymen, of their burnt villages, of their ruined prop-
> erty, of their extinguished ascendancy, and of their humbled
> nationality. To the Government and the English they ascribe these

wrongs, and nourish against both an indiscriminating and eternal animosity. Nor have the English inhabitants forgotten in their triumph the terror with which they suddenly saw themselves surrounded by an insurgent majority. . . . They find themselves still a minority in the midst of a hostile and organized people . . . and their only hope of safety is supposed to rest on systematically terrifying and disabling the French, and in preventing a majority of that race from ever again being predominant in any portion of the legislature of that Province.

"Radical Jack" Durham was a brilliant, vain aristocrat with excellent political connections who had been sent out by the British government with instructions to come up with a solution to the "Canadian question," which was taking up far too much of London's time and always carried the implicit risk of war with the United States. Political complications at home forced Durham to return to England after less than six months in Canada, but his monumental Report in January 1839 had a profound effect on Canada's relationship with the British Empire. At a bare minimum, he felt, it was necessary to solve the two problems that had caused the Rebellions of 1837 in Lower and Upper Canada: French Canadian nationalism, and popular resentment in both Canadas against the domination of politics by a wealthy minority.

The latter problem could be solved by granting the colonies "responsible government": that is, by giving them governments like that of Britain itself, drawn from an elected legislature and answerable to it. However, Durham also believed that if the French Canadians of Lower Canada were allowed fully democratic institutions, they would soon use them to take the province out of the empire. His solution was to reunify the two Canadas, which had been separated in 1791, in order to create a single colony with an overall English-speaking majority who would choose to stay in the empire.

English Canadian loyalties, Durham correctly assumed, were a foregone conclusion. The original large American element in the population was rapidly being diluted by direct immigration from the British Isles, and an explicit feeling of being "British" was adding a new sentimental bond to the old strategic dependence on Britain. There would never be any comparable sentiment in the French Canadian attitude towards Britain, but Durham failed to realise that if the ethnic oppression that had so alienated the French Canadians were ended by the granting of responsible government, it would not be necessary to submerge them in a united province of Canada. Their old pragmatism would almost certainly then return them to their former acceptance of British rule.

The Rebellion of 1837 was only the final experience (though much the bitterest) in the formation of a special French Canadian view on how their nation ought to behave in the world. In the space of eighty years the French Canadians had been conquered from one empire by another; they had been invaded and occupied by a revolutionary republic; they had been "liberated" by their former conquerors; they had been invaded again, less successfully, by the same republic in a less revolutionary mood; and they had finally had a bloody and unsuccessful nationalist uprising of their own.

As a result, French Canadians became prematurely sophisticated–one could almost say cynical – about the ways of the world. They were no longer taken in by fine words, either in the British imperial idiom or in the mouths of their own nationalist idealists. They would drive a hard bargain in matters concerning their own security, taking all they could and giving as little as possible in return, and for the rest they would try simply, like Voltaire's Candide, to cultivate their own garden. All the great crusades were delusions, if they were not indeed deliberate deceptions foisted on the unwary by the powerful.

English Canada, by contrast, was a wide-eyed innocent, with a shorter and gentler history – even its revolt was a play-school version of the real thing – that left it wide open to seduction by any likely crusade that came past its door. And it would enlist in various of those crusades over the next century, dragging the unwilling French Canadian minority in its wake. However, the restraining influence of French Canada may have saved the lives of tens of thousands of English Canadians who would otherwise have been sacrificed in these wars. Australia, with only three-fifths of Canada's population but no comparable domestic constraint, has contributed almost as many dead (94,000) as Canada to the various imperial wars both countries have participated in during the twentieth century.

Neither the dour isolationism and severe pragmatism of the French Canadian tradition nor the naive idealism and breathless enthusiasm of the English Canadian tradition constitute a desirable basis for Canadian defence and foreign policy in the late twentieth century – but this is to get very much ahead of ourselves. In 1839, the point was simply that the stark realism of French Canadians could very easily drive them back into the arms of the British, if only their existing disadvantages could be removed. Unfortunately, Lord Durham could only think in terms of overwhelming the French Canadians with an anglophone majority.

He is understandably loathed in French Canada for his wounding comments on French Canadian culture: "There can hardly be conceived a nationality more destitute of all that can invigorate and elevate a people than . . . the descendants of the French in Lower Canada, owing to their retaining their peculiar language and manners. They are a people with no history and no literature. . . . Much as they struggle against it . . . the English language is gaining ground, as the language of the rich and of the employers of labour naturally will." And Durham was not merely speaking as an observer; it was his explicit hope that his recommendations would result in the disappearance of the French Canadian identity into a larger "British" and English-speaking culture. That ambition was as futile as it was intolerant.

Unfortunately, few British politicians could comprehend how self-government in a colony would not inevitably lead to independence from Britain, so at first Canadians ended up with the worst of both worlds. Durham's reforms were not implemented as a package: in 1840 the British government unified the two Canadian provinces in order to subordinate the French to the English permanently – though for many legal purposes they remained separate entities, now known as "Canada East" (Quebec) and "Canada West" (Ontario) – but it did not grant responsible government. The result was a bitter eight-year struggle in the united colony of Canada over that question, in which the reformers in both parts generally had the good sense not to let themselves be divided by issues of language and religion. While Canadians were distracted by that struggle, the dormant American threat began to stir again.

### CHAPTER SIX

# Fifty-four Forty or Fight

Poor Mexico! So far from God, so close to the United States!
Porfirio Díaz, President of Mexico, 1877-1911

If Canadians ever had any doubts about their need for the British military guarantee, they had only to look at what happened to the other neighbour of the United States in the 1840s. Mexico achieved its independence from the Spanish empire in 1822, but by the 1830s American settlers were beginning to encroach on its loosely governed border areas. And then, between 1836 and 1847, the Mexicans lost almost half of their national territory to the Americans. Without a European empire behind them, they were no match for the power of the United States.

The territories that the Mexicans lost were on the southern edge of the wave of American settlement as it surged westward in the first half of the nineteenth century. It was an extraordinary mass migration, and Mexico was powerless to halt the influx of land-hungry American settlers who rapidly changed the population balance in its sparsely populated territories from Texas to California. The first major Mexican loss was Texas, which became an independent republic under the leadership of American settlers in 1836.

On the northern edge of the expanding area of American settlement lay half of what is now Canada: the future provinces of Manitoba, Saskatchewan, Alberta, and British Columbia. They were just as desirable to American settlers as the Mexican territories, equally bereft of natural barriers to divert the flow of homesteaders, and even more sparsely populated (the non-native population of British Columbia did not reach ten thousand until 1860, and the settlement of the Canadian prairies did not really begin until the 1870s). But as the wave of American settlement rolled west, there was relatively little seepage north across the utterly artificial boundary along the Forty-ninth Parallel, which had been drawn across the Great Plains to the Rockies in the convention of 1818.

When American settlers began to spill over the Rockies onto the Pacific coast in the late 1830s, however, they found that Britain, through its agent the Hudson's Bay Company, claimed all the territory north of the Columbia river (the southern border of the present state of Washington). They were deeply displeased, and in 1843 American squatters formed a provisional republic of Oregon and appealed for annexation to the United States. That provided the occasion for the next burst of American territorial expansion, which had been stalled since the Louisiana Purchase of 1803 by the controversy over whether new territories should become slave or "free" states. It now seemed possible to expand in both the northwest (against the British) and the southwest (against the Mexicans) at the same time, thus adding equal numbers of free and slave states and not upsetting the existing balance in Congress, so the Democrats picked the issue up and ran with it. In 1844 President James K. Polk was elected on two slogans: "the annexation of Texas and the re-annexation of Oregon" and (much more alarmingly) "Fifty-four Forty or Fight." That was a demand for the entire Pacific coast of North America up to latitude 54° 40′, the southern extremity of Russian Alaska.

Once Polk took office in 1845, Congress approved a treaty for the annexation of Texas, and the pretexts began to be prepared for a far bigger territorial grab from Mexico, taking in most of the territories that now form the states of Colorado, Utah, New Mexico, Arizona, Nevada, and

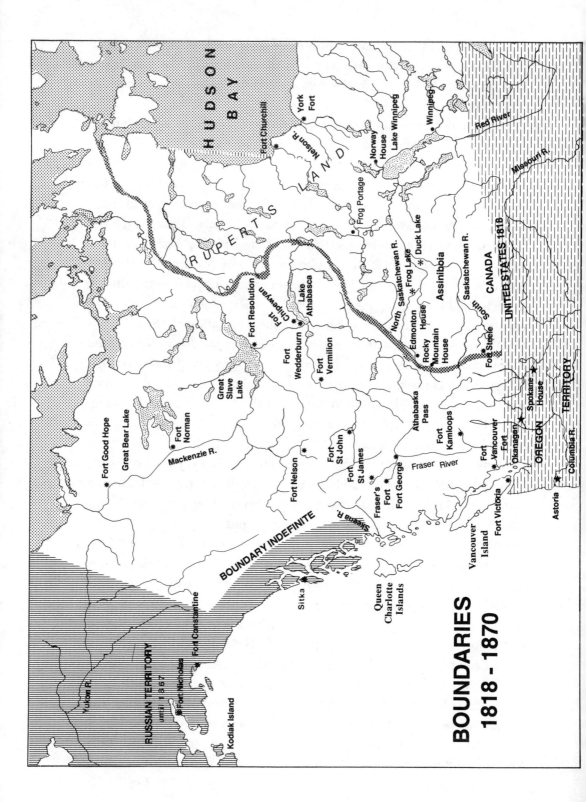

BOUNDARIES
1818 - 1870

California. But the parallel project on the northwestern frontier did not prosper. In 1846 American negotiators tamely agreed to a compromise that merely extended the frontier between the United States and British North America straight west along the Forty-ninth Parallel all the way to the Pacific, thus creating the "Oregon Territory" south of the line and "British Columbia" north of it.

American military provocations against Mexico continued, and in the end the Mexicans fought – and lost, of course. By 1847 U.S. troops commanded by General Winfield Scott had fought their way into Mexico City. But the territories that would one day comprise Western Canada did not suffer a similar fate, for they belonged not to an independent country but to the British Empire. An independent Canada would not only have lost all those territories to the United States; in the process it would probably have been goaded into a war that would have ended with U.S. troops occupying the entire settled territory in the East as well.

It was not a massive British military presence north of the frontier that enforced this restraint on the Americans. There were very few British troops in the West, and even the regular garrisons in the settled parts of British North America gradually declined as the last war receded into the past. But Britain was the unrivalled world power for at least four decades after 1814, and Washington, despite occasional outbursts of bluster, was nervous about the outcome of a war with such a formidable enemy.

During all this time the British North Americans enjoyed an extraordinary "free ride" in defence. There was a local, virtually untrained militia, for use in emergencies only, but their real defence consisted of regular British troops paid for by British taxpayers. Britain's total military expenditure for North America for 1846 was £645,000, almost a quarter of its total spending on imperial defence and about three percent of all British government expenditure on everything other than the national debt. At the same time, the proto-Canadians profited from the system of imperial trading preferences which guaranteed high prices and good markets for their exports. It was a very good deal – but nothing lasts forever.

❖

Electors of St. Denis, you gave proof of your courage when, on November 22, 1837, armed with a few pitchforks, guns and bludgeons, you repulsed the troops of Colonel Gore. I was with you, and I don't think I showed any lack of courage. Today I demand from you a greater, a better, a more patriotic action. I appeal to you to repel by your votes an army still more formidable – those who would continue to oppress you by depriving you of the advantage of responsible government.

> Georges Étienne Cartier (later a "Father
> of Confederation"), election speech, 1844

Despite the regressive measures taken in the years after 1837, the agitation for a genuinely democratic system never stopped in Canada – and in 1846, just as the immediate American threat to British North America was dying down, the government changed in London. Within a year, the Canadian colonies began to receive the responsible government Lord Durham had recommended eight years before. He had been dying of tuberculosis even as he wrote his Report, but the new Colonial Secretary, Lord Grey, was his brother-in-law, and the new Governor General of British North America, Lord Elgin, was married to Durham's daughter.

The grant of internal self-government resolved most of the unfinished business from the rebellions of 1837. By 1849 both Papineau and Mackenzie were back in Canada, and both re-entered Parliament, but the issues on which they had thrived had largely been settled and they never regained their former prominence (although four of Papineau's former aides eventually led Canadian governments). However, colonial self-government was only part of a far more sweeping change in Britain's attitude toward the empire, as it became increasingly aware that the real source of its wealth and power lay in its own burgeoning industrial base, not in its distant colonies.

The new Whig (Liberal) government in London was dominated by advocates of free trade who promptly set about dismantling the old imperial trading system that had allegedly made owning colonies worthwhile. The imperial trading preferences were a relic of the "first British empire" – the seventeenth- and eighteenth-century empire that consisted mainly of North American and West Indian colonies populated by British emigrants (and imported slaves, in most cases). The prevailing "mercantilist" economic doctrine had then held that you could maximize the national wealth by creating a closed, controlled, and self-sufficient economy. Canada had benefitted greatly from this doctrine, because the imperial trading preferences had given Canadian primary products like wheat, flour, and timber a privileged position in the British market, and a great deal of the Canadian economy had been developed on the assumption that they would always be there.

But by the mid-nineteenth century both politics and economics had moved on. The "second British empire," founded on the conquest of vast territories in Asia and Africa, was already taking shape (especially in India) even before Britain lost the Thirteen Colonies. Moreover, as Britain's prosperity and power came to depend more obviously on its own expanding industries, commercial and political opinion in England grew distinctly doubtful about the net economic advantage of owning an empire at all: foreign trade is a lot more profitable if you avoid the expense of defending and administering the foreign trading partners. This perception did not lead to the wholesale dismantling of the British Empire – there were far too many vested interests in its preservation – but it did mean that henceforward the bits of the empire that were particularly expensive to defend (such as Canada) were viewed by London with a rather jaundiced eye. And it certainly meant the disappearance of the old imperial trading preferences: why give Canada privileged access to the British market when the same products might be available more cheaply from somewhere else in the world?

The British North American colonies eventually repaired some of the economic damage caused by the abolition of the imperial trading system by concluding a "reciprocity" (free trade) agreement with the United States in 1854, but it meant that they no longer had any powerful economic reason to stay within the empire. Indeed, one of the early responses of a large part of the business community, both in Canada West and among the powerful English-speaking minority in Montreal, was to demand annexation to the United States. Far more importantly, once the imperial trading system was gone, why *should* Britain pay to defend British North America?

> I feel myself however, I must confess, somewhat in the position
> in which the master of one of those ricketty vessels which are
> sent to this quarter in quest of timber occasionally finds himself.
> By dint of much labor and watching he succeeds in conveying

ship and cargo safely through the tempests and icebergs which assail him on the voyage out and home, and he is not a little disappointed, poor simple minded man! when on reporting his arrival, he hears the owners mutter to one another "It would have been better for us if the whole concern had gone to the bottom, as we should have then realized the Insurance." Much in the same light are exertions made to maintain and perpetuate the connexion between this Province and the Mother Country, likely, I fear, to be viewed: – for Canada is beginning to be reckoned, I shrewdly suspect, by most English politicians, a bad bargain at any price.

Nevertheless, so long as I am in charge, it is my duty, I presume, to steer by the old lights, and to endeavour to keep things together as best I can.

Lord Elgin, Governor General of British North America,
to Lord Grey, Colonial Secretary, 9 April 1848

Successful empires are run on a combination of sentiment and cold calculation, but the sentiment predominates at the periphery while calculation prevails at the centre. In the particular case of British North Americans, there was an unusually large admixture of conscious self-interest in their sentiment (especially among French speakers), since loyalty to the British Empire gave them a free guarantee against annexation by the United States. But there was also a simple, unquestioning sentiment of "imperial patriotism" among most of the more recently arrived English speakers, who generally still thought of themselves as British – and that section of the population grew steadily more numerous and influential as the century progressed.

In London, however, the balance between sentiment and calculation was different, and by mid-century it was leading British governments to chafe at the responsibility for defending British North America. The British electorate still felt a certain kinship for people of British descent overseas, and the politicians were concerned that imperial prestige not be harmed by any loss of territory through military defeat. But most people in the British government secretly wished that British North America would just go away.

I confess that I think that now the Canadians have self Govt. so completely granted to them they ought also to pay all its expenses including military protection.

> Lord Grey, Colonial Secretary, to Lord Elgin,
> Governor General of British North America, 1848

We must seriously consider our Canadian position, which is most illegitimate. An Army maintained in a country which does not even permit us to govern it! What an anomaly! . . . Power and influence we should exercise in Asia; consequently in Eastern Europe; consequently in Western Europe; but what is the use of these colonial deadweights which we do not govern?

> Benjamin Disraeli, British Chancellor of the Exchequer,
> to Lord Derby, 1866

By the 1850s the North American colonies had come to be seen as a political, economic, and military liability. They were an inconvenient left-over from Britain's first empire, which had had the heart torn out of it by the American Revolution in the 1770s. Britain had cut its losses and gone on to build a second empire in Asia, centred on its possessions in India, and in the mid-nineteenth century British foreign policy, even in Europe, focussed on the protection of that Asian empire. If you are obsessed with protecting your lines of communication to an Asian empire from jealous European rivals, the last thing you need is a military commitment to unprofitable North American colonies thousands of miles away in the opposite direction – especially when they might drag you into war with the growing power of the United States.

So the British government began looking for ways to divest itself of this awkward commitment by urging its North American colonies to take responsibility for their own defence, even though they obviously lacked the men or the money to create a defence that would hold off a deter-mined American attack. However, the logical final step in this British policy – an open withdrawal of the imperial military guarantee and the abandonment of the North American colonies to the United States – was never actually taken. Even in London, sentiment counted for something, and prestige counted for a great deal. But basically, the British wanted out, and they soon took a significant first step in that direction.

In 1854, Britain went to war in order to stop Russia's southward expansion towards the Mediterranean, which was thought to threaten Britain's communications with its Asian empire. It was the first war between European great powers for forty years – and in order to find troops for the Crimean Expeditionary Force that London sent off to fight the Russians, it had to strip its imperial garrisons all over the world. Within twelve months of the Crimean War's outbreak, the number of British regulars in North America dropped by more than half, to only 3,284 men. The stark need to provide a credible military resistance to an American invasion – at least long enough for reinforcements to arrive from Britain – now forced Canadians to make at least a gesture towards self-defence. But the Militia Act of 1855 did much more than that: it also laid the foundations for Canada's eventual participation in wars that went far beyond strict self-defence.

❖

A few men, well mounted and dressed as lancers, in uniforms which were, however, anything but uniform, flourished backwards on the green sward, to the manifest peril of the spectators; themselves and their horses, equally wild, disorderly, spirited and undisciplined; but this was perfection compared with the infantry. Here there was no uniformity attempted of dress, of appearance, of movement. . . . Some had firelocks, some had old swords suspended in belts, or stuck in their waistbands; but the greater number shouldered sticks or umbrellas.

Mrs M. told me that on a former parade she has heard the word of command given thus – "Gentlemen with the umbrellas take ground to the right! Gentlemen with the walking sticks take ground to the left!" Now they ran after each other, elbowed and kicked each other, straddled, stooped and chattered; and if the commanding officer turned his back for a moment, very coolly sat down on the bank to rest. . . . [The day ended] in a drunken bout and a riot in which, I was afterwards informed, the colonel

had been knocked down, and one or two serious and even fatal
accidents had occurred, but it was all taken . . . very lightly.

> Mrs Anna Jameson, describing the annual militia muster
> at Erindale, Ontario, on 4 June 1837

The old military system of North America resembled that of medieval
Europe. There was no standing army, but every able-bodied man was
theoretically obliged to make himself available for military service in wartime. It was imported into North America by the first European settlers,
both English and French, and it continued to flourish here for a remarkably long time. Even in the early 1600s this system was already disap-
pearing in Europe, as the rising technical sophistication of warfare drove
European governments to depend on smaller professional armies of paid
volunteers. But right down past the mid-nineteenth century, small towns
all over North America were still the scene for the annual muster of militia
at which all the fit men of the district had to present themselves, with
whatever weapons they might possess, for a roll call, some perfunctory
drill, and generally a good deal of drinking and rowdiness.

However, the Militia Act of 1855 marked the tacit abandonment of
the myth of 1812, which pretended that the defence of Canada had been
and could be based mainly on the enthusiastic but amateurish efforts of
a militia that included the entire adult male population. Right down to
1950, Canadian law kept the theoretical obligation of all adult males for
military service if the "Sedentary Militia" were called out, but in practice
all the attention after 1855 went into creating a far smaller "Active Militia" made up of volunteers. These volunteers (about five thousand men
in 1855, rising to about twenty thousand by the end of the century)
actually received a couple of weeks' military training each year, and were
given more or less modern weapons and equipment. With the addition
of a small "Permanent Force" in 1883, consisting of a thousand or so full-
time professional soldiers whose main job was to train the Active Militia,
Canada's military forces took on the basic form they would retain until
only a few decades ago.

In terms of military efficiency, the old militia system had had huge
defects: both Britain and France always had to rely heavily on imported
regular troops for their wars in North America. However, the old militia

system did have one great advantage: it made it virtually impossible to send North American troops overseas to fight in foreign wars. The Militia Act of 1855 changed all that, by creating a smaller, more highly trained force of Canadian volunteer troops who could potentially be used outside North America. But before Canada could embark on a semi-independent military career as a supporting player in the great-power game, it had first to get through the most dangerous decade of the 1860s, and avoid being swallowed by the United States. It was a near-run thing.

❖

[I have acted] in a proper and prudent manner . . . for the protection of American citizens from foreign savages and wanton aggression of foreign officials.

Brigadier-General William S. Harney, U.S. Army.
Commander-in-Chief, Department of Oregon,
August 1859

[Harney is] a general who on his own authority has invaded our territory. His grounds for doing so were based on falsehood and were carried out clandestinely. What now can be expected of a man who has spent his lifetime warring with Indians?

. . . Instead of warring, Her Majesty's captains take to diplomacy. . . . We must defend ourselves, a militia must be formed. San Juan is the key to British Columbia.

Speaker of the British Columbia House of Assembly,
September 1859

[I will not] involve two great nations in a war over a squabble about a pig.

Rear-Admiral Robert L. Baynes, Commander, British
Pacific Fleet, September 1859

The island of San Juan, in the straits between Vancouver Island and what is now the state of Washington, was a piece of unfinished business left over from the 1846 Oregon Treaty that had defined the border between U.S. and British territory on the Pacific coast. The negotiators had agreed that the boundary would run along the Forty-ninth Parallel as far as the coast, and then south and west again down "the middle of the channel" separating Vancouver Island from the mainland. Unfortunately, the diplomats' knowledge of the local geography was so scant that they did not realize there were two channels that might plausibly be described as the "main channel": one ran to the east of San Juan Island, the other to the west. Whichever government controlled the island would therefore be in a position to dominate the seaward approaches to the lower mainland of British Columbia.

The British government had created the colony of Vancouver Island in 1849 to prevent the loss of "northern Oregon" to the incoming waves of American settlers. The colony of British Columbia on the mainland followed in 1858, mainly in order to impose British authority on the influx of American prospectors caused by the Cariboo gold rush. (The two colonies were united under the name of British Columbia in 1866.)

From the start, major efforts were made to bring in British immigrants to nail the vulnerable territories down, and particular attention was paid to San Juan Island because of its potential strategic importance. By 1855 the Hudson's Bay Company was operating a flourishing stock farm on San Juan Island. The British governor in Victoria, Sir James Douglas, also tried to induce British settlers to go to the island with offers of 500 acres of free land, but there were no takers. Instead, American squatters began to move in, and by 1858 there were twenty-three U.S. citizens on San Juan. One of them, Lyman Cutlar, made the error of homesteading 160 acres right next to the Hudson's Bay Company establishment. There were several hundred pigs on the Company farm, and pigs like potatoes.

On 15 June 1859, a pig belonging to the Hudson's Bay Company crawled under the fence and began rooting around in Mr Cutlar's potato patch. Cutlar, a man of very little patience, shot it. Adding insult to injury, he then cooked and ate it. When the local British magistrate arrived to arrest him, accompanied by Mr Dallas, Governor Douglas's son-in-law (who happened to be visiting the island), Cutlar jammed his rifle barrel up Mr Dallas's nose and ordered them both off his property. Cutlar then appealed for help directly to General William "Goliath" Harney, who commanded U.S. army forces on the Pacific coast – and that vehemently anti-British officer promptly sent a hundred troops of the Ninth U.S. Infantry to occupy the island.

The crisis escalated with astounding speed. The American soldiers landed on 26 July, and by 3 August four British warships with Royal Marines on board arrived from Victoria. Harney sent reinforcements to his outnumbered troops on San Juan, and called for armed volunteers from Oregon Territory and San Francisco to defend American rights. Rear-Admiral Baynes, the commander of the British Pacific Fleet, arrived all the way from Chile in mid-August in the eighty four-gun battleship HMS *Ganges* to take command of the British forces. By that time there were about five thousand soldiers and sailors, British and American, nervously confronting each other on and around San Juan Island.

On 16 September General Winfield Scott – the same man who had been captured at Queenston Heights in 1812, fought the British to a standstill at Lundy's Lane in 1814, and captured Mexico City in 1847 (and by now universally known in the American army as "Ole Fuss'n'Feathers") – was ordered west to take charge of the U.S. forces. But Washington didn't want war over San Juan, and Scott, now Commander-in-Chief of the U.S. Army, was instructed by President Buchanan to calm things down: "It would be a shocking event if . . . two nations were precipitated into a war respecting a small island."

London suspected that the Americans had initially decided to make a grab for British Columbia back in July because at that time it looked as if Britain was about to be sucked into a war between France and Austria that had suddenly broken out in northern Italy. Scott's less belligerent instructions in September, the British believed, were only due to the fact that by then the war in Europe had suddenly and unexpectedly ended. "Even the occupation of San Juan by General Harney was effected shortly after intelligence of the breaking out of war in Italy had reached the Pacific," noted the Duke of Newcastle, the Secretary of State for the Colonies. "And . . . it may be believed that [the early end to the war in Europe decided] the Cabinet of Washington to send General Scott on his Pacific Mission."

This was probably just the usual paranoia that infects every country's foreign policy. Unaware of the British suspicions, General Scott privately blamed the whole San Juan Island affair on Harney, who he thought had been trying to copy Andrew Jackson's feat of seizing Florida from Spain and using that successful act of robbery as a springboard for the presidency: "Harney probably thought he could make himself President too,

by cutting short all diplomacy and taking forcible possession of the disputed island." American generals have always had a penchant for running
for the presidency—Winfield Scott himself had had a try in 1852—so there
may be some truth in his surmise: General Harney had visited San Juan
in disguise only two months before the crisis began, and was clearly
itching to make a forward move. But as Scott remarked, President Buchanan, "well knowing the difference in power between Spain and Great
Britain," had sent his most senior officer out there to calm the dispute.

General Scott and Admiral Baynes managed to negotiate a gradual
reduction of forces in the area, and drew a temporary line across the
island to separate the British and American troops. But Scott himself
thought that it would probably be only a few years before events led to
"a separation of the Canadas, New Brunswick, etc., etc., from England,"
after which they would almost certainly join the United States – and
despite Scott's success in lowering the temperature of the confrontation,
he could not end it.

Each country suspected the other of planning war, and in 1860 Governor Douglas on Vancouver Island, having received instructions to
impress upon the colonists "the necessity of providing themselves with
arms and of learning to use them," had authorized the formation of the
"Victoria Pioneer Rifle Corps" (manned principally by the black residents
of the colony). By early 1861 some of the white inhabitants had been
persuaded to enroll themselves in the militia as well – and for the next
dozen years, British and American regular troops sat on San Juan glowering at each other, while the island, with no effective civil administration,
became "a depot for murderers, smugglers and whiskey-sellers."

The San Juan incident set the tone for the next decade: repeated
American invasion scares, with the British reluctantly supporting their
North American colonies but desperately anxious to avoid war with the
United States. It was a time when national unification was all the rage in
the Western world. The various Italian states were united in 1859, the
American Civil War was explicitly about the subordination of the various
states to the national government, and the German wars of national unification extended from 1864 to 1870. Given that wealth of example, plus
all the internal political difficulties that were troubling the united province of Canada, it was hardly surprising that the question of unification
should come up in the British North American colonies too – but in the

Canadian case, fear of the Americans was an indispensable part of the process.

❖

Secession first he would put down
Wholly and forever,
And afterwards from Britain's crown
He Canada would sever.

> popular American ditty of the 1860s, sung to the tune of
> "Yankee Doodle Dandy"

The hero of the ditty was William Seward, President Lincoln's Secretary of State. He had first advocated the annexation of British North America with the dual purpose of averting the imminent secession of the Southern states by distracting them with a triumphant foreign war, and of increasing the relative power of the "Northern" states in the U.S. political balance by the addition of the Canadian territories. Annexation of Canada continued to be a popular cause in the United States, for the "unnatural" division of North America had been deplored by influential American figures from Benjamin Franklin on down. And even after the Southern states actually seceded and the Civil War broke out in 1861, the absorption of the British territories stayed close to the top of the political agenda in Washington.

Indeed, the American Civil War actually heightened the threat of an invasion of Canada, because relations between London and Washington became so tense that they frequently verged on war. The first crisis, the *Trent* affair, occurred in October 1861, when the U.S. warship *San Jacinto* stopped the British mail steamer *Trent* near Havana and American soldiers abducted two Confederate representatives who were aboard. The British government was outraged at the behaviour of the Americans: "I don't know whether you are going to stand for them," shouted Lord Palmerston, the British prime minister, flinging his hat down on the Cabinet table, "but I'll be damned if I do." And in this crisis, with the two countries on the brink of war, London's response was extremely reassuring to the nervous inhabitants of British North America: the imperial government promptly hired ships and sent over fourteen thousand troops to Canada, quadrupling the regular garrison of the colonies.

Heartened by this show of strength and by the early defeats of the Union forces in the Civil War, Governor Douglas in Victoria even asked London for permission to drive the Americans out of San Juan Island and the entire Puget Sound area. He could do it, he said, using only the British forces already in the area and local militia units. He also promised that with the additional help of "one or two Regiments of Queen's Troops" he would be able to "push overland from Puget Sound and establish advanced posts on the Columbia River, maintaining it as the permanent frontier." But London told Douglas to observe strict neutrality toward the Americans and to make no forward moves in the region. Despite the increased number of British regiments in North America, the British government suspected that in the end any war with the United States would be disastrous for its North American possessions.

A war between the United States and Britain as early as 1861 would almost certainly have ensured the independence of the Confederacy, so Washington also worked to contain the crisis, but Anglo-American tensions remained high as a result of incidents like the operations of the Confederate commerce raider *Alabama*, which was fitted out in a British shipyard despite Washington's strenuous objections. By the time of the next real crisis in 1864, moreover, the odds had shifted sharply in Washington's favour in case of war. By that time the U.S. government controlled the largest modern-style army in the world, and its final victory over the South was only months away.

At this delicate juncture, in October 1864, a small band of Confederate soldiers operating out of a secret base in Quebec raided the town of St. Albans in Vermont. The United States erupted in rage. The raiders (cum-bank-robbers and murderers) were put on trial in Canada, but the trial proceeded very slowly. Eventually Judge C. J. Coursol decided he had no jurisdiction and released the men. This infuriated the Northern states once again: Congress brought in legislation to end the Reciprocity Agreement with Canada, and many Americans began talking of invading the Canadian colonies and eliminating the British threat once and for all. The British North Americans were sufficiently alarmed that the question of a confederation between all the North American colonies became, for the first time, a live political issue.

The subject of a narrower federation had been on the political agenda of the united province of Canada since 1858, when Alexander Tilloch Galt, the millionaire politician who was president of both the British

American Land Company in the Eastern Townships and of the Grand Trunk Railway, had succeeded in getting the project adopted by the Conservative government led by Georges-Étienne Cartier and John A. Macdonald. Galt, however, was initially interested only in escaping from the dilemma created by Lord Durham's decision to merge Upper and Lower Canada, which had been as pernicious in practice as it was wrong in principle. Indeed, far from being submerged in the united province of Canada as Durham had intended, the French Canadians had emerged as the dominant force in the provincial Assembly, since their minority status naturally enforced a greater unity on them than was the case for the fractious English Canadian political groupings.

It was not that collaboration between French and English speakers was impossible, either on an individual or an a group basis: Macdonald and Cartier (who had fought on different sides in the rebellions of 1837) were a splendid example of how close and how fruitful such political partnerships could be. But the particular form of collaboration represented by the structure of the united province of Canada simply wasn't working. The attempt to run a single provincial government catering to the very different expectations and demands of French-speaking Catholic Quebeckers and English-speaking Ontario Orangemen was imposing intolerable strains on the united province created out of Upper and Lower Canada in 1840: on matters like schools, for example, a government majority that depended primarily on French Canadian votes in the Assembly frequently had to decide on questions that were mainly of importance to English speakers, or vice versa.

As George Brown, editor of the Toronto *Globe* and a leading Reform politician, lamented in 1864: "We have two races, two languages, two systems of religious belief, two systems of everything, so that it has become almost impossible that, without sacrificing their principles, the public men of both sections could come together in the same government." Indeed, despite two elections and three governments between 1861 and 1864, the Canadian Assembly was unable even to pass the measures to strengthen the militia which everyone agreed had become necessary. So the idea of creating a federation in which Canada West and Canada East might re-emerge as the separate provinces of Ontario and Quebec, looking after their own local affairs while preserving a strong central government to deal with the larger issues, was a tempting solution to many in both French and English Canada.

This local political perception in the Canadas meshed quite conveniently, as it happened, with the growing British desire to see a broader federation of all the North American colonies. London's barely concealed hope, of course, was that having such an extensive country to run would strengthen the British North Americans' will to defend themselves – and ultimately, perhaps, might even get them off British hands. However, the four Atlantic colonies were distinctly cool toward this idea, and even the government of the Canadas might not have got around to doing anything about it if there had not been a serious American threat in 1864.

It was that atmosphere of impending crisis which enabled Macdonald and Cartier to send a delegation to Charlottetown in September to begin the negotiations with the other colonies that culminated in Confederation – and the near-panic north of the border did not subside even after the Civil War ended in April 1865. The question of annexation was kept on the boil by Washington's quite accurate perception that Britain's heart was not really in the defence of its North American colonies – and the spectre of an American invasion, looming constantly in the background, kept the colonial politicians committed to the difficult negotiations down to their successful conclusion two years later.

> A confederation of states on this continent, extending from ocean to ocean ... and founded upon monarchical principles, cannot be considered otherwise than in contravention of the traditions and constantly declared principles of this government.
>
> Resolution of the U.S. House of Representatives,
> March 1866

> I am more than ever disappointed at the tone of feeling here [London] as to the Colonies. I cannot shut my eyes to the fact that they want to get rid of us. They have a servile fear of the United States and would rather give us up than defend us, or incur the risk of war with that country.
>
> Sir Alexander Tilloch Galt, after a visit to London
> seeking British support for Confederation in 1865

Although the North American colonies were not worth a major war with the United States, Britain was still prepared to *pretend* that it would fight for them, in order to deter the United States – provided that the

Canadians were willing to pay for their share of the bluff. By an agreement of 1865 the united province of Canada promised to maintain a high level of spending on the militia, and to build new fortifications "at and west of Montreal." For its part, Britain promised to guarantee loans to the Canadian government for the construction work, to complete the fortification of Quebec City itself, and "in the event of war to undertake the defence of every portion of Canada with all the resources of the Empire."

On paper, it was an ironclad guarantee. In fact, however, a British military commission had already concluded by 1865 that a successful defence of Canada would require 150,000 men, the enlargement of the Rideau Canal to allow armoured warships to reach the Great Lakes, and elaborate fortifications around Montreal. Even then, everything from Niagara Falls west would have to be abandoned. So London brought every available pressure to bear on its recalcitrant North American colonies to unite. A successful Canadian confederation might be persuaded to provide most of the resources for this scale of defence itself – and if it chose not to, the British government would have a more plausible excuse for not fighting a war with the United States on its behalf. By early 1867, the confederation of British North America was about to come to pass.

> The first and most important of our duties will then be the speedy withdrawal of all British troops from the North American continent. . . . As long as these troops are shut up during half the year in an almost inaccessible Province, and exposed at all times to an invasion, the American government has so many hostages, as it were, for British good behaviour.
>
> *The Times*, London, 29 March 1867

The immediate threat of invasion that helped drive the various colonies into Confederation in 1867 came from the Fenian Brotherhood, a revolutionary group of Irish immigrants in America, most of them Civil War veterans. The Fenians had a crazy plan to take over Britain's North American possessions, where a large fraction of the English-speaking population were also relatively recent Irish immigrants, and then to use Canada as a base to wage war against Britain (probably in alliance with the United States) in order to force London to grant Ireland its freedom. In June 1866 ten Canadian militiamen were killed and thirty wounded in a bloody fight with Fenian raiders at Ridgeway (close to the Niagara River in Ontario). Fenian threats against New Brunswick helped to topple the anti-Confederation government there (which was the major obstacle to a union of all the larger colonies), and there were also raids on Quebec. But the Fenians were really just comic-opera stuff (although the British government took them seriously enough to rush three battalions of infantry and one of cavalry to Canada, with supporting artillery, by the first available ships): the more serious threat was the U.S. government itself.

The huge Union armies of the Civil War quickly melted away, but Congress was in a confidently expansionist mood. In 1866 General N. P. Banks of Massachusetts introduced a bill providing for "the admission of the States of Nova Scotia, New Brunswick, Canada East and Canada West, and for the organisation of the territories of Selkirk [Manitoba], Saskatchewan and Columbia." The perceived American threat grew even greater in 1867, when U.S. Secretary of State William Seward bought Alaska from the Russians for $7.2 million. It was, he said, "a visible step in the occupation of the whole North American continent" – and some Canadians recalled his even blunter remarks in 1861:

I can stand here and look far off into the North-west and see the Russian as he busily occupies himself with establishing seaports and towns and fortifications as outposts of the empire of St. Petersburg, and I can say: "Go in, build up your outposts to the Arctic Ocean. They will yet become the outposts of my own country, to extend the civilisation of the U.S. in the North-west."

So I look upon Prince Rupert's Land and Canada and see how ingenious people and a capable, enlightened government are occupied with bridging rivers and making railroads and telegraphs to develop . . . the great British provinces of the north, by the Great Lakes, the St. Lawrence, and around the shores of Hudson's Bay, and I am able to say to you: "It is very well. You are building excellent states to be admitted hereafter to the American Union."

After Seward's Alaskan purchase, American political pressures for a settlement of the San Juan Island dispute increased immediately, and Congress echoed with "Right, Proper and Desirable" demands for the "re-annexation" of the whole of British Columbia. The old "Fifty-four Forty or Fight" slogan came back to life.

❖

> The American war is . . . at length over, and the immense [American] army . . . will require employment on new battlefields. . . . As we at present stand, we would have no course but to surrender, and the whole of British territory west of the Rocky Mountains would fall like an over-ripe apple into the lap of the United States. . . . If we wish to retain possession of these colonies, we must, or rather the mother country must, adopt a more effective means of defence.
>
> *British Colonist*, Victoria, 9 May 1865

"Or rather the mother country must." The mother country would do no such thing. It was no longer the economic fashion to believe that colonies were a profitable undertaking, so British Columbia could not expect endless largesse from the British Exchequer to pay for its defence. Its only long-term hope of escaping annexation to the United States was if the Canadian confederation being discussed in the East actually got off the ground and gave it support and shelter. There was plenty of goodwill at the British Colonial Office, but not much more.

> It seems to me impossible that we should long hold B.C. from its natural annexation [to the United States]. Still we should give and keep open for Canada every chance and if possible get [Governor] Seymour to bridge over the present difficulties till we see what Canada may do.
>
> C.B. Adderley, Parliamentary Under-Secretary
> for the Colonies, 17 September 1867

The partial achievement of Confederation in British North America in 1867, taking in Ontario, Quebec, New Brunswick, and Nova Scotia, is now seen as a kind of watershed, but at the time very little seemed to be settled. The British were supportive, but they were "waiting to see what Canada will do." As for the Americans, they regarded Confederation as a mere constitutional fiddle – rearranging the deck-chairs on the *Titanic* (if you will pardon the anachronism) – and they set to work at once on those who had remained outside the new country, or were unhappy to be in it.

In 1868 the U.S. Senate sent a mission led by Senator (and former General) Benjamin F. Butler to Prince Edward Island, which had refused to enter Confederation in the previous year, to offer it a version of the Reciprocity Agreement which had just been abrogated with Canada. Butler also had talks with anti-Confederation diehards in Nova Scotia, which had joined but was having serious second thoughts. And American nibbling at the other extremity of the new country began as soon as the new administration of President (and former General) Ulysses S. Grant took office in early 1869.

Grant's secretary of state, Hamilton Fish, concocted fantastic claims for reparations from Britain for damage caused by Confederate shipping raiders that had been built or refitted in Britain during the Civil War. He then proposed that London should cede all of Rupert's Land and the North-West Territories (very roughly, Northern Ontario, the three Prairie provinces and the Yukon and Northwest Territories of today) to the U.S. in satisfaction of these claims. Grant and Fish even urged Britain to "withdraw" from North America entirely, in the expectation that the new Dominion would then fall into their hands sooner or later. It was not an unreasonable expectation, and the Dominion of Canada's first prime minister, Sir John A. Macdonald (who was knighted in London in 1867), was well aware that the country had to expand rapidly or see most of its potential inheritance slip away. "It is quite evident to me," he observed in January 1870, " . . . that the United States government are resolved to do all they can, short of war, to get possession of our western territory, and we must take immediate and vigorous steps to counteract them."

> Sir John Macdonald is a type of politician who has never failed to delight the English people – the man who, like Palmerston, can work hard, do strong things, hold his purpose, never lose sight for a moment of the honour and welfare of his country, and yet crack his joke and have his laugh, full of courage and good spirits and kindly fun.
>
> N. F. Davin, quoted in Willison, *Reminiscences*,
> pp. 187-88

Though he was sometimes a bit too full of spirits, the Glasgow-born lawyer from Kingston, Ontario, was Britain's unhesitating choice as the man to shepherd the North American colonies into self-reliance, if not eventual independence. In the following years the British government did everything possible to help him bring the rest of its possessions in North America under Canadian rule.

In the fall of 1869 Rupert's Land and the North-West Territories were transferred from the Hudson's Bay Company to Canada in return for a cash payment of $1.5 million, and in the following year the settled part of that vast area was hastily elevated to full provincial status under the name of Manitoba, even though its non-Indian population was only about seven thousand people. A majority of these people, the French-speaking Métis, led by Louis Riel, wanted nothing to do with Canada, and created a provisional government of their own in the Red River settlement, but the British government promptly made troops available to Canada to suppress the revolt. Colonel Garnet Wolseley (later to be the original for Gilbert and Sullivan's "I am the very model of a modern major-general") led a 1,041-man expedition across Lake Superior and up the rugged old canoe route to Fort Garry, Manitoba, in the summer of 1870 without losing a man, and the rebellion collapsed without resistance. Louis Riel fled to the United States.

In 1871 the promise of a transcontinental railroad within twelve years persuaded British Columbia to enter Confederation. Finally, in 1873, Prince Edward Island was gathered into the fold when a local railway-building venture turned into a financial disaster and the Charlottetown government asked to be bailed out. Within six years of Confederation Canada achieved its present borders (except for Newfoundland).

A most improbable outcome had been reached. In just a century, out of the odds and ends (mostly French-speaking) left behind by the wreck of Britain's first empire in North America, there had emerged a united "British" country of some three and a half million people controlling half the continent. It happened just in time, for Britain's rapidly waning commitment to its North American territories meant that by the 1860s, when American pressures peaked, nobody really knew if the British military guarantee was valid.

Even the British government itself could not know from year to year what it would do if confronted with a stark choice between war with the

United States and the surrender of its North American possessions. As the British commander-in-chief in North America, Sir John Michael, observed: "The worst that could happen to Canada would be annexation to a free and prosperous country. To Britain, pecuniary ruin and loss of prestige." If the United States had attacked, Britain would probably have fought in the end, even if defeat was inevitable, simply because that is how states generally behave. But the final decision would have depended on what other military problems London had on its hands at the time, and by the 1860s London was getting concerned about the growing military power of its European neighbours.

For the first time in over half a century, Britain felt vulnerable militarily right at the heart of the empire – and its reaction was to call the legions home. Edward Cardwell, the Secretary of State for War in Gladstone's new government, decided in 1868 that the British army had to be converted into a force suitable for field service in a European war and that it would therefore have to keep at least half its strength in Britain. The final withdrawal of the British garrison in Canada, after 110 years in the country, took place with indecent haste. The Canadian government was informed that the British troops were leaving in February 1870, and by late 1871 all were gone except for a garrison at the imperial naval base at Halifax. The defence of the new Dominion of Canada, at last until British reinforcements could cross the Atlantic, now lay entirely in the hands of its ramshackle militia.

Britain's overwhelming reluctance to do anything that might lead to war with the Americans was evident at the Joint High Commission which met in Washington in the same year to settle all outstanding Anglo-American disputes arising from the Civil War. Prime Minister Sir John Macdonald, who was allowed to attend as one of the British commissioners, remarked that "the U.S. Commissioners . . . found our English friends so squeezable in nature that their audacity has grown beyond all bounds." But in fact no irreparable harm was done to Canadian interests by the Treaty of Washington, and it did involve *de facto* American recognition of the existence of the new Canadian state (which had not previously been forthcoming). If the British were no longer prepared to sacrifice vast amounts of blood and treasure for their North American subjects, they were at least still willing to grunt and growl on their behalf.

As it turned out, that was all that was needed. The U.S. government did not officially close the "frontier" (of settlement) until 1890, but the new generation of Americans was already more likely to seek work in the growing industrial cities than to demand more land for homesteading. The old drive for territorial expansion was ceasing to be a major theme in American life, and the new imperialism that soon replaced it posed little threat to Canada: what Washington now wanted was overseas colonies just like the European empires had.

So the fortifications along the U.S.-Canadian frontier gradually fell into disrepair – and since no other country has ever shown any desire to invade Canada, let alone the ability to do so, that should have been the end of Canada's military history. It did not turn out that way, of course, but one can hardly blame the Americans for that.

As for San Juan Island – well, Canada lost it in the end. Britain and the United States agreed to submit the dispute to arbitration by the German Kaiser, and in 1872 he gave his decision: the island was American. On 21 November of that year the British flag was lowered on San Juan for the last time, the British troops embarked on HMS *Petrel*, and the Pig War finally came to an end. History does not record what finally became of Mr Cutlar, but the pig was definitely dead.

### CHAPTER SEVEN

# *Drifting Toward Commitment*

It is customary at this point, in books about Canada, to pause for a rousing cheer at the happy outcome: Confederation was a success and a new nation was born. Perhaps that is the appropriate response, but the reasons for it are not self-evident. The mere existence of yet another separate and sovereign state, in a world that does not suffer a scarcity of that commodity, is not a sufficient cause for anybody to rejoice (except, perhaps, federal government employees). Canada exists, but so what?

Obviously, Canadians are generally pleased that Canada exists, but then they would be, wouldn't they? They grew up here, and this is what they know. But if events had come out differently in the 1860s, and all the territories that now form Canada had been absorbed into the United States, the present-day inhabitants of the ten northernmost states would be equally fervent in the conviction that *that* had been the desirable outcome.

Ironically, French Canada has a more logical reason to rejoice in the existence of the Canadian state than anyone else. Even French Canadians who now incline toward separatism generally recognize that their language and cultural identity would be only a picturesque relic by now if Quebec had been absorbed by the United States one or two centuries ago. By contrast, as the biggest fish in what was left of Britain's North American possessions after the American Revolution, French Canadians could demand respect for their own laws, customs, and language. Although two centuries and a wave of English-speaking immigrants have now turned them into a minority even within the smaller pond of Canada, their political and cultural autonomy is still far greater than it would have been if they had joined the United States. Almost every generation of French Canadian intellectuals since 1867 has re-examined the question of whether being the minority nationality in a hybrid binational state, with all the restrictions and frustrations that involves, is really indispensable to its own community's interests. But so far, at least, every generation has reluctantly concluded (sometimes after much turmoil) that Confederation is the least bad option.

To justify Canada's existence in terms of French Canadian cultural survival, however, is to engage in a circular argument, based on the assumption that French Canadian culture is an irreplaceable treasure. This is not a self-evident truth to the millions of English-speaking U.S. citizens who are descended from French Canadian immigrants to New England. As for English Canadian culture, it would be hard to persuade the average French Canadian (or even the average Englishman) that it is an irreplaceable treasure. The English Canadian culture is only one of about twenty prominent sub-divisions of the global English-speaking milieu, and although English Canadians have contributed their fair share to the arts and sciences of mankind, it is not clear that the sum of that achievement would have been significantly less if there were not a separate Canadian state.

The world would not be a radically different place if northern North America were inhabited by an extra 25 million Americans, and only a nationalist would regard the perpetuation of the Canadian state as an end in itself. Nevertheless, Canada exists, and is likely to go on existing for at least some generations to come—unless, of course, its population is exterminated by war. And that is the context in which Canadian statehood is a potentially useful accident. Canada is a paid-up member of the international system which will almost inevitably produce a nuclear war in the long run (regardless of the present, moderately encouraging moves towards nuclear de-escalation by the superpowers) unless the system itself is changed quite drastically. But Canada is a rather untypical member, with the capacity to do untypical things. For this reason it is our belief, or at least our hope, that Canada could be of considerable use to a world which must eventually move beyond the traditional assumptions of sovereign national states in matters of "defence" if it is to survive.

That is the hope. The reality, it must be admitted, is that most Canadian decisions on war and peace since Confederation have mired the country ever deeper in the conventional wisdom about how a sovereign state must behave. As a result, Canada has played a loyal supporting role to the reigning great powers within its own cultural and economic orbit, the "Anglo-Saxon" world – first Britain, now the United States – in almost every major war and military confrontation of the twentieth century. Today, it formally stands ready to fight a nuclear war by their side.

The present Canadian orthodoxy on questions of defence depends heavily on shaky analogies with our military policy in the First and Second World Wars. National identity is necessarily founded on shared myths about the past, so Canada's policies, like any other country's, are shaped to a considerable extent by systematic delusions about the meaning of our own history. But the tradition we have acquired in defence policy was neither inevitable nor indisputably wise. It grew out of a series of decisions that were made in the first half-century of Confederation –and more often than not the leaders who made those decisions did so against their better judgement, under great pressure, and with enormous foreboding about the future consequences of the precedents they were setting.

❖

Here we must pause for a minor digression, for much of what follows, in this and succeeding chapters, will grate heavily on the sensibilities of many English Canadians. We argue in essence that London was able to inveigle Canada into a series of imperial wars that were none of Canada's concern, but in which millions of Canadians endured great hardship and a hundred thousand were killed, by playing on the gullibility of English Canadians who were blinded by their sentimental attachment to Britain.

Since French Canadians obviously had no emotional loyalty to Britain they were also spared the gullibility, and in the course of the narrative that follows they will often appear irritatingly wise and mature in their judgements (especially compared to the poor silly English Canadians). This is indeed their own view of the past, by and large, but there is no empirical evidence to support the hypothesis that speaking French makes you more intelligent. So, as an antidote to what is to come, let us indulge in a little story of French Canadian folly.

> *Nous touchons enfin aux murs, où nous sommes reçus par une salve effrayante; les coups de fusils étaient si nombreux que le bruit ressemblaient au roulement de tonnerre. Pendant quelques instants, nous avançons et nous retraitons tour à tour; la victoire paraissait indécise. Mais faisant un effort suprême, nous nous élançons en avant, baïonnette au canon, massacrant et culbutant tous ceux qui opposaient quelque résistance, et, du même élan, nous pénétrons dans la ville au milieu des applaudissements d'une foule innombrable des citoyens. Les Garibaldiens, échelonnés sur les murs de la ville, n'eurent pas le temps de se rallier; ils furent tous forcés de déposer les armes et de se livrer aux mains du vainqueur. A neuf heures, la guerre était finie, et le drapeau pontifical flottait de nouveau sur la ville d'Albano.*
>
> (Sergeant) C. E. Rouleau, *Soldat de Pie* IX

[We finally reached the walls, where we were received by a terrifying volley; there were so many shots that it sounded like a roll of thunder. For a few seconds we hesitated, milling back and forth; victory seemed doubtful. But making a supreme effort, we launched ourselves forward with fixed bayonets, slaughtering and hurling aside everyone who showed any resistance, and with the same dash we forced our way into the city amid the applause of a huge crowd of citizens. The Garibaldians, lined up on the walls of the city, didn't have time to rally; they were all forced to lay down their arms and deliver themselves into the hands of the victors. At nine o'clock the war was over, and the papal flag floated once more over the city of Albano.]

It was (perhaps needless to say) only a mock battle, pitting the French Canadian unit of the Pontifical Zouaves against an equally underemployed unit of some other nationality during the long, tense twilight of the Papal States between the Battle of Mentana in 1867 and the surrender of Rome in 1870. It was the closest that most of the French Canadians ever came to real combat. Of over five hundred men who left Canada to defend Pius IX's domains against the patriot Garibaldi and the other secular forces that were struggling to unite Italy, only two were wounded, eight died of fever, and one was drowned. But they were willing, even eager, to fight and die for the Pope – and so (at least in spirit) were those who sent them.

> *Dieu le veut, enfants du Canada, partez pour Rome.*
>> Monseigneur Ignace Bourget, Bishop of Montreal,
>>> November 1867

[God wills it, sons of Canada. Leave for Rome.]

Confederation was not yet four months old when the first military force of Canadian volunteers was recruited to fight overseas, and they were not English Canadians longing to lay down their lives for Britain. Just as loyalty to Britain provided a social cement and a sense of participation in a larger world for English Canadians, so did devotion to the Catholic Church serve most French Canadians as their primary focus for solidarity. The old radical republicanism of the 1837 rebellion had been pretty thoroughly extirpated by the Church over the succeeding generation, and of course France was still not viewed with much affection, having first abandoned Quebec to the British and then blotted its copybook irremediably during the Revolution by attacking the Church. So when Mgr. Bourget launched his call for volunteers to go to Italy and defend the beleaguered Pope, every bishop and parish priest in Quebec echoed his summons, and young French Canadians flocked to volunteer: five applicants were rejected for every recruit accepted in the first contingent, which sailed for Europe in February 1868.

It was all quite unofficial, of course, at least in the sense that the government of Canada was not involved. But the mobilization of French Canadian society to recruit, outfit, and pay for the expeditionary force (Mgr. Bourget sent out a pastoral letter asking for a contribution of thirty cents from every parishioner) depended on exactly the same kind of naïve enthusiasm that French Canadians would later deplore when English Canadians were preparing to offer sacrifices to *their* ancestral gods. The elite of French Canada associated themselves with the enterprise in whatever ways they could: the flag of the volunteers (featuring a beaver and *two* maple leaves) was designed by Napoléon Bourassa, son-in-law of Louis-Joseph Papineau of the patriote revolt of 1837 and father of Henri Bourassa, the leading French Canadian nationalist politician of the next generation. And the men who volunteered for two years' service in the Pontifical Zouaves (mostly well educated young men of "good family") were just as naïvely idealistic and enthusiastic as their English Canadian compatriots would be a few decades later.

When Bourget visited them in Rome in March 1869, they reportedly told him: "*Nous n'avons plus qu'une chose à désirer: c'est de verser notre sang pour le Pape. Nous espérons bien que . . . nous nous battrons avant que notre engagement soit fini, et que nous laisserons dans le cimetière de Saint-Laurent avant de partir, quelques-uns des nôtres, et que nous nous en retournerons dans notre cher Canada avec de glorieuses blessures.*" [We want only one more thing: to shed our blood for the Pope. We hope that . . . we will get to fight before our engagement is up, that we will leave a few of our own in the cemetery of Saint Lawrence before we leave, and that we will come back to our dear Canada with glorious wounds.] No doubt the volunteers raised the tone of their discourse when speaking to a bishop, and no doubt he rarefied it still further in his letter home, but nonetheless it rings essentially true. Young English Canadians of later generations would voice quite similar sentiments when they went off to war in response to the summons of their elders and betters – at least until they saw people actually getting killed in battle.

Alas for the first French Canadian expeditionary force, it never got to see a real battle. The volunteers marched around the Papal States looking like harem guards in their zouave uniforms (a style borrowed from the French army, which had acquired it from the Algerians), but they never got to do anything more exciting than chase bandits in the hills and stage an occasional mock battle. Right at the end, as the Italian armies closed in on the Holy City in September 1870, they made ready to die gloriously in their positions near the Porta Pia, but the Pope surrendered after only a token resistance to avoid useless bloodshed.

After eight days as prisoners of war, the Canadian volunteers were loaded onto a ship for England, then another to New York, and finally a train to Montreal. There they were greeted by a cheering crowd fifty thousand strong, and had a "Te Deum" sung for them in Notre Dame cathedral. With the passage of time, however, the whole "crusade" came to seem less heroic than embarrassing, or even comical, and it was decently interred among the footnotes of Canadian history: myth-making was not necessary, since hardly anybody had died. But a lot of young French Canadians *might* have been killed in Europe fighting for the Pope: there was a very serious battle the year before they arrived in Rome. And the French Canadian contingent in Italy, which was paid for solely by voluntary donations, was about a third as large, in proportion to its own population, as the force that all of Canada would manage to dispatch to the Boer War in the next generation, even with the federal government paying for it.

Since the Papacy finally gave up fighting wars after 1870, there was no further occasion for French Canada to translate its sentimental attachment to the Church into specific acts of military self-sacrifice. But it was mainly the temptation that was lacking – that, and the political clout needed to commit the entire country to a military adventure overseas. In terms of the innate ability to act foolishly, French Canadians have no cause to sneer at English Canadian reflexes in these matters. Just thought we'd mention it, given that French Canadians did have such great cause for resentment in succeeding decades as English Canadians repeatedly dragged them into British wars overseas.

❖

England will have in us a friendly nation – a subordinate but still a powerful people – to stand by her in North America in peace or war. (cheers)

The people of Australia will be such another subordinate nation. And England will have this advantage . . . that, though at war with all the rest of the world, she will be able to look to the subordinate nations in alliance with her . . . who will assist in enabling her again to meet the whole world in arms, as she has done before. (cheers)

Sir John A. Macdonald, Confederation debate, 1866

All the talk we have heard about Canada's fighting the battles of England is very silly and quite likely to be hurtful.

*Manitoba Free Press*, 1884

> We have enlisted for the European war six percent of our popu-
> lation. That is the equivalent of an army of 2,400,000 for France
> and 2,700,000 for the United Kingdom. . . . *How many French
> soldiers, or even British soldiers, would they send to America, if Canada
> was attacked by the United States?*
>
> Henri Bourassa, *Le Devoir*, 1916

Within a couple of decades of Confederation, as Britain's military preoc-
cupations on the European continent grew to overshadow everything else,
the idea of sending a huge army across the Atlantic to fight the United
States in defence of Canada became literally inconceivable to London. Yet
the ghost of that idea eventually seduced Canada into doing something
equally inexplicable.

By the mid-1880s the British Empire was well past its zenith in terms
of relative power, even though it would go on adding new territories in
Africa and Asia for another half-century. Britain was beginning to feel
vulnerable as it anxiously reckoned up the military and industrial power
of its continental rivals, France and Germany, so in 1885 influential private citizens founded the Imperial Federation League. Behind all the cant
about the virtues of the Anglo-Saxon race and the need to bind its scattered branches more closely together, the League was clearly aimed at
rounding up military support from the empire, and French Canadians,
in particular, were alarmed. Quebec Prime Minister Honoré Mercier
warned his countrymen that it presaged a future in which their sons would
be sent to die for the British Empire "from the icefields of the North Pole
to the burning sands of the Sudan."

The dramatic shift in Canada's population balance had virtually halted
by the 1880s, but by then the francophone share of the population had
already dropped to about 30 per cent. Almost all the rest were "British,"
and French Canadians were acutely sensitive to the fact that they were
now at the mercy of the new majority's loyalties. As *La Presse* stated in
1899, when the implications of this were becoming all too clear: "Canada
is for us the whole world: but the English Canadians have two countries,
one here and one across the sea."

However, to most Canadians in the 1880s the prospect of involvement in foreign wars still seemed only a very small cloud on the horizon.
Britain did put out tentative feelers in 1884 about imperial contributions

to a military expedition up the Nile to rescue an Anglo-Egyptian force commanded by Major-General Charles "Chinese" Gordon, who had advanced to Khartoum to extract a threatened garrison but lingered too long and got himself besieged there. Offers poured in to Ottawa from volunteers, but Prime Minister Macdonald's response was frosty. "The spasmodic offers of our Militia Colonels anxious for excitement or noto-riety have roused unreasonable expectations in England," he observed, and instructed the Canadian High Commissioner in London that all sug-gestions for Canadian military help in the Sudan should be firmly rebuffed: "Our men and money would be sacrificed to get [British Prime Minister] Gladstone & Co. out of the hole they have plunged themselves into by their own imbecility."

Ottawa did allow General Garnet Wolseley, the British officer who had commanded the Red River expedition fifteen years before and was now in charge of the Sudan operation, to recruit a contingent of 368 Canadian voyageurs to help his force make its way up the cataracts of the Nile, but they were hired entirely at the British government's initiative and expense. Most of them did very good work for the British (although General Gordon's force was overwhelmed and massacred before the res-cue expedition could reach Khartoum). But like the devout French Cana-dian Catholics who had gone to Italy in 1868 and joined the Pontifical Zouaves, or the English and French Canadians who would fight for the Spanish Republic in the Mackenzie-Papineau Brigade in the late 1930s, or the small but steady flow of Canadians who used to enlist in the British imperial forces (and now tend to enlist in the U.S. armed forces instead), the voyageurs who went to the Nile were not in any sense an official Canadian commitment. Canada is, if you will excuse the expression, a free country, and what individual Canadians do abroad for faith, money, or love of adventure is their own affair; it creates no obligations for the country as a whole.

In the 1880s that distinction was still quite clear not only to pragmatic French Canadians, but even to English Canadians who were emotionally attached to Britain. The old bargain still applied: Canada acknowledged its membership in the British Empire, but Britain was obliged to provide for Canada's defence as a *quid pro quo*. In any case, until quite late in the nineteenth century most Canadians continued to subscribe to the opti-mistic Victorian belief that great wars were a thing of the past. Canada's only real military task seemed to be the "pacification" of the native population of the prairie provinces – and that did not pose too much of a problem: the suppression of the North-West Rebellion of 1885 was accomplished entirely by Canadian militia.

❖

> We heard reports of guns, but thought they were firing in the air to frighten us, but they had shot Quinn, Dill and Gilchrist, whom I did not see fall. Mr and Mrs Delaney were a short distance ahead of my husband, I having my husband's arm. Mr Williscraft, an old grey-headed man about seventy-five years of age came running by us, and an Indian shot at him and knocked his hat off, and he turned around and said "Oh! don't shoot! don't shoot!" But they fired again, and he ran screaming and fell in some bushes.
>
> On seeing this I began crying, and my husband tried to comfort me, saying "My *dear* wife be brave to the end," and immediately an Indian behind us fired, and my husband fell beside me, his arm pulling from mine. I tried to assist him from falling. He put out his arms for me and fell, and I fell down beside him and buried my face on his.
>
> Theresa Gowanlock, Frog Lake, 2 April 1885

John and Theresa Gowanlock, married six months before at Tintern, Ontario, had come west to Frog Lake in Saskatchewan to build a sawmill. They understood little about the background to the massacre in which he was murdered and she became temporarily a captive of the Cree Indians, but it was basically the old story of Indians pushed to the wall by the advance of white settlement (the buffalo were gone, and both the Indians and the Métis were starving by the winter of 1884-85). However, it was complicated by the separate politics of the mixed-race, French-speaking Métis, many of whom had fled farther west after the collapse of Louis Riel's provisional government on the Red River in 1870. And for French Canadians, the Métis were becoming a symbol of the dying dream of a francophone West, whose future was rapidly being foreclosed by the endless waves of English-speaking immigrants.

If I had been on the banks of the Saskatchewan, I would myself have shouldered a musket to fight against the neglect of governments and the shameless greed of speculators.

Wilfrid Laurier, Montreal, 22 November 1885,
(Prime Minister of Canada, 1896-1911)

The return of Louis Riel from his American exile in 1884, half-mad and already half-dedicated to martyrdom, provided the leadership that had been lacking. In March 1885 Riel set up another provisional government at Batoche in the North Saskatchewan valley and invited the Indians to join his people in forcing the Canadian government to redress their grievances. But incidents like the Frog Lake massacre extinguished any slim possibility that Ottawa might have been willing to negotiate, and Sir John A. Macdonald's government sent troops instead.

For the very first time, it was an entirely Canadian military operation. The commanding general of the militia, Sir Fred Middleton, was, as always during the nineteenth century, a British general, but all the soldiers under his command were Canadian. It proved to be a reasonably competent operation organizationally: almost eight thousand militia troops were mobilized from all over the country and quickly sent to the North Saskatchewan to quell the revolt. The actual fighting, mercifully, was not exactly professional on either side, so few people were killed.

And then Gabriel [Dumont, the Métis military leader] shouts to his people: "Courage! Follow me!" And he runs towards the fleeing enemy. At that moment he falls down on the snow. A bullet had grazed the top of his skull and ricocheted, producing a whistling sound. Blood was spurting out. "Ah! They are killing you," cried Delorme. But Gabriel answers him: "When you don't lose consciousness, you don't die." And at the same time he shouted to Baptiste Vandal: "Cousin, come and take my rifle!"

Vandal drops his rifle and takes Gabriel's fourteen-shot rifle. "Come, take my bullets too," adds Gabriel. Vandal was undoing the cartridge belt for the revolver. "No! not that one," says Gabriel, "undo the other buckle."

"I was trying to get to my knees," says Gabriel, "but it was the belt holding the revolver bullets that held up my pants, and as Baptiste hadn't buckled it, my pants fell down."

> The Battle of Duck Lake, 25 March 1885,
> *Métis Memoirs*, Batoche

The breeds dashed up with a wild war-whoop when Major Short, springing to the front, cried "Who'll follow me?" and rushed at the advancing enemy. . . . The men sprang to their feet, fired a volley into the breeds, who turned tail within twenty yards of the guns and sought cover. Here was an opportunity not to be missed. . . .

A few seconds sufficed to get the Gatling at work. Its "growl" as the bullets streamed out reminded one more of the explosion of a huge bunch of firecrackers than anything else. The bushes were fairly mowed down, and how any flesh and blood could have lived through that leaden hail is a mystery.

> The Battle of Cutknife Hill, 2 May 1885
> Toronto *Mail* (19 May 1885)

But it was only bushes that were being mown down: the terrifying Gatling gun (an early hand-cranked machine-gun) claimed only one victim, a stray child, during the whole campaign. The inexperienced militia at Cutknife Hill, commanded by Colonel William Otter, were forced to withdraw after an inconclusive day of fighting, and were spared serious losses only because their Indian opponents were equally unable or unwilling to push the fighting to a conclusion. The only decisive battle was at Batoche on 10-12 May 1885, and even counting that, the total casualties of the entire campaign were fifty-three white and about thirty-five Métis and Indian dead. Insofar as Canadians worried about military matters at all, the North-West Rebellion of 1885 seemed to prove that they were doing everything just about right.

❖

The fact was that the Active Militia, all 45,000 "authorized strength" of them, were of great importance as a Canadian social and political institution, but only marginally significant as a military force. More than half the force existed on paper only: between 1876 and 1896, the average number of men who actually drilled each year was only 18,871. And there were almost as many chiefs as Indians: for every nine private soldiers, according to the 1894 figures, there were four officers, NCOs, buglers, and bandsmen.

Becoming a militia officer was the surest route to social acceptability: men otherwise unacceptable because of their origins or history could be received by the Governor General (the summit of social achievement in Canada) provided they were in uniform. And it was a status one could purchase, within limits: officers had to pay an entry fee to join a militia regiment, hand over their pay to the regimental fund, and buy elaborate and expensive ceremonial uniforms out of their own pockets. "An officer is useful to his regiment because he has the means to spend and the will to spend it; the regiment is useful to him because the paths toward social distinction are smoothed for the militia officer." It all had so little to do with military proficiency that the British officer commanding the Canadian militia in 1891, in a report to the Secretary of State for War in London, made no objection to recently deceased Prime Minister Macdonald's persistent refusal to spend much money on the militia:

> He looked upon money voted for militia purposes, only as a means of gaining political ends, but he was honest enough to keep that use of it within strict limits, and consequently cut down the militia estimates to the lowest possible figure. He knew that at any time he could obtain an increased vote but he also knew that any money so voted would not yield any corresponding efficiency, but merely add to the party claims which would have to be satisfied from that source.
>
> General Ivor Herbert to the Duke of Cambridge

Even the few professional military institutions in Canada were rather beside the point. The Royal Military College that had been created at Kingston, Ontario, in 1876 was supplying a large number of its graduates to the British regular army, and not many of the remainder were active in the Canadian militia. In 1887, the Canadian army's Permanent Force was formally expanded to a thousand men, but it was scarcely capable of fulfilling its designated role of being a model and a school for the militia:

out of an effective strength of 886 men in 1890, 345 were discharged, eight died, and 152 deserted during the year – and 128 men were convicted by court martial of military offences. Over half the Permanent Force had been in for less than two years.

The reason none of this mattered was that Canada, for about a quarter century after 1870, faced almost no military task more demanding than the suppression of a few hundred ill-armed Métis and Indian rebels. The real reason for the continued existence of the militia, apart from the fact that it was an excellent method of dispensing political patronage, was its usefulness as a means of providing "aid to the civil power." The militia were called out by various local municipalities eighty-five times between 1867 and 1900 to settle (among other things):

> a lumbermen's brawl in Pembroke; an affray during a hanging in St. Andrew's, New Brunswick; a reign of terror by railway navvies in the area of Tamworth, Ontario; an attempt to cut wood on Crown property surrounding the disused forts of Lévis, Quebec; the escape of a convict in Quebec City; the kidnap of a girl in Roberval, Quebec, by members of a visiting circus.
>
> Major J. J. B. Pariseau, *Disorders, Strikes and Disasters: Military Aid to the Civil Power in Canada, 1867-1933*

The militia served as an emergency police force in most of the country, which seemed to be all that was required. The United States had apparently lost interest in taking over Canada, at least for the moment. And if it changed its mind, or if any other military dangers arose – well, that was why Canada belonged to the British Empire. In the main, however, the imperial link came to be seen as a source of commercial advantage, a diplomatic guarantee against American encroachment, and (for English Canadians) as a source of "racial" pride. Canadian governments, assuming that war with the United States was unlikely and any other military threat inconceivable, therefore felt justified in allowing the militia to degenerate into little more than a fancy-dress party, and in rejecting occasional British blandishments to take part in the incessant colonial wars of the empire.

At this time the British were not even trying very hard to suck Canada into a military role in the empire, but the British officer commanding the

Canadian militia in 1895, Major-General Ivor Herbert, found out the hard way that Canadian governments were very sensitive on this subject. All General Herbert did was to propose that the Royal Canadian Regiment (the infantry part of the Permanent Force) go off on a temporary exchange with a British regular regiment in Hong Kong. There was no war on, and Herbert was only thinking of improving the Canadian regiment's military proficiency. Moreover, he had the support of the Canadian Minister of Militia, J. C. Patterson. Unfortunately, Patterson had neglected to clear the matter with his cabinet colleagues (Herbert once called him "the laziest man I ever knew"), and the rest of the cabinet saw it as a British plot to inveigle Canada into taking over part of the job of policing the empire. So the proposed exchange was vetoed, the Minister of Militia was punished by being made Lieutenant-Governor of Manitoba, and Herbert lost his job. Canada still refused any broader military responsibilities in the empire – but after 1895 attitudes started changing fast.

❖

Part of the forenoon might be occupied with a familiar talk by the teacher on the British Empire, its extent and resources; the relation of Canada to the Empire; the unity of the Empire and its advantages; the privileges which, as British subjects, we enjoy. . . . The afternoon . . . might be occupied with patriotic recitals, songs and readings by the pupils.

> Instructions for the celebration of Empire Day,
> Ontario Ministry of Education, 1898

In 1887 a rising young British politician called Joseph Chamberlain told an eager Toronto audience to be proud of "the greatness and importance of the destiny which is reserved for the Anglo-Saxon race . . . which is infallibly destined to be the predominating force in the future history and civilization of the world." Ten years later Joseph Chamberlain was Secretary of State for the Colonies – and it was exactly the job he had asked for, because the mission he had given himself was to unite the empire militarily. So he exploited the presence of the colonial prime ministers in London in 1897 for Queen Victoria's Diamond Jubilee celebrations to urge the idea of a permanent Imperial Council on them.

National defence could not be separated from imperial defence, Chamberlain told the newly knighted Canadian prime minister, Sir Wilfrid Laurier, and all the self-governing colonies ought to accept a share of the imperial defence burden. Canada, he pointed out, might find itself at odds with Russia, Japan, or the United States, and would need the help of the whole empire to preserve its security. In fairness and in self-interest, it ought to be prepared to offer help elsewhere in the empire, too.

Sir Wilfrid Laurier's knighthood was the crowning achievement in the stately political progress of a self-made man. He began building his political career in the late 1860s as a young lawyer in the small town of Arthabaska in Quebec's Eastern Townships, where he was initially viewed with some suspicion because of his republican and anti-clerical political sympathies, but by the time he became Canada's first French Canadian prime minister in 1896 he had turned into the very model of a Liberal English gentleman, patrician in appearance and infinitely courteous in manner. Behind that facade, however, was a highly skilled politician who knew that the idea of Canadian participation in imperial defence beyond Canada's borders would cause great alarm and offence among French Canadians.

Laurier fended off Chamberlain's proposal for what amounted to a military alliance of Britain and its Dominions with practised ease, but he returned to a Canada where a new mass-circulation yellow press led by the *Montreal Star* and the Toronto *Mail* (the *Toronto Sun* is the closest equivalent in style today) had discovered that strident imperial jingoism was an excellent way to sell newspapers. In English Canada, with its half-formed identity, early local stirrings of nationalism were easily transmuted (with semi-official encouragement) into "imperial patriotism."

In 1895 the Imperial Federation League opened a Canadian branch, and in 1898 the Ontario, Nova Scotia, and Quebec Protestant school boards proclaimed the 24th of May "Empire Day," to be marked by pseudo-religious ceremonies glorifying British rule over a quarter of the planet. It was a comforting way to smother the feeling of inferiority that came from being a mere outpost of a world empire. As Stephen Leacock put it: "I . . . am an Imperialist because I will not be a Colonial." However, the imperialists didn't notice that their loyalty was largely a one-way street: English Canadians might see themselves as British, but the British certainly did not share that delusion.

The doctrine of Anglo-Saxon racial superiority was very attractive to English Canadians, and the more bumptious ones even saw Canada as "the future centre and the dominating portion of the British Empire." As Rudyard Kipling observed, they had "a certain crude faith in the Empire, of which they naturally conceive themselves to be the belly-button" – and the belief that Canada would eventually rule the empire let them reconcile their imperial loyalty with their nascent Canadian nationalism. The notion was preposterous, given Canada's small population at the time, but imperial enthusiasts were offering confident predictions of one hundred million Canadians by the end of the twentieth century.

It was Stephen Leacock, with his quintessentially English Canadian talent for cloaking real ambition in humour (so that you can retreat without loss of face if you've gone too far), who got the Canadian imperialist mentality exactly right. England, he said, was like an aged and feeble farmer whose sons had reached maturity: "The old man's got old and he don't know it, can't kick him off the place, but I reckon that the next time we come together to talk things over, the boys have got to step right in and manage the farm."

All this loud talk and adolescent ambition would have been harmless buffoonery, except that the empire was already in decline. Nor was it just naïve Canadian enthusiasm: the original stimulus for this outburst of imperial sentiment came from London and from members of the English Canadian elite whose interests were closely linked with Britain, and its ultimate purpose was to prepare Canadians to participate militarily in the empire's long last stand. By the late 1890s Britain was utterly isolated in Europe, facing a collection of potential enemies whose industrial and military growth had already far surpassed its own. The whole idea of imperial federation was directed toward exploiting the "British" loyalties of the overseas colonies in order to commit their resources to Britain's defence. But Canada, the biggest and richest of those colonies, posed a particular problem, for the French-speaking third of its population had no emotional attachment to Britain.

Prime Minister Laurier, like most French Canadians, was perfectly prepared to support Britain politically in any confrontation with its enemies, and even to take any local military measures that might seem appropriate. When Britain came close to war with France in 1898, for example, Laurier had no objection to the proposed use of Canadian militia to seize the tiny French islands of St-Pierre-et-Miquelon in the Gulf of St. Law-rence. But he was well aware that his own people would never agree to send troops to fight in Britain's wars overseas, whereas English Canada's sense of commitment to the empire was growing stronger by the year. Any proposal to send Canadian troops abroad could therefore provoke a profoundly dangerous clash between the two cultural solitudes, and Lau-rier's entire fifteen years as prime minister would be characterized by the adroit evasions and compromises through which he sought to head off that clash.

Laurier's problems would have been a lot more manageable but for the apparent resurgence of the old American threat in the mid-1890s, which seemed to make the military link to Britain once more indispen-sable to Canadian independence. In 1895 a dispute between Britain and Venezuela over the boundary between that country and British Guiana erupted into a crisis when Venezuela appealed for American support. Washington responded with a brazenly offensive ten-thousand-word dip-lomatic note to London that effectively told the British that their presence in the Western Hemisphere, even in their existing colonies, depended on American sufferance.

> Today, the United States is practically sovereign in this conti-nent. . . .
>
> Why? . . . It is because . . . its infinite resources combined with its isolated position render it master of the situation and practically invulnerable against any or all other powers. . . . Dis-tance and 3,000 miles of intervening ocean make any permanent political union between a European and an American state unnat-ural and inexpedient.
>
> Robert Olney, U.S. Secretary of State, note to the British<br>Foreign Office, 1895

It was an enormous extension of the original Monroe Doctrine, which merely declared U.S. opposition to the European reconquest of inde-pendent ex-colonies in the Americas. A war scare swept both Britain and the United States, and General Nelson Miles, Commander-in-Chief of the U.S. Army, declared that in the event of war "Canada would fall into our hands as a matter of course." Canadians were shocked by this sudden reappearance of the old peril, and the government hastily sent an officer to England to order 40,000 rifles, twenty-four modern field-guns, and some machine-guns.

The Venezuela crisis ended peacefully, but the "American threat" did not subside. The Spanish-American War of 1898, in which the United States drove Spain out of its remaining American colonies, seemed to confirm Washington's willingness to act on its new doctrine, which could equally well be applied to Canada's "unnatural and inexpedient" union with Britain. This naturally worried Ottawa, and when the Klondike gold rush drew thousands of American prospectors into the Yukon in the summer of 1898 two hundred men of the Canadian army were formed into the Yukon Field Force and rushed north to back up the North-West Mounted Police in asserting Canadian sovereignty.

The influx of Americans into the Yukon also brought to a head the smouldering dispute over the border between Alaska and Canada, which dated back to Russian times in Alaska. Washington, like St. Petersburg before it, claimed that it had jurisdiction over the entire coastline of the Alaskan Panhandle, while Ottawa (and Britain) maintained that some of the fjords penetrated so deeply into the mainland that the land at their heads, including that at the top of the Lynn Canal, the main access point for the Yukon, was part of British Columbia. Ottawa's anxiety about American intentions deepened when talks with Washington over the disputed Canada-Alaska boundary broke down in early 1899.

Britain was also concerned, but after the 1895 crisis the War Office had reviewed its plans for a war with the United States. The British had learned (from Redfield Proctor, the former U.S. Secretary of State for War) that American planning during that crisis had envisaged a three-pronged attack on Canada. One column would have cut the Canadian Pacific Railway in Maine (thus effectively isolating the Maritimes from central Canada), one would have moved on Medicine Hat in the West, and the third would have launched the main attack on Quebec and Ontario via the Great Lakes after seizing the shipping canals at the outbreak of war. So Britain's Joint Naval and Military Committee took a fresh look at the problem of defending British North America – and was appalled by what it saw.

Major-General E. P. Leach, who was sent out by the War Office in 1896 to review Canada's defence plans, secretly warned London that the British army should avoid any involvement in the defence of Canada

unless and until all the costly measures he had recommended for expanding the Canadian militia and building new fortifications had been carried
out. Given the amount of money Canadian governments had available to
spend on defence, that was extremely unlikely, but even the best trained
and equipped Canadian militia imaginable would not change the fundamental nature of the defence problem. Viscount Wolseley, the British
commander-in-chief, put his finger on it at the very beginning of the
review: "The defence of Canada . . . turns very much upon what the
[British] navy can and will do upon the Lakes. Whichever side holds these
inland seas will hold Canada."

It soon became clear that if the war began in the wintertime, the
Americans would have time to build up their naval strength on the lakes
and seize the main shipping canals that connected them even before the
Royal Navy could get up the St. Lawrence when the ice broke up in the
spring, thus effectively foreclosing the issue. But even if war came in the
summertime and if the navy was willing to risk a significant fleet of warships on Lake Ontario and Lake Erie, any early British military successes
would inevitably be swamped sooner or later by the sheer weight of
American numbers. As Sir John Ardagh, Director of Military Intelligence
and author of the British army's report, concluded: "a land war on the
North American continent would be perhaps the most unprofitable and
most hazardous military enterprise we could possibly be driven to engage
in."

Knowing that soldiers are sometimes ordered to carry out even the
most hopeless military tasks, however, Ardagh carried his investigation
through to the bitter end. Since the most that Britain could possibly hope
for in the defence of central Canada (given brilliant generalship and a
great deal of luck) was a costly and precarious military stalemate, London
would have to look elsewhere for a way of exerting decisive pressure on
Washington to make peace. The only conceivable solution would be to
make a "vigorous offensive gesture" by exploiting British naval superiority
in the Atlantic: i.e., to land a British force on the American east coast and
threaten New York or Boston. Accordingly, an officer from British military intelligence was sent off to make a secret reconnaissance of the coasts
of Maine and Massachusetts and to identify suitable places for such a
landing.

On the surface it all seemed quite proper and serious, a token of Britain's continuing commitment to defend Canada regardless of cost. In reality it was merely a demonstration of how the military staff planning reflex will continue to operate even in the face of political and strategic realities that make the plans quite irrelevant. For the fact was that no British government was going to face war with the United States to defend any Canadian interest, however vital, nor was the British navy even theoretically willing to consider committing its ships to such a war. And the reason that the left hand seemed entirely ignorant of what the right hand was doing was simply human nature.

By the end of the nineteenth century British strategists and politicians were in the invidious position of hoping to extract Canadian military contributions for imperial defence while no longer being able or willing to supply the *quid pro quo* (British assistance in defending Canada from the United States) which the relationship still formally presumed. In such circumstances most people – and especially people in bureaucracies – tend to evade and procrastinate so that the awkward truth never gets addressed too squarely. Thus, for example, the secret British army report on possible landing sites on the U.S. eastern seaboard, drawn up by the spy sent by British military intelligence in 1896, landed on the British navy's desk in March 1898 – whereupon the navy studiously ignored its existence for almost three years, until December 1900.

At that point the navy stated that the report was no longer relevant, as the situation had changed and the American navy's growth in the intervening period now rendered the proposal infeasible. And even after that, although everybody in the War Office and the Admiralty knew that Britain would never again fight to defend Canada, nobody was willing to commit that conclusion to paper in so many words. But the U.S. Secretary of State, Robert Olney, had been quite right in his note to London in 1895: the United States was "practically sovereign" in North America, and there was effectively nothing that Britain could do about it.

This conclusion was never passed on to Ottawa, for obvious reasons. It was fortunate, in the circumstances, that the United States actually had no intention of attacking Canada despite all its bluster. It was less fortunate, perhaps, that Canadians did not know that Britain had no intention of defending them, for it meant that the ancestral conception of the old bargain was still part of Canadians' mental furniture when the Laurier government faced the momentous decision to send Canadian troops off to war in South Africa in 1899. That obsolete notion, plus the virulent sentiment of "imperial patriotism" that had infected much of the English-speaking population, proved to be more than Laurier could cope with.

### CHAPTER EIGHT

# *Just A Little Precedent*

The doctrine is new to me that under the British flag and under the Canadian flag, we should go and broaden people's minds with dum-dum bullets.

Henri Bourassa, House of Commons, *Debates*,
13 February 1900

Even at the very end of the nineteenth century, the colonial wars that the British army fought from time to time put no serious strain on British manpower or resources. What preoccupied the British government was the growing possibility of a war with its European rivals – and even Britain's thirty-seven million people might be inadequate to meet the demand for military manpower in that kind of war. The ten million people in the white dominions were an extra source of manpower that might be needed in the ultimate crisis, and they had to be accustomed to the idea beforehand. Britain asked Canada to send troops to the South African war because it needed to set a precedent.

> We do not intend to accept any offer from volunteers. *We do not want the men* and the whole point of the offer would be lost unless it were endorsed by the Government of the Colony and applied to an organised body of the Colonial forces.
>
> Joseph Chamberlain, British Colonial Secretary, to Lord
> Minto, Governor General of Canada, 4 October 1899

> [There was an attempt] to minimize the official appearance of Canada's offer, and to give it as far as possible the character of a volunteer expedition with a small amount of Government assistance.
>
> Lord Minto to Chamberlain, "Secret," 20 October 1899

The war in South Africa was caused by London's decision to bring back under imperial control the Afrikaans-speaking *Boers* (farmers) who had escaped British rule by trekking inland from Cape Colony in the 1830s. The land-locked Boer republics of the Transvaal and Orange Free State might have been left alone, but then the world's richest gold-fields were discovered in the Rand district of the Transvaal in 1885, and English-speaking miners and speculators poured in. They soon comprised a majority of the local population, but these *Uitlanders* (foreigners) were denied the vote and heavily taxed by the Transvaal government. They petitioned Queen Victoria for help – and their plea for intervention was backed by powerful British interests eager to gain direct control of the wealth now pouring out of the Rand.

As war approached in 1899, Israël Tarte, Prime Minister Laurier's right-hand in Quebec, asked in his newspaper, *La Patrie*, why French Canadians should be expected to fight the Boers, who were struggling to preserve "their independence, language and peculiar customs": the analogy with French Canada's own situation was painfully clear. But English Canada was burning with enthusiasm for the empire. On 30 September 1899, less than two weeks before the Boer War began, (militia) Colonel T. Denison, a prominent Toronto lawyer and founding member of the Imperial Federation League, told a special meeting of the Toronto Military Institute (in the presence of the provincial Lieutenant-Governor) why Canada should volunteer to fight in South Africa. It was not right to depend on Britain for defence without giving anything in return, Denison said – and besides, Canada could hardly expect to succeed in the dispute with the U.S. over the Alaska boundary "if we had not behind us the power of the empire." So the Canadian government should send a military contingent to South Africa at once: "We have been children long enough, let us show the empire that we have grown to manhood."

Lord Minto, the Governor General, had only been in Canada a year, but he already knew too much about the country's politics to imagine that it would be a simple task for Laurier's government to send Canadian troops to South Africa. Moreover, Minto knew enough about South Africa to suspect that "money was playing a large part in the game," and to believe that a war against the Boers, if it came, would be "the most iniquitous we had ever engaged in."

> The fact is, if we fight we fight for Rhodes, Beit & Co, and the speculators of the Rand, and it makes me sick. We shall win, and get all S. Africa, but how shall we have got it and what a nice heritage of bad feeling we shall have. . . .
>
> From the point of view of a Canadian statesman, I don't see why they should commit their country to the expenditure of lives and money for a quarrel not threatening Imperial safety. . . . Sir Wilfrid [Laurier] told me the other day that if the question were reconsidered he shd [sic] call a cabinet council and ask me to be present. I hope he won't, for I shd be in a nice muddle, my chief at home thirsting for blood, all my friends here ditto, and myself while recognizing Imperial responsibilities, also seeing the iniquity of the war, and that the time for Colonial support has hardly yet arrived.
>
> Lord Minto to Arthur Elliott, Private,<br>28 September 1899

However, Minto knew where his loyalty lay: he kept his doubts to himself, and dutifully pressed the Colonial Secretary's demands for Canadian troops on Prime Minister Laurier. He had an eager accomplice in Major-General Edward Hutton, the British officer commanding the Canadian militia, who as early as July had drawn up a secret draft plan for the dispatch of a Canadian contingent of about twelve hundred men to South Africa. But Hutton did not understand how such an act could split Canada along "racial" lines – whereas Laurier, whose majority in the House of Commons depended on Quebec seats, certainly did.

Nor was London's first official approach about Canadian troops a monument of tact. On 3 October, a week before the declaration of war in South Africa, the Colonial Office sent a circular telegram to all the colonies "acknowledging" their offer of troops for the forthcoming war. Canada was thanked for providing four units, which should embark for Cape Town by the end of the month. The telegram was released to the British press, and on the same day General Hutton's plan for a large Canadian contingent was leaked (with his prior knowledge) in the *Canadian Military Gazette*. Yet the Canadian government had made no offer of troops, and it was the last thing Laurier wanted to do.

Laurier was in Toronto at the time, and promptly told the editor of the leading Liberal newspaper, the *Globe*, that he had no intention of sending an official Canadian contingent to South Africa just to satisfy "the jingo spirit." Upon his return to Ottawa, he admitted to Lord Minto that he would allow privately raised volunteers to go if necessary, but that was all. (A self-important Tory militia colonel called Sam Hughes had been publicizing his personal plan for such a private force to fight in South Africa since the previous summer.) Laurier then left for a speaking engagement in Chicago, hoping that the uproar would have died down by the time he returned.

But a privately raised contingent was precisely what Britain didn't want, as Joseph Chamberlain had already made clear to Lord Minto. The Colonial Secretary wanted to create a precedent for the sending of official expeditionary forces from the colonies to the great European war that might one day actually require their manpower and resources – and Britain had no compunction in using its long-standing guarantee of imperial military support for Canada (which it had already implicitly decided never to fulfill) as a lever on Ottawa. On 6 October, General Hutton wrote confidently to Lord Minto: "Considering that the Laurier Gov$^t$. are expecting the Imperial Gov$^t$. to force the Alaska Boundary Question upon the U.S. Gov$^t$., and that Sir Wilfrid himself referred to arbitration or war (which latter can only mean armed intervention by the Imperial Gov$^t$.), I do not understand how they can hold aloof from giving material support to the Imperial Gov$^t$. in the present Crisis."

Minto applied the screws, sending Laurier a letter warning of "the

16  C.-E. ROULEAU, PONTIFICAL ZOUAVE.
The harem-guard style of uniform was borrowed from the French
Army, which had acquired it from the Algerians.

17 SON HONNEUR
BENJAMIN TESTARD
DE MONTIGNY.

MOTHER BRITANNIA.—" *See ! Why, the dear child can stand alone !* "
UNCLE SAM.—" *Of course he can ! Let go of him Granny ; if he falls I'll catch him !* "

18 "Canada would fall into our hands as a matter of course."
General Nelson Miles, Commander-in-Chief of the U.S. Army (1895).

19  GABRIEL DUMONT
The Métis military leader.

20 THE CANADIAN MILITIA, 1898.
Becoming a militia officer was the surest route to social
acceptability. Men otherwise unacceptable because of their origins
could be received by the Governor General provided they were in uniform.

21 HENRI BOURASSA.
"The precedent, Sir, is
the accomplished fact."
Bourassa broke with Laurier
over the Boer War because
he believed Canada should
not get involved in
Britain's wars.

22 The editor of the
Liberal *Globe* warned
Laurier privately that he
would have to "either send
troops or get out of office."

23 BOER WAR, 1899-1901.
Bivouac on Bloemfontein Common. Some of the Canadian
volunteers did not even know the first principles of drill and were
totally unfamiliar with army life.

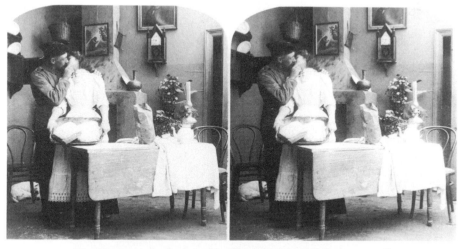

24 "Tommy asks for bread in Bloemfontein and finds sweets."
The Boer War was extensively photographed. Most pictures were
carefully posed for the voters at home. This one is from a set of
sterco (3-D) photographs.

25 The Boer Laager at Paardeberg: men ransacking wagons. The Royal Canadian Regiment lost 130 men killed and wounded at Paardeberg; it was the first British victory after four months of humilating defeats. The Canadians instantly became heroes.

27 IMPERIAL CONFERENCE, 1911.
L. to r.: Louis Botha (South Africa), Doris Harcourt, Sir Wilfrid Laurier, Prime Minister H. Asquith (Britain), Sir Joseph Ward (Australia). Seated on ground: Barbara Harcourt, Anthony Asquith

26 Wounded Canadian after Paardeberg. "Leavitt is not expected
to live. Boers surrendered to the Canadians. Roberts said we did
fine work . . . Men are horribly shot."
Albert Perkins, 27 February 1900.

28 Sir Wilfrid Laurier at New Westminster, B.C., 24 August
1910. It was difficult to get the various parts of the country to
agree about the Navy. British Columbia worried about the Pacific
and Asian masses; Ontario worried about the Royal Navy; and
Quebec worried about getting dragged into Britain's wars.

29  HMS *Niobe* in drydock *c.* 1911. This was half of Laurier's "tinpot" navy.

impression that may be produced in the Old Country by a decision on the part of Canada not to offer troops. It may be taken perhaps to indicate a certain want of loyalty here, which would be all the more unfortunate at a time when we are relying a good deal upon Imperial support in the Alaska question."

Even more alarming to Laurier than this British blackmail was the eruption of rage in the imperialist press in English Canada at his "cowardice." By 9 October, when Laurier got back to Toronto from Chicago, English Canada was up in arms and the yellow press was accusing French Canadians of treason. The *Toronto News* fulminated: "The French rulers of Canada are holding back the loyal Canadians. . . . This Dominion is in the grip of foreigners who have no taste for British advancement. Their ideas are not those of the Anglo-Saxon. . . . Only a wholesome fear of what would happen to them at the hands of the more virile people of Ontario and the West restrains them."

J. S. Willison, the editor of the Liberal *Globe*, warned Laurier privately that he had only two alternatives: "either send troops or get out of office." Laurier travelled on to Ottawa, and on the evening of 13 October held a meeting with leading members of the Liberal Party to try to find some solution that would not hopelessly alienate either English Canada or French Canada. A federal election was due within a year, and Laurier could not possibly regain office without the support of both Ontario and Quebec Liberals. Yet his Quebec lieutenant, Israël Tarte, and most other Quebec cabinet members were vehemently opposed to sending Canadian troops to the Boer War, while William Mulock, the Ontario Liberal leader, stormed out of the meeting in fury when Laurier appeared to be hesitating on the question.

Present at the meeting was Sir Wilfrid's close friend and political confidant, Henri Bourassa, who at the age of only thirty-one had already been three years in Parliament. "A bearded D'Artagnan of words rather than swords," Bourassa was the classically educated grandson of Louis-Joseph Papineau, the leader of the 1837 rebellion. He was every inch an aristocrat, but his ambition and intellect marked him out for a brilliant future in public life. Bourassa had already made his position on South Africa clear in Parliament, protesting against "this extreme spirit of militarism, which is entirely out of harmony with the public opinion of this country." But the public opinion Bourassa was referring to was *French*

Canadian, and Laurier had to contend with the realities of English Canada, too.

The Prime Minister had a compromise up his sleeve that he hoped would mollify all the conflicting demands on him – English Canadian, French Canadian, and British – though it would not fully satisfy any of them. He proposed that the Canadian government should authorize the formation of a Canadian contingent and pay for its equipment and transportation to South Africa, after which the British government would pick up its costs. Moreover, rather than sending regular troops or an existing militia unit, which would give the proceedings too official a character, it should be a special force made up entirely of volunteers who wanted to go to this particular war. It was pure hair-splitting, of course, but that is what most politicians reckon they are paid to do.

Henri Bourassa didn't think that, and when Laurier tried to placate him – "My dear Henri, the circumstances are difficult" – the young M.P. burst out: "It is because they are difficult that I ask you to remain faithful to your word. To govern is to have the courage, at a given moment, to risk power to save a principle." But Mulock and the Ontario Liberals accepted Laurier's compromise, and so did Israël Tarte, who had previously been threatening to resign from the cabinet if troops were sent. (Tarte did insist on a public statement that this decision would not constitute a precedent for future Canadian actions, however.) So Laurier proceeded to authorize a force for South Africa without calling Parliament. The Order-in-Council, dated 14 October 1899, read:

> The Prime Minister, in view of the well-known desire of a great many Canadians who are ready to take service under such conditions, is of the opinion that the moderate expenditure which would thus be involved for the equipment and transportation of such volunteers may readily be undertaken by the Government of Canada without summoning Parliament, especially as such an expenditure under such circumstances *cannot be regarded . . . as a precedent for future action.* [emphasis added]

Laurier fully understood Britain's long-range purpose in seeking Canada's agreement to send troops overseas to this little war: that was why the announcement stressed that it did not imply any future commitments. But four days later Bourassa, who quit his seat in Labelle in protest (and was re-elected by acclamation), summed up all the forebodings of French Canada in his public letter of resignation to Laurier. Bourassa wondered, somewhat ironically, whether the British Empire was really in danger:

> *Ou sommes-nous en présence d'une tentative de fédération militaire de l'Empire, projet cher à M. Chamberlain? . . . L'arrêté ministériel qui décrète l'enrôlement et l'expédition de nos troupes réserve, paraît-il, l'avenir, et empêche cette action d'être considerée comme un précédent. Le précédent, Monsieur le Ministre, c'est le fait accompli.* [emphasis added]

> [Or are we face to face with an attempt at military federation of the Empire, a scheme dear to Mr Chamberlain? . . . The Order-in-Council providing for the enlistment and dispatch of our troops seems to state a reservation about the future, and excludes the present action from being considered as a precedent. *The precedent, Sir, is the accomplished fact.*] [emphasis added]

Among English Canadians, swollen by "racial" pride and urged on by imperialist propaganda, there was little concern as to where this exciting little war might eventually lead Canada. The real debate was among French Canadians, who knew perfectly well where it was leading and didn't want to go there at all. But most of them still believed that their old bargain with Britain was essential to their national survival, even if the terms were being unilaterally changed by the British and the English Canadians. Laurier was considerably more than just an adroit political fixer, and there was real anguish in his reply to Bourassa's letter of resignation: "Tell me what attitude should the French Canadians take in the Confederation? . . . It is necessary that we choose between English Imperialism and American Imperialism. I see no other alternative. If there is one I wish you would indicate it to me." There probably was no alternative, given the state of English Canadian opinion at the time. But Bourassa was right: a precedent had been set.

❖

As soon as the proclamation had been issued the volunteers flocked in, and 1,061 men on a one-year enlistment sailed for South Africa from

Quebec City on 30 October 1899 as the 2nd (Special Service) Battalion, Royal Canadian Regiment. Before leaving, they were treated to a farewell oration by the Rev. Frederick George Scott, rector of St. Matthew's Church, Quebec (Church of England), and part-time poet, who reassured them that: "You are not a wild horde let loose in savage warfare, but Christian men armed in a great cause" and then proceeded to quote poetry at them:

> Though your only reward be a thrust of the sword
>> And a bullet in heart or brain,
> What matters one gone, if the Flag floats on
>> And Britain be Lord of the Main.

During the month-long voyage to Cape Town on the cramped little ship S.S. *Sardinian* (renamed the "Sardine" by the troops), the battalion commander discovered that few of his supposedly trained militiamen knew more than the rudiments of military drill. Lieutenant-Colonel William Otter, a native-born Canadian regular officer, had commanded militiamen in battle once before, during the North-West Rebellion of 1885, and he was determined not to lead raw troops into battle again. Although the Boer armies had inflicted a number of major defeats on the British by the time the Canadian troops arrived in South Africa, he managed to get two months at Belmont, near Kimberley, to turn his enthusiastic Canadians into soldiers before they were committed to battle.

The endless hours of drill and the relentless discipline did not win the tough, greying colonel many friends among the troops, but they did get the militiamen up to the minimum standard of training and fitness that was required in modern mobile warfare. Some of them may have begun to understand why Otter had been so harsh when they were sent marching north across the endless veldt in February 1900 to take the offensive against the Boer armies alongside British regular regiments. After marching twenty-three miles during the night, they arrived on the steep bank overlooking Paardeberg ford on the Modder River just after dawn on 18 February 1900. The Boer army of General Piet Cronje was caught in the act of crossing the ford, and since his men would not abandon their ox-wagons (which were their own property, and in many cases contained their wives and children), he turned to fight. It was the first time a Canadian military unit had ever gone into battle outside North America.

*Pour nous rendre à notre position, il nous fallut traverser la rivière Modder à pied, malgré le courant qui atteint une vitesse de neuf milles à l'heure. Vous comprenez si nous en avons arraché; de l'eau jusqu'au cou et même par-dessus la tête pour plusieurs; mais cela, ce n'était que le commencement. A peine étions-nous sortis de l'eau et avions-nous escaladé la côte, que nous voilà sous les balles de l'ennemi. Ça pleuvait dru, je vous le dis; il fallait voir cela. A cent verges plus loin, vers sept heures, le premier Canadien a été frappé à l'épaule.*

Captain J. E. Peltier (Montreal)

[To get to our position we had to wade across the Modder River, despite a current that reached nine miles an hour. It wouldn't have been surprising if we had been dragged away; water up to our necks and even over their heads for some; but that was just the start. We had hardly got out of the water and clambered up the bank when we came under the enemy's fire. The bullets came as thick as rain, I'm telling you; you should have seen it. A hundred yards farther on, around seven o'clock, the first Canadian was struck in the shoulder.]

*Vers les 10 heures du matin, le feu augmente; les Boers sont retranchés dans un coin de la rivière, abrités par des tranchées naturelles; d'autres sont montés dans les arbres et tirent sur nous sans être aperçus. Seuls nos canons peuvent les atteindre. Les balles pleuvent littéralement au-dessus de nos têtes; à chaque minute il tombe des morts et des blessés. . . . A onze heures notre ligne avance de quatre cents verges, nous ne sommes plus qu'à douze cents verges de l'ennemi. . . .*

Lieutenant Lucien Larue (died of his wound,<br>24 June 1900)

[Around ten in the morning, the fire gets heavier; the Boers are dug in on a bend of the river, sheltered by natural trenches; others are up in the trees and fire on us unseen. Only our artillery can hit them. The bullets rain literally over our heads; there's someone killed or wounded every minute. . . . At eleven our line advances four hundred yards; we're now only twelve hundred yards from the enemy. . . .

At one, we advance four hundred yards . . . The Boers' rifle-fire slackens, and we wonder if they aren't going to retreat. . . . At four the Boers start up again with a terrific fire. We're lying flat, and it's awful to hear the cries and moans of the wounded, but we can't go to help them. . . .

It's five o'clock and our gallant commander, Major Oscar Pelletier, orders F Company to double up to the first firing line. The company obeys. We can see death coming now, but we run forward like real soldiers. I had hardly gone twenty paces when a bullet struck my right shoulder and I saw the blood gush out of my wound.]

The temperature did not drop below a hundred degrees Fahrenheit that day until late in the afternoon, and there was no way of getting water to the troops. There was no cover from the lethally accurate fire of the Boers' Mauser rifles except tiny undulations in the terrain and the occasional anthill (and the Mauser bullets went right through the anthills without losing force). On this first day of battle the Canadian battalion lost eighty-three men killed and wounded – one-tenth of its total strength – and the Canadians were only able to withdraw from their exposed position after night had fallen. But Otter's relentless training had done its work: they held their own and did not panic – neither then, nor on the following days of the ten-day battle. It was on the last day of Paardeberg, however, that they became famous.

[Lord Roberts hesitated to attack], but agreed when the Royal Canadians volunteered to lead the action. Commanded by Colonel W. D. Otter, they were made up of "elegant extracts" from the best-known militia units in the Dominion, including a fine French company. . . .

In the dark of early morning they advanced to within sixty yards of the trenches before a withering fire compelled them to lie flat, but they kept up the attack for two hours. . . . Between 5 and 6 a.m. the Boers raised white flags above their trenches facing the Canadians. Other groups followed suit. . . . Roberts at once ordered the cease-fire.

Rayne Kruger, *Goodbye Dolly Gray* (London, 1959)

It was our turn to advance the trench. . . . At two we rose and advanced. Some had shovels and some had bayonets, for we did not know where we would need them. It was very dark, so dark that we were told to advance holding hands. . . . We had gone about 300 yards when orders came whispered along to entrench. We had only been at that a few minutes when again we got whispered word to advance. That order should not have been given.

We had gone about 100 yards when all of a sudden there was a blaze of rifles. We had walked right on top of the Boer trenches. In a flash we were on our faces hugging the ground. We dare not return the fire as it would give us away. To lift one's head would mean sure death.

Had the Boers not been afraid to rise up and fire low, not one of us would have escaped. . . . After a while we crawled or rolled back to our trench. . . . When dawn came the Boers found we had covered their position and so gave in. . . . Leavitt is not expected to live. Boers surrendered to the Canadians. Roberts said we did fine work. . . . Men are horribly shot. . . . Herb. Leavitt walked over four hundred yards after being shot. Anniversary of Majuba thus it was avenged.

Albert Perkins, Royal Canadian Regiment,<br>Battle of Paardeberg, 27 February 1900

Military historians depict battles in terms of logic and purpose, so Rayne Kruger's version of the final phase of the Battle of Paardeberg, written in 1959, is somewhat different from Albert Perkins's version, written in his diary on the day it happened. In fact, Colonel Otter didn't volunteer his regiment to do anything, and there was no planned attack. The Boer army of five thousand men was outnumbered six-to-one by the British, and it had been surrounded in open country and shelled incessantly for ten days. The Boers were hungry and demoralized by the time the Canadians went stumbling off into the dark to dig new trenches, and General Cronje had already decided to surrender. The Canadians just happened to be in the right place at the right time. But Paardeberg was the first British victory after four miserable months during which the British army had suffered one humiliating defeat after another at the hands of the Boers, so the imperialist press turned the Canadians into heroes, not just in Canada but throughout the empire.

After Paardeberg, the Royal Canadian Regiment took part in the great British advance that captured the capitals of both Boer republics by June 1900. A second contingent of one thousand men, once again raised at the Canadian government's expense, arrived in time to participate in the grim guerrilla war that followed the surrender of the main Boer armies, in which the Boers' farms were burned and their women and children rounded up and put in concentration camps, where about twenty thousand of them died of disease (or from being fed ground glass, according to the version still believed by most Afrikaners). Other Canadian units followed, although these were paid for not by Ottawa but by Britain or by private individuals like Lord Strathcona, the Canadian High Commissioner in London, who spent £200,000 of his own money to raise and equip a six-hundred-strong cavalry regiment called (of course) Lord Strathcona's Horse.

In a guerrilla war the whole population is the enemy, including women and children, and like most of the British Empire's troops in South Africa the Canadian soldiers frequently indulged in looting. Small portable items such as alarm clocks were especially popular: "We had no trouble getting up at the right hour. You could hear alarm clock bells in nearly every heap of blankets and the veldt hummed like a telephone office. (When a soldier loots a house the first thing he grabs is the clock.)" Nevertheless, most of the Canadians felt a certain sympathy for the people they were fighting, and often their rural instinct to help out people in distress mingled strangely with the ruthless nature of modern counter-insurgency warfare. One of the most vivid accounts of the confused behaviour that often resulted was a long letter published in the Ottawa *Citizen* by its editor, Lieutenant E. W. B. Morrison, who was serving in South Africa with the Canadian Artillery. He described an attack on the village of Dullstroom in the northern Transvaal by Canadian troops under the command of Major-General H. L. Smith-Dorrien.

> The Boers drove in our outposts on the flanks and began sniping the guns and we had all to turn loose and amid the row of the

cannonade and the crackle of rifle fire the sacking of the place began. First there was an ominous bluish haze over the town and then the smoke rolled up in volumes that could be seen for fifty miles. The Boers seemed paralyzed by the sight and stopped shooting. When the lull came Gen. Smith-Dorrien invited the artillery officers to go down into the place with him on a sort of official appearance – "just tell them that you saw me" style of thing. The main street was full of smoke and fiery cinders and as the flames belched out in huge sheets from one side or the other our horses shied and plunged from side to side. The place was very quiet except for the roaring and the crackle of the flames.

On the steps of the church were huddled a group of women and children. The children didn't seem to know whether to cry or to be diverted by the spectacle. The women were white but some of them had spots of red on either cheek and their eyes blazed. Not many were crying. The troops were systematically looking the place over and as they got through with each house they burned it. Our Canadian boys helped to get their furniture out, much as they would do at a fire in a village at home. If they saw anything they fancied they would take it . . . but they had not the callous nerve to take the people's stuff in front of their faces. Of course in the case of shops it was different. But you should see the Royal Irish on the loot! They helped the people out with their stuff by heaving bureaus bodily through the windows, putting pickaxes through melodeons. . . .

I went into a very pretty little cottage standing in a rose garden on a side street. The C.M.R.'s [Canadian Mounted Rifles] and R.C.D.'s [Royal Canadian Dragoons] were looting it, but really helping the woman out with her stuff more than sacking the place. The woman was quite a good-looking lady-like person and the house was almost luxuriously furnished. She was breathlessly bustling about saving her valuables and superintending the salvage operations. A big dragoon would come up to her and say in a sheepish sort of way: "What you want next, lady?" and she would tell them and they would carry it out. As I stood looking on she turned to me and said: "Oh, how can you be so cruel?" I sympathised with her and explained it was an order and had to be obeyed. She was a good-looking female in distress and had quite the dramatic style of an ill-used heroine.

I certainly was sorry for her – we all were – until the house began to burn and a lot of concealed ammunition to explode and nearly killed some of our men. But all the same it was a sad sight to see the little homes burning and the rose bushes withering up in the pretty gardens and the pathetic groups of homeless women and children crying among the ruins as we rode away.

Lieutenant E. W. B. Morrison, The Citizen, Ottawa,<br>2 January 1901

In all, over seven thousand Canadians enlisted for the South African war, of whom about five thousand arrived in time to see active service there. For most English Canadians at home, the war began as an exciting distraction and ended at least as a successful demonstration of Canada's military prowess and its unbounded loyalty to the empire. But there were a few nagging details that detracted from this cheery view of the war: of the eight companies of the Royal Canadian Regiment that had enlisted in the first rush of enthusiasm, for example, six flatly refused to extend their service when their year's contract expired in September 1900.

Even in English Canada the war was not without its critics (although the criticism tended to be limited to farmers' weeklies and radical labour journals). Goldwin Smith, the editor and owner of two small papers, was appalled by the brutalization of Canadian society. He particularly disliked the war toys being given to children: "puppets made by their distortions and squeaking to resemble the agonies of dying Boers." And the Woman's Christian Temperance Union (Ontario Branch) passed a strong anti-war resolution:

We place on record our deep regrets that our country has recently deemed it necessary to engage in war; that we earnestly recommend the women of our country to proclaim the principles of peace, and that we do all in our power to discourage the fostering of the military spirit in our families, in our schools and in our churches and also resolved, that we favor the settlement of international disputes by arbitration instead of war.

But the efforts of the Peace and Arbitration Committee within the Woman's Temperance movement and of individuals like Goldwin Smith were of little avail: even women generally accepted the values of their fathers, husbands, and clergymen and supported the war. The mainstream English-language press was overwhelmingly jingoist, and its readers had no quarrel with its view of war as a morally positive and virtually cost-free spectator sport.

In the late afternoon of January 12, 1901, two of the volunteers came home. To greet them, 2,000 citizens of Paris, Ontario gathered at the Junction Station "to welcome (in the words of the Paris Star-Transcript) Our Boys who had Done so well – Gunners Arthur Flanagan and Alex Hume."

When the locomotive came puffing and clanking into the station, the band struck up "See the Conquering Heroes Come!" and the crowd raised a series of mighty cheers. Then, "as the Kaki clad heroes alighted, there arose upon the air that familiar refrain, 'Home, Sweet Home'." . . . After greeting some of their relatives in the waiting room, the heroes, in gaily decorated sleighs, were driven home to embrace their mothers. . . . In the evening, at 8:15, a procession was again formed at the station. Its order was as follows:

> Mounted Marshall, Captain W. W. Patterson
> Rough Riders, six abreast
> Colours
> Visiting soldiers and firemen
> Our Veterans
> Citizens and visitors
> Colours
> Carriage containing Our Boys
> Burford Cavalry
> Rough Riders, six abreast
> Ambulance

After passing along streets of decorated and illuminated houses and through lines of cheering spectators, and after serenading the homes of the heroes and setting off a mass of brilliant fireworks, the procession wound its way to the town hall, [where]

> a number of long orations were delivered. . . . George Shepherd,
> John Vine, and John Jefferson, Paris boys who were still in South
> Africa . . . together with the two returned heroes, were praised
> for the part they had played in helping to defend "Truth, Justice
> and Christian Civilization."
>
> Donald A. Smith, *At the Forks of the Grand*, Volume II

After the speeches, the good people of Paris, Ontario, presented Alex Hume with a gold pin and Arthur Flanagan (more usefully) with a gold watch. Everybody congratulated themselves on how the town had helped to "defend the integrity of the British Empire and the honour of our beloved Queen," as Mayor Evans put it – but five volunteers was actually not a very impressive total for a town of over four thousand people. In fact, the average native-born English Canadian man was not nearly so eager to go off and die for the empire as his political leaders, his social betters, and his newspapers assumed.

Almost thirty percent of Canada's volunteers for the Boer War were British immigrants, though they made up only seven percent of the total population. Even more significantly, Canada's total contribution lagged far behind the other white dominions: it had a larger population than the Australian and New Zealand colonies put together, but they raised over three times as many men for the war. As for French Canadians – the "fine French company" of the Royal Canadian Regiment had francophone officers, but two-thirds of its men were actually English speakers. Only 3 per cent of those who served in South Africa were French Canadian, although francophones comprised 30 per cent of the Canadian population.

Individual French Canadians went to South Africa for the sorts of personal motives that will induce some men, at certain times in their lives, to go to a war almost regardless of what it is about, and once there they fought just as well as anybody else. But the war was almost universally unpopular in French Canada, where some of the young wore buttons bearing the name of Kruger, the Boer leader, to show where their sympathies lay. In March 1900 there were three days of rioting between English and French students in Montreal, and the militia had to be called out. Meanwhile, the more rabid sections of the English Canadian press called the French Canadians scoundrels and traitors and warned of civil war. Lord Minto, the Governor General, reported that some eastern

Ontario farmers went to bed at night with guns by their sides because they feared a French Canadian invasion.

Nevertheless, Laurier's compromise had succeeded. He won the 1900 election comfortably, and the country moved on to other concerns. In January 1903 the Alaskan boundary dispute was decided entirely in favour of the United States (because the British representative on the arbitration tribunal voted for the American case in order to avoid a clash with Washington). There was great fury in Ottawa and across the country, and the two Canadian representatives on the tribunal refused to sign the decision in protest, but Laurier's government survived. By then the South African War had been over for six months, and all the Canadian volunteers had come home except for the 224 who were buried there. It was a gentle enough introduction to the business of fighting foreign wars – and not too many Canadians were bothered by a little thing like a precedent.

Long after the war, John Jefferson, who was then 99 years old, was asked why he had been eager to risk his life in South Africa: "I was young and foolish," he said, "and I wanted adventure." Then thoughtfully he added, "If I'd known then what I know now, I'd not have gone. I risked my life so that a few rich men could have full control of the gold and diamonds of the Transvaal. I was taken in by a lot of propaganda."

Donald A. Smith, *At the Forks of the Grand, Volume* II

### CHAPTER NINE

# "This Conclusion Was Not Discussed with Canada . . . "

Gentlemen, we do want your aid. . . . The weary Titan staggers under the too vast orb of its fate. We have borne the burden many years. We think it is time our children should assist us to support it.

Joseph Chamberlain to the colonial prime ministers,
Imperial Conference, London, 1902

Having persuaded the colonial prime ministers to contribute troops to the Boer War, Colonial Secretary Joseph Chamberlain invited them all to another Imperial Conference in 1902. He now wanted to make the arrangement permanent by getting them to commit some of their forces to a special "Imperial Reserve" that would be available for service anywhere in the world.

Canada's contribution to the proposed Imperial Reserve would be one infantry brigade and one artillery brigade (about 4,500 men). That was only half the size of Australia's, but Chamberlain charitably explained the discrepancy by observing that Australia didn't have to worry about its own territory being invaded, whereas Canada had the United States next door. However, Laurier objected strongly to the whole idea, and the conference ended with no formal Canadian commitment.

> There is a school . . . in England and in Canada, a school which is perhaps represented on the floor of this Parliament, a school which wants to bring Canada into the vortex of militarism which is the curse and the blight of Europe. I am not prepared to endorse any such policy.
>
> > Sir Wilfrid Laurier to the House of Commons, Ottawa,
> > before the Imperial Conference of 1902

Laurier was equally unhelpful to the enthusiastic new British commander of the Canadian militia, Major-General the Earl of Dundonald, who had distinguished himself as a cavalry leader in the Boer War. That officer was full of grand ideas for building new training areas and fortifications in Canada and raising the strength of the peacetime militia to 50,000, with provisions for expanding it instantly to 100,000 on the outbreak of war. He also wanted to make cadet corps compulsory in Canadian schools, in order to facilitate the further expansion of the Canadian army to 200,000 men in the early months of a war: "It is an easy matter for the school boy to devote a good deal of time to drill in a cadet corps. . . . When in later life they join the militia regiments, they will be fit to proceed at once, without waste of time, to the more advanced branches of military training."

It was all still allegedly in the context of defending Canada against an American attack, but it is hard to believe that Lord Dundonald was not also thinking of other possible uses for a large Canadian army. Laurier was not amused: "You must not take the militia seriously, for though it is useful for suppressing internal disturbances, it will not be required for the defence of the country, as the Monroe Doctrine protects us from enemy aggression." By 1904 Dundonald had been dismissed, ostensibly for trying to stop political interference in militia affairs, but really for showing an excess of zeal. His parting advice as he left for Britain was: "Men of Canada, keep both hands on the Union Jack!" And yet, despite

Laurier's refusal to make any overt military commitments to imperial defence, he found it impossible to resist the undertow that was drawing Canada into deeper waters. A new Liberal government in Britain had more success in implicating Canada in imperial defence by subtle means than Joseph Chamberlain had ever had with his direct appeals, and the militia budget crept inexorably upward, more than quadrupling between 1898 and 1911.

It is hard to explain why this happened, for the key Canadian actors did not change. Laurier was prime minister continuously from 1896 to 1911, and his Minister of Militia throughout all fifteen years was Frederick Borden, a Nova Scotia physician, merchant, and politician who combined a gregarious fondness for the social aspects of militia life (he played the fiddle or performed Scottish dances at the slightest provocation) with a stern appreciation of the militia's severely limited military and political value to Canada. There was, it is true, a steady rise in imperialist sentiment in English Canada throughout this period, and any Canadian government concerned to stay in office had to cater to it to a limited extent, but there was certainly no popular demand for a direct Canadian military contribution to the imperial forces. Borden, the militia minister, had never shown himself vulnerable to British blandishments in this regard before the Boer War, nor did he tolerate Dundonald's attempts to shift Canada in this direction.

Yet something must have changed, and one is reduced to looking for the possible personal influences on Frederick Borden that could have made him respond more favourably to imperial claims on Canadian resources by the first years of the twentieth century. Borden's own son had volunteered for the Boer War and had been killed in South Africa, which (as any amateur psychologist will tell you) could have made him more supportive of the empire his son had died for. A less convoluted reason would be simply the warm friendship and easy working relationship that Borden enjoyed with Percy Lake, a British officer with strong Canadian family ties who had already served in Ottawa in the late 1890s, and who returned after Dundonald's abrupt departure in 1904 to serve as Chief of the (Canadian) General Staff until 1908. (He then remained on as Inspector-General, at Borden's request, until 1910.) At any rate, while there was no sudden and drastic change of direction in Canadian military policy during this period, there was a steady drift.

It began with Ottawa's response when Britain began to concentrate its navy in home waters in 1905. As a natural consequence, London decided to withdraw its garrisons from the imperial naval bases at Halifax and Esquimalt – and if Canada had not volunteered to take up the slack, the British would simply have abandoned these fortified bases. That is what certainly would have happened if this withdrawal had occurred as little as a decade before, when Canadian governments had still been quite clear in their conviction that the whole point of belonging to the empire was that *it* defended *you*. But by 1905 this simple formula was getting blurred, and so the Canadian government agreed to replace the British garrisons in Halifax and Esquimalt with its own regular troops, and increased the authorized size of the Permanent Force to four thousand in order to find the men. It was an ambiguous measure – you *could* argue that these bases were relevant to Canadian defence too, and not just imperial defence, if you really wanted to – and a pretty modest one. Besides, the Canadian government did not really expand its regular forces as promised: in 1908 the Permanent Force still numbered only 2,730 men. But it was the start of a trend.

Five years after Laurier's firm stand in 1902 against Canadian involvement in the "vortex of [European] militarism" there was another Imperial Conference in London, this time orchestrated by the much more congenial Liberal government of Sir Henry Campbell-Bannerman. There was no pushy Joe Chamberlain around in 1907 to queer the pitch with his demands for explicit military commitments from the overseas Dominions; just a soothing resolution that, without committing any of the governments at the conference to any particular action, affirmed the need for "a General Staff selected from the forces of the Empire as a whole, which . . . shall undertake the preparation of schemes of defence on a common principle." Each local section of the General Staff, in Ottawa and the other Dominion capitals, would advise the local government on military matters, but would exercise no powers of command.

There seemed no harm in that, no infringement of Canadian autonomy. Nor was there anything obviously objectionable about the special Imperial Defence Conference of 1909. There were no calls for Canada to earmark troops for overseas service, just a great deal of detailed work by the soldiers on the "standardization" of uniforms, weapons, and training throughout the armed forces of the empire. The aim, as Prime Minister

Herbert Asquith explained in the British House of Commons that year, was to ensure that "should the Dominions desire to assist in the defence of the Empire in a real emergency, their forces could be rapidly combined into one Imperial Army."

It was all carefully couched in conditional phrases, so as not to startle the prey, but in fact this was how Canada effectively became committed to defending Britain in Europe, even though there was never a parliamentary debate or a cabinet discussion of the question. After 1909 Canadian officers regularly attended Staff College courses in Britain, and British officers in Ottawa organized a Canadian branch of the General Staff. Even in English Canada, however, there were some alert observers who understood the implications of all this and had the gravest reservations about where it was leading. Dr O.D. Skelton, then a professor at Queen's University and later the founder of the modern Department of External Affairs, wrote to a friend in a public letter of 1909:

> you calmly assume that in all the wars in which Britain is engaged she is "assailed" rather than "assailing". A recollection of the process by which the British Empire has expanded . . . might suggest that she has had at least her share of attacking. . . . There are real difficulties in any plan of Canadian neutrality while Britain is at war, I admit, but they are not so serious as the problems presented by the proposal to accept all Britain's wars as ours.

But voices like Skelton's were very scarce in English Canada. For most English Canadians allegiance to Britain, even to the extent of automatic involvement in her wars, was not something to be weighed rationally. It was instinct.

> Politics wore a complexion strictly local, provincial or Dominion. The last step of France in Siam, the disputed influence of Germany in the Persian Gulf, the struggle of the Powers in China were not matters greatly talked over in Elgin; the theatre of European diplomacy had no absorbed spectators here. Nor can I claim that interest in the affairs of Great Britain was in any way extravagant. . . .
>
> It was recognised dimly that England had a foreign policy, more or less had to have it, as they would have said in Elgin; it

was part of the huge unnecessary scheme of things for which she was responsible – unnecessary from Elgin's point of view as a father's financial obligations might be to a child he had parted with at birth. It all lay outside the facts of life, far beyond the actual horizon. . . .

[But] belief in England was in the blood. . . . Indifferent, apathetic, self-centred – until whenever, down the wind, across the Atlantic, came the faint far music of the call to arms. . . . The sense of kinship, lying too deep for the touch of ordinary circumstance, quickened to that; and in a moment, "we" were fighting, "we" had lost or won.

Sara Jeannette Duncan, *The Imperialist*, 1904

Sara Duncan's "Elgin" was actually Brantford, Ontario, where she grew up. Her novel was a fair representation of what people felt in the small towns of English Canada (and Canada was still a country of small towns): a sentimental loyalty to Britain that didn't count the cost, and never even imagined there might be much cost to it. Their only example, after all, was the Boer War, which had been cheap and glorious. The unobserved drift toward a European military commitment in the Militia Department in Ottawa coincided with the drift of sentiment in English Canada, and would not rouse strong conflicting emotions in French Canada until and unless Canadian forces were actually sent to Europe.

If Laurier had realized what was happening, perhaps he could have stopped it. The Laurier of 1902 certainly would have. But as his prime ministership entered its second decade his political troubles (including a bitterly fought naval controversy) began to mount, and he wasn't looking for any extra fights. Besides, it was hard to put your finger on exactly what was happening unless you immersed yourself in the flow of paper across the militia minister's desk.

That was clearly not the prime minister's job, and after all Frederick Borden had been running his department for over a decade and could be trusted not to make any serious mistakes. So it is much to be doubted that Sir Wilfrid Laurier, preoccupied with preparations for an imminent election, even knew that in July 1911 his Minister of Militia approved the assignment of a staff officer to draw up plans for sending overseas a Canadian expeditionary force of 25,000 men – six times larger than the one Laurier had rejected a decade before. Let alone the fact that the staff officer in question was specifically instructed to assume that the force would be going to a war "in a civilized country with a temperate climate."

❖

*Alliances*, n. In international politics, the union of two thieves who have their hands so deeply inserted in each other's pockets that they cannot separately plunder a third.

Ambrose Bierce, *The Devil's Dictionary*

Canada wasn't alone in being drawn into the "vortex of militarism," of course. In Australia, New Zealand, and South Africa too, entire national communities of European descent were being psychologically prepared to sacrifice their young men in huge numbers in the forthcoming struggle between the European great powers. And although the United States had no allegiance to any European empire, its people would also find themselves sending troops to Europe before the First World War was over.

They would all believe that they were taking part in a unique event of great moral significance. In that, they were no different from the Europeans, who would soon start calling it "the war to end all wars." But the First World War was not a unique event: it was part of the cycle of "world wars" that stretches back to the beginning of the modern international system in seventeenth-century Europe, and still stretches ahead of us toward the nuclear precipice. The principal players have changed over centuries, but the basic rules of the great-power game have not. And although its origins may seem lost in the obscurity of the distant past, they are extremely important, for this game still rules our destiny.

The use of alliances, Sir, has in the last age been too much experienced to be contested. . . . By alliances, Sir, the equipoise of power is maintained, and those alarms and apprehensions avoided, which must arise from daily vicissitudes of empire, and the fluctuations of perpetual contest.

Sir Robert Walpole, House of Commons, London, 1741

During the 1400s and 1500s, powerful centralized governments began to extend their control over large areas of Europe. At the same time, rising wealth and better communications made it easier for large armies to operate far from home. Local wars had been constant in medieval Europe, and they would continue to occur frequently in the new "modern" Europe that was emerging, but now a new pattern was superimposed on the old: the entire continent was transformed into a unified political and military arena.

Governments had always sought allies in their quarrels – it is an obvious way of increasing your own side's power – but they could now make useful alliances with distant states. The ideal allies were countries that also had a quarrel with your own enemy, but it was almost as good if they had a quarrel with one of your enemy's allies. So gradually, all the local rivalries coalesced into an interlocking, constantly shifting kaleidoscope of alliances that incorporated every great power in the entire continent of Europe – which soon came to mean, in practice, every great power in the world, since by the seventeenth century Europe already effectively dominated the entire globe. The modern international system was born, and in 1618, it produced the first "world war": the Thirty Years' War.

Those who would baulk at the use of that phrase because their image of a "world war" involves trenches or bomber fleets are missing the point. That happens to be the technology employed in the world wars of our own century, but as a *political* phenomenon such wars have a much longer history. They are, to be precise, wars in which *every* recognized great power of the time is simultaneously involved. In that very important sense, the Thirty Years' War was the first world war: by the middle of it, Swedish troops were fighting Spaniards in the centre of Germany. And although it was billed as a religious war, the great powers actually chose their alliances on the basis of national advantage, not on shared belief.

The alliances that organized the great powers into a "system" rarely formed haphazardly: they were generally governed by the principle known as the "balance of power." This did not mean, however, that the various countries tried to create a balance that would make war less likely; "balance of power" politics was and is a far more dynamic process, in which alliances tend to be created against whichever state is seen to be the most dangerous (either the most powerful or the most rapidly growing) in the system. In the Thirty Years' War, the superpower was Spain, whose vast wealth and great military power put it head and shoulders above any other European state. But that automatically created a coalition of rival powers that felt threatened by Spanish hegemony, and Spain's resources ultimately proved unequal to its pretensions.

In the next three world wars, the aspirant superpower was France, which had become by far the richest and most populous of the European states: the Thirty Years' War was followed, at intervals of about half a century, by the War of the Spanish Succession (1702-13); the War of the Austrian Succession and the Seven Years' War (1740-48 and 1756-63), which for most practical purposes can be treated as a single long war interrupted by a lengthy truce; and finally by the Revolutionary and Napoleonic Wars (1792-1815). France, too, was ultimately thwarted in its ambitions by alliances between all the states it threatened, but the game did not stop. After 1815 Britain emerged as the dominant power in the system, but in due course another challenger appeared – Germany – and the result was the First World War.

None of these transient superpowers was out to conquer the world, or even to rule all of Europe (which would have come to much the same thing, since Europe collectively ruled most of the world). They were simply out to gain certain specific goals and to improve their relative power position to such an extent that they would be invulnerable to any challenge. Since invulnerability for one state meant an unacceptable degree of vulnerability for every other state, the alliance-forming process therefore never lacked fuel. But it should not be supposed that superpowers were the sole cause of the problem in the past, any more than they are in the present. All the great powers, and the lesser powers as well, are part of the same pattern. Moreover, the pattern is *cyclical*.

"World wars" have occurred, on average, about every fifty years throughout most of modern European history. They are not necessarily fought all over the world (though most of them have affected several continents); the criterion is simply that all the recognized great powers be involved. And unlike wars between two individual countries, world wars are not really about anything in particular. They are about everything in general.

Once large-scale alliances (often based on secret understandings and always prone to sudden changes of membership) became the European norm, the possibility existed for wars in which there would be a general settlement of accounts. In theory, all the members of the winning alliance could achieve their particular national objectives, while all the members of the losing alliance would have to grant the victors' demands. It was never quite that simple in practice, but these wars invariably brought about a general reshuffle of the deck. Even in the long intervals of relative peace, therefore, the next general war became the implicit focus of the great-power competition (as it still is). International politics became, and has largely remained, a zero-sum game in which any gain in power by one state is automatically a loss for all the others in the system. And as to why these general wars recurred with an interval of about half a century–that has to do, curiously enough, with the peace treaties.

> *Utrecht, Peace of:* a series of treaties (1713) concluding the War of the Spanish Succession. Philip V kept Spain . . . and Charles VI obtained Milan, Naples, Sardinia and the Spanish Netherlands. Britain gained Gibraltar, Minorca, Newfoundland and Acadia. . . . French expansion was halted.
>
> Longman's *Modern English Dictionary*

> Treaties are like roses and young girls. They last while they last.
>
> Charles de Gaulle, 1962

Once upon a time, schools taught European history as a succession of peace treaties at which everything was settled: the Treaty of Westphalia (1648), the Peace of Utrecht (1713), the Treaty of Paris (1763), the Congress of Vienna (1815), and so on. Fashions in teaching history have changed now, but so far as the causes of world wars are concerned, the old-fashioned history teachers were right–peace treaties did matter. They were the definitive record of what territories the victorious side had won and what the defeated alliance had lost. Equally important, they were an implicit statement of each state's power, and therefore its position in the international pecking order. However, there was always the possibility of a re-match.

At the end of each world war the relative rank of the great powers, together with all the borders that depend upon that, is defined and frozen. (We, for example, are still living in the world that congealed in 1945.) But after each war, as the years pass, some countries grow faster than others in wealth and population, and some change sides. At first the winners are still strong enough to enforce the peace treaty, but gradually the possibility arises for another roll of the dice. The interval of around fifty years between world wars is not a natural law like gravity, but simply the average time it takes for enough changes to occur that the last peace treaty is no longer enforceable.

By then, some countries reckon that their strength entitles them to more status, influence, and territory than they were allocated in the last treaty, and others no longer have the real strength needed to defend their gains under that treaty. The international system becomes increasingly unstable, and at that point it only takes a deliberate decision by just one country to attack a neighbour, or even a bluff that misfires, for the alliances to drag everybody into another general war. It ends in another treaty that readjusts everybody's "prestige" (which means, in plain English, the ability to frighten your rivals), and changes a good many borders.

North Americans were involved in all of these world wars in the seventeenth, eighteenth, and nineteenth centuries, but they didn't have to *go* to them, in the sense that we have sent troops off to war in this century. The European empires had overrun practically the entire world, including North America, so the wars came to us. What changed in the course of the nineteenth century, as almost all the countries of the Western Hemisphere gained their independence from the European great powers, was that they thereby escaped from the alliance system and became largely exempt from the world wars.

The alliance system is an open game, so any aspirant great power with the wherewithal to sustain its claim to that status – like the United States and Japan in the early twentieth century – could have a place in the system just for the asking: non-European powers were certainly not excluded on principle. The inclusion of Canada in the system was far less of a foregone conclusion, however. It derived almost entirely from its membership in the British Empire, for it was not a great power, nor did it have the remotest prospect of ever becoming one.

In 1914 Canada was in many ways comparable to Argentina: they were then countries of equal prosperity and apparently equal promise, both settled almost entirely by people of European origin. Both lived an ocean away from the European great powers and could theoretically have expected to be immune to their wars. And indeed the Argentines did not get pulled into the great-power wars of the twentieth century, for they were already independent – but the Canadians, with their British imperial ties, went off to fight for "God, King and Country."

Three things served to obscure the reality of their situation from most Canadians (including almost all English Canadians). The first was the sense of spatial disorientation in most English Canadians, too recently arrived in Canada to have broken their psychological ties with Britain or to realise where their new country actually was on the globe. The second, common to both English and French Canadians, was the false, or at least very faded paradigm whereby membership in the British Empire, and payment of whatever dues that might entail, constituted the only reliable way of fending off annexationist pressures from the United States. Thirdly, Canadians, like all the people of 1914, saw themselves as the heirs of the "long peace" that had lasted almost a century. Nobody understood that world wars were a cyclical phenomenon and that the "First World War" was therefore almost inevitable at some point in the early twentieth century, mainly because there had not been another world war on schedule in the mid-nineteenth century.

History does not run on rails. The mid-nineteenth century world war almost happened several times—that was what General Harney was counting on when he occupied San Juan Island in 1859—but it never quite got off the ground. Instead, there was a series of smaller wars in which all the European great powers fought each other not all at once, but in rotation: Britain, France, and Turkey against Russia in 1854, France and Italy against Austria in 1859, Austria against Germany in 1866, and Germany against France in 1870. They were quite big wars, but most were quite short. (That may partly explain why they didn't expand into a general war: there just wasn't enough time.)

In practical terms, however, these smaller wars had the cumulative political effect of a world war: some great powers rose in "prestige" and others fell, and territory changed hands in proportion. It was in these wars, for example, that the Austrian Empire ceased to be a power of the first rank, and the newly united German Empire became one. Political realities having been adjusted to conform to the actual strength of the various great powers, stability then returned to the system for around another half-century. Indeed, *no* great power fought any other between 1870 and 1914 (unless you count the war between Russia and the newest applicant for great-power status, Japan, in 1904-1905).

By the beginning of the twentieth century, however, world war was in the air again. Between 1898 and 1914, a crisis that brought Europe to the brink occurred almost every other year. Unfortunately for Canada, it all had a lot to do with the power and status of Great Britain – but Ottawa didn't really take it very seriously until the Naval Crisis of 1909.

❖

> If the problem of Imperial Naval Defence is considered merely as
> a problem of naval strategy, it will be found that the . . . maximum
> of power will be gained if all parts of the Empire contribute . . .
> to the maintenance of the British Navy.
>
> Winston Churchill, Admiralty memo, 1909

On 16 March 1909 Reginald McKenna, First Lord of the Admiralty, stood up in the House of Commons in London and frightened the British out of their wits. After declaring that Britain's supremacy at sea was being undermined by the German drive to build a large fleet of battleships, he called for a greatly increased programme of British naval construction to counter it. The panic soon communicated itself to Canada, where Prime Minister Laurier got unanimous support in Parliament for a resolution creating a Canadian naval service. It was the start of a five-year "defence" debate in Canada that finally dragged the question of the country's growing commitment to imperial defence onto centre stage – and ultimately did for Laurier despite his attempts to evade the issue.

McKenna's statement to the British House of Commons in 1909 was in fact a classic example of distortion and panic-mongering: anybody who has lived through the "windows of opportunity" and other manufactured crises of the Cold War should recognize both the technique and the intended beneficiary. For it was quite clear to anyone with eyes to see that the Germans were not planning to conquer the British Empire.

The document that people like McKenna invariably quoted to prove that the Germans intended to undermine British naval supremacy was the German Naval Law of 1900: "Germany must possess a battle fleet of such strength that even for the most powerful naval adversary a war would involve such risks as to make that Power's own supremacy look doubtful." However, if you read the law carefully, it was not a declaration of intent to build a bigger navy than the British. The Germans never aspired to that, being fairly realistic about how much money they could afford to divert from their army to their navy. What Berlin set out to build at the turn of the century was a "second-best" navy so powerful that the British would choose never to fight Germany, for fear of losing so many of their own ships in the course of destroying the German navy that Britain would no longer be able to control the world's oceans.

The Germans were just trying to make sure that Britain never took sides against them in a European war – and the German naval build-up proceeded so sedately that nobody took much alarm until the British launched a whole new kind of battleship in 1906. The trouble with HMS *Dreadnought*, the first fully armoured, all-big-gun battleship, was that it made every other battleship in the world instantly obsolete, including all the battleships which were the source of Britain's own naval supremacy. The day *Dreadnought* was launched, Britain had a single ship that could probably have defeated every old-style battleship in the world, but it also had a lead of precisely one in the only kind of battleship that now counted. For the first time, it seemed, Germany had a real chance to catch up. This was enough for the British naval strategists, who measured capabilities rather than intentions. In 1909 (with strong support from the navy and the shipbuilding industry) they pressed the panic button in London – and Canada jumped too.

However, the unanimous assent of Parliament in Ottawa in 1909 to the creation of a Canadian naval service concealed a deep divergence of purpose between Prime Minister Laurier and the Conservative opposition leader, Robert Borden (not to be confused with Laurier's militia minister, Frederick Borden). The prime minister felt that if it was now politically unavoidable to accept some sort of naval commitment, at the very least it had to be a *Canadian* navy so that the government could keep Canada's commitments in wartime under Ottawa's own control. By contrast for Robert Borden, a ponderous, painfully earnest Nova Scotian, there was no doubt that any Canadian warships should be fully at Britain's disposal in wartime. He accepted that Canada would be automatically involved in any British imperial war, and concentrated simply on trying to find ways to exert Canadian influence on British policy both before and, if necessary, during a war. He was even prepared, in the apparent emergency that had arisen, to postpone a separate Canadian navy in favour of an immediate cash contribution to the British naval budget.

When Ottawa's representatives arrived in London in the summer of 1909, that turned out to be exactly what the British wanted: a cash donation to build Dreadnoughts for the British Navy in British shipyards. Laurier's government demurred, and promised instead to build a "two-ocean navy" for the protection of Canada's coasts: five cruisers and six destroyers in all, which would be based at Halifax and Esquimalt. Although far from pleased, the British agreed on the grounds that anything was better than nothing. So in 1910 Laurier brought in the Naval Service Bill creating a Canadian navy, to be built in Canadian shipyards.

In an emergency, he said, it would be placed at the disposal of the British fleet by an order-in-council if the Canadian government so decided. However, Laurier added, if Parliament was not already in session, it would have to be called within fifteen days to confirm the decision. He conceded that Canada, as part of the British Empire, had no legal right to decide for itself on questions of war and peace. – "When Britain is at war, Canada is at war. There is no distinction" – but he was really saying that Canada itself would decide what to do, in practical terms, if Britain got into a European war.

> *Nous n'y prendrons part que si nous le jugeons à propos. . . . Ne monteront sur ces navires que ceux qui voudront y monter. Les jeunes gens prenant du service sauront qu'ils ne sont pas obligés de prendre part à toutes les guerres de l'Angleterre, mais qu'ils peuvent être appelés par le peuple du Canada, par le Parlement du Canada, quand il le jugera à propos, à prendre part aux guerres de l'Angleterre.*
>
> Wilfrid Laurier, Montreal, 10 October 1910

[We will not take part unless we think it appropriate. . . . Only those who wish to serve on those ships will board them. The young men joining up will know that they are not obliged to take part in all of England's wars, but that they may be called by the people of Canada, by the Parliament of Canada, when it thinks it is appropriate, to take part in England's wars.]

It was the opening of the last round between Laurier and the imperial patriots of English Canada. It was not just about naval strategy, but about loyalties, and jobs, and two very different views of the world and Canada's place in it. When the Royal Navy asked for ships (and meant money), they were still playing by the old rules. Laurier's response was to quote Kipling: "Daughter am I in my Mother's house, but Mistress in mine own."

In a way it was a phony crisis, for even as it raged the less dramatic decisions that would really commit Canada to send troops to fight for Britain in Europe were being made by obscure British and Canadian officers on the General Staff in Ottawa, to the complete ignorance of the public and with no political participation apart from Minister of Militia Frederick Borden's. Nevertheless, the naval crisis did give Canadians the opportunity to hold a public debate on the question of Canada's commitment to a European war (even if over the wrong service) – and it was a very bitter argument, for the ultra-imperialist wing of the Conservative Party was outraged by Laurier's attitude. How could Canada ignore the crisis that faced the mother country? Provincial Conservative leaders opted for cash contributions to the British fleet, either as an emergency measure or even as a permanent policy, and indignantly denounced Laurier's "tin-pot navy." Borden, the federal opposition leader, mockingly called it an "order-in-council Navy," and wondered whether a Russian or German "ironclad" would refrain from torpedoing a Canadian warship until Ottawa promulgated the order-in-council declaring that Canada, too, was at war.

Robert Borden embodied all the imperialist loyalties of English Canadian Conservatives, but his closest allies in the struggle against Laurier's compromise proposal of a Canadian navy, ironically, were at the other extreme of the argument. F. D. Monk, the Conservative leader in Quebec (and a francophone despite his name), and Henri Bourassa, by now the founder-publisher of *Le Devoir*, wanted Canada to have nothing to do with naval commitments at all, whether in the form of a Canadian navy or cash donations to the British navy – so they collaborated with Robert Borden in a campaign to bring the Liberal government down. In the first round, a coalition of Conservatives, Nationalists, and Bourassa supporters defeated the Liberal candidate in a by-election in Drummond-Arthabaska, the heart of Laurier's Quebec. They won mainly on the argument, strongly advocated by Bourassa in *Le Devoir*, that Canada's proposed warships would automatically involve it in any British war, since their mere presence at sea would make them just as much a target as any British warship.

But they also played on the vague fears of credulous rural voters (and of their voteless but influential wives) that French Canadians might be conscripted for the British fleet:

> *Dans quinze ans, vos femmes verront venir l'agent du gouvernement, ayant à la main cette loi maudite et leur disant à chacune: "Bonne mère, il faut que tu donnes tes fils non pas pour défendre le pays natale, mais pour se battre sur toutes les terres et toutes les mers du monde en faveur du drapeau anglais." Et quand vos femmes apprendront, quelques mois après, qu'un obus autrichien, un boulet japonais ou une balle allemande aura éventré leur enfant . . . pensez-vous qu'elles diront alors: "C'est bien, mon mari était rouge et c'est Laurier qui a fait passer cette loi, il a bien fait." Non, elles vous maudiront, et ce sera à bon droit.*
>
> Henri Bourassa, Farnham, 17 September 1910

[In fifteen years, your wives will see the government agent arrive, brandishing this accursed law, and he'll say to them: "Good mother, you must give your sons, not to defend their native land, but to fight in all countries and on all the seas of the world for the British flag." And when your wives hear a few months later that an Austrian shell, a Japanese bullet or German shrapnel has disemboweled their child . . . do you think that they'll say then: "Oh well, my husband was a *rouge*\* and it was Laurier who passed that law, he did the right thing." No, your wives will curse you, and rightly so.]

The *Toronto Star* warned that the next election might see the "solid French Canadian vote arrayed against the solid vote of the other elements of the community . . . a contingency which we must all look forward to with misgivings." Realizing that his government was in danger, Laurier seized on an American offer of "reciprocity" – the old Liberal nostrum of free trade with the United States – and went into the 1911 election hoping that the economic attractions of free trade would outweigh English Canadians' anger at him on the naval issue.

---

\**Rouge*: "Red" Liberal with republican, anti-clerical, and pro-American views.

While fears about the navy remained the dominant question in Quebec, reciprocity was indeed the big issue in English Canada, but it proved not to be a vote-winner for Laurier's Liberals, at least not in the populous province of Ontario where much of the population now worked in industries that thrived behind Canada's protectionist tariffs. Moreover, the old fears that free trade was the first step toward annexation had never been fully put to rest. Rudyard Kipling cabled from London: "It is her own soul that Canada risks today" – and it didn't help Laurier when American politicians declared that they backed reciprocity because they hoped to see the day "when the American flag will float over every square foot of the British North American possessions clear to the North Pole." That would have required quite a large American flag, but many Canadians took fright nevertheless.

President Taft denied that reciprocity was the preamble to annexation and Laurier pointed to the good relations between the two countries since the settlement of the Alaskan boundary dispute almost a decade before, but the old fears won out. "The result of the election was a matter of amazement throughout the country," wrote a delighted Robert Borden: Laurier held only the Liberal stronghold of Quebec, and there were now 133 Conservatives and Nationalists to only eighty-eight Liberals. Canada's first French Canadian prime minister had finally lost his extraordinary ability to bridge the gap between English and French. At the end of the campaign he sadly remarked: "I am branded in Quebec as a traitor to the French, and in Ontario as a traitor to the English. . . . In Quebec I am branded as a Jingo, in Ontario as a Separatist. . . . I am neither. I am a Canadian." However, the Liberals demanded that the seventy-year-old Laurier remain as head of the party.

The Conservative election victory of 1911 ended all talk of free trade, but the naval question remained. (Hardly anybody except a handful of officers on the General Staff in Ottawa realized that there was an army question too, and they certainly weren't going to bring it up in public.) Robert Borden simply ignored Laurier's Naval Service Act, and recruiting stopped for the two aged British cruisers, *Rainbow* and *Niobe*, which Laurier's government had bought from Britain in order to train the personnel of a future Canadian navy. However, as eloquent as Borden had been in 1910 in urging prompt action in an emergency that might rend the empire asunder, warning that "all beyond is chaos and darkness," he suddenly remembered the value of caution once he was in power. "It is infinitely better to be right than to be in a hurry," said the new prime minister (who had a number of anti-navy Quebec ministers in his coalition government). Nonetheless, he was forced into a new naval debate by the British Admiralty (which wanted the cash donation he had promised), by the jingoes in his own party – and by the Liberals, who saw a chance to split Borden's fragile cabinet.

Borden would have been fully justified in stepping even further back from his rash original commitment, for as early as 1909 the Germans began trying to interest the British in arms control schemes whereby both countries would limit their battleship building. It eventually became clear that Germany had neither the will nor the resources for an all-out naval building race with Britain, and by 1914, with the British well ahead in the race, London and Berlin were actually discussing a "naval building holiday." But by then a great deal of suspicion and hostility had been generated between the two countries – and in the intervening years there was enormous pressure on both the British and colonial governments to get more battleships into the water as quickly as possible.

In order to gain firsthand evidence that could convince his Nationalist and Conservative allies in Quebec of the seriousness of the naval crisis, Borden travelled to England in 1911. A couple of months earlier Winston Churchill, now First Lord of the Admiralty, had been defiantly declaring: "Whatever may happen abroad there will be no whining heard; no signals of distress will be hoisted, no cries for help or succour will go out." But in fact the British government was now practically fawning on the Canadians. The Royal Navy went all out to dazzle Borden: "In the yacht *Enchantress* they passed between the lines of this mighty fleet (315 ships), stretching for five miles of defensive naval power. . . . They watched a display of aeroplanes and hydro-aeroplanes performing marvellous evolutions against the blue-grey sky, saw the submarines make a snake-like attack on the Dreadnoughts and witnessed an almost terrifying attack by Destroyers."

Borden didn't disappoint his hosts. At a banquet at the Royal Colonial Institute he said that he understood the importance of British supremacy on the seas: "I have always held the conviction, and hold it today, that the sea defences of the Empire can best be secured by one Navy." (But then he added, in a characteristically Canadian footnote: "I would like you to understand that Canada does not propose to be an adjunct, even of the British Empire.") Churchill, ever the politician, told the Canadian prime minister that he was "ready to play the game," and in September 1911 he sent Borden a secret Admiralty memorandum for use in bringing his own cabinet around.

The arguments Churchill supplied to Borden in 1911 were very similar to those used to justify the nuclear arms race of our own time, with Dreadnoughts standing in for missiles. British naval supremacy, of course, was "defensive," while a German navy of even remotely comparable size would be offensive (in both senses of the word). Technological change was the real destabilizing factor, but it tended to be interpreted as an enemy plot, and both navies played the numbers game to prove to their public that they needed more ships. Larger questions, such as why two countries with no territorial claims against each other and little to gain from fighting each other should be in a naval race at all, were simply not discussed. Public opinion responded admirably in Britain – "The Admiralty had demanded six ships; the economists offered four; and we finally compromised on eight," as Churchill later recalled – and he hoped for a similar response in the ex-colonies.

In the secret memorandum he provided to Borden, Churchill stressed that Britain would soon lose its naval superiority entirely if it did not get more resources to build capital ships. The arithmetic was as dodgy as the logic – it was rather like the comparisons of military strength put out nowadays by the Pentagon at budget time – but Borden read it to his cabinet, hoping to swing them behind a $35 million emergency donation to Britain for three new Dreadnoughts. It didn't work: F. D. Monk, the Quebec Conservative leader, insisted that this matter must be decided by plebiscite. Borden quite rightly suspected that Monk was simply afraid of the furore his proposed Naval Aid Bill would arouse in Quebec, but no amount of pleading, bullying, or denouncing Monk's lack of "backbone" could induce the Quebecker to change his position.

In October 1912 Monk resigned on this issue, and his departure enabled the prime minister to convince his other Quebec ministers to go along with his Naval Aid Bill (although very reluctantly). In return for Canada's $35 million contribution, Borden hoped for increased Canadian influence on British foreign policy in the form of a permanent representative on the Committee of Imperial Defence. Laurier, now Opposition leader, was scathing about Borden's desire for a seat at the high table. "I understand," he said in the Commons, "that my Right Honourable friend proposes to the British Admiralty that there should be a representative of the Canadian government all the time in England to confer with the Secretary of State for Foreign Affairs on all questions on which war may probably arise. If this is done for Canada, it must be done for Australia, for New Zealand, for South Africa, and for Newfoundland, and I doubt very much that the Secretary of State for Foreign Affairs would receive much assistance from such a multitude of advisors." Faced with a Liberal filibuster Robert Borden rose in Parliament in December 1912, his neck swathed in bandages to cover a bad outbreak of boils, and introduced closure to force his Naval Aid Bill through the House.

On the question of a Canadian representative on the Committee of Imperial Defence, however, the British entirely agreed with Sir Wilfrid Laurier and Borden's other opponents. Later in December 1912 the Secretary of State for the Colonies gently explained to Prime Minister Borden that imperial defence policy "is and must remain the sole prerogative of [the British] Cabinet, subject to the support of the House of Commons." In other words: We asked for your money, not your advice.

❖

> With the mention of Canada, drinks were forgotten. Two or three Germans produced the noon editions of Berlin newspapers with large headlines announcing Canada's action. "Canada gives three battleships to Britain," "$35,000,000 voted by Canada for British Navy," etc. I was at once plied with questions demanding to know why the Canadian Parliament had voted such a large sum to the British Navy.
>
> Walter Riddell, *World Security by Conference*

Walter Riddell was a young Canadian, born in Ontario and educated at the University of Manitoba, who was travelling in Europe on the pretext of doing "further researches for . . . a doctor's degree at Columbia University" when Borden's Naval Aid Bill was passed by the House of Commons in late 1912. He was in Berlin, having lunch in a businessmen's restaurant, when the news reached Germany, and he had just contrived to make himself known as a Canadian to the whole restaurant through the simple device of ordering milk rather than beer with his meal.

Confronted with a barrage of hairy-chested mockery about consuming "baby food" by the dozen Germans sharing the long table with him, together with guesses that he must be English or American to be so effete, Riddell drew himself up to his full height and proclaimed that he was neither English nor American. He was a Canadian, the citizen of a country where one was not held up to ridicule for drinking either milk or beer, unless one drank too much of the latter. Whereupon the entire restaurant began listening, and the subject instantly changed to Canada's Naval Aid Bill.

As he was leaving the table after a lengthy argument, a tall, dignified-looking man who turned out to be a manufacturer invited Riddell to join him and two banker friends at the opening of a new beer-garden that evening. "All Berlin was talking about the amazing act of the Canadian Parliament," the German industrialist said; perhaps he could throw some light on it.

> Hardly were we seated in this huge new *biergarten* when they began to ply me with questions as to why Canada was presenting the British Government with $35,000,000 for the Navy. I began by saying that we felt we received a great deal of protection from the British Navy. . . . I then reminded them that after all we were largely British. . . . I remarked casually that if Germany attacked Great Britain she would have to fight Canada too.
>
> This was too much for the banker who damned the British for being a nation of cunning schemers, settling their surplus population in their overseas possessions in order, when occasion required, to be able to bring them back to help fight their battles in Europe. While the Germans, he bitterly complained, were compelled to see their large emigration being absorbed by other countries and forever lost to the Fatherland.
>
> After my hosts had consumed seven steins of beer each, the party broke up. It was about 2 a.m. when they dropped me at my hotel.
>
> Walter Riddell, *World Security by Conference*

Riddell would later come to understand a great deal more about why wars occurred, and as a Canadian diplomat in the 1930s he would finally and quite deliberately destroy his own career by making an extraordinary lone stand in favour of the kind of measures that might really preserve peace. But that was far in the future in 1912, and he was then pretty representative of educated English Canadian opinion: kinship with Britain was an argument that overrode all others and required no further elaboration or justification.

That was just as well, because the old pragmatic argument for the link with Britain was hard to buy any more without some kind of emotional assistance. The assumption that imperial defence included the defence of Canada itself was still accepted almost universally in Canada, but the old bargain was really long dead and starting to smell. By now the British had brought themselves to the point of admitting explicitly (but only in their secret documents) that they had no intention of helping Canada in the event of an attack by the United States, the only plausible military threat to Canadian interests.

The question of Britain's responsibility for Canadian defence had been repeatedly discussed (and generally fudged) by the Committee of Imperial Defence (C.I.D.) in London during the preceding decade, but it is safe to say that by 1905 any serious consideration of sending help to Canada had been abandoned. That was the year when the Foreign Secretary, Sir Edward Grey, prevented the C.I.D. from discussing American infringements of the Rush-Bagot Treaty that limited the number and size of warships on the Great Lakes by stating that "he had no desire to discuss the question of what action would be taken by us in the event of a war with the United States."

That was a perfectly reasonable foreign policy for Britain – nor was it particularly bad for Canadian interests, since in fact the United States was very unlikely to embark on the conquest of Canada. But the British were guiltily conscious of the fact that many Canadians had not yet figured that out, and that they were exploiting obsolete Canadian fears of American attack in order to get Canadian support in *their* wars. Thus, for example, Sir William Nicholson, the Chief of the Imperial General Staff, objected to sending Ottawa a document in 1912 saying that war with the United States was "in the last degree unlikely," and that Canadian coasts were safe from attack by any other power because *America* would intervene to protect them, on the grounds that this was inconsistent (to say the least) with London's continual encouragement to the Canadians to build up their own military power. That power was wanted for imperial defence purposes, and so the offending admission was deleted from the document sent to Ottawa.

The same conscious distortion of strategic realities was becoming British policy in personal contacts with Canadian politicians. In the summer of 1912, for example, when a joint C.I.D. meeting with Canadian ministers was being considered, Maurice Hankey, secretary of the C.I.D., warned Prime Minister Asquith that they must at all costs avoid discussing the possibility of war with the United States with the Canadians:

> The peculiar delicacy of this question is that in 1905 the Committee of Imperial Defence came to the conclusion that the Admiralty could not either themselves undertake the Defence of the Canadian Lakes, nor recommend any measures by which Canada could herself undertake their defence (a conclusion which vitiates any measure of military defence) – *and this conclusion was not discussed with Canada, nor communicated to her Government.*

The Canadian debate about contributions to British imperial defence continued in blissful ignorance of all this, even among Laurier's Liberals. Laurier, now leader of the Opposition, simply didn't believe there was really an emergency: "The armament of the great powers has compelled England . . . in order to maintain her security in her own waters . . . to withdraw some of her naval forces from distant seas." The solution, Laurier insisted, was to create a Canadian navy to protect Canadian waters, not to pay for a few British Dreadnoughts.

However, apart from French Canada and a handful of English Canadians, few "colonials" were willing to question the imperial government's judgement on questions of war and peace. By 1912 Australia, New Zealand, and Malaya had already commissioned twelve major warships for the imperial fleet. By 1913, when the naval psychosis was at its height, even the Fiji Islands and Newfoundland were offering contributions. Only Canada was dragging its feet, and Borden was desperate to bring the country into line. But it was to no avail: although the House of Commons had finally passed his Naval Aid Bill in late 1912, the Liberal-controlled

Senate killed it in May 1913. "This House is not justified in giving its assent to this Bill," declared the Senate (not without malice aforethought), "until it is submitted to the judgement of the country."

> *Honneur au Sénat! Il a bien mérité de la patrie Canadienne. . . . Ainsi, après quatre ans de projets de toute sorte, de propositions et de contre-propositions, de motions, d'amendements, et de sous-amendements, de multiples invocations au dieu de l'Empire . . . tous consacrés à faire valoir "le mode le plus efficace" de contribution canadienne aux guerres de l'Empire, il ne reste rien, rien – ni marine canadienne, ni dreadnoughts, ni contribution à l'Angleterre.*

Henri Bourassa, 1913

[Glory to the Senate! It is worthy of the Canadian fatherland. . . . Thus, after four years of all sorts of projects, of proposals and counter-proposals, of motions, and amendments, and sub-amendments, and of numerous invocations of the god of Empire . . . all destined to find "the best way" to make a Canadian contribution to the wars of the Empire, nothing remains, nothing – neither Canadian navy, nor Dreadnoughts, nor a contribution to England.]

Borden was still determined to make a contribution to the defence of the empire, but his fragile coalition might not survive another election on the naval issue. The prime minister muttered darkly about reforming the Senate, and both he and Laurier visited Toronto, each virtually campaigning. Laurier stuck to his guns: "I regret nothing. . . . It seems to me that defence, like charity, begins at home." The seven thousand Liberal supporters who had come out to see the old leader cheered, but it was a self-selecting audience; the general mood of English Canada was really one of enthusiastic jingoism.

When Prime Minister Borden visited the city two weeks later, staid Toronto let itself go. According to some estimates, one hundred thousand Torontonians lined the streets, and ten thousand people jammed into the Toronto Arena, all waving Union Jacks, to hear Borden speak. He described the tensions in Europe, explaining that there was simply no time to wait for ships to be built in Canada. Laurier's concept of a Canadian Naval Service was "an absolute negation and refusal of any direct voice or influence by Canada in the Councils of the Empire."

He warned his audience that the Liberal policy "pointed first to neutrality and then to independence." Both ideas were utterly alien to the good people of Toronto, many of whom had close family links to Britain. But while independence, to conservative English-speaking Ontarians, seemed a merely frivolous notion, neutrality was quite shocking: being neutral was letting the side down. And although Laurier's stance in 1913 was not really neutralist, it was beginning to sound that way in order to be more acceptable to French Canadians. The racial split was widening.

Borden stayed with his theme right through 1913. When he spoke in Halifax (his home riding) in September, he harshly condemned Laurier's Naval Service Act of 1910, saying that it "contemplated the separation of Canadian Naval forces from the Empire and their neutrality in time of war." He was certain that his own Naval Aid Bill would eventually be reinstated: "The union of the Empire cannot be maintained if its greatest Dominion adopts the policy of scampering under the cover of neutrality in time of danger or trouble." As things turned out, though, neutrality might not have been a bad idea.

Both Borden and Laurier were Canadian nationalists in their different ways: Borden seeking more Canadian influence at the heart of the empire and Laurier trying to retain as much decision-making power in Ottawa as possible. Perhaps Henri Bourassa would not have accepted either one as a nationalist, but then he didn't have to deal with the political realities of English Canada. It was the fantasy world of the *Boy's Own Annual*: the great majority of English Canadians were convinced that any war Britain got involved in would be just, and very many believed that war, or at least militarism, was a positive moral good. And although Borden himself was not a militarist, he had little choice but to give the portfolio of Militia and National Defence to Colonel Sam Hughes, a Conservative politician and part-time soldier who most certainly was.

Hughes had founded an entire political career on being an enthusiastic promoter of the militia, and during the Boer War, when his offer to raise a volunteer force was rejected by the British, he had invented a job for himself with the railway line of communications forces there. The British commander-in-chief, Field Marshal Lord Roberts, tried beyond endurance by Hughes's bumptious and loudly stated conviction of his own inestimable military worth (especially compared to the plodding and limited intellects of mere professional soldiers), had eventually sent him home, but that simply confirmed Hughes in his lifelong belief that the only thing wrong with the British Empire was the fact that it was run by the English. It was, nevertheless, the best game in town for a militarist, and in 1913 Hughes told an audience in Napanee, Ontario, why Canada needed a strong militia and an unconditional commitment to take part in the wars of the empire:

> To make the youth of Canada self-controlled, erect, decent and patriotic through military training, instead of growing up as under present conditions of no control, into young ruffians or young gadabouts; to ensure peace by national preparedness for war; to make the military camps and drill halls throughout Canada clean, wholesome, sober and attractive to boys and young men; to give that final touch to imperial unity, and crown the arch of responsible government by an inter-Imperial Parliament dealing only with Imperial affairs.

In 1913 an unprecedented three-quarters of the 74,000 men enrolled in Canadian militia regiments actually received a couple of weeks' training in camp – and Sam Hughes (who had recently promoted himself to major-general) was not in the least ambivalent about the fact that they would almost certainly be sent to fight overseas if war came. He delighted in sub-Nietzschean formulas that exalted mass action and war: "The old Saxon days have returned," he was wont to exult, "when the whole nation must be armed." And his audiences lapped it up; English Canada was ready to "fight the good fight." Like the hymn, however, that was an English, Protestant view of things – and the larger forces in the world were moving strongly against England.

❖

> If there is ever another war in Europe, it will come out of some damn silly thing in the Balkans.
> Prince Otto von Bismarck, 1898

It is customary nowadays to attribute the coming of the First World War to the interlocking European alliances, and the even more intricately interlinked railway timetables for delivering millions of mobilized troops to the frontiers of the great powers. Once a Balkan spark set the machinery in motion, nobody could stop it. That is perfectly true, in the same sense that if you slip on a banana skin, then the banana (or its former owner) can be blamed for your fall. But you also fall because of the law of gravity.

By 1914 everything had been in place for a world war for years: the alliances, the huge armies of reservists, and the mobilization plans. Psychologically, too, everybody was ready for a war – and it was basically going to be about whether Britain would remain the superpower of the international system.

For the preceding hundred years Britain had dominated Europe by commercial means far more effectively than Spain and France, its predecessors as reigning superpower, had ever managed to do by military means. The industrial revolution began in Britain fifty years before it spread to the rest of Europe, which gave the British a huge lead in wealth and technological expertise. Moreover, as an island, Britain could pour most of its military spending into a navy that made it invulnerable at home and dominant in all the world's oceans, while its continental rivals also had to pay for large land armies to protect themselves against their neighbours. As a result, Britain was able to pursue a policy of splendid isolation throughout most of the nineteenth century: it simply didn't bother making long-term alliances on the continent. (In fact, the invulnerability and sheer lack of involvement of Britain, the dominant power in the system, may be a major reason why the mid-nineteenth-century wars never coalesced into a world war in the usual way.)

It was only toward the end of the century that the rapid industrial growth of continental powers like France, Russia and, above all, Germany, finally caused alarm in Britain. That was what prompted Joe Chamberlain's attempts as Colonial Secretary to create a unified military system drawing on all the empire's resources – and soon afterward, Britain began to make alliances in Europe. Its skills in this art were rusty, but Britain had after all been the nucleus and paymaster of all the alliances that had denied France hegemony over Europe in three previous world wars, and it did not take British diplomats long to get the hang of it again. When they made their first overtures, shortly after the turn of the century, *every* major power was Britain's potential enemy: there had been war scares with both France and Russia in the preceding few years, and the German Empire's aspirations to a "place in the sun" made it a possible opponent, too. The essential task (although the diplomats never put it so coarsely) was to decide which country was most dangerous to British supremacy in the long run.

> The question which calls for an answer is whether Germany is to become a world-power or is to decline. . . .
> The political position of the German Empire does not in any way correspond with the pre-eminence of German civilization and with the economic importance of Germanism abroad. . . . We must obtain an unshakeable foundation for our position on the Continent of Europe by enlarging the sphere of our power in Europe itself.
>
> General Friedrich von Bernhardi, *Our Future –*
> *A Word of Warning*

Britain's choice of enemy fell quite naturally on Germany, the newest of the great powers. Having been united only in 1870, Germany had missed out on the division of the world among the European empires, and ended up with nothing except a few unpromising African colonies, half of Samoa and a quarter of New Guinea. This did no discernible harm to Germany's economy (whose output overtook Britain's about 1900), but many Germans nevertheless felt deprived and wanted a "fairer share." Not only was Germany Britain's major rival for the position of Europe's greatest industrial power, but certain aspects of Germany's national ambition, like its drive to build a great navy, directly challenged the foundations of Britain's own power. So, with the main threat identified, the British Foreign Office set about making alliances with Germany's potential enemies.

> The basis of the Entente is the necessity that no single power shall succeed in dominating the Continent.
>
> Yves Guyot, London *Standard*, July 1914

The Austrian Empire had been allied to Germany since 1879, because it was a Balkan power that needed support against Russian ambitions there. That made Germany and Russia potential enemies, so it followed that Russia was a potential British ally. France was also a potential ally for Britain, despite the centuries-long history of war between the two countries, because the French had lost the provinces of Alsace and Lorraine to Germany in the war of 1870, and were still seething with resentment.

It all happened quite swiftly. The French and the Russians were already allies. Britain and France took some time to end their differences over colonial spheres of influence (they had gone to the brink of war over the Sudan as late as 1898), but once they had settled who was to get which bits of Africa, nothing stood in the way of a military agreement between them (the *Entente Cordiale*) in 1904. It took Britain rather longer to come to terms with Germany's other potential enemy, Russia. There had been intense rivalry between Britain and Russia for decades over the control of Central Asia, since London was convinced that Moscow was trying to creep up on Britain's empire in India. However, by 1907 the two countries had defined the boundaries of their respective spheres of influence in Asia, and the alliances were complete: Britain, France, and Russia against Germany, the "have-not" on the way up, and Austria-Hungary, the ramshackle "have-not" on the way down. After that, it was just a question of waiting for the starting gun.

The alliances had nothing to do with a common political ideology: France was a republic, Britain was a constitutional monarchy, and Russia was an incompetent pre-totalitarian autocracy. In the past, the consequences of the wars fought by such alliances had been messy but tolerable –a few hundred thousand lives snuffed out, or at worst a few million, and a few borders rearranged, followed by a peace treaty that ratified the changes wrought by the war. By 1914, however, the world was a different place, even if its statesmen hadn't noticed.

### CHAPTER TEN

# A Long Way from Home

Anyone going to the Yugoslavian town of Sarajevo today will find two brass footprints set into the sidewalk near the bridge. They mark the place where the youthful Serbian terrorist Gavrilo Princip stood when he shot Archduke Franz Ferdinand, the heir to the Austrian throne, and his wife, Sophie, on 28 June 1914. As the open car accelerated away, Ferdinand cried, "Sophie, Sophie, don't die. Live for the children," but soon they were both dead. The double murder made the headlines even in Canada, but the Foreign Office in London thought it was just one more Balkan assassination.

The whole previous decade had been filled with crises and war scares, but in 1914 relations between the great powers were actually better than they had been for many years. The Baghdad Railway, which had long been a major cause of Anglo-German friction, was now supported by both British and German finance. Far from quarrelling over colonial territories, Britain and Germany had recently revised their secret agreement of 1898 in order to give Germany a bigger share of Portugal's colonies if the Portuguese sold out. The German Reichstag was considering Churchill's proposal for a "holiday" in the Dreadnought race, and it seemed more concerned about the industrial side effects of stopping the German naval building programme than about the strategic consequences. Meanwhile the German and British navies jointly celebrated the opening of the Kiel Canal, the Russian Tsar was planning a summer holiday in Germany, and the German Kaiser was coming to England for the regatta at Cowes.

In Canada, people and politicians were mainly concerned about the depression that was putting an end to Canada's exuberant growth. At the end of the spring sitting of Parliament, which was taken up almost entirely with railway questions, Laurier taunted Prime Minister Borden about the alleged "Naval Crisis" that had dominated so much of the House's time in the past few years: "Emergency? Who speaks today of an emergency?" Laurier asked. And the highlight of the summer was supposed to be the farewell tour of the popular Governor General, the Duke of Connaught.

❖

It is difficult . . . to discover any cause of hostility between the European Great Powers in 1914. But there was one cause of estrangement. This was the system of Alliances which distanced the Great Powers unnecessarily. These Alliances dragged Powers into wars which did not concern them.

A. J. P. Taylor

Nobody intended to have a great war in 1914, but the Austrian Empire was determined to punish Serbia, where many senior officers and politicians were involved in the Black Hand, the secret society that had armed and briefed the terrorists who killed Franz Ferdinand. Terrorist assassinations of prominent people were even more common in the decades before 1914 than they are now, and the violent hatreds of the various Balkan nationalities were as fertile a source of crises then as the Middle East is today. Serbia and its semi-official terrorists in 1914 had a reputation in the world comparable in many respects to that of countries like Libya and Syria in contemporary international affairs, and the Austrian response – outrage, and an eager grasping of the long-awaited pretext for massive retaliation – can be compared without too much distortion to the American air raids on Libya in 1986. Most of the time, such events fill the headlines for a few weeks, and then vanish leaving few traces behind. There is always, however, the question of alliances.

A war against Serbia was quite popular with most Austrians, but they were afraid that Russia, which saw itself as the protector of the Slavs, would come to Serbia's aid. So Austria waited until it got a guarantee of support from its German ally before handing Serbia an ultimatum. That took almost a month.

> Germany cannot and must not give Russia time to mobilise, or she will be obliged to maintain on the Eastern frontier a force which would leave her in a position of equality, if not of inferiority, to that of France.
>
> General Helmuth von Moltke, quoted by M. Cambon,
> the French ambassador to London, 1914

The German guarantee to Austria was intended to deter Russian military intervention and confine the war to the Balkans – but if by chance deterrence failed and a general war broke out in Europe, Germany's plans were fairly well known. Faced with powerful enemies both east and west, the Germans planned to knock France out of the war quickly, before the Russians were ready to invade them. Since the Franco-German border was heavily fortified, the Germans intended to gain time by attacking France through neutral Belgium. If France was to withstand the German attack, British help was essential, but although secret plans for cooperation had been drawn up by the British and French general staffs, there was no formal British guarantee that troops would actually be sent. The French were understandably anxious.

On 23 July, the day that Austria sent its ultimatum to Serbia, the Duke of Connaught and his family left for Western Canada. On the twenty-eighth, Austria declared war on Serbia. The Governor General was in Banff when the alarming news arrived on the following day that Russia had mobilized against Austria. It was just a Balkan quarrel, but both Austria and Russia had allies elsewhere. Germany demanded that Russia demobilize again within twelve hours, but the Tsar refused. On 31 July the German ambassador to France officially asked what Paris would do if war broke out between Germany and France's ally, Russia. President Raymond Poincaré of France, who knew that his country would fight in order to preserve its Russian alliance, promptly wrote to King George V asking for a public statement of British solidarity. Poincaré was afraid that a general European war was now inevitable unless Britain frightened Germany into backing down by openly stating that it would fight alongside France. And while Poincaré approached the King privately, Colonel François Rousset of the French Higher War College publicly reminded Britain of its implicit commitments in the columns of the London *Standard*:

(1) The British Expeditionary Corps should number at the very least 100,000 men, in order to . . . [counter] the effects of an almost certain violation of Belgian territory.

(2) This same Expeditionary Corps should be landed on the Continent from the very beginning of the operations, if not before . . .

But King George hedged, and meanwhile Russian troops were moving toward the borders of Austria. Germany declared war on Russia on 1 August, and on France on the third. The Germans then sent an ultimatum to Belgium demanding free passage across its territory; when the Belgians refused, Britain's dilemma was solved. The German violation of Belgium's neutrality, which had been guaranteed by Britain, gave London an unassailable reason for doing what its secret pre-war talks with the French had already envisaged, and what its fear of a victorious and more powerful Germany impelled it to do anyway. At midnight on 4 August, Britain's ultimatum to Germany expired, and the empire was at war.

As I was leaving, [the German Chancellor] said that the blow of Great Britain joining Germany's enemies was all the greater that almost up to the last moment he and his Government had been working with us and supporting our efforts to maintain peace between Austria and Russia. I admitted that that had been the case, and said that it was part of the tragedy which saw the two nations fall apart just at the moment when relations between them had been more friendly and cordial than they had been for years.

Last interview of the British Ambassador, Sir Edward Goschen, with Chancellor Theobald von Bethmann-Hollweg, Berlin, 4 August 1914

Every step in the crisis was a logical response to the one before, in orthodox military and diplomatic terms; but seen as a whole, it hardly seemed a good reason for eight million people to die.

> The Alliances were supposed to promote peace and to protect their members. The First World War, and its outbreak, demonstrated that the Alliances were the cause of great wars. This was not the last time this was shown.
>
> The deterrent is the contemporary version of the Alliances. It, too, will be the cause of great wars. Men will ask afterwards: "Why did they do it?" There will be no convincing answer.
>
> A. J. P. Taylor

❖

In Montreal, on 1 and 3 August, huge crowds paraded in the streets waving British and French flags, singing "La Marseillaise" and "Rule Britannia." In Winnipeg, Regina, Edmonton, Vancouver, and Victoria cheering crowds filled the streets. In Paris, France, *Le Temps* (a now defunct newspaper that was rather like the *Globe and Mail*, only more so) saw something deeply poetic in the fact that English Canadian blood would now be shed for France, while French Canadians bled for England. And in Paris, Ontario, it was the Boer War all over again:

> A crowd began to mill about Grand River Street. Prominent citizens trumpeted their considered opinions. One said: "The war will be over within three months. The Russians will roll in from the east and the British and French from the west, and they'll meet in Berlin before Christmas." The crowd vigorously cheered his perspicacity.
>
> Then the Citizens' Band formed up in front of the fire hall and began to play martial music. The crowd grew larger. It sang "The Maple Leaf Forever", "Rule Britannia", and "God Save the King". Members of the Scout Bugle Band ran home for their bugles. As Bugler Grenville Whitby rushed from the house, his father said: "War is a serious thing. You shouldn't be out tonight making a noise." Grenville heedlessly ran down the street, blow-

ing shrill blasts. The crowd formed itself into a procession, and led by blaring bugles and thumping drums, paraded along William, Willow, and Dundas Streets. Torches smoked and flared, and in their light, eyes gleamed with exultation.

Donald A. Smith, *At the Forks of the Grand, Volume II*

"We are British subjects," said Sir Wilfrid Laurier in the House of Commons on 18 August, "and today we are face to face with the consequences which are involved in that proud fact." By then Borden's government had already offered to send one division (22,500 men) to Europe, had secretly bought two submarines that had just been built for the Chilean navy, and had placed Canada's two decrepit training cruisers at the disposal of the Royal Navy. Perhaps the government could have responded a little less eagerly, but it could not really have stayed out of the war unless it had decided to declare its independence then and there. Nobody had that in mind, not even the most ardent of Quebec Nationalists.

Canada, an Anglo-French nation, tied to England and France by a thousand ethnic, social, intellectual and economic threads, has a vital interest in the maintenance of the prestige, power and world action of France and England.

Henri Bourassa, *Le Devoir*, 8 September 1914

It is doubtful whether sentimental ties can justly be called "vital interests," and there were no practical reasons why Canada's long-term interests depended on the maintenance of British power and prestige (except that old shadow of concern about the United States). But plenty of short-term interests were involved – many Canadian and British business interests were intimately linked, for example – and in any case Canada was not a fully independent nation in 1914. It was automatically at war when the empire was. Henri Bourassa, like many French Canadians, would probably have preferred to emulate the policy of the United States and declare Canada neutral, but he recognized that emotional, commercial and legal factors meant that Canada had to support the Entente. However, he stressed that it should do so "to the measure of its strength, and by appropriate means" – which did not include sending troops to Europe.

> The Canadian territory is nowhere exposed to the attacks of the
> belligerent nations. As an independent nation, Canada would
> today enjoy perfect security. . . . It is then the duty of England to
> defend Canada and not that of Canada to defend England.
>
> Henri Bourassa, *Le Devoir*, 8 September 1914

But it was no use to argue. The Boer War had created the precedent
for sending Canadian troops overseas. The military staff work in the intervening years had created both the assumption that it would be done again
and the organization for doing it. And the national mood, at least in
English Canada, would not have stood for anything less. There was probably not a single person in Canada in August 1914 (indeed, there were
not even very many in Europe) who genuinely understood how the war
had come about, but it didn't matter. It was this sense of loyalty and
identification with Britain and France (as Pogo would say: "them is us")
that brought the crowds out. Besides, nobody had the faintest idea what
a twentieth-century European war was going to be like.

> Q. *Do you remember why you joined up?*
> Spirit of adventure, mostly, I think, at that time. Because I don't
> think one knew, had any idea what was ahead, you know. And I
> think that was the only thing that interested me then, was to see
> the world.
>
> Mabel Rutherford, Toronto, Nursing sister

> Q. *Did you feel at the time that there was any distinction between
> Canada and Great Britain?*
> No, no. The Empire was at stake. . . . They were peace-loving
> people, but the thing was on the barrel-head, and you almost
> unquestioningly said: "Well, if they need me, I'll go."
>
> Ted Watt, Victoria, Royal Canadian Navy

Although there was a tiny handful of pacifists in Canada, English
Canadian popular culture was quite overtly militarist and jingoist. The
young had no doubts about the war – nor did most of their elders. In 1914
they were not just English Canadians; they were *British* Canadians. So
were some of the French Canadians, at least rhetorically.

> When the call comes, our answer goes at once, and it goes in the
> classic language of the British answer to the call of duty: "Ready,
> aye, ready".
>
> Sir Wilfrid Laurier, 8 August 1914

There was no real debate about whether Canada should be in the war. The avowals of profound loyalty to the empire from politicians like Laurier and Borden were echoed quite sincerely by ordinary English Canadians like Ted Watt and Mabel Rutherford. But the response of ordinary French Canadians was another story entirely.

❖

It was not a question of language or culture, basically, but simply of geographical perspective – of where people thought they lived in the world. When the call for volunteers went out, recent immigrants from France enlisted just as readily as the most enthusiastic English Canadians: the town of Trochu in Alberta, which had been settled by French ex-cavalrymen in the years before the war, virtually emptied in 1914 as the men went back to fight for their mother country. But French Canada itself had long ago abandoned the delusion that it was part of Europe, and few French Canadians saw any reason to fight in its wars. They also soon became aware of a particularly good reason for remaining civilian: the Minister of Militia and National Defence, Colonel Sam Hughes.

Hughes was a bullying Ontario Orangeman who neither knew nor trusted French Canadians. Colonel Willoughby Gwatkins, on loan from the British army as Chief of the General Staff, had prepared careful mobilization plans in 1912 that would have included French Canadian participation, but Hughes was determined to do everything his own way: finally he had a real war and the power to run it.

Casting aside the existing mobilization plans, which would have carried out the first phase of the process at the local militia centres, Hughes simply sent telegrams directly to every battalion in the militia, inviting the hundred-odd part-time colonels who commanded them to show up with as many volunteers as they could find. They were invited to bring them, moreover, not to the perfectly adequate training area already in existence at Camp Petawawa in the Ottawa valley, but rather to a wilderness area at Valcartier near Quebec City. (This served no military purpose, but it did serve the business interests of Sir William Mackenzie and Donald Mann, two good friends of Hughes who happened to own the only railway link to Valcartier.) And the colonels received no guidance about how many officers and men might be required from their area for the First Contingent, nor any instructions about bringing equipment and supplies with them.

Hughes personally supervised the creation of a central training depot at Valcartier, transforming woods and sandy valleys into a huge training camp with streets, buildings, telephones, and four miles of rifle ranges in about three weeks: his ability to bring order out of chaos was almost as great as his propensity for creating chaos in the first place. As a staff officer – not really his job, but one he promptly appropriated – he was a prime example of the category that the German military philosopher General von Moltke classified as the most dangerous of all: industrious and stupid.

Hughes considered himself a military genius, despite the fact that he had no serious military training or experience. Indeed, he considered his ignorance of conventional military procedures and practices to be a positive virtue, since he completely believed the southern Ontario myth, a hallowed relic of 1812, which maintained that the sturdy, independent-minded Canadian volunteer, however lacking in training, was intrinsically superior to the over-trained and unimaginative regular soldier. Throughout his career he seized every opportunity to demean and publicly humiliate Canada's relatively few professional soldiers – so in 1914, instead of using the Royal Canadian Regiment, which contained most of the trained infantrymen in Canada's three-thousand-strong Permanent Force, to train the flood of volunteers, he immediately sent it to Bermuda to replace a British regiment heading for France. (It did not reach France itself until 1916.)

At Valcartier, therefore, it was the blind leading the blind, and Hughes largely ignored even the structures and skills that were available in the militia. He simply disregarded the existing militia units and their traditions, creating entirely new battalions for the Canadian Expeditionary Force (C.E.F.) that were identified solely by their numbers and trained from scratch at Valcartier. In his appointments of commanders personal favouritism was the only visible criterion: at least one-third of all the officers who went overseas in 1914-15 had not yet met even the very modest militia training standard for their rank. And since many more militia officers and men had shown up at Valcartier than would be needed for the single infantry division that was to sail for Europe in October, there was tremendous chaos.

In fact, one rather suspects that it was Sam Hughes's instinct to create chaos quite deliberately, since that was the environment that afforded the most scope for the kind of behaviour he revelled in. The autumn of 1914 presented him with the opportunity to dispense patronage on a scale that he had never previously dared to imagine, and he seized it with both hands. The relatively scarce jobs for officers in the First Canadian Division were allocated almost entirely on the basis of friendship rather than professional competence (with the inevitable result that "everybody was at everybody's throat," as one militia officer put it) – and Hughes even created an entire parallel structure of "supernumerary officers" who would go overseas with the division although they had no jobs to do. Units were created, disbanded, and reformed again at Hughes's whim. He spent most of his time at Valcartier, and when he wasn't holding court to receive the petitions of officers seeking posts of command he was often to be found galloping around the camp, shouting orders and impartially cursing everybody as he went.

> From time to time during the mobilization and training of the First Contingent at Valcartier, there were disturbing reports as to the conduct of the Minister of Militia at Valcartier. On September 16, the Governor-General reported to me that Hughes' language to his officers had been violent and insulting.
>
> Prime Minister Robert Borden, *Memoirs, Volume 1*

> Mr Borden is a most lovely fellow, as gentle-hearted as a girl.
>
> Sam Hughes, 1914

Borden did not have a high opinion of Hughes: "while he was a man of marked ability and sound judgement in many respects, his temperament was so peculiar, and his actions and language so unusual on many occasions, that one was inclined to doubt his usefulness as a Minister." But whether because of his gentle heart or his fear of Hughes's powerful allies in the "militia lobby" and the Ontario wing of the Conservative Party, Borden did not remove Hughes. Instead the "general" was left free to swagger around in uniform, blustering and posturing – and he did not even consent to organize the relatively few French-speaking volunteers who risked placing themselves in his power into a single francophone battalion. Out of some thirty-three thousand men who sailed for Europe in the First Contingent on 3 October 1914, only 1,245 were French-speaking – and by the time the contingent reached France as the First Canadian Division, only one of its forty-eight infantry companies was French-speaking. French Canadians were profoundly unimpressed.

Out of personal conviction or self-interest, individual French Canadians tried to swim against the tide. Dr. Arthur Mignault of Montreal, for one, offered to contribute $50,000 towards raising a French-speaking regiment. Borden's government went along with the proposal, and Mignault's efforts were blessed by Sir Wilfrid Laurier and a number of other French Canadian politicians, but it wasn't quite enough. When the 22nd Battalion sailed from Quebec in 1915 with the Second Contingent, it had to be brought up to strength by drafting in French Canadian recruits from other units raised in Quebec.

But it wasn't just the French Canadians who were reluctant. Right from the start, there were very big differences in the rate of volunteering: far more came from English-speaking areas than French, of course, but also more from the West than the East, and more from the rootless cities, where the newspapers had the greatest influence, than from the settled rural areas. In fact, native-born Canadians of every sort, apart from the very young, the adventurous, and the economically desperate, seemed somewhat reluctant to go and fight the Germans.

At the start, too, it was easy to find socially acceptable reasons not to volunteer. In 1914, for example, farmers still needed their children's labour, and since Britain depended heavily on Canadian agricultural products, they could always argue that their sons were more valuable to the war effort at home. And if all else failed, you could pretend you wanted to enlist and then get your mother to write you a note. In the early days of the war, volunteers would be turned away if their wives or mothers wrote a letter proving that their menfolk were needed at home.

Our Canadian women should realise that their objections, unless made for good cause, are highly unpatriotic. The privilege of objection was granted to prevent abuse in enlistment by married men, but if Canada is to maintain her independence the Canadian soldier must do his duty and his wife should not restrain him from selfish motives.

Colonel E. W. B. Morrison, in a public protest,
19 August 1914

But many Canadian women, blinded by selfishness, did not want their husbands and sons killed in order to protect Canada's "independence." Lacking Colonel Morrison's training in strategy, they failed to perceive that the result of their treachery would be a German victory parade up Yonge Street. Despite all the public oratory and flag-waving, the imperialist *Montreal Star* noted with some dismay on 10 August that only 20 per cent of the volunteers so far were Canadian-born. A month later the *Canadian Military Gazette* somewhat peevishly complained that there were 800,000 men eligible for military service in the country, so there should have been hundreds of thousands volunteering. There weren't. In the Toronto area one regiment, the Mississauga Horse, was said to have only one native Canadian for every six or eight British-born volunteers. Montreal couldn't meet its quota for the First Contingent at all and the difference had to be made up with men from Winnipeg and the West. And the pro-British establishment's fears were correct: a large majority of those who joined the First Contingent were not Canadian-born.

I came from England, Folkestone, down in Kent. I came in '12.
Q. *And when did you join the army?*
In '14.
Q. *Did you go overseas at once?*
At once, yes, the First Contingent. We went down to Montreal and we shipped from Quebec–thirty-two boatloads. At that time, we were one of the biggest convoys that had ever crossed the Atlantic.
Q. *Why did you join in '14?*
Well, I think it was, as I look back at it, genuine patriotism. Maybe I changed my mind afterwards, after we got there. But at the time it was genuine.

Q. *But you'd only been in Canada two years.*
Two years, yes. So I was looking at it probably from an English point of view.

George Turner, Edmonton, Canadian army

George Turner survived the trenches and came back a devout Canadian (there's nothing like a war for moulding a national identity), but people like him formed a very high proportion of Canada's volunteers, especially in the early years. In fact, during the three years to October 1917, when all enlistments were voluntary, 49 per cent of the people who joined the Canadian forces were British-born immigrants, although they were only 11 per cent of the population. And that was why the West bore such a huge burden in the war. In 1914 there were barely a million and a half people in the four western provinces, a mere fifth of Canada's total population–but almost two-fifths of the soldiers who served overseas came from the West: that was where the bulk of the recent British immigration had gone, so that was where the volunteers were.

Yes, I was at the station, because I can remember how far they leaned out of the windows, waving to the people. And the way the mothers and the wives tried to clasp their hands as they went, as the train drew out very slowly, and this lament going on in the background: "Will ye no' come back again?"

Naomi Radford, Edmonton

The most extreme case was Alberta, which had been settled almost entirely during the preceding fifteen years. In the first year of the war Alberta contributed 22,325 men to the Canadian army (in addition to 5,600 British, French, and Belgian reservists who went back to fight for the Old Country in its own army), out of a total population of less than half a million. From the Edmonton city area alone seven thousand men enlisted, and the little town of Strathmore, east of Calgary, gained the distinction of being the most patriotic town in Canada. There, *every* eligible man joined the army in the fall of 1914, except one – and he went as soon as the harvest was over. But then Strathmore had only been settled nine years before, and most of the settlers were from Britain.

I remember the start of it. I remember when they assassinated the Archduke. And I remember all the boys around, you know, joining up – the older ones.

There were an awful lot of people from the town went. . . . My people were all very patriotic about the whole thing, and that. But I don't think anyone expected it to go on as long as it did. I think, you know, in those days people thought the British Empire was pretty well invincible.

Serres Sadler, Strathmore, Alberta (too young for<br>the First World War, so he went next time)

There was, in fact, a fairly consistent pattern in the rate of volunteering in Canada, a curve sloping down from west to east. The longer a region had been settled, the more aware people were of their own separate identity and interests as Canadians, and the less they tended to see Britain's war as their own (however many flags they waved). The split between immigrants and native-born was very noticeable in a town like Paris, Ontario, where just about half the population was Canadian-born, while the remainder were English immigrants attracted by the booming textile industry there. By mid-1915, the English-born in the town were openly accusing the Canadian-born of being "slackers." One person wrote to the local paper:

In the present great war for the freedom of our beloved Empire, it behooves us in Canada to spring up from this drowsy slumbering attitude that the Canadian born are assuming towards our Motherland. . . . What is our little town of Paris doing in its share to win from the uncivilized, barbarous Hun? They, if we are beaten in this war, would come over from the United States and Germany in their millions, to take everything over from a pin to our federal government.

If the Germans are victorious, the very first thing they would do would be to take over Canada. . . . They would fill every city, town and village, and hold drunken, debauching orgies, in celebrating their victory, and our women and children would be the victims of these drunken, barbarous wretches.

> Every minister of the church, every woman and girl, should
> do all they can to encourage all young men who have any grit in
> them to put on the King's uniform. . . .
>
> Donald A. Smith, At the Forks of the Grand, Volume II

The clergymen of the Paris Ministerial Association did their best,
organizing a great public rally as part of an approach that became known
as "coercive recruiting": coercion by public opinion. The drums banged,
the buglers played, and the speech-makers orated, but only twenty-eight
more recruits marched up to the platform "as though at a revival meeting," to be sent off with the usual "crisp 10-dollar bill" and a parcel of
comforts from the Ladies' Patriotic League. And further east in the Maritimes, where there were virtually no recent English immigrants, recruiting was even harder.

> Must we say hereafter with bated breath that this is the city and
> Province of the Loyalist? Must we say at this momentous period,
> fraught with the gravest responsibilities ever cast upon British
> people, that there exists within the borders of this Province at
> least 5,000 men, physically fit, and from whom a bare 800 have
> displayed sufficient courage and patriotism to unsheath the sword
> in defence of their homes?
>
> Mayor Frink, Charlottetown, Prince Edward Island,<br>29 June 1915

Prince Edward Islanders might be "Loyalist" by tradition, but by 1914
they had been there long enough to notice which continent they lived in,
and they did a lot less volunteering than British Columbians. As for the
one big dip in the curve, Quebec–as Laurier said in Parliament, defending
the French Canadians' evident reluctance to die for Britain: "Enlistment
[varies inversely] with the length of time that the men have been in the
country. . . . French Canadians . . . have been longer in the country than
any other class of the community."

❖

*Q. Were you excited at the time, about going to war?*
Oh yes, it was an adventure, you know. We were all a bunch of young people, eh? I was about the youngest in the crowd, but I took it as an adventure, you see. Because the story was that we'd never see the war, because it would be all over by the time we got to England.

Leslie Hudd, Sherbrooke, Quebec, Canadian Army

After three months of training in England in the winter mud of Salisbury Plain, the Canadians began to move to France. The first unit to enter the trenches, in January 1915, was "Princess Patricia's Canadian Light Infantry" (named after the daughter of the Governor General). It was a special battalion made up mainly of ex-British regulars and Canadian veterans of the Boer War, which had been raised and equipped with $100,000 donated by Captain A. Hamilton Gault, a Montreal millionaire and militia officer who had fought in South Africa. (Gault served in France with the battalion himself, and eventually lost a leg in battle.) But even the large number of experienced soldiers in the P.P.C.L.I. were at a loss for how to deal with this very new kind of battlefield, with its barbed wire and machine-guns and crushing artillery barrages.

The generals had expected a classic short war of swift movement and decisive battles, but the machines for efficient mass killing produced by industrial societies created a quite different war. The soldiers were driven to take shelter below ground level in what used to be called "field entrenchments," in order to escape from the lethal hail of bullets and shell fragments that swept away anyone who exposed himself on the surface. Within months Europe was divided by two great lines of trenches: the Western Front, where the British and French faced the Germans, and the Eastern Front, where the Germans and Austrians faced the Russians. The grim stalemate of the trenches had already set in when the Canadians reached the Western Front.

Of course you have read about the trenches in the papers. Well, our battalion has had four spells in them. Three or four days is usual. No charges made or repulsed, but we have had a number of casualties. . . .

Our trenches are from 75 to 120 yards from the German
trenches. Wise lads, too. The first night in, they called out to
know if we were Canadians. How are things on Hastings Street?
They also sang an English song or two.

The English Tommies that were here last fall are the ones who
had it bad. We have come to trenches all prepared and drained,
and in some places, paved with boards, brush, galvanized iron or
even bricks. There are dugouts built and floored with straw.

The cooking and smoking, with a little would-be witticisms
with Fritzies across the way . . . while away the tedious hours.

> Jairus Maus (Paris, Ontario). Enlisted in P.P.C.L.I. in
> Vancouver, January 1915 (*At the Forks of the Grand,*
> *Volume II*)

During the wettest English winter in living memory, the Canadian
troops had already got rid of some of the more useless bits of equipment
foisted on them by the political patronage that infested the Canadian
militia organization (such as boots that disintegrated in the wet). But when
the battalions of the First Canadian Division began to cross over to France
in mid-February, their men were still carrying the Ross rifles that were
Sam Hughes's pride and joy. He'd been warned by the British army that
they were excellent target rifles but useless for sustained fire in combat –
but nobody could ever tell Sam Hughes anything. The Canadians first saw
heavy fighting at Ypres in March:

How the Germans knew a bunch of green Canadians were going
to take over this part of the Ypres front, I don't know, but . . .
they opened up on us, and that was our first baptism of fire as a
unit.

So the troops on our right, the British, put up this rapid fire
with their Lee-Enfields. They were so disciplined that it sounded
like a hundred machine-guns going off at one time. So at our
front, the Canadian front, we tried to do the same thing. [starts
to cry]
Q. *What happened?*
Well, the boys were fighting away there and trying to do the rapid
fire, but you see the Ross rifle had a lock bolt with grooves in it.

So it went all right for a while, but then we noticed that we couldn't bring the bolt back. When the rifles got hot, they jammed.

So what did we do? 'Course we were under cover, eh? We'd sit up and try to use our foot to push the bolt down. That's when it started. Over that rifle I bet we lost about 1500 or 2000 men either wounded or killed, just over that silly damn thing. It was a lovely target rifle, but as an active service rifle, no, no.

Leslie Hudd

I have been seeing a bit of real warfare recently. Three nights ago we charged and took a German trench.

Under the flare of rockets they put up, they sent a terrific rifle fire into us. But almost immediately on our reaching their trenches, they fled. Our Battalion, the 16th, was only supposed to be supporting another battalion, which was to do the charging, but a great many of our boys reached the trench as soon as any.

When we were first told to take a German trench, my nerves were a bit jumpy, otherwise one is warmed up and excited and doesn't care. But it was a sad, sad roll-call. Half or more of my chums were missing. Some, no doubt, will recover.

After getting through this bout alright, I was mug enough to volunteer yesterday morning to leave a trench for a building some distance off, where the cook had some soup for our boys, who needed something bad enough. The shell fire was heavier than I anticipated, and so I'll have a little holiday. One in my right forearm and two in my left leg, but all clean wounds, although my leg is broken. . . . In all probability, I will convalesce in England.

Jairus Maus, letter home of April 1915<br>(At the Forks of the Grand, Volume II)

Maus left the line just before the Canadians were among the first troops in the world to experience a new horror. From the middle of April there had been persistent warnings that the Germans were going to use poison gas. There were reports of a German rush order in Ghent for 20,000 mouth protectors "to protect men against the effects of asphyxiating gas," and Belgian intelligence estimated that the attack would come on the front where the German 26th Reserve Corps were dug in. "All this gas business need not be taken seriously," replied French headquarters. And it wasn't.

Facing the German 26th Reserve Corps were colonial troops: Canadians of the First Division and Algerian troops of the French African Light Infantry. When the Germans released the greenish-yellow gas on 22 April, the Algerians fled and the Canadians had to stretch their line out to cover that part of the front, too.

> Instead of being two or three men every two or three feet, we were one man to about four or five feet. . . . I was gassed, but you see, we had no idea what it was.
>
> We saw this stuff coming over, it was sort of mist. The wind was blowing our way, towards the trenches. So next we knew it was gas, chlorine gas. The only thing we could do, we covered our mouths. So we took a piece of shirt, anything you could get, and wet on it. I don't know if I should say how we wet on it, but we wetted it, anyway, and wrapped that around our faces, and we had to take a chance on our eyes.
>
> Anyway, it worked some, but we lost a lot of men over that. It was hell, that gas. . . . We did what we could, and when we were taken from the trenches, we got a big name over in England over this . . . The papers were full of what the great, brave Canadians . . . [cries]
>
> Leslie Hudd

> It was a screeching of shells, men falling on all sides, Frenchmen retreating in disorder, yelling all kinds of things we could not understand, until they saw our gallant boys in khaki advancing in one thin line at the double, and they rallied with shouts of 'Brave Anglaise'. . . . We drove the Germans back, a few hundreds of Canadians against thousands of Germans. But I don't think they knew there was only such a small number of us. It was getting dark . . . anyhow, we gained the situation and dug holes into the ground, and neither the Germans nor their terrible shelling could move us, and wasted out and tired as we were, doing without

sleep and not much food, we stuck to them five days and nights, until we were relieved. . . . We have now got pads to put over our nostrils and mouth, ready for the poisonous gas that those German curs use. . . .

You would hardly know me now. I have aged quite a bit in looks, also in feelings, and got very thin. It is all with the continued hardships and nerve-racking things we have to endure. Well, dear mother, I will close, hoping I am alive to receive your answer to this letter.

John Carroll (Paris, Ontario), machine-gunner,

3rd Brigade, C.E.F.

The 1st Canadian Division did all that was asked of it and finished with a desperate bayonet charge. But the cost was terrible. Hundreds of good, willing lads gave up their lives without a murmur. Personally, I suffered from a bullet wound in the right side of my body and two in my right leg. Those in my leg are healing fine, but the one through my body, of course, is not doing well. . . . I was lying on my side firing when I got the first bullet through my leg, followed shortly after by another in the right side, and a second in the leg. . . .

Ask Lorne to find out for me how Knill, Larin, Cullum and Murray are. Never saw any of them after the fight started, and am anxious about the fellows. I do hope that the Paris boys come through alive, for it was terrible work.

I heard a good joke while lying on the road at Ypres. One of our stretcher bearers asked a severely wounded Irishman if there were many dead on the field, and he answered, "Sure, it's alive with dead men."

A.D. Fraser (Paris, Ontario), April 1915

(Napoleon Larin and A. E. Cullum were wounded, and

Ivor Murray was dead. Fraser survived the war.)

The Canadians lost 6,341 men at Ypres, and two weeks later, at Festubert, they were asked to do it again. They were short of high-explosive shells and the map of the objective was printed upside down, so Brigadier-General Arthur Currie, the ranking Canadian officer, asked for a postponement of the attack. He was refused. The Canadians managed to advance six hundred yards and captured the eastern hedge of an orchard. Their casualties were 2,468.

Prime Minister Borden stood up in the House of Commons and said: "They have proved themselves equal to any troops in the world, and, in doing so, they have brought distinction and renown to the Dominion." It was all true, but the gap in comprehension between those at home and those at the front was growing as wide as the Atlantic. Talbot Papineau (grandson of the leader of the 1837 rebellion), who was serving in Princess Patricia's Canadian Light Infantry, did not think in terms of distinction and renown any more:

> I hate this murderous business. I have seen so much death – and brains and blood – marvellous human machines suddenly smashed like Humpty Dumpties. I have had a man in agony bite my finger when I tried to give him morphine. I have bound up a man without a face. I have tied a man's foot to his knee when he told me to save his leg and knew nothing of the few helpless shreds that remained. He afterwards died.
>
> I have stood by the body of a man bent backward over a shattered tree while blood dripped from his gaping head. I have seen a man apparently uninjured die from the shock of explosion as his elbow touched mine. Never shall I shoot duck again or draw a speckled trout to gasp in my basket – I would not wish to see the death of a spider.
>
> Talbot Papineau letters, Public Archives of Canada

In early December 1915, Jairus Maus died of the "clean" wounds he had received at Ypres about seven months earlier while going for soup. His mother and sister, who had gone over to Britain to be with him, brought his body home to Paris, Ontario for burial.

❖

We should say something at this point (perhaps we should have done so before) about the way we are treating the very serious subjects of heroism and sacrifice. The death of a person in battle, however little dignity it is

30  Soldiers leave for W.W.I.

31

32  Newfoundland officers taking a rest in their dugout, Suvla Bay, Gallipoli. "There's only one reason any of us enlisted, and that's pure, low-down, unmitigated ignorance."

33  SIR EDWARD MORRIS.
"Sir Edward never hesitated, but offered his people to the Army and Navy and pledged the Colony's credit for their maintenance."

34  NEWFOUNDLANDERS IN THEIR TRENCHES AT GALLIPOLI.
"Nobody in the front line trenches ever expected to leave the Peninsula alive."

35  MAJ.-GEN. SIR SAM HUGHES
INSPECTING THE GUARD OF HONOUR IN PARIS.
"The Canadian Baron Munchausen will be to less effect. . . .
The greatest block to the successful termination of the war
has been removed. Joy, Oh joy!" J.C. Crcelman
on hearing the news of Hughes' resignation.

36  Woman at work in the assembly department, British
Munitions Supply Co. Ltd., Verdun, Quebec, 1916-18.

37  Wounded soldier in France.

"Just in the measure that the French in France are under an obligation to fight for us, just in so much are we under an obligation to go to France to fight for them." Henri Bourassa, May 1916.

"You will bring dishonour and disfavour upon our race, so that whoever bears a French name in Canada will be an object of suspicion and possibly of hatred." Open letter from Papineau to Bourassa, 1916.

38 HENRI BOURASSA, 1917.

40 TALBOT M. PAPINEAU, APRIL 1916.

39 A seventeen-foot shell hole in the Main Square, Ypres. Brig.-Gen. Burstall and Capt. Papineau, July 1916.

41 The enthusiasm of the early days was long gone, but in its place was an inflexible determination to win the war and to make sure that the suffering was shared by all.

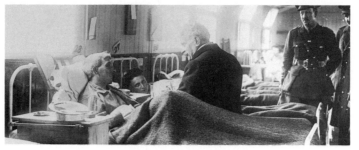

42   BORDEN ON THE WESTERN FRONT.
Sir Robert Borden chats with a wounded man at Base
Hospital, March 1917.

43   Anti-conscription parade, Victoria Square, Montreal, 24 May
1917. One placard "A bas la conscription" is visible in the centre
of the photograph. Some of the spectators are carrying British
flags, which are also draped from the windows.

44   "The King had a great many Canadian soldiers to dine at Windsor
and . . . their language about the French Canadians had been lurid.
*'When we get back we will shoot Laurier and every d—d French Canadian—
cowards and traitors . . . '.*" Walter Long, 18 September 1917.

# Women of Canada
### and the
# War Franchise Act

In response to a request from the Government early in August, women leaders of several organizations undertook to glean from throughout the Dominion an expression of opinion as to the advisability of granting the full federal franchise to women at the present juncture.

The result of numerous enquiries convinced these women that considering the peculiar conditions which prevail at the present time in certain provinces and the uncertainty of the results in granting a full franchise it would be desirable that a limited franchise should be given as a war measure in order that Canada may do her full part in the war and remain true to her sacred trust to the Canadian men now fighting the battle of freedom.

While the fighting men of Canada have made Canada's name glorious for all time through the great sacrifices they have made, it has at the same time become evident during the past three years that the women of Canada are willing to make any sacrifice for the winning of the war.

(Signed)
MRS. F. H. TORRINGTON,
*President National Council of Women.*
MRS. ALBERT GOODERHAM,
*President Daughters of the Empire.*
MRS. A. E. STEVENS,
*President Women's Christian Temperance Union.*
MRS. L. A. HAMILTON,
*President Equal Suffrage League.*

*Vote Union Government*  45

Issued by the Union Government Publicity Bureau, 47 Slater St., Ottawa
Modern Press, Print.

46   Nurses voting at the front.

47   LESTER B. PEARSON, SPRING 1918. "Mike" was the invention of Pearson's Royal Flying Corps squadron commander who thought "Lester" an inappropriate name for a fighter pilot.

48 Canadians in Vladivostok, 15 November 1918. Borden
arranged that a Canadian officer should command the
British Empire contingent in Vladivostok, which was
80 per cent Canadian.

49 In the Upper Ausable Valley, east of Lake Placid, planning to
invade the U.S.A.

50 Col. J. Sutherland Brown CMG, D.S.O. Director
of Military Operations and Intelligence, with Lt.-Col.
F.O. Hodgins and Lt.-Col. J.M. Prower on the road between
Keene and Upper Jay, New York.

51 THE CHANAK CRISIS. "I should be glad to know whether Dominion Governments wish to associate themselves with the action we are taking." Lloyd George, 15 September 1922.

Canada:—If I am needed I'll be there. The Empire Must be kept together.

52 AT THE LEAGUE OF NATIONS, GENEVA, 1928.
L. to r.: Dr. O.D. Skelton, Under-Secretary of State for External Affairs;
Philippe Roy, Canadian Minister to France; Senator Raoul Dandurand;
Prime Minister W.L. Mackenzie King; Charles Dunning, Minister of
Railways and Canals; Dr. W.A. Riddell, Canadian Advisory Officer, Geneva.

granted by the actual events, has a moral dignity that should not be denied. However mixed his motives for enlisting may have been in practice, and regardless of the cause for which he is killed, the soldier is actually laying down his life for his people. Jairus Maus would not appreciate his sacrifice being made the vehicle for gratuitous irony, nor would the men whom Papineau watched die – nor would we choose to exploit their deaths for the sake of a literary effect.

Nevertheless we do not intend to deal in terms like "glory" and "national honour," although the people we are writing about often did. The fact that Canadians proved to be as good at war as the people of any other industrialized country should be the cause neither of surprise nor of pride. And it would be wrong to conceal our belief that the war was folly and waste, although many of the dead did not think so, for it *was* a folly, part of an old pattern of folly that had suddenly grown to monstrous proportions.

The young Canadians who entered the trenches in 1915 were submitting themselves to an ancient and in many ways a familiar institution. Organized warfare is as old as civilization itself, and even the specific pattern of periodic world wars between the great powers, as a sort of regulatory device at the heart of the international system, had been going on for some three centuries. But they had the ill fortune to be drawn into the ritual just at the time when the institution of warfare itself reached a point of no return. It was the first great war to be fought between industrialized societies, and it provided the first solid evidence – there has been another, even more convincing demonstration since – that warfare and industrialized societies are, ultimately, fatally incompatible. The level of destruction they can wreak on each other is just too great.

The soldiers of the C.E.F., together with millions of young men from other nations, were in a sense the scouts we sent out to bring this information back, and they paid a desperately high price for it. There was great courage in the trenches, but it availed little against the killing machines – and there was no possibility of glory.

To be fair, Prime Minister Borden was not being deliberately insensitive when he spoke of Canadian troops "proving themselves" in 1915: he just didn't know what it was like at the front. And his own motives for sending Canadian troops to Europe were certainly honourable. But there is still room for outrage at the fate of so many young Canadians, for many of the men involved in sending them overseas were moved by crude considerations of self-advancement.

This was particularly true after the departure overseas of the Second Contingent (which was cobbled together, like the First, from enthusiasts who made their own way to Valcartier). For subsequent contingents, Hughes turned to the startlingly ramshackle device of placing recruiting almost entirely in the hands of "public-spirited citizens," generally prominent businessmen, who undertook to raise a battalion of volunteers in their area (and were often created honorary colonels in the C.E.F.). Many were his own cronies and political allies, and even in Quebec many were unilingual English speakers. Not all of Sam Hughes's pals profited directly from their work in recruiting and equipping the C.E.F., but some certainly did; indeed, one of the honorary colonels, J. Wesley Allison (whose shady business activities were partly responsible for Hughes's ultimate downfall), boasted publicly of the wonderful profits he had made in his dealings with the British government.

In most cases, to be sure, the businessmen and politicians who exhorted other men to join up for the war (and sometimes spent their own money to help found new regiments) were not out for profit. They were not unaware, however, that their efforts might be rewarded with British knighthoods, honours, and distinctions, which still played a large part in social advancement in Canada at the time. The most blatant example of this trade between London and eminent colonials, with imperial honours as the payment for colonial soldiers, was in Newfoundland, where the prime minister offered Britain an entire regiment at the outbreak of the war.

> The bulk of His Majesty's subjects in Newfoundland had then been steeped in ease for hundreds of years and imbued with an instinctive aversion to war, albeit the bravest of people in their own seafaring conditions. Neither did they understand the causes which compelled His Majesty's Government to declare war, nor did they consider themselves directly interested in the issue.
>
> The larger part . . . were on the whole inclined – living in the misty atmosphere of past centuries – to side with the King of Prussia, as the champion of Protestantism, and they remembered France only as the traditional enemy. The old memories of the

press-gang still lived in the outports, and the recollection of soldiering was that the wastrels of the hamlets enlisted for life and
never returned home. War signified to them . . . that those who
went out to fight went out to die.

Sir Basil Davidson, Governor of Newfoundland, 1912-17

Sir Edward Morris had been prime minister of Newfoundland since
1909. He was an Irish Catholic politician who had prospered mightily by
trimming his sails to catch the prevailing wind from Britain (he had a
standing order in London for the latest guide to the British peerage). But
by 1914 his Newfoundland People's Party seemed bound to lose the next
election, and the war came as a godsend: if he played his cards right, he
might restore the government's popularity – or better yet, use the war as
a stepping-stone to better things than Newfoundland politics.

Newfoundland volunteers had helped to save Quebec City during the
American siege of 1775-76, but the last Newfoundland regiment to serve
off the island had been disbanded in 1816, and in 1914 Newfoundland
had no military institutions whatever. Nevertheless, on 7 August 1914
Prime Minister Morris sent a telegram to London offering a land force,
and two days later London accepted Newfoundland's offer. Morris and
Governor Davidson then created the Newfoundland Patriotic Association
to raise, equip, and finance the contingents dispatched from Newfoundland. It was composed of prominent St. John's businessmen, religious
leaders, members of Morris's People's Party (including his brother), and
some politicians from the Liberal Party, but it carefully excluded Morris's
real political opposition, the Fishermen's Protective Union. The British
governor was chairman of the Association and controlled committee
appointments: in effect, he directed Newfoundland's war effort.

In a self-governing dominion, Governor Davidson's position was unusual if not unconstitutional. Davidson, however, had come to Newfoundland after twenty years in the civil service in Ceylon and ten years as
governor of the Seychelles Islands. In 1913, shortly after his arrival in St.
John's, he growled that "no man worth his salt" would consent to be a
mere representative of the crown and a mouthpiece of imperial interests.
He wanted to run the show, and Morris let him do so because he needed
Davidson's support in order to remain in power. The Newfoundland
Patriotic Association duly raised a contingent for overseas service, and

the "First Five Hundred," recruited mainly from St. John's (baymen tended to be more doubtful about the whole enterprise), sailed for England in the steamship *Florizel* in October 1914.

They then spent ten months training in England – and they had only volunteered for a year. Finally, in August 1915, as they were being reviewed by the King and by Lord Kitchener, the British war minister, they were given the option of returning home or enlisting for the period of the war. Most of them, unable to face the social disgrace of quitting, chose to stay, whereupon Kitchener announced that they were just the people he needed in Turkey. A week later they were sent to the Gallipoli peninsula, where imperial forces had landed earlier in the year in an attempt to break through the straits at the Dardanelles and capture Istanbul.

By now, the legendary early battles between the Turks and the Anzacs (Australians and New Zealanders) were largely over. What the Newfoundlanders had to face was four months of grinding, stalemated trench warfare where more men died from disease and exposure than from enemy action.

> All over the Peninsula disease had become epidemic, until the clearing stations and the beaches were choked with sick . . .
>
> By sickness and snipers' bullets we were losing thirty men a day. Nobody in the front line trenches or on the shell-swept area behind ever expected to leave the Peninsula alive.
>
> John Gallishaw, Royal Newfoundland Regiment,
> *Trenching at Gallipoli*

Those who survived Gallipoli and were unlucky enough still to be fit for war were sent to the Western Front, where the Royal Newfoundland Regiment was virtually wiped out at the battles of Beaumont Hamel and Gueudecourt in 1916.

Back home in Newfoundland, things were not going all that well for Sir Edward Morris and his People's Party, either. The economy was in disarray, the government was near bankruptcy, and after the carnage in France in the summer of 1916 recruitment became very difficult. Governor Davidson had become so unpopular that the Newfoundland Patriotic Association didn't even use his name any more – and the People's Party had no hope of winning the election due in late 1917.

However, throughout the war Morris had been exploring two possible escape routes from his impending defeat in Newfoundland politics. One was confederation with Canada, which could bring his political associates lucrative legal fees from the sale of the Newfoundland railway to the federal government. After that, an appointment to the Canadian Senate would ensure Morris himself a comfortable sinecure in retirement. Alternatively, if this "Canadian option" failed to perform as planned, Morris might provide for his future by an appointment as Newfoundland's High Commissioner in London, with a salary large enough for an expansive style of living; his political allies and enemies in Newfoundland would both be willing to pay a considerable price to see the back of him, and his hyperbolic loyalty to the Crown should ensure him a warm reception in London.

By late 1916, with Borden's government in Ottawa showing no interest in acquiring Newfoundland on Morris's terms, all his hopes centred on the "British option." Governor Davidson, anxious to maintain Newfoundland's flagging support for the war effort, was more than ready to cooperate.

The first step, in December 1916, was to extend the life of the Assembly for a year on the excuse that Morris had been appointed to the Imperial War Cabinet in London. Then, in July 1917, with various of Morris's political associates in the Newfoundland Patriotic Association under investigation for war profiteering and the issue of conscription looming on the horizon, Morris brought the opposition parties into a coalition "National Government." (Three prominent politicians who opposed the arrangement were bought off with knighthoods.) Morris promised his own party that he would stay in the government, but in a secret deal with the opposition party leaders he agreed to resign by the end of 1917 in return for being appointed High Commissioner in London on the then large salary of $10,000 a year. However, even his colleagues did not know that Governor Davidson was also working on a peerage for Morris as a reward for his obliging ways.

> Sir Edward Morris . . . now feels weary of the burden of leadership . . . and he has expressed to me his hopes that he may shortly retire from public life and reside in England.
>
> [By 1914, in Newfoundland], the proud tradition of attachment to the King and the Royal House had become almost lip

service, not involving the conception that loyalty might involve sacrifice. Despite these discouraging conditions Sir Edward never hesitated, but offered his people to the Army and Navy and pledged the Colony's credit for their maintenance.

[I wish] to press for your advocacy before the King in granting to Sir Edward Morris the unprecedented Honour of a Peerage, as a fitting reward for a man who has so well served the Cause of the British Empire. Sir Edward has sufficient means to maintain the Dignity of a hereditary title and a seat in the House of Lords.

Governor Davidson to the Colonial Secretary,<br>September 1917

Morris was already in London by September. On Christmas Eve he finally wrote to two of his former colleagues to announce his resignation as prime minister of Newfoundland, and a few days later he received his peerage. His former political associates then vetoed his appointment as Newfoundland High Commissioner, but he didn't need their money any more – a grateful imperial government arranged for him to be appointed to the boards of a British insurance company and an aircraft-building firm. His heir still sits in the House of Lords today.

Hardly anything in his public life that he did was what it professed to be. We will pass over the whole of it, in which he was ostensibly a Prime Minister and in reality a tool and agent of monopolists, up to the events that have so transformed the public life of the country.

St. John's *Evening Telegram*, 3 June 1918,<br>on publication of Lord Morris's letter of resignation

Seventy years after the Royal Newfoundland Regiment fought at Gallipoli, the steep slopes and eroded gullies of the peninsula are heavily wooded again. The Mediterranean pines cast the kind of shadows that drive cameramen mad, and storms come whipping across the bay with astonishing speed. Gallipoli is a deserted, haunted place: the invisible presence of all the nineteen-year-olds who came halfway round the world from Sydney and Auckland and St. John's to die there makes the hair on the back of your neck stand on end. Yet it is also a curiously gentle place.

On the 9th. January [1916] the final evacuation took place off Cape Helles. Thirty-two of the Newfoundland Regiment were honoured as rear-guard to remain in the trenches, and rifles and flares continued to go off at intervals. But it was recognised that the element of surprise would not serve and the rear-guard was thought doomed. The Turks would be apt to take toll for their former napping. But they proved sportsmen.

Our men said they stood four ranks deep on a narrow strip of beach which could have been enfiladed from the heights with great slaughter. Not a shot was fired, however. The Turks had called across the hill the previous day: "Goodbye. We know you're going. So are we. Good luck!" . . . They were a decent foe. They cared for British graves and there were no atrocities. Of the 32 [Newfoundlanders] who had been dedicated to an almost certain fate, all escaped.

Nursing Sister Mabel B. Clint, No. 1 Canadian Field
Hospital, Lemnos (near Gallipoli), 1916. (*Our Bit*)

Gallipoli is a sacred place for the Turks: hundreds of thousands of their young men died there to stop the British Empire from conquering Istanbul. The old Turkish guide who took us to the cemeteries (they are miles apart, linked by roads that barely cling to the cliffs) scratched at the soil with his boot-tip whenever we stopped to film, turning up old bullets and buttons and pieces of shrapnel from every square foot of ground. He asked us why we were there, and we explained about the Newfoundlanders who had died while invading his country in 1915. He wasn't at all resentful. Gravely, but with considerable kindness, he told us how sorry he was for them, because they had also been the victims of the British Empire.

"I'd like to know," said one chap, "why we all enlisted."

"I wish you fellows would shut up and go to sleep," said a querulous voice from a nearby dug-out.

"It doesn't do any good to talk about it now," said Art Pratt, in a matter of fact voice. "Some of you enlisted so full of love of country that there was patriotism running down your chin, and some of you enlisted because you were disappointed in love, but the most of you enlisted for love of adventure, and you're getting it."

Again the querulous subterranean voice interrupted: "Go to sleep, you fellows–there's none of you knows what you're talking about. There's only one reason any of us enlisted, and that's pure, low down, unmitigated ignorance."

John Gallishaw, Trenching at Gallipoli

CHAPTER ELEVEN

# *The Great Crusade*

Most Canadian troops were sent to the Western Front in France and Belgium, but as part of the British imperial forces Canadians ended up in every theatre of the war: there were Canadian fighter pilots in Italy, Canadian river pilots and marine engineers in Mesopotamia (Iraq), and Canadian sailors on all the world's oceans. In October 1915 Private Lester B. Pearson, # 1059, Canadian Army Medical Corps (who would one day become Secretary of State for External Affairs and then Prime Minister of Canada), landed in Macedonia in northern Greece with a new British expeditionary force. Britain and France had decided to violate Greek neutrality in order to bring help to their Serbian allies against the Austrians and the Bulgarians, and Pearson was part of the help. He was eighteen years old.

> My impressions of those first few days are of a vast muddy plain with our half dozen tents the only sign of human habitation; of

ceaseless rain and fierce winds; of horse ambulances coming
down the road with their loads of human agony; of the bugle
blowing the convoy call; of the boom of guns; of struggling in the
mire with wounded soldiers of the Tenth Division slung over our
shoulders – we had no stretchers as yet. . . . They had been
undergoing terrible experiences up in the hills. The weather was
below freezing, but through official mismanagement, they had
only tropical clothing. Practically all of them were frostbitten and
some in addition badly wounded, but not one complained.

   We pitched our tents, spread straw over the mud and laid the
casualties down on that, till there would be forty or fifty in a tent.
Then the medical officer would come around with his lantern,
the dead and dying would be moved to one side, the dangerous
cases would be attended to at once and the less serious ones
simply cheered up. All the while the wind whistled over the Mace-
donian plain and the sleet beat against the canvas. Nightmare days
when we all worked till we dropped . . . but the chance for real
service, the goal of our months of training.

letters home, October 1915, quoted in Lester Pearson,<br>
*Mike: Memoirs, Volume 1*

For the first time in Canada's history, there were also women in uniform: 2,504 Canadian nurses served in every theatre of the war. The first
Canadian women arrived behind the lines in France in early 1915, and
by the autumn of that year hundreds of Canadian nurses were struggling
to keep sick and wounded soldiers (and themselves) alive in the pestilential
conditions of the Eastern Mediterranean theatres of war as well. In August
M. B. Clint of No. 1 Canadian Field Hospital arrived on the island of
Lemnos, just off the Gallipoli battlefield, to find "sanitary conditions
appalling, food scarce and bad, heat great, small quantities of water, and
a frightful plague of flies."

Then one by one the Officers, sisters and orderlies succumbed to
dysentery, till only three out of thirty-five nurses were on duty in
No. 1. Canadians seemed to feel the change of climate particularly, but lack of food, water and the general environment was
the determining factor. . . . No. 3 suffered still more. . . . Within

a few days of each other, their Matron and a sister fell victim to the scourge.

As the little cortège of those well enough to attend followed the flag-draped coffins on wheeled stretchers, with the Sisters' white veil and leather belt laid on them, some of the patients in my ward were moved to tears. . . . It was expected that other nurses would die, and . . . the order went forth that other graves must be ready. . . . A trench to hold six was dug in the Officers' lines. A laconic notice-board bore the legend: "For Sisters only." At the moment, as one of our Mess remarked, you could almost "pick the names of the six."

Nursing Sister Mabel Clint, Lemnos, 1915, (*Our Bit*)

In fact, only thirty-nine Canadian women died overseas, but it was nevertheless a sign of the times. Even the strict rules of a traditional male-dominated society were collapsing before the war's voracious demands for manpower and, even more importantly, for total commitment.

❖

They would have little flags in the window. I can remember one house with three flags, that they had sent people overseas. One flag for each son, yes, or husband.

Naomi Radford, Edmonton

It is difficult to place a limit on the numbers of men that may be required in this devastating war. No numbers which the Dominion Government are willing and able to provide with arms and ammunition would be too great.

British War Office to Ottawa, May 1915

A second Canadian division had followed the First Contingent to France by the spring of 1915, and there was certainly no limit being placed yet on the numbers that the Dominion Government might send. But in June the Chief of the General Staff in Ottawa, Colonel Willoughby Gwatkins, passed a warning to the prime minister's legal adviser, for transmission onward to Borden, that the Canadian Expeditionary Force was already nearing the maximum strength that could be maintained by voluntary enlistment. Given the casualty rates that he was seeing from the first major battles, Gwatkins warned, any attempt by Canada to commit more than three divisions to the fighting would eventually force the government to adopt some form of conscription to keep the units up to fighting strength.

It is not clear that Prime Minister Borden fully understood what he was being told, but in July 1915 he went to England to try to find out more from the British about their war plans. They were vague. The war was consuming munitions in quantities far greater than anybody had anticipated in peacetime, and nobody was sure when the factories would be geared up to produce enough ammunition for a decisive offensive. Estimates of when the British would be ready to exert their full force ranged from a year to eighteen months. It was going to be a long war.

Trapped between the British and French in the west and the Russians in the east and seriously outnumbered, the Germans went over to the defensive on the Western Front in early 1915. They stayed in that posture for most of the next three years, depending on the impassable barrier of trenches, barbed wire, machine-guns, and artillery stretching from the Belgian coast to the Swiss frontier for protection in the west while they tried to knock the Russians out of the war in the east. It was the British and French who launched almost all the great offensives on the Western Front, but their overall strategy consisted of little more than an attempt to wear the Germans down gradually by attrition.

Even though the Allies almost invariably lost more men attacking the German trenches than the Germans did in defending them, the prevailing doctrine still required that they launch huge, forlorn offensives at regular intervals. The generals, and even the politicians they advised, were well aware that they had more men to put into the field than the Germans: if enough people were killed, the Germans would eventually have to stop fighting, because they would run out of men first. However, nobody had the faintest idea how long it would take to wear the Germans down, or how many Allied soldiers would have to die in the process. In October 1915, Borden passed an order-in-council increasing the Canadian force to 250,000 men:

> The war brought with it the necessity of organising great armies
> upon a scale unexampled in our history and of arming and equip-

ping them. During the past twelve months the response in all parts of the King's Dominions has been most encouraging but the need is still great and a supreme effort is now necessary. If that effort is made there can be no doubt as to the issue of the present struggle, for the allied nations are notably superior in numbers and resources to the enemy nations.

In return for this great contribution to the imperial war effort, however, Borden wanted Canada to have a voice in determining the conduct of the war. After his visit to Britain in mid-1915 and his shock at the confusion that reigned there, he noted that the old relationship between Britain and Canada had "in some measure passed away. Once for all it has been borne in upon the hearts and souls of all of us that . . . the issues of war and peace concern more than the people of these islands." The British Colonial Secretary, the Canadian-born Andrew Bonar Law, complacently informed Borden in late 1915 that he fully recognized "the right of the Canadian government to have some share in the control of a war in which it is playing so big a part. I am, however, not able to see any way in which this could practically be done. . . . If no scheme is practicable, then it is very undesirable that the question should be raised."

Bonar Law's reply drove the normally gentle Borden to fury, but his method for forcing the British to reconsider was quixotic. In his 1916 New Year's message, Borden doubled the planned strength of the Canadian Expeditionary Force to 500,000. Among the people who were astonished by this move (Borden had decided on it alone while bedridden with the 'flu) was the Governor General: "His Royal Highness cannot but feel considerable doubt as to the possibility of increasing the Canadian Forces to 500,000 men. His Royal Highness understands that of the 250,000 men at present authorised some 50,000 are still deficient and he fears that the magnificent total of 500,000 may be beyond the powers of the Dominion of Canada to provide under voluntary enlistment."

The Duke of Connaught (whose departure from Canada had been indefinitely postponed because of the war) was quite right in his assessment: Borden's target, if maintained, would eventually require conscription. On the other hand, the prime minister was sure that the men would be needed, since the monthly "wastage" of troops showed no sign of decreasing. He also hoped that his announcement would end the criticism of his government by those English Canadians who didn't think he was doing enough for the war. But above all, Borden believed that it would compel the British to give Canada a share in the direction of the war: "It can hardly be expected that we shall put 400,000 or 500,000 men in the field and willingly accept the position of having no more voice . . . than if we were toy automata. . . . It is for [the British] to suggest the method and not for us. If there is no available method and we are expected to continue in the role of toy automata the whole situation must be reconsidered."

By announcing that Canada would raise half a million troops before London had even asked for them, however, Borden had given the imperialist establishment in English Canada a pledge from which it would never release him – and since Canada had offered the troops of its own accord, he had not really strengthened his bargaining position with London. The gesture was in any case unnecessary: by December of 1916 the new British prime minister, David Lloyd George, had realized that the Dominions must be granted a share in policy-making. "We want more men from them," he told the Colonial Secretary. "We can hardly ask them to make another great recruiting effort unless it is accompanied by an invitation to come over and discuss the situation with us." He then invited the Dominions and India to send representatives to London for an Imperial War Conference at which they could "discuss how best they could cooperate in the *direction* of the war. They were fighting not *for* us, but *with* us."

What was never seriously discussed at these meetings of the Imperial War Cabinet, however, was the question of a compromise peace. There had been numbers of secret contacts between the two sides for a negotiated settlement in the first two years of the war, but by now the sheer scale of the losses incurred by all the combatants had moved it far beyond its original petty causes and limited aims. It had become something new: a "total war" in which *all* the available manpower and resources were devoted to the sole aim of achieving military victory: the entire workforce of wealthy industrial societies – including millions of women who were drawn into industry for the first time – was mobilized for war production. And since everyone was at least theoretically involved in the war effort in one way or another, everybody, whether in uniform or not, soon came to be treated as a legitimate military target: the first air attacks on civilians came in 1915, with the Zeppelin raids on London.

It was not the supreme importance of the issues at stake that made the First World War the first total war: as a diplomatic phenomenon it was no different from all the preceding great-power world wars. It was simply the first time that that kind of war had occurred since the great powers had acquired the vast resources and the technological and organizational capabilities of fully industrialized states. Once these capabilities existed it was inevitable that they would be used, since the side that showed restraint would surely lose. But the mass slaughter had such a powerful psychological effect on the combatants that it became impossible to end a world war in the old way.

After millions of ordinary citizens had died (most of them in uniform, but some not), the traditional outcome of such wars – a fairly modest reshuffle of territories and readjustment of influence among the great powers–was no longer acceptable to the populations of the warring countries. It became necessary to elevate the war to the status of a moral crusade, or at least to define it as a struggle for sheer national survival, in order to justify the sacrifices that were being demanded. This was in the nature of a self-fulfilling prophecy: as the only war aim acceptable to the people of each nation became total victory, the war did become something close to a life-and-death struggle for the European great powers, or at least for their governments. It was nothing of the sort for Canada, of course, but a great many English Canadians were also swept away by the rhetoric of the time.

❖

An extraordinary feature of enlistment in British Columbia as, indeed, wherever English families are to be found in Canada, was the spirit of sacrifice and patriotism which ran right through them. . . . Of the Mathieson family of Victoria, 5 brothers were on active service, and . . . Arthur Green and three sons of Victoria. . . . 7 boys of the Kerridge family of Vancouver were all at the Front. Of the George family, Victoria, in 1916, three were killed, one was missing, one a prisoner, two were at the Front, and two waiting till they were old enough to go . . .

*Canadian Annual Review*, 1916

It was the English Canadian families whose sons and husbands had already volunteered in large numbers who welcomed Borden's call for 500,000 men at the beginning of 1916: they rushed out and enlisted in even larger numbers. During the first three months of 1916 men were joining up at the rate of over a thousand a day (if you didn't count Sundays). The government heaved a sigh of relief: Canada might be able to raise half a million men without having to resort to compulsion. The Third Canadian Division had already joined the first two in the trenches, and there were plans for a Fourth and Fifth to follow.

But then enlistment began dropping rapidly. In December 1916, there were only 5,791 enlistments for the entire month. At that rate the country would fall far short of the target of enlisting 30 per cent of all males of military age.

By now the unemployment of 1913 was long forgotten. Farmers needed all the help they could get, and munitions factories were employing a quarter-million workers. The war had stimulated an unprecedented growth in Canadian industry. In 1914 Canadian arms manufacturers produced little more than small arms and ammunition, but in the last two years of the war the Imperial Munitions Board, created by Borden in late 1915, was spending more than the Government of Canada itself, and had 675 factories working for it in 150 different towns in Canada. By 1917 Canadian industries were turning out warships, military aircraft, and between a quarter and a third of all the shells fired by British guns on the Western Front: twenty-four million shells were shipped to Europe that year. Arms production was probably the most effective use that could be made of Canadian manpower, but it caused great difficulties for the army recruiters.

Newspapers, politicians, and Brigadier James Mason, the director of recruiting, spent much time trying to figure out how many eligible men were left in the country, and why they were not enlisting. Some thought it was because the average Canadian was wanting in loyalty to the empire: "If he lacked imperial sentiment, he lacked stimulus in the war, and was in the same state of mind which prevailed in the neutral masses in the United States – by which trend of thought, also, he was indirectly influenced" (*Canadian Annual Review*, 1916). Others thought that horror tales about the front were frightening young men and their mothers. Both interpretations were probably correct.

Brigadier Mason presented the Senate with a mass of statistics and a very depressing conclusion for the government. There were, he reported, one and a half million eligible men in Canada (half of them unmarried). By February 1916, 249,000 men had enlisted, but it was going to be much more difficult to get the next quarter-million:

> Moreover, this large number, if and when sent to the Front, must be maintained, and it has been estimated that the casualties will not be less than five percent monthly of the total force. This means that we shall have to provide each month, to maintain our Army's strength, at least 25,000 new men – or 300,000 a year.
>
> There can be no question that the additional 250,000 to bring our quota up to 500,000, and the 300,000 required annually to keep it at that figure, will not be obtained under the present system of enlistment.

By now the British tradition of voluntary enlistment was falling by the wayside elsewhere: in January 1917 Great Britain introduced conscription, and New Zealand had already done so. The feeling persisted in Canada that there was a great untapped mass of men of the right age, but no actual data existed: some parts of the country had only recently been settled, and until the war there had been no need for this detailed information. The obvious solution was a national registration system, so two million large cards were printed and sent to all the post offices in the country for distribution. (Originally they were going to be mailed to every male citizen in the country, until somebody realized that if you already had the name and address of every male in Canada, you might not need a registration system.) But the government shrank from making registration compulsory, and it was estimated that about 20 per cent of the males between eighteen and sixty-five didn't fill in the cards. There was a strong suspicion that the government was moving toward conscription, even if it said it was not, and many men felt it prudent not to draw themselves to the army's attention.

By now, too, it was apparent to the labour movement that the burden of the war was being borne very inequitably: almost 65 per cent of manual workers had enlisted, compared to only 6 per cent of professionals (slightly ahead of farmers), and a mere 2.5 per cent of employers and merchants. It was all very well for the government to say that it was enlisting wealth through taxation (a modest Business Profits Tax was introduced in 1916), but tax demands do not kill people. The labour leaders were convinced that registration was the prelude to conscription, and Borden did little to calm their fears:

> I repeat once more that the proposals. . . . are not connected with Conscription. Rather the idea was to make an appeal for voluntary National Service which would render unnecessary any resort to compulsion.
>
> You have asked for an assurance that under no circumstances will Conscription be undertaken or carried out. . . . I must decline to give any such assurance. I hope that Conscription may not be necessary, but if it should prove to be the only effective method to preserve the existence of the State and of the institutions and liberties which we enjoy, I should consider it necessary and I should not hesitate to act accordingly.
>
> Borden to labour leaders, 27 December 1916

Despite this reply, the Trades and Labour Congress executive did urge their members to register, but it made little difference. Not only did many men not fill out the cards, but when the army, seeking volunteers, canvassed the men who had registered, most of them felt that they were doing their duty by working in industry. By now even the West had run out of young, single, unemployed men with strong British loyalties, and nobody thought the war was an adventure any more. In Winnipeg, out of 1,767 men registered, nobody was willing to volunteer. Out of a pool of 4,497 men registered in Quebec, four enlisted. Most eligible Canadian men seemed curiously unconvinced that there was any threat to "the existence of the State and the institutions and liberties" they enjoyed.

❖

Meanwhile, nothing had improved in the management of the Canadian forces. Sam Hughes, now "Sir Sam," emphasized that the goal of 500,000 men was a target for which the prime minister alone had to take responsibility, but he was scarcely a model of responsibility himself. In August

1916 he cabled Borden from England to suggest that Canada should put eight or ten divisions in the field (it then had four). His motive appeared to be the pure spirit of competition: Australia, with a much smaller population than Canada, already had five divisions in France, and it was rumoured that there were enough Australian troops in England and Egypt to form four more.

On the same day, as an after-thought, Hughes cabled asking to have "sixty or eighty thousand troops sent over immediately." He assured Borden that this would still leave over one hundred thousand troops in Canada. (Even at this point in the war, the government thought it necessary to keep a fairly large "home defence" force to guard against an attack by the United States and to prevent industrial sabotage.) Besides, Hughes added helpfully, more men could easily be made available if clergymen helped out in the fields to release more farmers' sons for military service. And he wanted to send the Fifth Canadian Division (commanded by his very own son, Garnet) to France at once, even though the War Office felt that the Canadian troops still in England should be kept as reserves: the need for reinforcements to replace casualties in the four divisions already at the front seems to have eluded Hughes entirely.

The worst thing about Sam Hughes – much worse than his venal "friends" in commerce and industry, his absurd pretensions to military genius, or his random enthusiasms for new models of service rifle or entrenching tool – was his relentless, reflexive determination to do favours for his friends in the militia. He was the epitome of the "good ol' boy" politician whose sole method for extending his influence over his political environment is to create an ever-widening network of people who are indebted to him for their jobs. Professional military competence was therefore quite irrelevant to Hughes when he chose officers (and he had his "militia" ideology to rationalize his disdain for formal military qualifications). In the Post Office, this kind of management policy means that the mail gets delivered late and the organization runs a deficit; in an army at war, it means that large numbers of people get killed because of the incompetence of their superiors.

All the officers selected for the First Contingent of the Canadian Expeditionary Force were appointed by Hughes more or less as a personal favour, and many of them were not capable of organizing a binge in a brewery: the latterly famous military critic J.F.C. Fuller, then a young

British officer, remarked on seeing the First Canadian Division debark at Devonport in England in 1914 that they would be fine soldiers only "if the officers could be all shot." Most of the officers of the Second Canadian Division, and many of those commanding subsequent contingents, also got their jobs through Hughes's reflex cronyism: if you were a Canadian who wanted a combat command in the war, there was no other way. And yet, once they had actually seen battle, Hughes's own appointees tended to turn against him.

From mid-1915 on, there was unremitting guerrilla warfare between the Canadian divisions in France and the tangled web of competing Canadian military authorities in England that Hughes created to administer them. It was much more than the usual friction between the front and the rear: the key question was always whether the commanders in France had the right to choose their own replacement officers (mostly by promoting them from the ranks of their own battle-hardened troops), or whether they must accept replacements from among the horde of "supernumerary" officers, all promised a job by Sir Sam but utterly lacking in combat experience, who languished in England waiting for the call.

Combat experience changes people – and it also winnows them. The men Sam Hughes had chosen to officer the Canadian divisions in France in 1914 and 1915 were almost all deficient at the start in the military knowledge they would need, and there was a disproportionate number of sycophants among them. But time and battle weeded out the weak (there are almost always ways for an officer to escape the front, if he is determined to avoid it) and taught the survivors to act and think like real officers. The ex-lawyers and farmers and insurance salesmen turned into competent majors and colonels who understood exactly what it means to be responsible for your countrymen's lives – and that while it is your duty as an officer to spend the lives of some of them in order to achieve your country's objectives, the rate at which they die will be determined largely by your own military competence.

The toy soldiers turned into professionals, and they became contemptuous of Hughes's bluster. More than that, they became determined to stop him from parachuting his new crop of patronage appointments (ironically, "officers" who were in the very same situation they themselves had been in a year or eighteen months before) into positions of command where through their inexperience they might waste the lives of veteran

Canadian soldiers who had survived the battles of Ypres and the Somme.

The first evidence of this transformation of perspective among Canadian officers at the front came right at the end of 1915, when Hughes made one of his typical proposals for finding more jobs at the front for his cronies. He suggested that all the British staff officers serving with the Canadian Corps should be replaced by Canadians, even though his own bias against professional military education for militia officers had prevented all but a handful of Canadian officers from being properly trained for staff appointments. Faced with the prospect of having incompetent Canadians replace the trained British staff officers who were currently doing the vital staff planning jobs in the Canadian divisions, however, the Canadian senior commanders at the front unanimously backed the British corps commander, Lieutenant-General Sir Edwin Alderson, in protesting against it, and Hughes's proposal was dropped.

It was nearly a year later before Hughes himself was dropped, and many administrative tangles, of the sort that he was a master at producing, contributed to his ultimate downfall. One of the messiest was the consequence of his eccentric recruiting methods. The "honorary colonels" raised about one hundred and fifty battalions in excess of the number that could be fitted into the Canadian army's field establishment, each with its own local or ethnic loyalties, plus badges, buttons, bagpipes and kilts or whatever – and its own complement of officers. Hughes had known even as he encouraged people to create these battalions that they would have to be broken up before they reached France, where there were already quite enough units. What was needed was individual reinforcements to replace the horrendous casualties in those units.

So when the Moose Jaw Fusiliers, the Bay Street Old Pals' Battalion, or the Chicoutimi Highlanders reached England, there immediately ensued the long and painful process of breaking the unit up again–which, since each battalion's officers generally resisted dismemberment by every administrative trick and delaying tactic in the book, could take up to a year. Thus there was the permanent spectacle of large numbers of potential Canadian reinforcements sitting in England, unable to be sent to France because the struggle over disbanding their particular battalions was not yet concluded. And when the inevitable finally happened and the enlisted men of the battalion were sent to France piecemeal to reinforce depleted units at the front, the ex-battalion's officers mostly went to swell the mountain of unemployed Canadian officers in England who constantly besieged the authorities for appointments (at their existing exalted rank, of course) at the front.

This kind of nonsense was beginning to undermine Hughes's credibility at home even with his most avid supporters in the Conservative party by the latter part of 1916, and since the great man himself was almost constantly in England meddling with the forces there or else dashing around Canada on various urgent missions he invented for himself, Borden was gradually able to hand over more and more of the administration of Hughes's department in Ottawa to other, more competent people. However, the biggest factor in bringing Sir Sam Hughes down at last was the fact that his own former appointees in France had learned enough about war to reject his methods entirely.

Eventually enough information about attitudes at the front got back to Ottawa that Borden was able to get rid of Hughes without facing a political revolt in his own party. Much of this information came in private letters and in other informal ways, but there were also some very explicit and official protests. For example General Arthur Currie, then commanding the First Canadian Divison, had to play host for two weeks in December 1915 to a number of Hughes's favourite majors and colonels who behaved "as if they were on vacation" during their tour of the front. Once they had gone back to England he telegraphed to the Canadian authorities in London pointedly asking when the Canadian government would "stop playing and realize that we at least are serious."

Gradually the evidence built up against Hughes, and the final confrontation came in late 1916 when Prime Minister Borden decided to order him home from England and created a new Department for the Overseas Military Forces of Canada, quite separate from Hughes's Militia Department in Ottawa, to be run by Sir George Perley in London. Hughes was furious. In his own mind he was perpetually beleaguered by the plots of jealous rivals and incompetent subordinates, and now he accused Borden of being a plotter, too. Borden had had enough: on 9 November 1916 he demanded Hughes's resignation as Minister of Militia and National Defence. When he heard the news J.C. Creelman, an artillery brigade commander in the Canadian Corps in France who owed his original appointment to Hughes, wrote in his diary:

There is a new contentment among us all. We walk with spright-lier step . . . clear eyes . . . cleaner cut. . . . The Mad Mullah of Canada has been deposed. The Canadian Baron Munchausen will be to less effect. . . . The greatest soldier since Napoleon has gone to his gassy Elbe, and the greatest block to the successful termi-nation of the war has been removed. Joy, Oh Joy!

19 November 1916

And it did make a big difference: Sir George Perley in London loyally served as a kind of blocking force, protecting the troops in France from the patronage requests that still flowed copiously out of Ottawa, and by the spring of 1917 almost all the new junior officers in the Canadian Corps were being commissioned from its own ranks. The internecine battles among the Canadians overseas were mostly over. At home, how-ever, they were just getting underway.

❖

All of the men seemed to have gone. You had a tremendous rate of enlistment here, and my father at the newspaper was working overtime all the time, and he would come home absolutely exhausted.

You have to remember there was no TV, there was no radio, but a dispatch would come through that, say, the Somme Battle was in progress. . . . And the phone rang incessantly – these poor, anxious voices: "We're so sorry to bother you, but is there any news?"

So at the age of, I suppose about eight or nine by then, I was part of the chain of communication, because I would let my father rest. And I remember what a dreadful time I had pronouncing the names of these various battles. And Daddy would tell me what dispatch had come through, and I'd just repeat it.

Naomi Radford, Edmonton

By the end of 1916 Canada was a divided country: divided between those families who had a son, a husband, or a brother serving overseas and those who were still essentially living in the atmosphere of peacetime. The latter group might follow the progress of the European war in the newspapers, but they could not share the quiet terror of those who spent their days waiting for the official message that it was time to dress in mourning.

> The sight of a telegraph boy was a thing of horror . . . because they were never allowed to phone bad news. And you'd see the boy come down the street on his bicycle, and you'd watch what house he stopped at. And then, later, probably my mother would go over, one of the neighbours would go over.
>
> Naomi Radford

The resentment against men who had not volunteered was greatest in the West, where a large majority of families had a close relative in the trenches. At times it had a very bitter edge.

> The odd person, mostly old people, would go around, and they'd see a chap that they felt should be overseas, and they would bounce up and put a white feather on him. And of course, as the war went on these were often chaps who'd come back wounded, or had a heart condition or something. It was a very cruel thing to do. . . .
>
> Oh no, there was no organization as far as I know. They were just "public-spirited" people.
>
> Naomi Radford

By now, too, hatred for the Germans (helped along by atrocity propaganda) had begun to extend to German Canadians as well. Early in the war the town of Berlin in the German-settled part of southern Ontario had taken the precaution of renaming itself Kitchener (after the British field marshal and war minister), but as the times grew harsher such simple remedies no longer sufficed. The German social club in Kitchener was ransacked and its piano thrown out into the street, the Lutheran pastor serving the German community came under enormous pressure to preach only in English (although some of his older parishioners spoke little but German), and occasionally some unfortunate German Canadian was tarred and feathered for his opinions, or simply on principle. No German-speaker entirely escaped the label of "enemy."

> Looking back, when I think of the dear little butchers at the corner, man and wife, and how we all stopped dealing with them because they were German. It was a great loss to the children because they always gave us a piece of baloney when we went in.
>
> And I had been given two large dolls, sort of rag dolls, Mr and Mrs Katzenjammer (which was a cartoon at that time), and I hung Mr and Mrs Katzenjammer outside our attic window which faced on 107th Street. This was my way of winning the war against the Germans.
>
> Naomi Radford

But far more than for the German Canadians or the "shirkers" in their own communities, English Canadians with relatives in the forces reserved their deepest feelings of resentment for French Canadians. It was universally felt in English Canada that French Canadians were not carrying their share of the burden – and of course they weren't, for they didn't think it *was* their burden.

❖

> Canada being part of the British Empire, it is the sacred duty of the Canadian people to assist Great Britain in her heroic defence of liberty. This was the position taken by the Episcopacy of French Canada at the outbreak of the War, and this is the attitude Bishops . . . will continue to maintain to the very end. The obligations we owe the British Crown are sacred obligations.
>
> Archbishop Bruchési of Montreal, Laval, 7 January 1916

The Catholic hierarchy in Quebec almost unanimously supported the British cause during the war, in fulfilment of the Church's part in the old bargain. However, it was fighting an uphill battle against its own *curés*, who shared the general conviction that the Kaiser was not casting lascivious eyes on Trois Rivières and that the war was none of French Canada's business. But there were some French Canadians who joined up anyway.

*4 heures 15 a.m.*

*Dix minutes seulement avant l'assaut. . . . A l'horizon apparaît une bande grisâtre. C'est l'aube qui s'annonce et je me sens soudain le coeur plein d'amertume que le jour qui va luire bientôt sera probablement le dernier de ma vie. . . . Le sifflement d'un projectile déchire l'air et une explosion secoue la tranchée. Un soldat est blessé à deux pas de moi. Un éclat d'obus lui a brisé la jambe. Des brancardiers lui font un pansement sommaire puis il est évacué vers l'arrière. "Encore un qui aura la chance de ne pas participer à l'attaque," dit quelqu'un. . . .*

Signaller Arthur Lapointe, 22nd Battalion, C.E.F.,
*Souvenirs d'un Soldat du Québec*

[4.15 a.m.

Only ten minutes now before zero. The horizon shows a line of grey. Dawn is coming; and my heart is filled suddenly with bitterness when I realize that the day may be my last. . . . A shell bursts in our trench, breaking the leg of a man a few yards away. Stretcher-bearers apply a dressing and carry him to the rear. "There goes one man who won't die in the attack," remarks a soldier, almost enviously.

Our company commander, Capt. J. H. Roy, appears. "Ten rounds in your magazines and fix bayonets!" he orders. There is a click of steel on steel. Only two minutes now remain. . . . Yesterday, I believed I could die with something approaching indifference. Now I am aware of an intense desire to live. I would give anything to know beyond doubt that I had even two whole days ahead of me. . . . I see things . . . differently than I did yesterday.]

At one time or another thirteen battalions destined to join the C.E.F. strove to attract French Canadian recruits in Quebec, but apart from the 22nd Battalion, only the 163rd "Poil-aux-Pattes" and the 189th (recruited mostly in the Gaspé) reached Europe – and after the dreadful losses suffered by the 22nd Battalion at Courcelette in September 1916, the others were broken up to refill its ranks. The 22nd was a remarkable formation, with possibly the most distinguished fighting record in the entire Canadian army, but there were scarcely enough French Canadian volunteers to keep that single battalion up to strength.

*4 heures 25 a.m.*

*C'est l'heure . . . Un lourd roulement de tonnerre se fait entendre et vers nos arrière-lignes, le firmament vient de s'illuminer comme en un immense incendie. . . . Les obus passent par rafales au-dessus de nos têtes et à travers le bruit de canon, je saisis le crépitement de mitrailleuses. En deux bonds j'ai escaladé le parapet et me voilà, avec Michaud, un des premiers au-dessus de la tranchée. Notre compagnie prend deux ou trois minutes à se former en ligne de combat et ces minutes me paraissent ne plus finir. . . .*

Arthur Lapointe

[4.25 a.m.

Zero hour! A roll as of heavy thunder sounds and the sky is split by great sheets of flame. . . . Through the deep roaring of the guns I can hear the staccato rat-a-tat of machine-guns. I scramble over the parapet and, with Michaud, am one of the first in No Man's Land. Our company is forming up and the moments of delay seem endless. . . . A shell strikes a few yards away, and Lieut. Gatien is seriously wounded. We are not allowed to help him; that is the stretcher-bearers' duty. The noise of the barrage fills our ears; the air pulsates, and the earth rocks under our feet. I feel I am in an awful dream and must soon awake. . . .

We reach the enemy's front line, which has been blown to pieces. Dead bodies lie half buried under the fallen parapet. The wounded are writhing in convulsions of pain. . . . Through clouds of smoke, I catch sight of German soldiers running away. Shall I fire at them? I pity the poor devils and have seen enough dead lying in the mud; but this is war, so I open fire. A German soldier falls. Did one of my bullets find a mark, or was he struck down by a shell? I shall never know.]

There were some practical reasons why so few French Canadians joined the forces: they tended to marry younger, and the army that was seeking their services had become an almost entirely "English" institution (among some eighty Canadian brigadier-generals in the First World War, only four were French Canadian). But these obstacles were unimportant compared to the fundamental French Canadian disinclination to die for the British Empire.

For a while Borden tried to use his French Canadian ministers to drum up support for the war in Quebec, but they were never happy to be out recruiting. Henri Bourassa would attack them with the argument that this was not Canada's war and with unanswerable criticisms about the "fanaticism of Ontario" (where the provincial government had just restricted teaching in French in the schools), while the influential Abbé Lionel Groulx warned that *"une vague de fanatisme impériale soulève le Canada."*[a wave of imperial fanaticism is sweeping Canada away.]

> We are told that French Canadians should enlist to fight in the present war because the existence of France, the centre of French culture, is at stake. But . . . suppose that, tomorrow, civil war should break out between the French Canadians and the English Canadians.
>
> Suppose that the French Canadians, reading the words of Mr Asquith, Mr Lloyd George and others to the effect that the present war is to establish the rights of small nationalities . . . should decide to fight to gain their right to have their own children taught in French in the schools of Ontario; in other words, to get equal rights with their English Canadian fellow-citizens.
>
> In such a case would France declare war against Great Britain? . . . Just in the measure that the French in France are under an obligation to fight for us, just in so much are we under an obligation to go to France to fight for them.
>
> Henri Bourassa, Speech at St-Henri, 30 May 1916

So far as most French Canadians were concerned, the sentimental tie to France was not strong enough to justify dying for her, and loyalty to Britain had become a one-way street in which they were being asked to die in Britain's wars although they no longer needed Britain to defend them against the United States (nor could expect it to do so even if that became necessary). But English Canadians were coming to see all French Canadians as cowards or traitors, while French Canadians who had enlisted found themselves regarded as dupes by many of their own people. After a year at the front Talbot Papineau (who must have felt doubly isolated as he was serving in an English-speaking regiment) sent an open letter to his cousin, Henri Bourassa:

Can a nation's pride be built upon the blood and suffering of others? . . . If we accept our liberties, our national life, from the hands of the English soldiers, if without sacrifices of our own we profit by the sacrifices of the English citizen, can we hope to ever become a nation ourselves?

. . . Yet the fact remains that the French in Canada have not responded in the same proportion as have other Canadian citizens. . . . For this fact . . . you will be held largely responsible. You will bring dishonour and disfavour upon our race, so that whoever bears a French name in Canada will be an object of suspicion and possibly of hatred.

Papineau to Bourassa, 21 March 1916

But Papineau was as much American as French Canadian (his father, like Henri Bourassa's, was descended from Louis-Joseph Papineau, but his mother was American). Bourassa replied in another open letter, pointing out that even in English Canada it was the relatively recent arrivals, the "blokes" from Britain, who had done much of the volunteering. Moreover, he added, "the floating population of the cities, the students, the labourers and clerks, either unemployed or threatened with dismissal, have supplied more soldiers than the farmers," whose roots were in the land. Even if he changed his personal position, Bourassa said, he could not persuade French Canadians to enlist. French Canadians "look upon the perturbations of Europe, even those of England or France, as foreign events. Their sympathies go naturally to France against Germany, but they do not think they have an obligation to fight for France."

> *Je reviens de retrouver mon camarade Michaud sain et sauf. . . . Nous venons d'enlever le deuxième support allemand où nous avons fait une cinquantaine de prisonniers. Tous ont la figure hagarde, les yeux fous comme s'ils sortaient d'un enfer. La plupart d'entre eux sont blessés. . . .*
>
> Arthur Lapointe

[I have just found Michaud safe and sound. . . . We have taken the German second support line and captured about fifty prisoners, all haggard and wild-eyed, as though they had traversed a hell on earth. Most of them are wounded. One young lad with a badly torn face is raising awful cries. Another, with a leg torn away, is groaning; and his moans rend one's heart. Further away lies one of our men, a young soldier, a comrade of mine from the old 189th. He is terribly wounded, and holds his beads in his one remaining hand. Time and again he calls for his mother, and when his sufferings are more than he can endure prays for death. I can't stand the sight of his suffering, and walk away, with a great lump in my throat.]

Apart from the 22nd Batallion, however, it had become an almost entirely English Canadian war, and as the casualties mounted, so did the pressures from English Canada to *compel* French Canadians to "do their share." Only a few English Canadian politicians, like R. B. Bennett, the Director of National Service, whose recruiting work brought him into regular contact with French Canadians, were fully aware of the dangers this entailed. Bennett frankly told his English Canadian audiences that for the sake of national unity it might be better if the burden of sacrifice remained unequal: "We don't want to have our forces spent in quelling riots at home." But that was not what the audiences wanted to hear, nor were there many English Canadian politicians with the wisdom or the courage to say it to them.

❖

The Canadians played a part of such distinction [on the Somme in 1916] that thenceforward they were marked out as storm troops; for the remainder of the war they were brought along to head the assault in one great battle after another. Whenever the Germans found the Canadian Corps coming into the line they prepared for the worst.

David Lloyd George, *War Memoirs, Volume VI*

Once we got there we were strictly Canadian – there was no fooling around at all. We thought we were quite superior to everybody else, you know.

George Turner

By the end of 1916, despite all the political infighting and the disastrous losses (the Canadians had 24,029 casualties during the Battle of the Somme), the Canadian Corps in France had become a competent, highly professional army – and despite the very large proportion of English-born volunteers in its ranks, everybody in the Corps developed a strong Canadian identity. But as the politicians at home struggled to find enough men to send to the front as replacements, the Canadians in the field ran into a new problem. The reinforcements were sent out so hastily that they were sometimes virtually untrained.

> I found myself in a shell hole with some infantryman, and looking over a hundred yards or so away there was a German who was standing up out of a shell hole and shooting as if he was shooting at rabbits. I don't know whether he hit anybody, but any rate he was there. And I sort of said: "Why don't you shoot? Why don't you fire at that man?"
>
> "Oh, I don't know how to fire. . . . "
>
> He just couldn't use a rifle. So I took the rifle from him and took a shot, and the man disappeared. I don't suppose I hit him, but at any rate he wasn't there any more.
>
> "Tommy" Burns (later General, then a junior officer
> in the Eleventh Brigade)

The rate of losses in the Canadian army was already the major problem, and in 1917 it became critical. The last straw, ironically, was the greatest Canadian success in the war, the capture of Vimy Ridge. It was a long escarpment dominating an industrial plain, from which "more of the war could be seen than from any other place in France," and no significant advance was possible along the most important part of the British front so long as it stayed in enemy hands. The Germans had held most of the ridge since October 1914, and two hundred thousand men had already been killed or wounded in previous British and French attempts to capture it. In April 1917 the job of taking it was given to the Canadian Corps.

It was the first time that all four Canadian divisions had fought together as a corps, and the Canadians prepared for the assault with the meticulous care that was becoming their trademark in battle. They spent weeks studying a scale model of the battle area and practising the planned manoeuvres. More than a million artillery shells–fifty thousand tons–fell on the Germans in the week before the attack (they called it "the week of suffering"). Even now Vimy looks like a partially reclaimed moonscape, and signs still warn of unexploded shells.

Very early on 9 April, Easter Monday (having spent Sunday at church services), the men of the four Canadian divisions were given a stiff tot of rum and began moving forward under cover of a heavy barrage. For once the weather was in their favour: the snow-storm in which the Canadians crept forward across no man's land was unusual for April, but the snow was flying into the Germans' faces, concealing the Canadian advance. The Canadian *Official History* says the attack "went like clockwork," but *nothing* in battle goes like clockwork: some regiments in the Eleventh Brigade, which had suffered heavy losses in other recent fighting, had just "lost their confidence" (as the saying went):

> When they were supposed to get up, out over the top and go forward, they tended, after some casualties had occurred, to just not go on any further. And actually, with many of the troops being quite green, you couldn't expect them to do any better than that. When you got a bit forward, you found that the advancing troops had sort of stuck in the mud, somehow or other, and the attack as planned just fell apart.
>
> "Tommy" Burns

Nevertheless, the bulk of the Canadian army swarmed up over the ridge and seized the German trenches, and although the Germans were very well dug in, a lot of the forward positions were taken by surprise. But that does not mean that the attackers were not taking heavy losses. They were.

> I got bowled over nearly at the start, but picked myself up and ran on with the boys towards the German trenches, and believe me it was some fighting. It was like hell let loose. I was through the Somme but that was nothing compared to this one. . . . It was at the second line that I was knocked out by the concussion of a high explosive shell that burst right near me. By this time there were only two of us left of our machine gun crew.
>
> The shock of the explosion threw me into a shell hole. Cor-

poral Lang . . . came into the hole after me and gave me a drink of rum and water, which soon pulled me around and we started off for Fritz's third line. By this time the enemy were calling for quarter and surrendering fast.

J. M. Thompson (Paris, Ontario), April 1917

We went over Vimy Ridge just at dusk. The Canadian attack . . . had left it a jungle of old wire and powdered brick, muddy burrows and remnants of trenches. . . .

Two hours later we found Fourteen Platoon, hardly recognising it. The sergeant was there, and MacDonald, but most of the others were strangers. . . . MacDonald told us our company had gone straight through to the objective in spite of sleety snow and mud and confusion, but a flanking fire from the left, where the 4th Division had been held up, had taken a heavy toll. Belliveau and Jenkins and Joe McPherson had been killed in one area. One shell had wiped out Stevenson and two others.

MacMillan had been shot in the stomach and had died after waiting hours in the trench. Gilroy and Westcott and Legge had been killed by machine-gun fire. Herman Black had run amuck. They found him almost at the bottom of the Ridge, near a battery position, with eight dead Germans about him, four of them killed by bayonet.

Will Bird, Ghosts Have Warm Hands

After two days of futile counter-attacks the German commander, Crown Prince Rupprecht, ordered the withdrawal of his troops onto the plain below. He had lost a dominating position, and 4,000 Germans had been taken prisoner. But the Canadians had suffered 10,602 casualties, including 3,600 dead.

On April 10, word reached us of the splendid victory of the Canadians in taking Vimy Ridge on the preceding day.

Fine tribute from Haig [the British commander-in-chief]. Some mention in editorials, but none in "Times", which is disgraceful. . . .

Despatched telegrams of congratulations to General Byng.

Robert Borden, Memoirs, Volume 2

It was partly in recognition of the Canadian Corps' achievement at Vimy that it was finally given a Canadian commander in the early summer of 1917, and so became the first completely Canadian field army in the country's history. But while Lieutenant General Sir Julian Byng, the British officer who had commanded the Corps since May 1916, was well liked by the troops, his Canadian successor, General Sir Arthur Currie (who had been an insurance agent and part time militia officer when the war broke out), was not. Leslie Hudd, by now a seasoned veteran, met Currie after he was recommended for a French Croix de Guerre and a British Military Medal for single-handedly taking a German machine-gun post.

> I was just a buck private. So the [French] General came down and he embraced us all, and I was kissed on both cheeks. Currie came, and he shook hands with the officers and sergeants, but he just pinned it on the privates. . . . I never had much use for Currie. I thought it was his job to congratulate us the right way. All the privates thought that; thought they were worth a handshake from their commander. Not that I've got anything against him as a general, but you could say he wasn't too popular.
>
> Leslie Hudd

Currie was a shy, corpulent, ungainly man who had none of the actor's skill at currying favour with the troops that is cultivated by so many successful generals. But although his later life was blighted by a campaign of slander directed by Sam Hughes and his cronies, who claimed that he wasted men's lives needlessly, Currie actually worked very hard at keeping them alive. He was an excellent and conscientious commander who was once considered by Prime Minister David Lloyd George as a possible replacement for Sir Douglas Haig, the British commander-in-chief in France.

However, despite Currie's success in his unending struggle to keep the Canadian Corps together and prevent it being frittered away in small packets by the British high command to plug weaknesses in various sectors of the front, he could exercise little control over the way the Corps as a whole was actually used. Nor was there any senior Canadian military voice in Ottawa to give Prime Minister Borden strategic advice from the point of view of Canada's own interests: during the entire war the Chief of the General Staff of the Canadian army was a British officer, elevated by the end to the stately rank of Major-General Sir Willoughby Gwatkins. As in all Canada's wars down to the present, the strategic thinking was being done elsewhere.

❖

The victory at Vimy Ridge confirmed Borden's belief that the Canadian army was the finest of the allied armies, and this was not just nationalist pride. The four divisions of the Canadian Corps had subtly, almost surreptitiously, evolved first into a professionally competent fighting force and then into one of those tightly-knit field armies with a clearly defined character (which are actually quite rare, especially in big wars) that can always be relied on to get the job done or die trying—and that are seasoned and cunning enough that they generally do the former, not the latter. You may not admire armies, and you should certainly never romanticize them, but the Canadian Corps of 1917-18 was a classic of its kind.

Borden, of course, did romanticize it, and this made it all the more difficult for him to contemplate reducing the Canadian commitment. However, no army could afford to go on taking such losses unless it received a steady flow of reinforcements –and voluntary enlistments were drying up. The prime minister had also been much affected by his visit to the front, where he was shocked by what he saw, and by the nerve-racking visits he insisted on paying to all the Canadian military hospitals. (He visited fifty-seven during his 1915 trip.)

> On the one hand, I was inspired by the astonishing courage with which my fellow-countrymen bore their sufferings, inspired also by the warmth of their reception, by a smile of welcome, by the attempt to rise in their beds to greet me. In many cases it was difficult to restrain my tears when I knew that some poor boy, brave to the very last, could not recover.
>
> On the other hand, the emotion aroused from these visits had an exhausting effect upon one's nervous strength: and frequently I could not sleep after reflecting upon the scene through which I had passed.
>
> Sir Robert Borden, *Memoirs, Volume 2*

He felt a tremendous obligation to the troops in this army. . . .
He thought that having "his boys" reinforced was necessary for
Canada's defence, which he regarded as being across the ocean.

On the other hand, he also, being the man he was, felt what
a terrible disgrace it would be to Canada and the people of Canada
if this wonderful army that had been built up, that had fought at
the Somme, at Ypres and Vimy, and so forth, had to be disbanded,
in effect, because of the terrible casualties which they had
suffered.

Henry Borden (nephew of Robert Borden)

Not only Borden's solicitude for "his boys" but also the deteriorating
military situation of the Allies in general were now pushing him very
strongly towards conscription. He spent from the middle of February to
early May 1917 in England attending the first Imperial War Cabinet meetings. He was appalled by what he learned. The Allies' situation was growing worse: they might even be losing the war.

Astonishing news of the abdication of Czar and revolution in
Russia. Evidently due to dark forces, the Monk Rasputin, the pro-
German Court and bureaucratic influences, the meddling of the
Empress, the weakness of the Czar, and his inability to realize or
comprehend the forces of liberty and democracy working among
the people.

Robert Borden, *Memoirs, Volume 2*

The early optimism that the Russian Revolution would improve matters soon turned to fears that Russia would withdraw from the war. If
that happened the whole weight of the German army could be concentrated on the Western Front, and things were bad enough there already.
The French offensive that had begun at the same time as Vimy Ridge in
the spring of 1917 had pushed their army past the breaking point. One
French regiment went to the front making bleating noises like lambs being
led to slaughter, and when the offensive collapsed fifty-four divisions –
almost half the French army – mutinied. It took one hundred thousand
court martials to restore discipline, and even after that the French army
seemed to be finished as an offensive weapon, perhaps for years.

Meanwhile, German submarines were sinking a million tons of Allied shipping a month, and the First Sea Lord, Admiral Jellicoe, had concluded: "It is impossible for us to go on with the war if losses continue like this." Only one bright spot loomed on the horizon: the German campaign of unrestricted submarine warfare, by sinking neutral shipping, was pushing the United States into the war on the side of the Allies. (Washington declared war on Germany on 6 April 1917.) But it would take almost a year before American troops reached Europe in large numbers, and meanwhile France, Britain, and its overseas dominions had to hold out somehow on the Western Front. There was only one solution, and Lloyd George put it very bluntly to the Imperial War Cabinet on 20 March 1917:

> Let us look quite frankly at the position. [Germany] has more men in the field than ever she had. . . . She is in a very powerful military position. . . .
>
> The Allies are depending more and more upon the British Empire. . . . We started with 100,000 men, we now have 3,000,000 in the field. . . . What is it necessary for us to do in order to achieve the very sublime purpose which we have set before us? The first thing is this: we must get more men.

Lloyd George's "very sublime purpose," of course, was to make sure that the British Empire won the war – no matter what the cost to Britain or anybody else. By 1917, the first total war had brought a new breed of men to power in Britain, France, and Germany: Lloyd George, Clemenceau, and Ludendorff owed their positions to promises that they would wage the war unrelentingly and uncompromisingly until total victory. In fact, there was probably no choice by 1917: it was not only in Russia that revolution was a danger. After so much sacrifice, *any* major European government that stopped the fighting short of victory now faced the risk of overthrow by an angry and disillusioned populace: only victory could make them safe. Even in Britain the cabinet was seriously worried about domestic political stability.

In Canada, there was no danger of revolution, but the English-speaking majority would not forgive any government that failed to prosecute the war to the utmost, while the French-speaking minority would not forgive any government that resorted to compulsion. Four days after he returned to Ottawa from the Imperial War Cabinet meeting, Borden made his decision. He announced that the government would impose conscription.

### CHAPTER TWELVE

# A Country Divided

Bullets went through my main spar on the lower starboard wing and before I knew it I was in a steep dive but upside down, hanging onto the cowling openings beside the guns with both hands and my toes pressed up against the toe straps on my rudder bar for all I was worth. My seat belt had too much elasticity and did not hold me fast.

German machine guns were rat-tat-tatting away as the different pilots took turns shooting at me.

I went from 12,000 to 3,000 feet in this position, swearing at the Huns for shooting at me when I was obviously going to crash in a few minutes. I was panicky. At about 3,000 feet I went into heavy cloud, collected my panicked brains, reached up into the cockpit with one hand, caught the spade grip on the joystick, pressed the blip switch cutting the engine and slowly pulled back on the stick, coming out of the cloud right side up with no German pilots around.

I was over the German lines, did not want to be a prisoner, did not know whether the wing would stay together if I put the engine on or not but decided it was the only thing to do. . . . I put the engine on slowly, the wing held together, and with no one shooting at me from the air I stooged back home, a very thankful and less cocky fighter pilot.

> Flight Sub-Lieutenant W. A. Curtis (Toronto, Ontario)

The one aspect of the war which still retained some glamour for Canadians by 1917 was the war in the air. Once aerial warfare really got into high gear in 1916 and the British air services began to expand at a breakneck rate, Canadians flocked to join. Many young men already overseas wanted to escape the impersonal slaughter of the trenches, even if it just meant a lonelier death in a burning airplane a few months later, and many in Canada simply joined for the adventure. They were all slightly crazy.

A French squadron had its airfield not far from our hospital camp [in Macedonia, and] one or two of us had struck up an acquaintance with a young pilot of this French squadron. . . . On one visit . . . my friend was getting ready for a flight, and asked me if I would like to come along; there was room for one passenger. So I left my heart and courage on the ground and he took the rest of me up into the air.

After the first spasm of fear passed, I found that I liked flying. . . . My pilot friend may have sensed this, for he . . . gave me more flying than I expected, heading his machine, a Voisin monoplane, all canvas and string and wooden struts and a 90 hp engine, northwards to where the enemy were. When he indicated that he was going to do a little reconnoitring of the Bulgarian positions, my exhilaration diminished . . . [but] I have always claimed since that I was the only man in the history of military aviation whose first flight was over enemy territory.

> Lester Pearson (who applied to join the Royal Flying
> Corps as soon as he landed), *Mike: Memoirs, Volume 1*

One practice [at Camp Borden] was for a pilot to wait in the air at the time the Toronto express for Barrie was due, and then to come in from behind at a fast clip, low down over the tracks. As he and his plane swept by over the length of the train, the crazy man at the plane's controls would deliberately bump his wheels on the roofs of several of the coaches before reaching the engine, when he would speed over the top and actually dip down in front of it along the tracks far enough in front to swing away and yet not have his identifying numbers on the rudder seen by passengers or train crew.

Frank H. Ellis, Canada's Flying Heritage

Canadian trainee pilots were being killed off in accidents at the rate of more than one a day in the spring of 1917, which was a suitable preparation for the casualty rates they would face when they reached the front. For many men, becoming a pilot was a death sentence: in mid-1917 there were 240 Canadian pilots flying in combat squadrons over the Western Front, and during the next six months about 220 more joined them. Yet at the end of 1917, the number of Canadians still alive and flying over the Western Front was just 240. But it was at least an individual death, not the anonymous slaughter of the trenches–and those who lived to become aces provided wonderful material for the propagandists.

Ten of the top twenty-seven aces in the British forces were Canadians, and they included four of the twelve leading aces in the entire war. This extraordinarily high Canadian quotient was partly a reflection of the Canadians' remarkable enthusiasm for flying: by the time the various British air services were amalgamated into the Royal Air Force on 1 April 1918 there were 22,000 Canadians serving in them. (Indeed, the main reason that a separate Canadian Air Force was not created until the closing months of the war was the British concern that it would tear their own squadrons apart. "Thirty-five per cent of our total strength in pilots is Canadian," remonstrated a British officer, Lieutenant-Colonel R. C. M. Pink, in May 1918. "Under the Air Force Act every one of these can walk out of the door tomorrow and return to the Canadian service unless this service is definitely part of the Royal Air Force.") But the pilots themselves mostly didn't care what flag they saluted: they lived in an intense, closed world where the only thing that counted was the respect of their peers.

Major W. G. Barker, DSO, MC, and the officers under his command, present their compliments to Captains Brumowski, Ritter von Fiala, Havratil and the pilots under their command, and

request the pleasure of a meeting in the air. In order to save
Captains Brumowski, Ritter von Fiala and Havratil and the gentlemen of their party the inconvenience of searching for them, Major
Barker and his officers will bomb Godega Aerodrome at 10 a.m.
daily, weather permitting, for the next fortnight.

> leaflets dropped over the Austrian lines in Italy by 139
> Squadron (Major Barker commanding) in mid-1918

In late 1918 Major William Barker of Dauphin, Manitoba was already
one of the leading aces of the war, with forty-six confirmed victories
accumulated in two and a half years of fighting over the Western Front
and in Italy. (The Austrian Air Force sensibly kept its leading aces on the
ground during the daily bombing of Godega airfield despite Barker's generous invitation.) But Barker was also, at the age of twenty-three, a man
living on borrowed time, for even very good pilots rarely survived as long
as he had in combat.

By late 1918 the Allied authorities well understood the propaganda
value of live aces in boosting their populations' flagging morale, so Barker
was eventually posted to command an air-fighting school in England in
order to keep him alive. His protests were unsuccessful, but he did manage to get himself appointed to a squadron in France for ten days on the
way home, on the grounds that German aerial tactics over the Western
Front were now different from those he had become familiar with in his
more recent experience against the Austrian Air Force over Italy. He had
still seen no enemy aircraft when he took off alone for England on 27
October at the end of his ten days' stay in France, however, so he decided
to take one last peek over the front.

He was in luck, sort of. As his Snipe fighter climbed to 21,000 feet
over the Forêt de Mormal he spotted a Rumpler two-seat observation
aircraft on a reconnaissance flight high above the British lines. But as he
concentrated on the Rumpler he failed to notice the entire "flying circus"
of sixty Fokker D-VIIs, the latest and fastest type of German fighter, that
was flying beneath him stacked up in three or four echelons. As the
Rumpler broke up before Barker's guns one of the German fighters, climb-
ing in a near stall, raked his plane from below with machine-gun fire and
shattered his right thigh with an explosive bullet. Barker threw the Snipe
into a spin and levelled out several thousand feet below, only to find
himself in the midst of fifteen more Fokker D-VIIs. He got in quick bursts

at three of them, setting one on fire at ten yards' range, but then he was wounded in the other thigh and fainted.

Barker spun down to 15,000 feet before he recovered consciousness and pulled his fighter out of its dive once more – only to find himself in the middle of a lower echelon of the same German formation. By sheer instinct he got on the tail of one of them, but by the time it burst into flames his own aircraft was being riddled with bullets from behind; one bullet shattered his left elbow and he passed out again, dropping to 12,000 feet before he came to amidst the lower echelon of the flying circus. As the German fighters milled around his smoking machine, taking turns to attack from every point of the compass, it was clear to the thousands of British and Canadian troops watching from the trenches below that Barker was finished.

He must have thought so too, because he aimed his tattered Snipe at one of the D-VIIs and flew straight toward it as if to ram, firing as he went. But at the last instant it disintegrated and Barker hurtled through the wreckage; in the clear for a moment, he dove for the British trenches and crossed them at tree-top height, finally crashing into the barbed-wire entanglements around a British balloon site just behind the lines.

"The hoarse shout, or rather the prolonged roar, which greeted the triumph of the British fighter, and which echoed across the battle front, was never matched . . . on any other occasion," recalled Colonel Andy McNaughton, a militia officer who had risen to command the Canadian Corps Heavy Artillery and watched the fight from his advanced headquarters near Valenciennes. (McNaughton became commander of the entire Canadian army in a later war).

Billy Barker's lonely last fight, in which he added four more aircraft to his score, won him the Victoria Cross and failed to dampen his ebullience even slightly. "By Jove, I was a foolish boy, but anyhow I taught them a lesson," he told the newspapers from his hospital bed near Rouen ten days later. Although his leg wounds never properly healed and he had to walk with the aid of canes for the rest of his life, Barker stayed in aviation after the war, founding Canada's first (spectacularly unsuccessful) commercial airline in collaboration with another Canadian ace and Victoria Cross winner, Billy Bishop, briefly becoming director of the new Royal Canadian Air Force, and continuing to fly personally until he was killed in a crash at Ottawa's Uplands Airport in 1930.

The exploits of Barker and men like him, in a kind of combat that seemed, at least from a distance, to retain some of the honour and glory that had traditionally been associated with warfare, provided Canadians with virtually the only relief from the bitter news arriving daily from the trenches. But it was on the ground that the war would ultimately be won or lost, and by late 1917 the demand for fresh cannon-fodder had become so great that the government was knocking on the door of every family in Canada.

❖

Prime Minister Borden's decision in May 1917 to bring in conscription was greeted with grim satisfaction in much of English Canada. The enthusiasm of the early days was long gone – too many families had already lost a son or a husband – but in its place, especially in the homes of the bereaved, was an inflexible determination to win the war and to make sure that the suffering was shared by all.

> The casualty lists were never printed until during the next week, and I can remember the appalling lines down the paper. And you'd look at it, you know, watching for the names that you knew.
> Q. *How did people in the West feel about conscription?*
> Well, I think they were all for it. Because after all, the flower of the flock had already been taken.
>
> Naomi Radford, Edmonton

Borden could in all honesty argue that the voluntary system was no longer working. In the fighting of April and May 1917 the Canadian Corps in France suffered 24,000 casualties, and recruitment at home was only 11,000. At that rate the army would run out of men fairly soon, so compulsion seemed to him the only solution. His government had long outlived its popularity: even the dismissal of Sam Hughes had not removed the impression that the government was badly organized and that its recruiting methods were hopelessly out of date. But Borden's problems were greatly eased by the serious split over conscription that now began to tear the Liberal opposition apart.

French-speaking Liberals unanimously opposed conscription, but most of the prominent English-speaking Liberals were conscriptionists by conviction, and the rest were hedging out of political necessity. Even William Lyon Mackenzie King, Laurier's protégé and probable successor, who had opposed conscription all along precisely because it would split both the Liberal Party and the country, was starting to waver, fearing that there might be no future for an English-speaking politician who didn't line up with the English-speaking majority on this issue. "I have changed my views on conscription as the war has progressed and I have seen freedom threatened," he announced.

Borden's Conservatives split on English-French lines over conscription, too: the few remaining prominent French Canadian Conservatives in his cabinet (like E. L. Patenaude, the Minister of Inland Revenue, who resigned over the issue) warned him that if the Conservative Party brought in conscription, it would be destroyed in Quebec for twenty-five years. But the Conservatives depended much less heavily than Laurier's Liberals on French Canadian votes, and Borden was under too much pressure from conscriptionists in the rest of the country, and from the war itself, to back down. Moreover, he was convinced that conscription was what the men at the front wanted. Indeed, that *may* have been his most powerful motive:

> If we do not pass this measure, if we do not provide reinforcements, with what countenance shall we meet them on their return? . . . They went forth splendid in their youth and confidence. They will come back silent, grim, determined men who, not once or twice, but fifty times, have gone over the parapet to seek their rendezvous with death.
>
> If what are left of 400,000 such men come back to Canada with fierce resentment and even rage in their hearts, conscious that they have been deserted or betrayed, how shall we meet them when they ask the reason? I am not so much concerned for the day when this Bill becomes law, as for the day these men return if it is rejected.

While there was an element of melodrama in Borden's speech, he was not misrepresenting the mood at the front. A few months later Canadian officers visiting the King in London shocked him by the violence of their hostility toward French Canadians:

The King had a great many Canadian soldiers to dine at Windsor and . . . their language about the French Canadians had been lurid. "When we get back we will shoot Laurier and every d—d. French Canadian–cowards and traitors. We will have civil war and exterminate the whole lot. Especially the R.C. Bishops and Priests." So [the King's private secretary] came by command of H.M. to see me and tell me he thinks the situation very serious and begged me to get some influence to bear on the R.C. Church.

Walter Long, Colonial Secretary, to the Duke of Devonshire, Governor General of Canada, 18 September 1917

In fact, King George had even asked if the Pope could be persuaded to do anything to urge French Canadians to take a more active part in the war. However, the British Foreign Office apparently didn't follow up on the suggestion, since it believed that the Vatican's sympathies lay with the Catholic Austrians and "they may not wish to do anything to produce more soldiers to fight against their friends!"

❖

Both Borden and Laurier realized that the country was heading into a crisis, and Borden hoped to weather it by forming a coalition government. However, Laurier's unwavering opposition to conscription made that impossible, and he demanded a referendum on the issue (like the one that had recently rejected conscription in Australia).

The law of the land which antedates Confederation by many generations, and which was reintroduced at the time of Confederation, emphatically declared that no man in Canada shall be subjected to compulsory military service except to repel invasion for the defence of Canada. My honourable friend says the first line of defence for Canada is in France and Flanders. I claim there never was any danger of invasion on the part of Germany. Nobody can say that Canada, for one instant during the last three years, was in danger of invasion.

Sir Wilfrid Laurier

Henri Bourassa had been saying for years that Laurier was a secret conscriptionist, but he was wrong. In English Canada, there was an impression that if the French Canadians would only stop listening to Bourassa – if only Laurier would give them a lead – then they would *en masse* see the error of their ways and start joining the army in large numbers. But that was nonsense: Laurier was compelled to oppose conscription both by his own long-held political principles and by the urgent need to provide some legitimate political voice for the very large number of Canadians (not all of them French Canadians, by any means) who vehemently disapproved of conscription.

It was especially important to show French Canada that there was at least the possibility of resisting conscription within the bounds of the existing Canadian constitution. If Quebec's mainstream political leader had not provided a model of principled democratic opposition for the majority of French Canadians who loathed conscription but still basically supported Confederation, Canada might literally have been torn apart. It was a bitter end to Laurier's lifelong role as a bridge between English and French Canada, but it was perhaps the greatest service he ever did for the country.

> Now if I were to waver, to hesitate or to flinch, I would simply hand over the Province of Quebec to the extremists. I would lose the respect of the people whom I thus addressed, and would deserve it. I would not only lose their respect, but my own self-respect also.
>
> Sir Wilfrid Laurier, letter to Newton Rowell,
> 8 June 1917

Even with Laurier's Liberals providing a legitimate political vehicle for opposing conscription, the customary Quebec phenomenon whereby political moderates are outflanked in public by nationalist extremists soon made itself felt with a vengeance at the anti-conscription political meetings and demonstrations that proliferated in Quebec's cities. From the start these were marked by blood-curdling threats and occasional street violence. On 25 May Colonel Armand Lavergne, a former commander of the militia regiment at Montmagny and a well-known Nationalist, told a great throng in Quebec City that "I will go to jail or be hanged or shot before I will accept [conscription]. The Conscription of 1917 had its origin in 1899, when Canada sent men to assist in crushing a small nation in the Transvaal. . . . It is not for Canada to defend England, but for England to defend Canada." The crowd cheered lustily, and then went and smashed the windows of *The Chronicle* and *L'Événement*, the two pro-government papers in the city.

Throughout the long summer of 1917, as the Military Service Bill dragged its slow way through Parliament, the political atmosphere in Quebec grew steadily more poisonous. On 1 June 1917 *Le Soleil* advised Albert Sévigny, one of Borden's only two remaining French Canadian cabinet ministers, that if he really supported the government's policy he should avoid his riding of Dorchester: "*Si vous êtes en faveur de la conscription, ne retournez jamais dans Dorchester, car non seulement vous perdriez votre mandat de député, mais vous risqueriez d'y laisser votre peau.*" [If you are in favour of conscription, never come back to Dorchester, for you will not only lose your seat, but you run the risk of leaving your skin there.] Almost every warm evening during June and July crowds of young men surged through the streets in the French-speaking quarters of Montreal breaking windows, firing off blank rounds, and shouting "*A bas Borden*" and "*Vive la Révolution.*"

"Revolution" was a common theme in the oratory of the young firebrands who quickly rose to fame through their ability to command the crowds in the streets, despite (or perhaps because of) the fact that they were thereby courting a charge of sedition. Tancrède Marsil, whose anti-war newspaper *Le Réveil* had closed down in March 1917 after a warning from Ottawa, got his second wind from the government's decision to bring in conscription and soon exercised a powerful influence through his new paper *La Liberté* and his impassioned speeches. In late June in Waterloo, in the Eastern Townships, he told the crowd: "before we have conscription, we will have revolution," and added that the people of Quebec would prefer to see "*deux ou trois milles hommes tués dans les rues plûtot que d'envoyer en Europe trois cent mille hommes*" [two or three thousand men killed in the streets rather than send three hundred thousand men to Europe]. His angry audience responded by breaking nearby windows and cursing the Quebec Conservatives.

Talk like that made people very nervous in 1917, when real revolutions were breaking out in some other parts of the world: it was scarcely a year since the Easter Rising in Dublin, and only a couple of months since the Russian revolution in Petrograd. And the pressure in Quebec just went on building: on 15 July Colonel Lavergne declared before 15,000 people at Quebec City:

> *Si la loi de conscription est mise en vigueur, les Canadiens n'ont qu'un seul choix, mourir en Europe, ou mourir au Canada. En ce qui me concerne, si mon corps doit tomber dans un pays quelconque, je veux que ce soit sur le sol canadien.*

> [If the Conscription law is enforced (French) Canadians have only one choice – to die in Europe or to die in Canada. As far as I am concerned, if my body is to fall in any land, I want it to be on Canadian soil.]

On 24 July Ottawa moved to close down Tancrède Marsil's new newspaper, *La Liberté*, after it had called for a general strike, a run on the banks and, if necessary, a revolution – but by that time a certain Elie Lalumière, a dealer in electrical fixtures and one of Marsil's many rivals in street rhetoric, was claiming to have five hundred men under training in Montreal to resist conscription by force of arms.

The first phase of the crisis peaked in August, as Borden's Military Service Bill finally passed into law with the support of more than twenty English-speaking Liberals who had deserted Laurier to vote for it. Lord Atholstan, the publisher of the *Montreal Star* and a vocal supporter of conscription, had received numerous threats, and at four o'clock on the morning of 9 August his house at Cartierville, a rural part of Montreal Island, was dynamited. It was a large stone house and none of the family or servants was hurt, but the explosives were found to be from a load of 350 pounds of dynamite that had been stolen from a quarry by a gang of masked men at the beginning of the month. A terrorist campaign was feared, and so the Dominion Police* were brought in. They offered a

---

* The Dominion Police were founded in 1867 to provide security in Ottawa, but they were pressed into service during the First World War to supervise the enforcement of conscription. They were ultimately amalgamated with the R.C.M.P. in 1921.

large reward for the culprits, twelve men were arrested – and one of them turned out to be the regular anti-conscription speaker, Elie Lalumière.

Lalumière detailed plots to blow up the *Star* offices, the *Gazette*, and the Mount Royal Club, and to assassinate Sir Robert Borden and other well-known political figures. The English-language press described his associates as "desperadoes, cocaine fiends, wanted for several murders and crimes". By the end of the summer of 1917 many members of the public in Montreal were signing an anti-conscription "Declaration" which warned that "if the Bill is enforced Borden and his men will have to suffer the penalty of death," and on 30 August the city was swept by demonstrations, marches, outbreaks of looting and clashes with the police during which revolvers were freely used and at least seven men were wounded.

But the proto-insurrectionary character of the street violence and the growing number of attacks on property in the anti-conscription protests began to worry the French Canadian establishment. The higher clergy of the Catholic church in Quebec, in accord with tradition, had supported the British from the start and now reluctantly backed conscription too, but hitherto the French Canadian political and cultural élites (and the business élite, such as it was) had mostly turned a blind eye to what was happening in the streets because of their sympathy for the anti-conscriptionist cause. Matters were now clearly getting out of hand, however – and at the same time they were offered a safer and more moderate way of opposing conscription, in the form of an imminent federal election.

In September the Montreal police began to break up anti-conscription meetings and several well-known nationalist orators were arrested (although they were soon released on bail again). By the end of the month the momentum of the campaign in the streets was broken, and its passions were diverted into the federal election campaign that began in October. For there did, after all, seem to be a chance of defeating conscription through the ballot box.

By October 1917 Prime Minister Borden had succeeded in forming a "Union" government, which incorporated most of the English-speaking Liberals, especially from Ontario and the west, as well as his own Conservatives. However, he had failed to win bipartisan support for an extension of Parliament past its normal term. That meant that he had to call an election before the end of 1917, and he was by no means certain of winning that election. Even in English Canada organized labour and farmers were dead against conscription, and the popular magazine *Everywoman's World* found that a six-to-one majority among its readers opposed it (although that mattered less, since women didn't have the vote). What worried Borden's government most, however, was "French, foreigners, slackers."

Quebec was a lost cause for the Conservatives: the entire Nationalist movement, with Henri Bourassa in the lead, placed itself at the service of the Liberal opposition. "We ask nothing better than to assist Laurier to throw out of power the Government which has proved itself a traitor to the Nation," Bourassa wrote in *Le Devoir* – and the Nationalists ran practically no candidates of their own in Quebec in order not to split the anti-conscription vote.

The Conservatives had good reason to worry about the prairie provinces, too. They could more or less count on the "British" element of the western population, especially in the towns, since most of those families already had relatives at the front (although farmers who depended on their sons' labour were a rather less predictable factor). But the great surge of immigration that had rapidly populated the prairies in the two decades before the war had also included a high proportion of "foreigners" – particularly Ukrainians – who felt even less enthusiasm than French Canadians for sending their sons to die for Britain: all three Prairie provinces had voted Liberal in the most recent provincial elections.

But in the West (unlike Quebec), the "Union" government was presented with the temptation to shift the voting balance radically by disfranchising the Ukrainians, most of whom came from Austrian-controlled Galicia and therefore technically counted as enemy aliens. Nor would such a flagrant act of electoral manipulation alienate those Prairie voters, mostly "British," who were potential Conservative supporters. The Ukrainians were not actually sympathetic to their former Austrian imperial masters, of course, but Anglo-Saxon jealousy at the growing prosperity of Ukrainian homesteaders, and fury at the refusal of Ukrainian farm labourers to accept the low pre-war wages at a time of booming grain prices, easily translated into racism.

The Ukrainians' technical status as "enemy aliens" provided a socially acceptable facade for this prejudice. From the harvest of 1916 on, western farmers were demanding that enemy aliens – indeed all "foreigners" – be conscripted to work as farm labourers for $1.10 a day (the pay of a Canadian soldier in France), supporting their demands with rationalizations like the following piece of doggerel published in a Saskatchewan weekly farmers' newspaper. Farmer "John Reaper" tries to hire four "Austrian" labourers–"Bohunkis," "Ruffneck," "Hoboko," and "Tuffguysky" – only to have them dance around him singing:

> Hoch, hoch, hoch
> We laugh at you, old sock;
> We hope your grain will freeze and rot;
> We hope your farm will go to pot;
> Us fellers, Kaiser Bill und Gott
> Will work at harvest for you not.
> The Austrians we left behind
> Are always present in our mind.
> You do not like it very well
> But you and yours can go to hell.

The same racism prevailed at more exalted levels: one Alberta M.L.A. told the *Toronto Telegram* how sad it made him to see "the country being cleared of our fine Anglo-Saxon stock and the alien left to fatten on war prosperity." The Wartime Elections Act of 1917 adroitly exploited this prejudice–and destroyed the mainstay of Liberal anti-conscriptionist sentiment in the West – by taking the vote away from all naturalized Canadians born in enemy countries who had arrived in Canada after 1902. It was election-rigging on a breath-taking scale. Borden's government also generously gave women the vote – but only to women who might be expected to support conscription: those serving as nurses with the Canadian forces, and the far larger number of female relatives of serving soldiers. (One angry suffragette leader wrote to Borden suggesting that it would have been simpler if he just disqualified everyone who didn't promise to vote Conservative.)

The Military Voters' Act was designed to take care of any remaining difficulties the government might have in winning the 1917 election. According to the Act, soldiers' votes could be assigned to any electoral district that they chose (and government polling agents were often on hand to offer helpful suggestions). The beauty of this procedure was that, since the troops overseas voted after the election was over in Canada (and could be trusted to vote for conscription), their ballots could then be allocated to those marginal ridings where just a few hundred more votes would let the Unionist candidate win. It was Arthur Meighen, the Conservative party's chief fixer (who became Solicitor-General in 1913, added the portfolio of Secretary of State in 1915, and was Minister of the Interior by 1917), who came up with the cynical strategy to "shift the franchise from the . . . anti-British of the male sex and extend it at the same time to our patriotic women," but both he and Borden insisted that this wasn't gerrymandering, and that in any case the end justified the means:

> Our first duty is to win at any cost the upcoming elections, in order that we may continue to do our part in winning this war and that Canada not be disgraced.
>
> Robert Borden, diary, September 1917

The election was held in December, six months after conscription had been introduced. The pro-Borden *Colonist* in Victoria warned voters against "Bolsheviki intoxicated with the hope of power" (the Liberals, presumably), and the Toronto *Daily News* printed a map of Canada with Quebec outlined in black, labelled "The Foul Blot on Canada." Meanwhile it was practically impossible for Union government candidates to get their views heard in Quebec. Albert Sévigny was shot at, stoned, and unable to say a word at St-Anselme, in his former riding of Dorchester, and he was howled down even in Westmount. Another Union meeting, this time in Sherbrooke, turned into a three-hour riot.

After a while Unionist candidates in Quebec gave up because of inadequate police protection, and Borden cancelled his one scheduled Montreal appearance. But the predictable hostility of French Canadians in Quebec worried Borden and his Union supporters far less than the favourable reception that Laurier's anti-conscription campaign was getting in rural Ontario and the West. Many English-speaking farmers did not like the Military Service Act any more than French Canadians did: they called conscription "a conspiracy of the rich and powerful against the lowly." So to win back the farmers' votes from the Liberals, Borden passed an order-in-council decreeing that "farmers' sons who are honestly engaged in the production of food will be exempt from military service."

All the careful stacking of the deck paid off. In the December 1917 election, most of the female relatives of serving soldiers (who had been promised that none of the remaining men in their families would be conscripted) voted for the government. In the Prairie provinces, where most voters of Ukrainian, German, Austrian, Hungarian, and Croatian descent had been disfranchized, Unionist candidates swept the board, winning forty-one out of forty-three seats. Despite all Borden's massaging of the voting lists, the Conservative majority among civilian voters was still barely a hundred thousand votes. But soldiers voted almost twelve-to-one for the government, tripling its majority and changing the outcome in fourteen ridings (although the scheme to shift their votes into marginal constituencies was largely foiled by the Chief Electoral Officer). In the end, Borden's Conservatives won 115 seats and his "Union" Liberal allies took thirty-eight – but only three of those seats were in Quebec. Laurier's Liberals took sixty-two seats in Quebec, and only twenty in all the rest of the country. Canada had never been so divided.

Only one Liberal did well out of the 1917 election, and it would have taken some foresight to realize it at the time. Mackenzie King had wavered on the conscription issue for a time: he rebuffed an approach from the Union government, which was having great success at recruiting pro-conscriptionist Liberals, but did consider simply not running. But he finally returned to his original convictions and waged an apparently suicidal anti-conscription campaign in North York (the old seat of his grandfather, William Lyon Mackenzie, before the 1837 rebellion). Election day was the worst of King's life: he was overwhelmingly defeated and his beloved mother died. But as he watched Laurier's political destruction spelled out in the election returns, he was also aware that Quebec would remember the Conservative imposition of conscription long after the war was over: "This will make me prime minister," he told a friend.

❖

Just after the election, Sir Wilfrid Laurier wrote to a Liberal friend commanding a regiment in France to explain why the English-speaking Liberals who had deserted him had been wrong: "Your reason to take the stand which you took is: 'To us speedy reinforcements seem to take precedence of all else.' I appreciate the point of view, but you will see how far wrong you were. The conscription measure was introduced in the first week of June [1917]. We are now in the third week of January [1918] and not ten thousand men, if indeed half that many, have been brought into the ranks by this measure."

The defect in the Military Service Act was the numerous exemptions that could be applied for – but without those exemptions, Borden would probably never have won the election. Of the 400,000 unmarried men in Canada aged between twenty and thirty-four, the so-called "first class," 380,000 had claimed exemptions by the end of 1917 (and Ontario, for all its electoral support of the government, claimed more exemptions than Quebec: 118,000 for Ontario, 115,000 for Quebec). Exemption tribunals were staffed by local people and reflected local loyalties and prejudices. The Quebec tribunals were accused of granting almost blanket exemptions to French-speaking applicants, while "they applied conscription against the English-speaking minority in Quebec with a rigor unparalleled," according to the chief appeal judge, Mr Justice Lyman Duff of the Supreme Court. Military representatives took to appealing virtually every exemption, and Laurier began to worry out loud about what the government would do next – and about how Quebec would respond:

It is now felt on the Treasury Benches that conscription was a failure, and that coercion will not produce the results which its authors anticipated. There are strong reasons for believing that the government would quietly let the Act pass into oblivion, but the blind, the fools and the miscreants [of English Canada] who coerced the government to coerce still hold the whip high over their heads.

And now the band of the blind, the fools and the miscreants is being strengthened by those other blind, fools and miscreants who at this moment are stirring up the people of Quebec to violence and riot.

In early 1918 the Military Service Act was toughened. Nineteen-year-olds were ordered to report for service, and men between twenty and twenty-two were exempted only if they were the sole remaining son of military age in the family. Every young man in the first class had to carry a written proof of exemption or be liable to arrest. All over the country, young men vanished into the woods:

> A mounted policeman once told me of the men who had gone way deep into the Peace River country or the Athabaska country and hid out. He would be searching around, and find them in a cabin someplace or other. And I remember him telling me of a mother that practically scratched his eyes out–she had three sons hidden around the country, and saw that they got food.
>
> Naomi Radford, Edmonton

In Quebec, opposition to the new regulations was spectacular, especially since a hasty marriage was no longer a way out of the draft (men now had to have been married prior to 6 July 1917 to claim exemption). There were still thirty thousand appeals before the courts, but the Minister of Justice was making arrangements to speed the process up and feelings were reaching fever pitch: the popular resistance that seemed to have crested in August 1917, and to have been almost completely dissipated by the December election, came roaring back to life.

> *C'est un petit conscrit,*
> *Que l'on prend dans son pays,*
> *Parce qu'il faut sur une terre lointaine*
> *Encore bien du sang qu'à la guerre inhumaine.*
> *C'est un bien triste sort,*
> *D'aller risquer la mort,*
> *Si loin des siens, si loin de son pays.*
> *Plaignez le petit conscrit!*
>
> Popular Quebec song, 1918

[There's a little conscript
Taken from his home
Because the cruel war needs still more blood
in a distant land.
It's a bitter fate
To go and face death
So far from his people, so far from home.
Pity the little conscript!]

The delayed-action conscription crisis of 1918 was quite inevitable. During all the protests of 1917, the subject had been emotional but almost entirely theoretical: the machinery ground into action so slowly that few conscripts actually disappeared into the army before the end of that year. By early 1918, however, everybody in Quebec knew someone who had already been conscripted, or who was facing the near-certainty of conscription at any moment. It put the issue in a very different light, and things came to a head at the beginning of Easter weekend in Quebec City, when the Dominion Police detained a young man named Mercier who was unable to show proof of an exemption.

Mercier finally managed to get permission to go home and produce his papers, and he was then duly released – but meanwhile a crowd of several thousand had gathered, angered at "the tactless and grossly unwise fashion in which the Federal Police in charge of the Military Service Act did their work" (as the jury put it at the subsequent inquest). To vent their anger, the crowd proceeded to burn down the police station. The mayor tried to get them to disperse – but the mob, singing "O Canada" and "*La Marseillaise*," attacked the offices of the *Quebec Chronicle* and *L'Événement* instead. The following evening another mob attacked the offices of the Registrar of Military Service and burned all the files.

In an act of singular ineptitude, the local military authorities then brought in a battalion of Toronto soldiers as reinforcements. The officer in charge of the operation was one of the army's few senior French Canadians, Major General F. L. Lessard, but mutual incomprehension and suspicion between francophone crowds and anglophone troops did not help matters – nor did charging at the crowds with bayonets. On Sunday, 31 March, the army also resorted to cavalry charges, driving back the crowds with axe handles. By then, military discipline was breaking down and some soldiers were firing at the mobs. Charles "Chubby" Power, the young Liberal M.P. for Quebec South, a veteran who had served overseas, reported hearing an officer from his own regiment admit that he had been unable to prevent some of his soldiers from opening fire. He had not seen any wounded, he said.

On Easter Monday, the Old Town looked like a battlefield. Using snow banks and ice barricades for shelter, the crowds were throwing bricks, stones, blocks of ice or whatever else they could lay their hands on at the soldiers. There were a few shots heard from the direction of the mob, and at first the troops replied with volleys over their heads.

*Après le deuxième coup tiré dans la direction de la rue Bagot, il a été dit:* "Come on, you French sons of bitches, we'll trim you!" *Les soldats étaient pas mal dispersés. Ils disaient:* "Go back, you French Cock-suckers", *et* "Go back, you French Cunt-lickers". *Et puis dans l'intervalle, il y a un officier qui est arrivé. Il dit:* "I will fix the machine gun. We will do better work."

Testimony of Wilfrid Dion at the Coroner's inquest,
Quebec, 12 April 1918

[After the second shot fired in the direction of Bagot St., they said: "Come on, you French sons of bitches, we'll trim you!" The soldiers were quite spread out. They were saying: "Go back, you French Cock-suckers" and "Go back, you French Cunt-lickers." And then, during a lull, an officer arrived. He said: "I will fix the machine gun. We will do better work."]

So I started the machine gun, and stopped it just like that (the witness snaps his fingers). It ran about three-quarters of the drum: so 36 shots were fired.

Testimony of Major George Rodgers, Quebec,
10 April 1918

There were two more bursts of machine-gun fire. An estimated thirty-five civilians were wounded, and four were killed. One of them was only fourteen years old. It was not exactly the storming of the Bastille, but the authorities feared insurrection in Quebec, and on 4 April 1918 the Governor-in-Council was given the power to call out the troops whether the civil authorities asked for them or not. In such a situation martial law would be declared; habeas corpus would be suspended and "persons disobedient to such military orders shall be tried and punished by court martial."

❖

*Bailleulval. 18 mai 1918.*
*Réveil ce matin à trois heures. Toute l'arrière-garde du 22ème se met en marche pour assister à une des plus tristes scènes de ma vie en*

*soldat: celle de l'exécution d'un malheureux camarade coupable de désertion et de lâcheté en face de l'ennemi. . . .*

Arthur Lapointe, *Souvenirs d'un Soldat du Québec*

[Bailleulval. May 18, 1918.

I got up at 3 o'clock this morning. The rear details of the battalion were ordered to take part in one of the saddest scenes I have ever witnessed, the execution of a soldier, guilty of desertion and cowardice in face of the enemy.

After marching for an hour and a half, we reached a little village whose name I do not know. We entered a big court-yard, surrounded by a stone wall. In a house at one end of the yard were military police. The condemned man appeared suddenly between two policemen. In passing, he cast a glance at us, so hopeless that the tears rose in my eyes. He disappeared behind a screen, erected to conceal him from sight. Behind this screen, the firing squad was in place. All of a sudden, a volley rang out. . . .

Now, we have to march past the body of the executed man, who is still tied to the chair in which he died. Blood has stained his tunic and his head has fallen on his chest. His face reveals complete resignation and on his lips is the trace of a smile.]

Twenty-five Canadian soldiers were executed in the field during the First World War, all but two of them for desertion or "misbehaviour before the enemy." The executions were a direct measure of the mounting strain on the Canadian army. Canadian soldiers convicted of desertion or cowardice all had their sentences commuted to terms of imprisonment until the war was almost two years old, but then there were seven executions in seven weeks after the Battle of the Somme in July 1916. Executions "to encourage the others" then continued at a steady pace until the war's end – with one particular group being, in historian Desmond Morton's words, "conspicuously over-represented": seven of the twenty-five men executed had French names, and five of them were from the sole French-speaking battalion, the 22nd.

The military machines everywhere were starting to show the strain. By 1918 both the French and the Italian armies had come close to disintegration, and the Russian army had collapsed utterly. The Bolshevik coup of November 1917 had taken Russia entirely out of the war, and the Germans were moving large numbers of troops from the former Eastern Front to the Western Front for a make-or-break offensive. With British forces worn down by the Passchendaele offensive (which had been launched partly to distract the Germans from noticing the terrible state of the French army), Prime Minister Lloyd George of Britain sent a request to Borden on Easter weekend 1918 for still more Canadian troops. In France, General Currie broke his own rule and sent Canadian reinforcements to British units. And in England Lester Pearson, recently commissioned a lieutenant after two years' service in the ranks, was recuperating from an accident that had interrupted his training in the Royal Flying Corps.

> I spent much of that sick leave with a Canadian friend, Clifford Hames, who had just finished his abbreviated flying training and was on leave before going to France. We spent hours trying to get some understanding of what we were being asked to do; to bring some reason to the senseless slaughter. For what? King and country? Freedom and democracy? These words sounded hollow now in 1918 and we increasingly rebelled against their hypocrisy. Cliff Hames and I came closer together in that short time than I have ever been with any person since, outside my family. He knew where he was bound within a few days. He could not know it was to his death within the month. I did not know what was to happen to me. . . .
>
> We both assumed that our generation was lost. The war was going badly in France. The great German March offensive was about to begin. The fighting would go on and on and on. We, who were trapped in it, would also go on and on until we joined the others already its victims. All this had to be accepted. It never occurred to us that we could do anything about it. We might as well make the best of it, getting what pleasure we could.
>
> Lester Pearson, *Mike: Memoirs, Volume 1*
> ("Mike" was the invention of Pearson's Royal Flying
> Corps squadron commander, who thought "Lester" an
> inappropriate name for a fighter pilot.)

For Germany, the spring of 1918 was the last chance for victory. The Allied blockade was causing severe shortages of food and raw materials at home, and the arrival of large numbers of American troops at the front within a few months would leave the Germans permanently outnumbered. So General Ludendorff deliberately stripped his divisions of all their best remaining troops and concentrated them into assault units that would, he hoped, gain a decisive breakthrough and end the war. They almost succeeded.

On 21 March 1918 the Germans struck on the Somme. Within a week the British and French armies lost more ground than they had won in the previous three years of offensives, and were in danger of being split apart. In Canada, Borden called a secret session of Parliament to explain the peril, and passed an order-in-council effectively cancelling all exemptions for single men, including farmers. In mid-May, five thousand farmers arrived in Ottawa to protest the new policy. Troops prevented them from approaching the Houses of Parliament, but Borden spoke to them and told them bluntly that the government had taken a solemn pledge to reinforce the Canadian Corps. As long as he was prime minister, that pledge would be fulfilled.

But long before any further reinforcements reached the Canadian Corps, the Germans' spring offensive ran out of steam. Although they had gained a good deal of ground, they never got their breakthrough, and in trying for it they had used up most of their remaining good troops. It was the Canadians and Australians, attacking side by side near Amiens, who made the great breakthrough on 8 August, the longest advance that any Allied attack had yet achieved in the war. Ludendorff called it "the black day of the German army." From August on, the Germans were in almost constant retreat – and the Canadian and Australian divisions, whose condition was still far better than most of the British units, were consistently used to spearhead the attacks. Between 22 August and 11 October 1918 the Canadian Corps lost over 1,500 officers and 30,000 casualties in the other ranks.

I guess you have heard now of the Big Push, of the battle of Amiens, in which the Canadians took a prominent part. . . . It was a terrible battle, our Division winding up the advance and holding the ground gained. Our battalion took the last objective. The Company I am with went into the attack 140 strong, and when the roll was called, only 32 answered. I am sorry to say I lost two dandy chums – one missing and one killed. I tried to help bandage Aubrey but it was no use, as the bullet had gone through his head. . . .

Corporal Walter Cullen (Paris, Ontario), August 1918

(*At the Forks of the Grand, Volume 2*)

I got wounded on the Saturday, and the War ended on the Monday morning. I had a rather nice time during the war: I was in the Cycle Corps, we weren't up the line, we weren't in the mud all the time. We were mobile infantry, and they started to use us at the last, so I had a rougher time towards the end than I did earlier on in the war.

I was on a patrol that was trying to get into Mons, and there were four on the patrol. Two were killed, I was wounded, and one got away scot-free – he'd been sent back with a message.

George Turner (Edmonton)

The Third Canadian Division, at the price of many sacrifices, penetrated the city at three o'clock in the morning, avenging thus by a brilliant success the retreat of 1914. Glory and gratitude to it.

Proclamation of the Town Council of Mons

On 11 November 1918 Robert Borden was at sea, on his way to England to discuss with Lloyd George and the Imperial War Cabinet what position the British delegates to a peace conference should take after the war was won:

At 12.30 ship's time purser in tremendous excitement came to my room with startling announcement that Germany signed armistice at 5 a.m.; hostilities to cease at 11 a.m. today. . . . This means complete surrender. The Kaiser is reported as seeking refuge in Holland, but the Dutch don't want him. Rumours that several of German princelets and kinglets have abdicated or fled. Revolt has spread all over Germany. The question is whether it will stop there.

> Robert Borden, *Memoirs, Volume 2*

❖

The old international system should have died after the First World War – and there was certainly a determined attempt to kill it. Four years of the most devastating war in European history, over a Balkan quarrel whose protagonists had mostly disappeared by 1918, were enough to convince large numbers of people (and even their governments) that there was something dreadfully wrong with the traditional way of running the world. War had become far too costly a means of settling disputes between the great powers, and so the nations began to cast around for an alternative.

(1) Open covenants of peace openly arrived at . . .
(2) Absolute freedom of the seas . . .
(4) General disarmament consistent with domestic safety . . .
(14) Creation of a general association of nations for the purpose of providing international guarantees of political independence and territorial integrity for all nations.

> President Woodrow Wilson, *The Fourteen Points*,
> 8 January 1918

The Lord God had only ten.

> French Prime Minister Georges Clemenceau,
> about Wilson's Fourteen Points

Woodrow Wilson's formulation of Allied war aims for the U.S. Congress at the beginning of 1918 was light-years distant from what those aims had been in 1914, but the war had greatly changed the way people saw the world. "If it ain't broke, don't fix it" – and so the international system had staggered on for centuries, periodically producing a general war, but never doing irreparable harm to its major players. By 1918, however, it *was* broke: it had delivered all the great powers into a war grotesquely out of proportion to the purposes for which they had entered it (insofar as they had any clear aims at all). They had fought it to the bitter end because they did not know how to stop it, and dared not admit to their own peoples that it was not about anything worth fighting for.

But at the same time it was quite clear to both the leaders and the led that this must be "the war to end all wars". And since only the naïve and the ignorant believed that defeating their enemies in this particular war would suffice to abolish war itself, many people were prepared to contemplate the radical idea that the international system itself would have to be changed.

The notion of an international organization to prevent war had been floating around for half a century, but it fell to Woodrow Wilson, the rigid and sanctimonious university professor who became president of the United States, to put it on the agenda of the world's governments. His idea for a League of Nations was gravely flawed, but it was an idea that would never go away again. However reluctant governments and peoples might be to change their old ways, there was a general recognition that it had to be tried, because the alternative – a future of ever more destructive technological wars – was even worse.

❖

We are the Dead. Short days ago
We lived, felt dawn, saw sunset glow,
   Loved and were loved, and now we lie
    In Flanders fields.

Take up our quarrel with the foe:
To you from failing hands we throw
   The torch; be yours to hold it high.
   If ye break faith with us who die
We shall not sleep, though poppies grow
   In Flanders fields.
      John McCrae, Canadian Expeditionary Force (died 1918)

That never-to-be-forgotten day, 11 November 1918, saved the rest of my generation and gave the world not peace, but a reprieve.

1939 was only twenty years away; we did not keep the faith with those who died; the torch was not held high.

Lester Pearson, *Mike: Memoirs, Volume 1*

The First World War remains the most profound trauma in Canada's history, although it all happened long ago and thousands of miles away. The names of our quarter-million dead and wounded are mostly forgotten now, but the effects of that collective act of self-immolation still reverberate in our national life today. However, keeping faith with the dead of the First World War has more often been interpreted by Canadians as an injunction to go and fight the Germans again (or the Russians, or whomever) than in Pearson's more perceptive sense, as a call for Canadians to play their part in the immense task of abolishing war.

The fact that we fought the First World War on other people's territory for other people's purposes has contributed greatly to the confusion Canadians feel about their role in the world: for many English Canadians the great lesson of the war was that international politics is a crusade of good nations against evil ones. Their consequent willingness to place the country at the disposal of Britain in the great-power struggle (a loyalty subsequently transferred virtually intact to the United States) has been the single most powerful influence on our foreign policy down to the present. For Canada's experience in the First World War is the foundation of English Canada's national identity.

The orchestra at dinner greeted the entrance of the Canadians with the strains of "O Canada", and the guests, nearly all themselves in uniform, stood to honour it. The stately air has become the distinctive national song of the Dominion during these months . . . as a symbol of a united will and a common birthplace.

It is a matter for much surprise and regret that even now no official English form of words has been selected for general use, among the many translations of the original that have been printed at various times. It is time that it should be sung as well as played, though it must of course remain secondary to "The King", the anthem of the British Empire.

Nursing Sister Mabel Clint, Folkestone, England,

July 1915, (*Our Bit*)

The First World War saw the birth of a distinctive English Canadian national consciousness (with a borrowed French Canadian anthem), but French Canada was not present at the birth. The great irony is that a lot of English Canada wasn't present either, although it later pretended it had been. Even after vigorous and repeated recruiting drives and the ultimate imposition of conscription dragged many native-born English Canadians into the army, the proportion of native born in the Canadian forces rose to only 51 per cent by the end of 1918. The great bulk of the remainder were drawn from the relatively small fraction of first-generation British immigrants in the population, who volunteered for the war at a rate at least as high as that of the New Zealanders or the British themselves.

In Canada as a whole the rate of enlistment was lower even than in Australia (with its large Irish population) or in English-speaking South Africa. English-speaking Canadians had, on average, been in their own country longer than the populations of the other "white dominions," and had had the time to get their bearings. Their sentimental attachment to the "Motherland" remained, but they knew that their practical interests were different, so they did not volunteer as readily to fight for Britain. Nevertheless, the fact that so many people fought in Canadian uniform, and suffered so greatly, had a profound effect on English Canadians' subsequent view of themselves and the world. The "British Canadians" who went off to the trenches, whether English-born or native-born, returned simply as Canadians – but they were a very different kind of Canadian from those who spoke French.

> I venture to think that the French Canadians who have fought and died in France and Flanders are more truly representative of the spirit and ambitions of their race than those who, like [Bourassa], have remained in Canada and refused to share in the glory and agony of this our national birth. It was as a Canadian that I appealed to him, not as an Imperialist.
>
> Talbot Papineau, after he had read Bourassa's reply to his
> open letter, August 1916

Talbot Papineau was a gallant figure, but desperately out of step with his compatriots. French Canada's war was mostly at home, against the demands that it fight in Britain's war in Europe. The exact figures cannot be determined, but of the more than 600,000 men and women who served in the Canadian forces during the war, only around 35,000 were French Canadians (a proportionate share would have been around 200,000) and fewer than half of the French Canadians who did enlist ever saw the front. Moreover, although Quebec contains about seven-eighths of Canada's French-speaking population, almost half of the 15,000 French Canadian volunteers serving in April 1917 (before conscription began to distort the figures) were from the French Canadian communities *outside* Quebec, which were much more exposed to the influence of English Canadian public opinion.

> *9 juin 1918.*
>
> *Dans la tranchée bouleversée par le bombardement, règne maintenant le calme. L'artillerie, fatiguée de la rude besogne de cette dernière nuit, se repose.*
>
> *Quelques soldats allongés dans un trou recouvert d'une toile, l'air sombre et abattu, méditent sans doute sur les péripéties de la vie guerrière. Je reconnais quelques conscrits rencontrés hier. Je les plains de tout mon coeur. . . .*
>
> Arthur Lapointe, *Souvenirs d'un Soldat du Québec*

> [June 9, 1918.
> In the trench, wrecked by the bombardment of last night, all is now quiet and peaceful. The gunners are now taking things easily.
>
> Several men are lying in a shelter, thinking probably of the strange vicissitudes of a soldier's life. I recognize some of the conscripted men who joined us yesterday. I am sorry for them from the bottom of my heart. They have been sent out here against their will, while the rest of us have voluntarily assumed our task. A dozen of the conscripts were killed last night, their first night in the line. They lie now in a corner of the trench, waiting until someone moves them to the rear for burial.]

Conscripts, including a handful of French Canadian conscripts, began to reach the army in France only in the closing months of the war. For all the tumult it caused, the Military Service Act had raised only 83,355 men by November 1918, of whom 7,100 were absent on compassionate leave and 15,333 on agricultural leave. Seventeen months' operation of the conscription law therefore produced only 61,000 soldiers, of whom most never reached France.

The many delays and errors involved in the application of conscription were certainly a blessing, for if the war had lasted long enough for conscripts from Quebec to begin dying in the trenches in large numbers – and the British generals were planning for a war that continued into 1920 – then the events of Easter Monday 1918 in Quebec City might have been repeated and magnified a hundredfold. By 1920 the war might really have come to Canada, and Quebec might have been occupied territory. As it was, French Canada's legacy from the war was bitterness at having been isolated and reviled for taking a position that even English Canadians would now concede to have been justifiable. French Canadians owed their loyalty to Canada alone, and would have fought to defend it, but the European war did not threaten Canada.

What French Canadians learned from 1914-18 was to distrust the instincts of English Canadians in matters of war and peace, and to resent and fear the majority's willingness to impose its views on the whole country in a crisis. What the conscription crisis was about, in Quebec's eyes, was the ruthless determination of English Canadians to order French Canadian young men to die for an exclusively English Canadian cause.

> *C'est un petit conscrit*
> *Qui meurt pour son pays,*
> *Sans même savoir pourquoi là-bas il tombe,*
> *Aucun ami pleurera sur sa tombe.*
> *Pour remplacer les pleurs,*
> *Gardez en votre coeur*
> *Le souvenir de tous les petits conscrits*
> *Qui meurt pour leur patrie!*

> [There's a little conscript
> Who dies for his country
> Without even knowing why he dies "over there."
> No friend will weep on his grave.
> Instead of tears
> Keep in your heart
> The memory of all the little conscripts
> Who die for their fatherland.]

Although few conscripts actually died, the bitterness of that memory has never quite gone away. As for those French Canadians who did volunteer for the war, out of a sense of adventure or a misplaced idealism, they are simply forgotten.

Dear Madam,

In confirmation of my telegram to you of yesterday's date, I regret exceedingly to inform you that an official report has been received to the effect that Captain A/Major T. M. Papineau, M.C., P.P.C.L.I. was killed in action on October 30, 1917.

Yours truly,

J. M. Knowles, Lieut.

### CHAPTER THIRTEEN

# *The Fireproof House*

On 11 November 1918, as the armistice finally descended on the Western Front, a group of Canadian gunners were fighting for their lives in northern Russia. Having advanced over a hundred miles up the Dvina River from Archangel to the village of Tulgas, they were surprised from the rear by a force of six hundred Soviet infantry. The Bolsheviks ("Bolos," as the Canadians called them) were seen only when they got within two hundred yards of the 67th Battery, and the artillerymen would have been overrun if their drivers and signallers had not managed to slow the attackers down with rifle fire until the gunners could get one of their 18-pounder guns out of its gun-pit, turn it around, and fire a quick-bursting shrapnel shell straight into the charging Russians at seventy-five yards' range. In those early days the intervention in Russia generally had a rather impromptu spirit about it.

> The first military operation at Soroka ... was a dashing reconnaissance carried out by Captain Adams, Canadian Engineers,

who was sent to Ruguzero in Karelia with a detachment of six Canadian sergeants and six Karelian soldiers . . . attached to the Canadian Syren Party.

. . . Although they had information that the village was occupied by a Red garrison of at least 150 soldiers, they decided to make an attack. Captain Adams sent Lieutenant Hordliski and the six Karelians with a Lewis gun to the southern end of the village. He and his six Canadian sergeants waited at the other end for zero hour. Then both parties dashed forward, firing and shouting, and the Bolsheviks, thinking they were surrounded and greatly outnumbered, capitulated without a fight. They were all herded into the village square, where they got the surprise of their lives when they discovered that a dozen determined men had killed or captured their whole garrison.

A big celebration was held at Canadian Headquarters when Captain Adams and his party returned with their prisoners, a dozen sleigh-loads of rifles, and all the documents of the Bolshevik headquarters in that district. The patrol had left Soroka on January 14th [1919] and returned on the night of January 17th, having covered 120 miles in horse-drawn sleighs.

John Hundevad, "A Saga of the North,"
*The Legionary*, 1936

The Allied intervention in northern Russia began with purely military motives in early 1918. It was aimed at bringing Russia back into the war, and although it quickly turned into an attempt to overthrow the Bolshevik regime that had signed a separate peace with the Germans, that was only a means to that end. The first Canadian soldiers who were sent to northern Russia in March 1918 as part of the "Syren Force," a multi-national concoction of British, French, Italian, American, and Canadian units, were part of that effort, and nobody in Canada objected to it.

A considerable number of Canadian airmen also fought for the counter-revolutionary forces in southern Russia in 1918-19: the 47th Squadron, Royal Air Force, a mixed squadron of fighters and bombers which provided air support for General Denikin's White armies, was commanded by Major Raymond Collishaw, Canada's second-highest-scoring ace in the First World War, and fifty-three of the sixty-two pilots he

296 The Defence of Canada

chose for the squadron were Canadian. But that too had nothing to do with policy-making in Canada. It was London's decision, not Ottawa's, since most Canadian airmen were still serving in the (British) Royal Air Force.

However, the decision to send five hundred Canadian reinforcements to Archangel, the capital city of northern Russia, in September 1918, and in particular the decision to dispatch four thousand Canadian troops to Vladivostok in the Russian Far East in October, were different from the start. Ottawa was playing its own hand there, for its own political ends.

> Intimate relations with that rapidly developing country [Russia] will be a great advantage to Canada in the future. Other nations will make very vigorous and determined efforts to obtain a foothold, and our interposition with a small military force would tend to bring Canada into favourable notice by the strongest elements in that great community.
>
> Sir Robert Borden to General Mewburn,
> Minister of Militia, 13 August 1918

The major Canadian intervention in Russia began when the Germans were on the brink of defeat, and continued well after their surrender. Borden, a nationalist who had come more and more to see Canada as a "principal power" in the war rather than a mere British hanger-on, had observed how the great powers used their military forces to advance their national interests abroad, and was tempted into trying Canada's hand at the game. So, on the assumption that the Bolsheviks would lose the Russian civil war and that the White Russian leaders would be duly grateful to those countries that had helped them win, Borden committed Canadian troops to Russia. He even arranged that a Canadian officer should command the entire five-thousand-strong British Empire contingent in Vladivostok, which was 80 per cent Canadian (largely conscripts).

Although the contingent in the Russian Far East never exchanged a shot with the Bolsheviks, the Canadian troops in northern Russia saw much heavy fighting. The Butch Cassidy flavour of the entire enterprise was much enhanced by the background of the commander of the Canadian "Syren Force" which advanced six hundred miles south along the railway from Murmansk to Petrograd (St. Petersburg to its old friends, but soon to become Leningrad). Colonel Jack Leckie had filled in the time between service with Lord Strathcona's Horse in the Boer War and the command of the 16th Canadian Infantry Battalion on the Western Front in the First World War by fighting as a mercenary in revolutions in Mexico and Venezuela. Leckie had personally picked the officers and men of "Syren Force," visiting the various Canadian camps in England to solicit volunteers for "a special mission to an unknown destination abroad," and by February 1919 he and the kindred spirits in his force were having the time of their lives:

> Early that morning, fearing that an attempt might be made to run an armoured train into the town [of Segaja, some 400 miles south of Murmansk], the Canadian Commander sent Captain R. M. Hodd and Sergeant R. J. Forbes, both of the Canadian Syren Party, across the river with two Russian railway workers. They jumped into a sleigh, galloped across the river and removed a rail at a spot where the enemy could be prevented by machine gun fire from the town from replacing it. Then, the job completed, they galloped back and returned safely, although they were under heavy short-range fire during the whole trip. The Bolsheviks made many attempts to replace that rail during the day's fighting but were unable to do so under the fire of 20 machine guns converged on this spot.
>
> The whole operation under Colonel Leckie's leadership was a complete success. The recruiting area for new Russian levies had been extended by over 3,000 square miles; the Bolsheviks had been taught a most salutary lesson . . . and feasibility of winter operations had been amply demonstrated. . . . The [Soviet] killed left behind, and prisoners, totalled nearly 200. . . . No wonder the Canadians had visions of reaching Petrograd before many months.
>
> John Hundevad, "A Saga of the North"

The Canadian airmen in southern Russia were having lots of fun, too. Raymond Collishaw scored his sixty-first and final victory by shooting down an Albatross D-V of the Red Air Fleet near Tsaritsyn (now Stalingrad) on the Volga. The intervention had now turned into an anti-Bolshevik crusade, but almost none of the airmen bothered their heads with political thoughts. They were there to improve their chances of gaining a permanent commission in the post-war Royal Air Force or Canadian Air Force, or just to continue their love affair with the airplane. And they did have some splendid adventures.

> [Captain W. F.] Anderson [of Toronto] and his observer, Lieutenant Mitchell, distinguished themselves on 30 July [1919] while carrying out a photographic reconnaissance along the Volga. When Anderson's fuel tank was punctured by fire from the ground, Mitchell climbed out on the port wing and plugged the leaks with his fingers, while Anderson jettisoned his bomb-load on a gunboat in the Volga. Meanwhile, Anderson's escort, a DH9 flown by Captain William Elliott . . . had been shot down by machine-gun fire; Anderson thereupon landed close by. "Several Squadrons of Cavalry attempted to surround our machine," he reported, "but they were kept clear by our machine-gun fire." Elliott set fire to his aircraft, he and his observer tumbled into the other DH9, and with Mitchell still plugging the holes in the fuel tank with his hand, Anderson flew home.
>
> S.F. Wise, *Canadian Airmen and the First World War*

Eventually, though, the intensely political character of what their troops were doing in the Soviet Union, and the fact that they had no business playing that sort of role in somebody else's country, began to dawn on Canadians. As discontent with the Russian commitment grew at home and the likelihood of a Bolshevik victory in the civil war became clearer, Borden started to back-pedal, and by April 1919 he was trying to get the Canadian troops home from Russia as quickly as possible. Not before time, because things were turning increasingly grim in Russia.

At Maselga [over four hundred miles south along the railway from Murmansk], the four Canadians stationed there – Lieutenant-Colonel L. H. MacKenzie, Major C. P. Fee, Captain Victor Weldie and Lieutenant J. F. Baker – had a rather "close shave". On July 5th 1919 one of the Russian privates whispered to an officer that a plot was being hatched to kill all the officers and stampede the men into going over to the Bolsheviks in a body. The ringleaders, whose names were obtained, were immediately arrested and, after being subjected to the usual, by no means gentle, "third degree" of their White fellow-countrymen, the details of the projected uprising were secured, together with the names of all who were implicated. The entire group were given prompt court-martial and, an equally prompt verdict having been rendered, the inevitable punishment was meted out on the spot by the White Russians, while a squad of Serbian instructors stood by with a Lewis gun to see that justice was properly dispensed.

The leader of this plot was found to have in his possession six pounds in weight of Soviet paper roubles with which to buy over the White soldiers. His plan, his confederates confessed, had been to murder the officers, including the four Canadians, while they slept; then assemble the men and tell them the Reds would welcome them with open arms, but that, if they refused to go over, the British would punish them for the murder of their officers.

John Hundevad, "A Saga of the North"

No doubt the British would have done exactly that, and one feels pity for the plight of the Russians who had enlisted (or had been press-ganged) to fill out the local regiments that the British and their Canadian allies were busily creating in north Russia: fighting in the service of a foreign power in the midst of a civil war is not the healthiest of occupations. But in fact, the issue was about to resolve itself. On 7 July 1919 there was a major mutiny in one of the new Russian regiments that had been created on the Archangel front, when its British and Russian officers were murdered and most of the men went over to the Bolsheviks, and on 20 July 1919 all the Russians on the Onega sector of the front mutinied simultaneously, thus isolating the foreign forces based on Archangel from those based on Murmansk. After that, it was just a question of getting the foreign forces out of Russia as quickly as possible, and the last Canadians left Murmansk in August.

❖

Canadian intervention in Russia was a foolish aberration, not at all typical of the behaviour of Canadian governments before or since. In 1917 Professor O. D. Skelton of Queen's University, observing Canada's rapid growth into a fully sovereign country, worried publicly about what kind of state it would become: "Surely Providence has something better in store for Canada than to become a nasty, quarrelsome little nation," he said – and by and large, Providence did.

The First World War was Canada's education in the art of being a sovereign state, and it was a very good time to learn. There is only one way to become a sovereign state: by gaining recognition from the other states in the club and accepting the rules by which they run the international system. By the time Canada joined, however, it was already obvious that the club was becoming a lethal madhouse, and that the rules would have to be changed if the members were to survive. The traditional anarchic behaviour of each state – the principle that Mussolini called "sacred selfishness" – was no longer tolerable in an era of industrialized warfare, and Canada paid its full share in blood for that lesson.

Canadians imbibed a basic mistrust of unlimited national sovereignty and power politics as part of the same experience by which we achieved statehood. As a result, the traditions and reflexes of the Canadian state are not fundamentally hostile to the creation of new international institutions beyond and above the national state, and that is all to the good. On the other hand, it was not to be expected that Canada would take a leading role in 1919 in the enterprise of reforming the international system, especially if it involved any significant price to the country itself. For one thing, Canada's geographical isolation from Europe, then the main theatre of great-power wars, made it easy (and therefore tempting) to evade the commitments we would have to accept if we took our full share of responsibility for changing the international system. For another, we were distracted and confused by the nature of our remaining links with Britain.

> The British Government could not call upon Canada to come into another war with regard to the causes of which she had had no voice. Canada was a nation of 8,000,000 people, twice as large as the United States when they became independent, and . . . unless she could have that voice in the foreign relations of the

Empire as a whole, she would before long have an independent
voice in her own foreign affairs outside the Empire.

> Sir Robert Borden, Minutes of the Imperial War Cabinet,
> 23 July 1918

Canada's view was that as an Empire we should keep clear, as far
as possible, of European complications and alliances. This feeling
had been immensely strengthened by the experience of the war,
into which we had been drawn by old-standing pledges and more
recent understandings, of which the Dominions had not even
been aware.

> Borden, Minutes of the Imperial War Cabinet,
> 30 December 1918

Borden was deeply hostile to the kind of alliances that Britain had
forged before 1914, which he saw as a contributory cause of the war, and
he was damned if he would ever let his country be dragged blindly into
another war like that. If Canada stayed in the Empire, he told the Imperial
War Cabinet, it was on condition that Ottawa have a voice in the conduct
of imperial affairs.

> He regarded the U.K., England, as the Mother Country, no ques-
> tion about it, and he was a great believer in the British Empire,
> but those views did not prevent him from being a very strong
> nationalist Canadian. . . . He did not regard Canada as a col-
> ony. . . . It was he who came up with the word "Commonwealth",
> rather than Empire. . . . He gave a great deal of credit to [the
> South African prime minister, General] Smuts, but Smuts did say
> to him after that Conference: "Borden, you and I have trans-
> formed the Empire".
>
> > Henry Borden, Sir Robert's nephew (who was with him
> > at the time)

The transformation was, in fact, only a way-station on the road to the
peaceful dissolution of the empire. The idea of a concerted imperial foreign policy, worked out in consultation between Britain and the Dominions and binding upon all of them, would not long survive the realities of

distance and differing interests. But it *was* working in 1918-19, and that was why Canada was able to achieve its major aim at the Peace Conference in Paris.

Prime Minister Borden was in Europe continuously from November 1918 to May 1919. His main preoccupation was to ensure that the wartime recognition of Canada's independent status within the empire, even in questions of defence and foreign policy, should be maintained in peacetime and accepted by the rest of the world as well. The first step was taken at the Imperial War Conference in December 1918, which was to decide on the form of imperial representation at the Paris Peace Conference. It was a subject about which Borden felt very strongly:

> Canada and the other Dominions would have regarded the situation as intolerable if they, who numbered their dead by the hundred thousands in the fiercest struggle the world had ever known, should stand outside the council chamber of the Conference while nations that had taken no direct or active part in the struggle stood within and determined the conditions of Peace.
>
> Borden, *Memoirs, Volume 2*

Borden, in co-operation with the prime ministers of the other Dominions, managed to get Britain's agreement to separate representation for the Dominions at Paris (plus a place for Canada on the joint imperial delegation). But that was only half the struggle; there remained the task of extracting the same recognition of Canada's new status from the other countries present. The main opposition came from the United States, whose Secretary of State, Robert Lansing, was "somewhat arrogant and offensive and desired to know why Canada should be concerned with the settlement of European affairs. . . . Mr Lloyd George replied that [they] believed themselves to have the right because . . . Canada as well as Australia had lost more men than the United States in this war." It was a difficult argument for an American to rebut, and in the end Canada was permitted to sign the peace treaties in its own right (although its name was indented, as were those of the other Dominions, to reflect its continuing membership in the British Empire).

There was a similar clash over the question of separate Canadian membership in the League of Nations, the new international body created by the Treaty of Versailles to keep the peace. Again the main opposition came from the United States, which affected to believe that the Dominions were not free to take an independent stand and that the whole issue was simply a British plot to get six votes (Britain, Canada, Australia, New Zealand, South Africa, and India) instead of one. However, American objections were again overridden, and Canada became a founding member of the League. By the middle of 1919 Canada for all practical purposes had received international recognition as a sovereign state, although some confusion remained in most capitals about the precise nature of the obligations and loyalties that still linked Ottawa to London.

Canadians, too, were rather confused about what was happening. There were certainly no celebrations about the country's new status. But some of the confusion even in Canada was understandable, for the achievement of sovereignty came as part of a package that was intended to abolish the most important single aspect of sovereignty: the independent right to make war.

❖

Even if I thought the proposal for a League of Nations absolutely impracticable, and that statesmen a hundred years hence would laugh at it as a vain attempt to accomplish the impossible, nevertheless, I would support the movement because of its supreme purpose and because it might succeed. . . .

Sir Robert Borden to the Imperial War Cabinet,
August 1918

If war is to be prevented or its likelihood to be diminished, that end can be attained only by there existing somewhere, if not a power that will control, at least an influence that will restrain the absolute sovereignty of the organised States in their dealings with each other.

Charles J. Doherty, Canadian Minister of Justice, Secret
Memo on the League of Nations, Paris, 27 January 1919

It has long been fashionable, with the privilege of hindsight, to dismiss the League of Nations as an abortive creation (and, by extension, to deride the United Nations as well). There has also, since the late 1940s, been a massive and largely successful attempt in the industrialized world to reinstate the pre-1914 belief in the value of alliances as a means of creating security and keeping the peace. But the statesmen of 1918 were still too close to the grim realities of the war to subscribe to that fallacy, and their glimpse of hell had finally persuaded them that something had to be done about the International system. "The psychological and moral conditions are ripe for a great change," General Smuts wrote in December 1918. "The moment has come for one of the great creative acts of history. . . . The tents have been struck, and the great caravan of humanity is again on the march."

It was not really the "great caravan of humanity" that demanded the creation of the League of Nations, however. It was mainly people in government, who understood that the war had been an inevitable product of the international system and that the system itself now had to be changed. It had served the victors well enough in the past (and the losers had no vote on how the system was run). But that past had been swept away by the advent of industrialized mass societies.

When the cost of a victorious war was far less than the advantages to be gained by it – as was still the case down to the mid-nineteenth century – then the dominant powers in the system were quite content to live with the recurrent great alliance wars (the phrase "world war" did not come into general use until the 1940s) that were an intrinsic part of that system. By the time of the First World War, however, the price of victory in warfare between industrialized countries had begun to race far ahead of any conceivable benefits that victory might bring.

The technology of killing, the economic resources to produce abundant quantities of that technology, and the political and social organization needed to keep entire populations committed to the enterprise of mass warfare – all the things that made the First World War such an atrocious experience for the countries that stumbled into it – were all the inevitable concomitants of an industrial civilization. And so a war that was, in its political dimension, scarcely distinguishable from the War of the Austrian Succession in the eighteenth century, ended up killing not a couple of hundred thousand regular soldiers but between eight and eleven million ordinary citizens.

Perhaps even worse (from the point of view of traditionalist statesmen and diplomats), the popular passions that were bound to be aroused by such mass slaughter had turned the war into a total war, even politically: *all* the losing great powers in the First World War had their regimes overthrown and their empires entirely dismantled. Indeed, the strain of total war had even destroyed the regime in one of the great powers on the winning side, Russia, and both the French and the Italians had had some anxious moments in 1917. The traditional zero-sum game with limited risks and rewards, and a guaranteed place in the next round for almost all the players, had unexpectedly turned into a no-holds-barred struggle that killed *regimes*–and that, of course, was bound to concentrate the minds of those who ran governments quite wonderfully. The cost-benefit equation of the existing international system had suddenly lurched deeply into the red, and something drastic had to be done to change it.

Perhaps we sound a trifle too cynical here. We certainly do not mean to imply that the people who created the League in 1918 were not genuinely appalled by the waste of life that they had just witnessed: the great majority of them had lost relatives or close friends in the holocaust themselves. They realized, moreover, that the price of war between industrialized societies would inevitably go on rising (although few could have guessed how far and how fast), and they were concerned for the fate of their own children or grandchildren in the next round, or the one after that. But the League would never have happened if the sovereign states that created it had not feared for their own future survival – nor could any amount of political and historical analysis have persuaded whole populations to accept the decisive break with deeply rooted national reflexes that the League represented if they had not experienced the First World War. Those who wanted to change the international system had a receptive mass audience for their views in 1918 – but they knew they had to move quickly.

> The great force on which we must rely is the hatred of the cruelty and waste of war which now exists. As soon as the war is over the process of oblivion will set in. . . . The chauvinists who believe that all foreigners are barbarians, the bureaucrats who think that whatever is, is right, the militarists who regard perpetual peace as an enervating evil, will . . . say "Can't you leave it alone." It is only, therefore, while the recollection of all we have been through

is burningly fresh that we can hope to overcome the inevitable opposition and establish at least the beginning of a new and better organisation of the nations of the world.

Lord Robert Cecil, British War Cabinet, 5 October 1918

In every country there were people who greeted the League of Nations with all the enthusiasm of feudal barons in twelfth-century Britain or France confronted with a proposal to establish a central government and domestic peace. It could never work, they insisted, and perhaps they were right – in which case we are condemned not just to perpetual war, but to terminal war. However, people like President Wilson, Lord Robert Cecil, and Prime Minister Borden were not naive idealists trying to create a "world government": they fully recognized the primacy of the sovereign state, the inevitability of conflicting interests, and the fact that military force is the final international sanction. What they were trying to do was to *regulate* the ways that force was used and conflicts were settled, in order to break the cycle of great alliance wars – world wars – that was coming to threaten civilization itself.

The essence of their approach, to put it crudely, was to replace the competing alliances that had flourished in traditional "balance-of-power" politics with One Big Alliance – the League of Nations – with universal membership. This all-embracing alliance of sovereign states would be bound together by quite new international rules: that no existing borders could be changed by force, and no aspects of the international *status quo* altered except by negotiation or arbitration. *Status quo* powers are always the large majority in the international community, so the new rules appealed to the fundamental interests of most nations.

These rules were to be enforced by a principle known as "collective security." Members of the League pledged to "renounce war as an instrument of national policy," and disputes between countries would be submitted to arbitration by the judicial organs of the League. But if any country defied the new rules and attacked another, *all* members of the League were bound to join in repelling the attack – and with this overwhelming preponderance of power at its disposal, the League should be able to deter or pick off aggressive governments one by one as they emerged. The basic purpose of the League was not to abolish sovereign states, but to safeguard every state's independence while averting the world wars that had been the traditional result of that independence: it was really a pragmatic association of poachers turned gamekeepers.

Collective security *could* work, in theory. So long as all the members were prepared to unite against any nation that transgressed the rules of the League, their combined weight would almost certainly be enough to overawe and deter potential transgressors, perhaps by the threat of economic sanctions alone – and if the ultimate sanction of military force were necessary, then their collective military strength would at least ensure that it was a brief and relatively confined conflict. In fact, they *had* to make collective security work, because the only alternative was to revert to the old pattern of competing military alliances and international anarchy, which would inevitably lead eventually to another world war.

There was, of course, a significant political price involved in accepting collective security (and perhaps even a moral price), since it meant that no country could legally resort to the unilateral use of force even to rectify what it felt to be a flagrant injustice. In order to gain the cooperation of existing governments, the League had to guarantee all their possessions and borders – and so, in seeking to outlaw war, the League of Nations was automatically committed to slowing down the pace of change to whatever could be achieved by peaceful means. In a world whose borders were largely defined by past acts of military violence, that implied the indefinite perpetuation of a great deal of injustice.

Moreover, the peace treaties of 1918 created a whole host of new injustices by blaming the war entirely on the defeated nations, stripping them of much of their territory, and imposing crippling "reparations" payments on them. The League's Covenant meant that all those injustices would have to be defended against violent international challenge – even to the extent of going to war over them if necessary. It couldn't be helped: any attempt to change the international system has to start from existing reality, which will always contain a great deal of injustice. But that is not, in principle, a valid objection to the creation of an international rule of law, especially if the result is an end to war. We have all made a similar compromise within our various national states, where we have outlawed private violence – even at the cost of denying some people "justice" – because the rule of law is the price of domestic peace.

Collective security makes a high demand on the capacity of nations to act with enlightened self-interest, even at the cost of some short-term sacrifices. Nevertheless, in the immediate aftermath of the First World War the surviving European governments were so badly frightened by the ultimate consequences of *not* changing the international system that they were at least determined to try. However, the duty of League members to defend *everybody's* borders against armed aggression, regardless of where they were or how those borders had originally been achieved, seemed particularly onerous to Canadians.

Canada, after all, had no disputed borders itself, and its geography made it virtually invulnerable to the effects of wars elsewhere if it chose to stay out. Prime Minister Borden supported the League in principle, but he tried hard to water down Article 10 of the Covenant, the clause which obliged all members to take automatic military action against any aggressor. As his adviser in Paris, Justice Minister Charles Doherty, warned him: "A way must be found, said and says Canadian Public Opinion, whereby Canada shall have . . . control over the events that in the future might lead her into war. If this be her view [even about] England's wars, what will be her attitude to [a promise] that France's Wars, Italy's Wars are in future to be hers wherever and whenever such a war is initiated by territorial aggression?"

But if the League's members were not willing to mobilize their forces against *any* aggressor, even when their own loyalties or interests were not directly involved, then the concept of collective security fell apart. It depended entirely on a far-sighted recognition by each government that it had to resist aggression against any member state in order to establish a principle and strengthen an institution that might one day protect it, too, from aggression. Borden's reservations about accepting this duty for Canada (which were shared by some other governments that also felt relatively safe from potential aggression) were disregarded, and the Covenant of the League was adopted unchanged. By it, Canada was formally bound to defend peace anywhere in the world.

❖

The Europeans clearly had no choice but to try something like the League of Nations after 1918, no matter how slim its chances of success. But Canadians lived in another continent, and they seemed to have two options.

Our policy for the next hundred years should be that laid down by . . . Sir Wilfrid Laurier: "freedom from the vortex of European militarism."

C. G. "Chubby" Power, MP for Quebec South, in the
Commons debate on the League of Nations,
September 1919

There are 60,000 [Canadian] graves in France and Flanders, every one of which tells us that, for good or ill, we are in the world and must bear our part in the solution of its troubles.

John W. Dafoe, editor of the *Manitoba Free Press*, 1919

In terms of short-term Canadian self-interest, Chubby Power was right in advocating what became known as "isolationism," for it would be at least another generation before technology would end Canada's physical immunity from European wars. (Americans, who enjoyed a similar geographical security, actually erected isolationism into a policy. The United States Senate saw no reason why Americans should make sacrifices to defend peace in areas of no immediate importance to them, and refused to ratify U.S. membership in the League.)

But in the longer term, it was John Dafoe who was right, for the "one world or none" dilemma we face today was already implicit in the military, economic, and technological trends of his own time. Dafoe was arguing specifically for a Canadian commitment to the League of Nations, *not* for the kind of reflex loyalty to the British Empire that had killed 60,000 Canadians in France and Flanders. It was, however, a new idea in 1919, and a distinction too subtle for many to grasp – a lot of Canadians simply didn't want Canadian troops to serve overseas ever again, whether in support of the British Empire or the principles of the League of Nations.

French Canadians were especially unenthusiastic about the League, or indeed *any* foreign commitments. Their attitude was to have a lasting effect on William Lyon Mackenzie King, who was chosen as Liberal leader on Laurier's death in 1919. King owed his position to the solid support of Quebec, and he knew that it depended as much on his avoidance of foreign military commitments in the future as on his record of opposition to conscription in the past. In 1922, after a brief interval when Arthur

Meighen succeeded the ailing Sir Robert Borden as prime minister and leader of the Conservative Party, King and the Liberals came to power.

> The fox knows many things; the hedgehog knows one *big* thing.
>
> Archilocus, *circa* 650 B.C.

Mackenzie King was a dumpy, fussy bachelor with few close male friends (although power, as Henry Kissinger was to remark in later and franker times, is the ultimate aphrodisiac, and King did not suffer from a lack of feminine companionship). Intellectually, he was both confused and confusing. He was a product of late nineteenth-century Ontario, and so was sentimentally attached to the idea of the British Empire – but he was also intensely proud of his grandfather, William Lyon Mackenzie, who had led a rebellion against that empire. Politically, he was a manip-ulator, perpetually balancing the conflicting demands of Britain and Anglo-Canadian imperialists against the instinctive isolationism of French Canadians. Personally, he was a fruitcake, communing regularly with his dear, dead mother and other denizens of the spirit world. But he knew One Big Thing: Canada must be kept united for the sake of its own future, the Liberal party's cohesion, and his own political prospects – he was not a man to make petty distinctions among the three – and that meant keep-ing Canada's foreign commitments down.

In September 1922, eight months after he assumed office to begin a prime ministership that would run, with only two interruptions amount-ing to five years, until 1948, Mackenzie King found the perfect occasion to display his new approach to Canada's international commitments. It came, bizarrely, over Turkey.

> STOP THIS NEW WAR!
>
> Cabinet Plan for Great Conflict with the Turks!
> France and Italy Against It!
> Extraordinary Appeal to the Dominions!
>
> *London Daily Mail* headlines, 18 September 1922

I confess [the British government's appeal for military support] annoyed me. It is drafted designedly to play the imperial game, to test out centralization vs. autonomy as regards European wars. . . . I have thought out my plans. . . . No contingent will go without parliament being summoned. . . . The French Canadians will be opposed, I am not so sure of B.C. . . . I am sure the people of Canada are against participation in this European war.

Mackenzie King's diary, September 1922

The crisis came out of the peace treaty that had been imposed on the defeated Turks after the First World War. Most of Turkey had been handed over to Greece and the European empires, but the Turks, under the leadership of Mustafa Kemal (Ataturk), refused to submit. Withdrawing to the interior of Anatolia, Kemal launched a war of resistance in 1919 (it was the struggle for which the Soviets coined the now hackneyed term "national liberation war"), forced the French and Italians to resign their claims in Anatolia, and finally crushed the Greek army after it had advanced almost all the way to Ankara. By the autumn of 1922, all that stood between Kemal's army and the reconquest of Istanbul and the European part of Turkey was a small British military force in the dingy town of Chanak, on the Asiatic shore of the Dardanelles.

Prime Minister Lloyd George knew perfectly well that the British public would not tolerate a full-scale war to stop the Turks from reclaiming their homeland, so he decided to run a bluff. His real aim was to force Kemal to accept an international conference on Turkey's future: Kemal would still end up with most of what he wanted, but there would be some restrictions on Turkish sovereignty, and a great deal of face would be saved (much of it Lloyd George's). To force the Turks to accept such a compromise, however, he needed a show of force at Chanak – and he could not look to the League, for the other great powers had already effectively repudiated the 1918 Treaty of Sèvres that had divided most of Turkey up among the victors. Lloyd George had to come up with the force to overawe Kemal all by himself, and his bluff would be a lot more convincing if he seemed to have the whole British Empire behind him, and not just Britain.

Cabinet today decided to resist Turkish aggression upon Europe . . . I should be glad to know whether Dominion Governments wish to associate themselves with the action we are taking. . . .

> The announcement that all or any of the Dominions were pre-
> pared to send contingents even of moderate size . . . might con-
> ceivably be a potent factor in preventing actual hostilities.
> Lloyd George to Mackenzie King, 15 September 1922

It was not exactly a peremptory imperial summons to war, but it was just the kind of thing Mackenzie King dreaded. What would French Canadians think if he sent Canadian troops to Turkey? (What would English Canadians think, for that matter, if their sons actually started getting killed there?) Nor were matters helped by the fact that the British cabinet leaked news of the request to British newspapers even before King saw the decoded official telegram: King first heard about the request when an Ottawa journalist asked him what he was going to do about it.

The Canadian General Staff, ever eager to be helpful, began making plans for the immediate dispatch of the entire Canadian regular army to Turkey, to be followed within a few months, if necessary, by an expeditionary force of 200,000 Canadian volunteers. However, King simply told Britain that Canada would take no action until Parliament had been consulted – and made no preparations to recall Parliament. It was, perhaps, the most muted declaration of independence any government has ever made, for King had to be careful not to anger English Canadian imperial patriots. (Arthur Meighen, for the Conservative opposition, declared that Canada's reply should be the traditional "Ready, Aye, Ready.") But King's message to London was quite clear: "Don't call us; we'll call you."

In the end, the crisis was defused and there was no war over Chanak. Lloyd George's government fell, and Turkey regained its territory and its independence. At the Imperial Conference in London the following year Mackenzie King was openly defiant. If the report of the conference committed the Dominions to the automatic support of British foreign and defence policies, he insisted, he would have to insert a special clause exempting Canada. So the conference closed with a statement that it was not an imperial cabinet but a conference of separate governments, each responsible to its own Parliament. Over the next few years King nailed down Canada's separate and sovereign status by concluding the first foreign treaty that was not also signed by a British representative (the unromantic U.S.-Canadian Halibut Treaty of 1923), and by appointing Canada's first diplomatic legations to foreign capitals (Washington, Paris, and Tokyo) in 1927.

By the time the Statute of Westminster formally recognized the independence of all the Dominions in 1931, Canada had already had it for
years. In 1927, when Canada was elected to the Council of the League of
Nations, Senator Raoul Dandurand, the Canadian delegate to Geneva,
replied to American criticism that Canada was the puppet of Downing
Street by declaring that Canada was "the spokesman of the North American continent's ideals." That was true enough, bearing in mind that the
predominant North American ideal at the time was isolationism – for one
of the first things King had done with Canada's independence was to
undermine the League.

> [If the Council of the League should] recommend the application
> of military measures in consequence of an aggression . . . the
> Council shall be bound to take account . . . of the geographical
> situation and of the special conditions of each State. It is for the
> constitutional authorities of each Member to decide . . . in what
> degree the Member is bound to assure the execution of this obli-
> gation by employment of its military forces.
>
> The "Canadian Resolution" on Article 10,
> League of Nations Assembly, 24 September 1923

Article 10 was the heart of the Covenant, committing all members
not only to respect "the territorial integrity and existing political independence of all the members of the League," but to defend each member's
rights by military force if necessary. That automatic obligation was exactly
what King objected to, but he was more subtle than Borden, who had
mounted a direct attack on the article and failed. Instead, the "Canadian
resolution" appealed to every country's secret desire for a private escape
route from the general duty of maintaining the peace, by declaring that
each member could decide independently whether it would take part in
economic sanctions or offer troops to support any military action decided
upon by the League.

After a year-long struggle, King's "interpretation" was accepted, and
Article 10 was effectively destroyed. (As Senator J. P. B. Casgrain of Quebec remarked: "Whenever lawyers desire to insert an interpretation
clause, the purpose is to make the document mean something other than
what people read in it.") Senator Raoul Dandurand, one of King's few
really close associates, was brutally frank about the selfish rationale

behind the Canadian resolution. Collective security was like fire insurance, he told the Assembly in 1924, and Canada should not be called
upon to pay the heavy premium of military sanctions against a possible
aggressor because Canadians faced little risk to their own property: "We
live in a fireproof house, far from inflammable materials."

This first attempt to reform the international system and break the
cycle of world wars was probably doomed to fail in any event – almost as
certainly as a child's first attempt to ride a bicycle – but King's wanton act
of sabotage was a premature and unnecessary blow to the League. And it
was supported by the Canadian opposition parties as well: wars, most
Canadians believed, were caused by wicked governments in Europe, and
it was possible for Canada to stay out of them thanks to its fortunate
geography. But since no serious crises came along to test the weakened
machinery of the League for quite a while, it would be almost a decade
before any Canadians began to worry about war again. Apart, that is, from
war with the United States.

### CHAPTER FOURTEEN

# Descent into War

Lt. Col. Forde and Lt. Col. Hodgins and myself left Ottawa in a motor driven by Colonel Forde about 6:45 a.m. on the 10th July, 1922 . . . and crossed the St. Lawrence by ferry to Ogdensburg, New York at 10 a.m. The American Customs and Emigration Authorities passed us without delay . . . We then took the highway to Canton through a generally rolling country. . . . The country everywhere is passable by infantry.

Extract from *Special Reconnaissance by the Director of Military Operations and Intelligence*, marked "Secret," H.Q. C.3487, Ottawa, 17 November 1922.

Colonel J. Sutherland ("Buster") Brown, Director of Military Operations and Intelligence of the Canadian army from 1920 to 1927, was convinced, like his ancestors before him, that the main military threat facing Canada was an American invasion – and he had a plan for dealing with it. We should invade *them* first. If war with the United States seemed likely, his Defence Scheme Number One ordained that the Canadian army would launch pre-emptive attacks deep into the United States. Canadian forces from British Columbia would "advance into and occupy the strategic points including Spokane, Seattle and Portland." Our troops from the Prairie provinces would "converge towards Fargo, North Dakota and then continue a general advance in the direction of Minneapolis and St. Paul." In the east, the Canadian army would cross the St. Lawrence and the Quebec border to occupy upper New England.

Preparing contingency plans for every conceivable conflict is the occupational disease of military staff planners. The U.S. armed forces still had a plan for war with Britain in the 1920s in which the invasion of Canada figured prominently (and they may well have one for dealing with an invasion from outer space today). But "Buster" Brown wasn't just covering all his bets. Defence Scheme Number One was *the* Canadian war plan throughout the 1920s, and the Director of Military Operations and Intelligence took it with the utmost seriousness. Indeed, Sutherland Brown even used to masquerade as a tourist and drive around the northern United States, accompanied by other senior Canadian staff officers in disguise, to survey the positions he wanted to capture. (He also encouraged all the commanders of Canada's regional military districts to do the same across their own parts of the frontier.)

> July 12th. We left Glen Falls at 9 a.m. Near French Mountain we entered the Adirondacks. It is about this point that troops from the North would enter an open rolling country lying between Glen Falls and Albany.
>
> Sutherland Brown, *Special Reconnaissance*

Sutherland Brown's military strategy was not at fault: his purpose in planning to seize large parts of the northern United States by surprise at the very outbreak of war was to win time for reinforcements from Britain to reach Canada before U.S. troops could pour across the Canadian border and overwhelm us. A similar strategy had been applied, with successful results, in the War of 1812: small contingents of troops from Upper Canada had crossed the frontier as soon as the United States declared war and seized Detroit and the Upper Peninsula of Michigan, thus slowing the main American invasion significantly. The problem lay only in Sutherland Brown's grasp of contemporary reality. The British could not have sent reinforcements to Canada even if his strategy had won them the necessary time – and in the 1920s Canada did not have one-tenth the number of trained troops that would have been required to carry out his plan.

❖

What I want to accomplish, if I possibly can, is to have a well-organised, snappy defence force that will be a credit to Canada without being too expensive.

George Graham, Minister of Militia, 1922

The huge Canadian army of the First World War had been dissolved with great speed. The 350,000 Canadians who were overseas on 11 November 1918 were almost all home and out of uniform by mid-1919 (although not before impatient veterans had turned to violence in the holding camps in Britain. A riot at Kinmel in north Wales in March 1919 left five dead and twenty-seven injured). The Canadian General Staff's post-war plans were for a regular army of twenty or thirty thousand men plus a militia force of fifteen divisions, able to mobilize a further three hundred thousand men at short notice. These forces were to provide the military resources both for home defence against an American invasion and for an expeditionary force of seven divisions to be sent abroad to fight in the empire's wars, and were to be kept up to strength by peacetime conscription of all Canadian males (though only for a four-month training period). As grandiose as it was ludicrous, this whole scheme quickly ran aground on the rocks of reality.

The fifteen militia divisions survived on paper, but with fewer than fifty thousand active members. Nobody was willing to tolerate the idea of conscription in peacetime, and the regular forces wound up with around five thousand men. Most of the numbered battalions of the Canadian Expeditionary Force and their hard-won traditions disappeared in the post-war reorganization of the armed forces, although a few were permitted to convert into militia regiments, with regimental names replacing their old numbers. Only two unique infantry units survived to join the

Royal Canadian Regiment as permanent elements of Canada's regular army: Princess Patricia's Canadian Light Infantry and the 22nd Battalion, the only French-speaking battalion in the C.E.F., which had so distinguished itself that it was even allowed to retain its number, becoming the Royal 22$^{\text{ème}}$ Régiment ("Van Doos," in English).

Such courtesies cost very little, but post-war Canadian governments were not willing to spend real money on the armed forces. The Canadian defence budget in 1922 was $12 million – just under a dollar and a half per Canadian – and it did not grow much until the late 1930s. Given the country's remarkably secure strategic situation and the absence of identifiable enemies, this parsimony was not an unreasonable attitude on the part of the government. But it was rather demoralizing for the remaining regular soldiers.

> When the three-inch mortar came into use . . . there were only three of them in the whole of Canada. Well, I was keen on mortars because I had just been at the Small Arms School and thought I knew something about it.
>
> So we decided to make our own . . . and we had the company pioneer build a wooden mock-up of a three-inch mortar – quite illegally, we paid for it out of the company's sports fund – and we had wooden bombs that we shoved down this black pipe and hoped for the best. At least we learned the drill.
>
> Dan Spry (later general, then a junior officer in the Royal Canadian Regiment)

What would have been even more demoralizing for the soldiers, had they allowed themselves to dwell on it, was their sheer uselessness to the country that paid their wages. The only possible invader of Canada was still the United States, but the American threat was no longer very plausible politically: the time had passed when the United States seriously wanted to annex Canada. Moreover, by the Washington Naval Treaty of 1922 London agreed to limit the Royal Navy to the same size as that of the United States, which meant that there was now absolutely no chance that Britain would ever again send troops west across the Atlantic to defend Canada against an American attack.

It was not just that avoiding war with the United States was such a high priority in Britain's general strategy that it would even dictate the abandonment of Canada to its fate, should that turn out to be the price of peace with Washington. That was true enough, but there are, after all, examples in British history when rational strategic calculations have been cast to the winds in favour of considerations of emotion and prestige (as the Argentines learned to their cost when they invaded the Falklands in 1982). Nor was it simply a question of dwindling British resolve, as it had been during the latter part of the nineteenth century. By the 1920s Britain literally *couldn't* send troops to assist Canada militarily against the United States.

Britain had large naval commitments elsewhere. Having accepted overall naval parity with the United States in the Washington Naval Treaty, henceforward it would always be inferior to the U.S. Navy in the Western Atlantic. London simply no longer had the ability to get troops west across the Atlantic against American opposition. However, Canada's professional armed forces took no notice whatever of this new strategic reality.

The foundation of Canadian military planning continued to be a militia force which, on mobilization, would amount to eleven infantry divisions and four cavalry divisions (though they were now only planning on having 130,000 men available to man these divisions)—all for fighting the United States. And by the time the "flying columns" of Canadian militia that had been thrown across the American border in a controlled penetration of a few hundred miles had been forced to retreat back to Canada's own frontiers, Colonel Sutherland Brown's Directorate of Military Operations and Intelligence calculated, British military operations should be well underway against America's east coast, while Australian and Indian expeditionary forces would be on their way to attack California. The Americans would sure be sorry that they had picked a fight with the British Empire.

Sutherland Brown's paper force of 130,000 volunteers who were to receive a month's military training each year contrasted sharply with the real Canadian militia, which in 1923 only succeeded in giving eight or nine days' training to 38,000 men. Even discounting awkward political realities like the fact that the British reinforcements he was counting on would never be sent (not to mention the wholly imaginary Australian and Indian contingents), Colonel Sutherland Brown's Defence Scheme Number One had not the slightest link with military reality unless the full

Canadian force envisaged on paper was actually available for the pre-emptive Canadian invasion of the United States. "I consider that the most difficult point in the Scheme is the fact that it is drawn up for forces which are to a certain extent non-existent," the commander of Military District No. 4 (Montreal) observed drily. In fact the plan was the purest moonshine, but it satisfied the armed forces' need to be needed.

It is tempting to speculate on what would have happened if some alert American policeman had stopped those Canadian "tourists" of military bearing who made meticulous notes about the terrain near the border and took photographs of every bridge, crossroads, and barracks (the "reconnaissance" reports are heavily illustrated). Here were senior Canadian officers brazenly spying on the parts of the United States they planned to invade in case of war. But the fact that it never occurred to any American to inquire into this activity is perhaps sufficient comment on its realism.

> Q. *What inspired Sutherland Brown to think that way in the 1920s –*
> *I mean, a war with the United States?*
> A. Well, I don't know. I think possibly there wasn't any other war
> to think about. (laughter)
> > General E. L. M. Burns, Commander of Canadian forces
> > in Italy, 1944; Commander of U.N. Emergency Force in
> > Suez, 1956.

General "Tommy" Burns served with Sutherland Brown in the 1920s, and his observation is very close to the bone. A professional military force needs enemies to justify its existence, and Lord Salisbury's famous observation about experts applies as much to Canada as anywhere else: "If you believe the doctors, nothing is wholesome; if you believe the theologians, nothing is innocent; if you believe the soldiers, nothing is safe." The First World War's lasting institutional bequest to Canada was a full array of professional armed forces staffed by native-born regular officers who were paid, quite literally, to identify foreign threats to Canadian national security.

The threats they identified would vary from time to time, as would the measures they advocated to deal with them, but they were as unlikely ever to declare that there was *no* threat to Canada as they were to admit that there was nothing useful they could do about the threats that they did identify (like that of an American invasion). *Of course* they found threats, whether from the United States or elsewhere, and *of course* they asked for money to maintain their own profession as a 'deterrent' to those threats.

❖

The regular military forces we inherited from the First World War received barely enough money to keep them going as institutions, certainly not enough to equip them to any militarily useful standard. By 1925 the Royal Canadian Navy had only two small destroyers left, and the Royal Canadian Air Force numbered fewer than a thousand men. The Permanent Force of the army amounted to only 4,125 troops, and the militia organization was somewhat smaller than the one that had existed before the First World War. Deprived of resources and largely irrelevant to the nation's concerns, Canada's regular forces fell to fighting among themselves.

Soon after Mackenzie King's Liberals came to power in 1922, in a sequence of events that prefigured the more celebrated integration battles of the 1960s under Defence Minister Paul Hellyer, the Canadian army, navy, and air force were "integrated" under a single Department of National Defence, run by a single minister. The Chief of the General Staff, Major-General J. H. MacBrien, was a dyed-in-the-wool army officer who promptly tried to exploit his position at the top of the newly integrated tri-service chain of command in order to exclude the navy's and air force's senior officers from any serious influence on policy-making and from direct access to the minister, with the transparently obvious objective of subordinating the other two services' interests to those of the army. The resulting inter-service war was waged without quarter until 1927, and got so silly that on one occasion Commodore Walter Hose, the navy's commander, forebade naval units to participate in the country's Armistice Day ceremonies because the administrative order for the parade had been written by the army. MacBrien finally resigned in 1927, but the war resumed with almost equal ferocity after General Andrew McNaughton became Chief of the General Staff in 1930. It continues, in one form or another, to this day.

Although Canada's small regular forces were preoccupied with fighting each other, they also remained under constant attack from governments hunting for economies. Savage cut-backs in air force personnel in 1931 prompted 250 laid-off officers and men to offer their services to Chiang Kai-shek in China as mercenaries in the war against his Communist rivals, and the navy was very nearly abolished entirely in 1933. Only the army was somewhat safer from extinction, since in addition to its alleged role in defending the country it was seen as a barrier against "communism" at home.

The regular army or the militia were called out to "keep the peace" on a number of occasions from the Winnipeg General Strike in 1919 and a major strike in Quebec City in 1921 to the Cape Breton coal-miners' strikes in 1922-23. But the "red menace" then receded, and the troops were not used in the streets of Canadian cities again until the Depression, when they were sent to quell disturbances in Oshawa and St. Catharines in 1932 and to contain a bitter strike by the furniture-makers and meat-packers of Stratford, Ontario, in 1933.

> Frequently I had the job of leading my platoon around the meat-packing plant, where all the female employees (whom the troops called "chicken-pluckers") would lean out the windows and call us far worse words than that. In fact, I learned some foul language from those chicken-pluckers that I hadn't heard before, even in the army. But it was a great delight to the soldiers to hear their officer being called all sorts of things.
> Q. *What did you actually do in the town?*
> Oh, we patrolled and marched about and sort of made our presence felt, at least visibly. Also socially, because after the thing was all over, it turned out that quite a number of our soldiers married Stratford girls. So it wasn't completely a waste of time.
>
> Dan Spry

Stratford was such a pointless exercise that the army was never again deployed "in aid to the civil power" until the Quebec Crisis of 1970. Deprived even of a domestic rationale for their existence, the Canadian armed forces struggled on, devoting most of their energies to sheer institutional survival, in the hope and expectation that they would one day be needed again by their country. Or if not precisely by their own country, at least by Britain – and since they were entirely British-oriented in their training, equipment, and strategic thinking, they had no doubt that any British war would be theirs as well.

> The British regular division is the prototype of all the forces of the Empire, it having been agreed long ago at Imperial Conference that organization and training should be uniform. Hence, a Dominion officer who feels it his duty to suggest improvements in military organization must argue the case for a change in all the Empire's forces, taking cognizance of the whole range of that army's duties, from first-class warfare to the suppression of religious maniacs in abominable deserts.
>
> Lieutenant-Colonel E. L. M. Burns, *Canadian Defence Quarterly*, April 1938

For Canadian military professionals in the 1920s and 1930s, the big league was the British Empire, abominable deserts and all, and so they never questioned its relevance to Canadian security. Defence Scheme Number One, with its hypothesis of an American invasion, provided a rationale for Canadian military allegiance to the empire that soldiers of the time chose not to examine too closely. In retrospect it is hard to resist the thought that its real attractiveness to the professionals was the justification it provided for the plans that eventually became known as Defence Schemes Number Two, Three, and Four. These planned for scenarios in which Canada would pay its dues for British "protection" by taking part in a war against Japan; sending another expeditionary force to Europe (seven divisions had been more or less promised to the British in 1919, and that promise was never officially retracted); or sending a brigade to deal with such emergencies within the empire as an uprising by "subordinate coloured people": tribesmen on the North-West Frontier of India, for example, or South African blacks.

"Buster" Brown himself truly believed in the American threat, but as his successor wrote in 1928, when asked if Defence Scheme Number One would be updated: "it is difficult to get the powers that be to take any real interest in anything beyond the organisation of an Expeditionary Force." Sending Canadian forces to Europe has been the prime focus of concern for most Canadian professional soldiers ever since 1914, because Europe offered them realistic possibilities for challenging professional employment. Military professionals not only have the usual bureaucratic instinct for finding reasons why they are "useful" to the government that employs them (even if the strategic realities actually make them fairly irrelevant); in the soldiers' case, those reasons will generally tend to justify their involvement in the biggest and most professionally interesting military league available.

Given Canada's geographical invulnerability to attack by anybody apart from the United States, however, our military professionals would probably have found Canadian governments unwilling to contemplate any more "Expeditionary Forces" to Europe if Canadian civilians had not got such a powerful psychological hang-over from the First World War. It was the myths that were forged to justify that first slaughter of Canadians in Europe – the pretence that it had somehow been in defence of Canada – that made the English Canadian population ready to believe the soldiers when they talked about European "threats" to Canadian security. That mind-set was indispensable to the future of the military profession in Canada, since few Canadian civilians (nor even very many soldiers) could really bring themselves to believe in the traditional American threat any more.

The old strategic and psychological equation of dependence on Britain to protect us from American invasion had lasted just long enough to deliver us smoothly into our new obsession with playing a role in the European balance of power. Once Sutherland Brown left his post as Canada's senior strategic planner, his Defence Scheme Number One rapidly fell into disrepute. In 1933, every military district in Canada was instructed to burn all documents connected with the plan (which would have caused severe embarrassment if they had somehow fallen into American hands). However, alternative plans already existed to send Canadian troops to fight in Europe again in case of war – and those plans did not change.

❖

Of all the members of the League, Canada was the first to . . . have torpedoed the organization, or to use another metaphor, to rob it of any teeth it had.

> Senator W. A. Cheesbach (Conservative, Alberta),
> Senate *Debates*, 1934

The descent into world war again at the end of the 1930s was premature in terms of the normal cycle: only twenty years had elapsed since the last one, rather than the more typical half-century. And while the failure of the League may have hastened events – a fully-fledged alliance system might have postponed the war for some years past 1939 – the drastic shortening of the cycle was due in larger part to the way the First World War ended. It had been the first total war, and such wars do not end in negotiated peaces. They tend to be fought to the bitter end, concluding in a crushing defeat for the losing side regardless of how evenly matched the opponents may have been at the start.

The German defeat in 1918 had been of that nature, and the Treaty of Versailles heaped punishments on Germany – loss of territory, a large measure of compulsory disarmament, demilitarized zones, massive reparations, and a "war guilt" clause that purported to justify it all by blaming the war exclusively on the Germans – that were neither defensible in terms of justice, nor (more importantly) sustainable over the long term. The peace treaties at the end of the First World War created an international order that could not be maintained once Germany began to recover from its defeat. Britain and France were simply not capable of depriving Germany permanently of great-power status.

However loyally the League's members upheld the principle of collective security – even if they did not take the escape route prepared for them by the Canadian "interpretation" of Article 10 in 1923 – the League system was bound to come under severe pressure from Germany's resentment at its artificially subordinate status. If the great powers in the League did not move fast enough in removing what the Germans perceived as injustices (and they did not), then they were eventually certain to face a German challenge that could only be stopped by invoking Article 10 and resorting to military force. In fact, however, the challenge that effectively destroyed the League came a little quicker than that, and not from Germany.

The collective security system faced no serious challenges during the

1920s; it first came under threat in 1931, when Japan suddenly seized Manchuria from China. The League conspicuously failed to rise to the occasion, but there were some extenuating circumstances: the attack was unexpected and quickly became a *fait accompli*, as the Chinese themselves were unable to offer any substantial resistance to Japan; and neither of the two great powers that had military bases available nearby, the United States and the Soviet Union, was a League member. Hitler's rise to power in 1933 was another blow, as he took Germany out of the League the following year on being denied recognition as a great power, and denounced the disarmament provisions of the Treaty of Versailles in March 1935. But the Soviet Union, alarmed by these developments, actually *joined* the League in 1934, and the collective security system still seemed a potentially useful tool to halt aggression and prevent world war when the great crisis struck in 1935: the Italian invasion of Ethiopia.

Mussolini's crime was no worse than what every other great power had done in the late nineteenth century. Ethiopia was one of the last independent bits of Africa, and Italy, only lately arrived on the great-power scene, was belatedly seeking its share of the colonial spoils. But the international rules had been changed by the creation of the League in 1919, and Ethiopia was a member: either the rules were enforced or the organization was meaningless. Moreover, this was a crisis the League members could actually deal with—there was plenty of time to organize a response, since ten months elapsed between the first indication of Italy's intention and the actual attack; the Ethiopians themselves were determined to fight; and Italy's sea communications with Africa were highly vulnerable to the stronger British and French navies.

On 2 October 1935 Mussolini invaded Ethiopia, and an overwhelming majority of League members promptly declared Italy an aggressor. Within a week, the League began to consider economic sanctions against Italy: nobody was talking about military measures yet, but economic sanctions could easily be the first step along that road. And Canada, to everybody's surprise, actually sought and got a seat on the committee that had to decide what those sanctions would be.

> We went into the League, took benefits, must assume responsibilities, or get out, not try to hornswoggle ourselves out.
> Prime Minister R. B. Bennett to Dr. O. D. Skelton,
> Permanent Under-Secretary for External Affairs, 1935

In 1935 Richard B. Bennett, a former Calgary lawyer "of large dis-placement" (as they used to say of ocean liners), had been prime minister of Canada for five years. Bombastic in public and autocratic with his colleagues, he was one of those rare Canadian politicians (Trudeau is the only other one to achieve prime ministerial rank since) who followed their private convictions quite heedless of popular opinion. In Bennett's case, his intellectual independence was buttressed by considerable wealth and excellent connections in Britain (after he retired from politics he moved to England and acquired a peerage through the help of influential friends), but his support for collective security was quite genuine.

This brought him into permanent conflict with most senior members of his own External Affairs Department, and most notably with Dr. O. D. Skelton, the Permanent Under-Secretary, a gaunt scholar who had had a brilliant academic career before being seduced into government by Mack-enzie King ten years before. Skelton had originally supported the idea of the League, since he believed it was necessary to build up "some inter-national organization to control rampant nationalism and to provide for orderly growth and peaceful adjustment." But he had concluded that this particular League was not going to succeed, and he had no confidence whatever in the ability of British diplomacy to avoid another war. So, in practice, Skelton was an isolationist, convinced that Canada at least might be spared the horrors of the next war if it kept out of overseas commitments.

Skelton did his best to talk Bennett out of having anything to do with League sanctions against Italy, but the prime minister simply wouldn't hear of it. In one bitter discussion in September 1935 he called Skelton and his colleagues at External Affairs "welshers" because of their desire to evade Canada's commitments under the League Covenant, and in Octo-ber he heatedly overrode External's attempt to have the Canadian dele-gation in Geneva abstain from the vote condemning Italy for aggression: "No one in Canada is going to deny Italy guilty or object to our saying so. If they did, [I'm] not going to wriggle out of it if it meant I didn't get one vote," he shouted down the phone to Skelton. But Prime Minister Bennett was deliberately ignoring Skelton's quite plausible reason for wanting Canada to abstain: in early October 1935 Canada was nearing the end of a long federal election campaign and Bennett was almost certain to lose that election to Mackenzie King–who would certainly not want to honour Canada's commitments to the League.

No interest in Ethiopia, of any nature whatever, is worth the life of a single Canadian citizen. No consideration could justify Canada's participation in such a war, and I am unalterably opposed to it.

Ernest Lapointe (Mackenzie King's deputy),
campaign speech, 9 September 1935

Do honourable members think it is Canada's role at Geneva to attempt to regulate a European war?

Mackenzie King to the House of Commons, 1935

That was precisely Canada's role (and everybody else's) under the League's Covenant. Only collective security offered any hope of preventing another great war from occurring in Europe sooner or later – but it did involve running the risk of at least a small war to deter aggression. Canadians had paid a high price for their intervention in the last European war, and an isolationist policy was a tempting alternative. The Atlantic was a broad moat, and Canadians could still shelter behind it if they wished.

Isolationism, as practised by the Americans, was an ungenerous but logical policy, declaring that the United States could and would protect itself from the consequences of European wars while avoiding the duties and costs of collective security. Canadians were strategically in the same position as the Americans, but they were trapped in a sentimental paradox. The Canadian version of isolationism was severely undercut by the loyalties of English Canadians, which could well draw the country into any European war involving Britain regardless of cold calculations of national interest. That logically made the task of preventing a European war a very high priority for Canada, and it should have made Canadian governments very supportive of the League and the idea of collective security. But a great many Canadians preferred to dodge that conclusion; instead, they wound up in the kind of contradictory stance best typified by Mackenzie King.

King instinctively distrusted the League of Nations, and during his previous prime ministership in the 1920s he had done everything he could to weaken the collective security obligations that might involve Canada in military commitments overseas. This was a perfectly rational position if Canada really intended to stay out of any European war that occurred because of the failure of the League (although it would have been more honest, in that case, simply to quit the League). Staying out of overseas commitments was also seen by King as a stark political necessity for the Liberals, since French Canadian opinion was virtually unanimous in its opposition to foreign military involvement of any kind (not a single French-language newspaper in Quebec supported Canadian participation in League action over Ethiopia).

The problem was that King was not really a convinced isolationist. As early as 1923 he had declared: "If a great and clear call of duty comes [to fight by Britain's side], Canada will respond, whether or not the United States responds, as she did in 1914." He needed English Canadian votes too, and he was English Canadian himself. King was unwilling to risk even the remotest chance of war for the right cause, the League. Yet he was ultimately willing to fight for the wrong one, British imperial interest, if he had to.

With King's overwhelming election victory on 14 October 1935 (the Liberals won 173 seats out of 245), Canada's man on the League sanctions committee at Geneva, Walter Riddell, was put in a very awkward position. Riddell, two decades older and a good deal wiser than the outspoken student who had staunchly defended Borden's naval bill in a Berlin beer-garden in 1912, had been Ottawa's permanent representative at Geneva for ten years, and he saw the way things were going: everybody was afraid to ban the export of really vital commodities to Italy for fear of driving Mussolini into a corner and provoking a war. It was one of those situations, not uncommon in diplomacy, where each nation knew what its duty was, but hung back nervously for fear that other countries would not do their duty and it would find itself out front all alone. But mere wrist-slapping would not stop the Italian dictator, so Riddell decided Canada should take a lead.

> By this time I had become thoroughly convinced that this was the last and best chance that the Member States would have of preventing a European collapse and another world war; that it was therefore imperative that the Member States should accept their obligations not only willingly but generously, as any losses they might suffer would be a mere bagatelle in comparison with the losses in the event of a break-up of the Collective System.
>
> Walter Riddell, *World Security by Conference*

Riddell took a very big chance. He knew perfectly well that Mackenzie King, in full harmony with his old appointee, the isolationist Skelton, would forbid any Canadian initiative that might ultimately involve Canada in the application of military sanctions by the League. Yet he feared that if nobody took a strong line in Geneva, the principle of collective security would slide ignominiously into oblivion amid timid half-measures and shabby compromises. So on 2 November he leapt in at the deep end: he formally proposed that League members ban the export of oil, coal, iron, and steel to Italy, knowing full well that Mussolini was threatening to go to war with anybody who applied such pressure to Italy.

Riddell's initiative put some spine into the hesitant members of the committee. On 6 November they unanimously recommended the full list of Riddell's sanctions to all League members. If those sanctions had been applied, Italy would have had to stop its attack on Ethiopia or grind to a halt, since it produced no oil itself and had only about two months' reserves. But meanwhile Riddell was having to play a double game, disguising the extent to which he had committed Canada in his telegrams back to Ottawa and pretending to misunderstand the instructions he was getting from there to do nothing conspicuous. It could not last, for newspapers around the world were calling the initiative that had galvanized the committee into action the "Canadian proposal."

> Had a few words with Mr King re the Italo-Ethiopian settlement and he spoke with surprising frankness. . . . King complained bitterly about Dr Riddell's gasoline, steel and coal proposal. "I am certainly going to give him a good spanking," was the way he put it. . . . He is very dubious about foreign commitments, and, also, about getting into the League too deeply.
>
> Ottawa correspondent to J. W. Dafoe, editor,
> *Winnipeg Free Press*, December 1935

King, shocked by his representative's daring action, instinctively ducked for cover. He and Skelton were on vacation together in Sea Island, Georgia, but he sent instructions back to his deputy, Ernest Lapointe, to repudiate Riddell. On 2 December 1935, while the League was still waiting for all the members' replies to the "Canadian proposal" on sanctions, Lapointe issued a press statement: "The suggestion . . . that the Canadian

Government has taken the initiative in the extension of the embargo upon exportation of key commodities to Italy . . . is due to a misunderstanding. . . . The opinion which was expressed by the Canadian member of the Committee – and which has led to the reference to the proposals as a Canadian proposal – represented only his personal opinion . . . and not the views of the Canadian Government."

> To make a suggestion and then run away is not helpful to the more exposed members of the League.
>
> > Sir Robert Vansittart, British Under-Secretary for Foreign
> > Affairs, December 1935

It was an act of gross vandalism, motivated by sheer timidity. It cannot be said for certain that King's disavowal of the Riddell proposal was the decisive factor in the League's ultimate failure to impose sanctions on Italy. The British and the French, who would have to do most of the fighting if an oil embargo against Italy led to war, were wavering in their commitment anyway, especially as they still hoped that Italy might be an ally if they ultimately had to fight Hitler. But King's action was certainly a major factor – and once the impetus given by Riddell's initiative and the apparent (although nervous) unanimity with which it was met had been lost, so was the League of Nations. The question of effective sanctions was repeatedly postponed until Mussolini completed his conquest of Ethiopia in mid-1936 and it became simply irrelevant. The League staggered on for a few more years, but it was only a husk. Collective security had been put to the test, and everybody had run away.

> I went over as a delegate [to the League] in '38. . . . By then it was dying, if not dead . . . but as a young man I was never prepared to admit that it was that bad. I could hardly accept that the League wasn't going to carry on as Smuts and Wilson and others, Lord Robert Cecil, hoped that it would, but in retrospect one can't conclude anything else.
>
> It didn't invalidate the Covenant and the richness of its contribution, but it certainly was – as the UN is now – an ineffective operation. Not because the idea was wrong, but because of the

failure of its members to live up to their obligations. And Canada
was one of those that did not.

> Paul Martin, M.P. for Essex East (Windsor, Ontario),
> later Secretary of State for External Affairs, 1963-68

The attempt to build a new international system had collapsed, and
the great powers went back to doing what they had centuries of experience at: building up their armies, giving away bits of other people's territory to buy time or allies, and preparing for the next world war.
Canadians wondered what they would do when it came – and so did the
British. In the aftermath of the sanctions fiasco, the British High Commissioner in Ottawa reported to London:

> Isolationist opinion in Canada is now normally of such strength
> that no Dominion Government can pursue a policy involving any
> appreciable risk of military commitments in Europe unless the
> isolationists have first been submerged by a wave of intervention-
> ist sentiment.

> Sir Francis Floud, British High Commissioner in
> Ottawa, to the Dominions Office, 13 December 1935

Only forty-five months later Canada entered the Second World War.

❖

> The idea that every 20 years this country should automatically
> and as a matter of course take part in a war overseas for democ-
> racy or self-determination of other small nations, that a country
> which has all it can do to run itself should feel called upon to
> save, periodically, a continent that cannot run itself, and to these
> ends risk the lives of its people, risk bankruptcy and political
> disunion, seems to many a nightmare and sheer madness.

> Mackenzie King to the House of Commons, March 1939

Mackenzie King wholeheartedly supported the British policy of appeasement. When Germany remilitarized the Rhineland in 1936, he showed
not the slightest public inclination to do anything about it: "I believe that

Canada's first duty to the League and to the British Empire, with respect to all the great issues that come to us, is, if possible, to keep this country united." His cabinet raised the defence budget by 20 per cent for the following year, the start of a slow process of rearmament in Canada, but the air force and the navy were emphasized at the expense of the army, which could be taken as an expression of intent to isolate Canada from a European war rather than to participate in it. Certainly the rearmament programme was not aimed at sending another large Canadian expeditionary force to Europe: "I think that is now wholly out of the question," King noted in his diary.

King's diplomatic statements deliberately left Canada's intentions in case of war obscure, and even in his private dealings with the British government he went out of his way to avoid military co-operation that might imply automatic commitment. There was no Canadian representative on the Committee of Imperial Defence in London, and King turned down a British request to establish Royal Air Force training schools in Canada in the spring of 1938. There could be no military establishments in Canada, he said, that were not maintained and controlled by the Canadian government.

He never openly challenged the legal doctrine that Canada, as a member of the British Empire, was automatically at war whenever Britain was at war, but in response to all attempts to pin him down, he took refuge in his favourite evasive tactic, saying that "Parliament will decide" (as though Parliament would not do whatever he and his cabinet decided). Refusing to allow a vote in 1939 on a resolution declaring Canada's right to remain neutral, King told the House: "Why divide Canada to provide against a contingency that might not arise? . . . The same consideration of the overwhelming importance of national unity which has led this government to decline to make premature and inappropriate statements of possible belligerency prevents it from recommending actions to declare possible neutrality." Since he never said publicly what Canada would do if war came, there was no focus around which a destructive national debate could get started.

Two groups in Canada wanted nothing whatever to do with a European war. A large number of Canadian nationalists (including almost all French Canadians) thought solely in terms of Canada's own interests, and were quite content to sit the war out on the sidelines since no vital

Canadian interests were involved. There were also those, particularly in English Canadian intellectual circles, who believed that the coming war was simply further proof of the failure of the existing international system. The war would have to run its course, and afterward everybody would have to resume the effort to build some new international institution like the League to prevent future wars. But neither the rationalists nor the nationalists had the final say; Mackenzie King did, and he was infuriatingly reluctant to say anything definite.

The reason Mackenzie King devoted such effort to dodging the issue lay in the ambivalent attitudes of most English Canadians toward fighting for Britain again. French Canadians were unambiguously opposed to the whole idea, of course, and as late as 1938 a majority of English Canadians were also probably isolationist in their conscious political opinions. But King was well aware that their emotions would lead most of them toward intervention if the crisis actually arrived. So his political strategy in the final years before the war was to hope that it would never happen, and in the meantime to dissimulate to everybody: to the British, to the public, even to most of his own colleagues.

> [King] saw long before a lot of the rest of us did, who were dubious about getting into a war, that with the composition of our population as it was in 1939, it would have been impossible to stay out; that it would have nothing to do with interests, it had to do with emotions.
> Q. *English Canada would not have stood for it?*
> No. Well, enough of English Canada would not have stood for it and, after all, English Canadians as late as 1939 were the dominant element. Much more than their numbers, their influence and their importance were such that it would have been, I think, quite impossible to stay out. I think I recognized that myself in 1939. Very sadly, but I recognized it.
> Jack Pickersgill (Secretary to Mackenzie King, 1937-48)

King, for all his obfuscations, was never really in any doubt that Canada would have to go in if war came. He thought it was a bad idea, and he was determined to go in only up to his ankles if he could get away with it, but he understood the nature of Canada at the time too well to imagine that his government could safely remain neutral. Although pro-British sentiments were much weaker in the English-speaking population as a whole than in 1914 (another generation had passed, and the cost of the First World War was graven in everybody's mind), the instinctive British loyalty was still strong in the business and professional elite, and those were the people who mattered.

At their worst, they were the sort of people whom the Conservative opposition leader, Dr. R. J. Manion, described to his son as "the usual crowd of old bachelors and childless parents." They certainly had enough influence to destroy any government that stayed out of the war, but even they would not have been powerful enough on their own to make Canada's entry into the Second World War inevitable. What gave their demands irresistible force was the almost unconscious sense of compulsion in ordinary English Canadians to take part in the war.

> If you were to ask any Canadian, "Do you *have* to go to war if England does?" he'd answer at once, "Oh, no." If you then said, "*Would* you go to war if England does?" he'd answer, "Oh, yes." And if you asked "Why?" he would say, reflectively, "Well, you see, we'd *have* to."
>
> Stephen Leacock, *Atlantic Monthly*, June 1939

For most English Canadians by 1939, the decisive motive was no longer a helpless tug of loyalty to Britain; at least, not a loyalty strong enough to die for her. It was more a sense of debt to their own past, and to their dead of the First World War. English Canada is the only part of the Western Hemisphere where almost every little town and village has the kind of haunting war memorial that you find all over Europe, with a list of the dead that sometimes seems to outnumber those still living in the place.

The terrible sacrifice of the First World War – a third of all English Canadian males of military age had served overseas, and one in seven had actually been killed or wounded – was the very foundation of English Canada's national identity, and to deny that Canada's duty was to fight at England's side in the wars of the great powers would have seemed somehow to devalue that sacrifice. The dead would not necessarily impose that duty on us for all time if they could speak, but that was the psychology of it. So to justify their past, English Canadians would feel that they must act in the same way the next time a European war came along: "Well, you see, we'd *have* to."

But since they would not feel that way until the crisis was upon them and their emotions swept them away, King had to avoid any clear position pro or con until the last moment. If there was no war, he would have neatly evaded a potentially fatal political controversy – and if war did come, English Canadians could probably be brought into it more or less united by such methods.

The same was not true for French Canadians, however. French Canada's attitude would *not* shift when the crisis arrived, for it had no comparable debt to the dead to pull its emotions around. There was never any doubt that French Canadians would fight to defend *Canada*, but the issue of conscription for service overseas was as explosive as ever – and unless that fear was laid to rest, French Canada would resist the war from the start, the country would split along "racial" lines, and King's government, heavily dependent on Quebec support, would probably fall. He was particularly unhappy that war, if it came, would likely take the form of a British and French declaration of war against Germany arising out of a German attack on Poland. Just after the Anglo-French guarantee to Poland in March 1939, King told the British High Commissioner in Ottawa that he believed the people of Canada would not consent to enter a war "which would appear to have been due solely to a Balkan dispute." (His geography was shaky, but the analogy was clear.)

Happily for King, English Canadian politicians of all parties were much more conscious of the French Canadian loathing for conscription than they had been in 1917 (and could detect some nervousness about it among their own constituents). It was the opposition leader who took the initiative. In March 1939, when war in Europe had become almost certain, Dr. Manion declared that Conservative policy would be "no conscription of Canadians to fight outside our borders in any war." King gratefully associated the government with this formula – and in the spring of 1939 he pulled one last rabbit out of his hat: the Royal Tour.

It is a spontaneous, inspired tribute – a moment of mass and individual exaltation. The tremendous throng is suddenly identified with the spirit of the monument that has just been unveiled. And in the words just spoken by the King, the very soul of the nation is here revealed.

Newsreel commentary on the unveiling of the Cenotaph
in Ottawa by King George VI, May 1939

King George VI and Queen Elizabeth were the first reigning monarchs ever to visit Canada, and in two months they were seen personally by two and a half million Canadians – almost a quarter of the population. The purpose was transparently to revive pro-British sentiment in Canada and that sense of identification with Canada's own past most strikingly displayed in the emotional scenes at the unveiling of the national war memorial in Ottawa. To a considerable extent it worked, even in French Canada. "By the smile of a Queen and the French words of a King, the English have conquered once more the cradle of New France," Omer Héroux noted crossly in *Le Devoir*, and it was largely (if only temporarily) true.

In Montreal, huge throngs of people lined the 23-mile parade route to cheer the British king and queen, and Mayor Camillien Houde, a lifelong enemy of British imperialism, was so moved that he gave the royal couple a warm personal welcome. When he accompanied them out onto the Windsor Hotel balcony overlooking Dominion Square, the crowd erupted into thunderous cheers and Houde told the King teasingly: "Listen, Your Majesty. Some of that applause is for you!" Soon after, the King conferred on Houde the title of Commander of the British Empire. The sheer astonishment of discovering that the English King and Queen spoke fluent French did more to calm French Canadian suspicion of Britain than years of reassurance offered by unilingual English Canadian politicians.

My two sisters and I were presented to Their Majesties at a reception up in the chalet on Mont Royal. We were all young girls, and we had to serve the royal table.

When I handed the Queen her cup of tea my hand was shaking so much I spilled some into the saucer. But if she noticed, she didn't let on. She turned to me and said in impeccable French: "*Vous êtes toutes tellement charmantes.*"

She is such a beautiful lady. Such blue, blue, blue eyes and

such a soft smile. I was surprised, though, to see the King, who
was smoking, casually deposit his cigarette butt into a teacup. He
was very human.

Marthe Handfield (née Houde),
daughter of Mayor Camillien Houde

As the "royal recruiting tour" proceeded westward, however, the size
and enthusiasm of the crowds dropped off steeply: despite the deeply felt
obligation to the dead, people in Ontario and the West remembered what
the last war had done to their families with a depth of emotion that French
Canadians could not share. The phenomenon was most marked in the
Prairie provinces, where many people were not of British origin, and
where those who were had paid the highest price of all for the last outburst
of pro-British military fervour. But even in small-town Ontario, although
the crowds came out to see the show, many of the people waving the flags
felt a deep sense of unease.

In the bright morning sunshine, at 10:15 Peter and I drove to
Paris High School. On our way up the hill, he said hopefully, "Will
the King and Queen be wearing a crown?"

"No," I said, "they don't always wear them." Obviously disappointed, he gazed up at me. Some of the luminosity was fading
from his grey eyes. For him a king was not a king without a golden
and bejewelled headpiece.

In front of the school, about 150 girls and boys, in their
Sunday best, were sitting and standing about in groups. The air
quivered with waves of excited talk and laughter. . . .

When the pupils had lined up for their march to the Junction,
Miss 'X' and Miss 'Y' asked me for a ride. On our way along
Capron Street I said lightly, "I suppose you two patriots are see-
thing with loyal anticipation."

"Not I," said Miss 'X' coldly. "Mark my words! A war is
coming. They want our boys to die for them and the Empire."

I was so astonished that I almost ran the car off the road. To
me, she had long been a symbol of the ultra-conventional.

"I guess," said Miss 'Y', "you won't be doing any wild cheering."

"Not much," said Miss 'X'.

Paris, Ontario, 7 June 1939, Donald A. Smith,
*At the Forks of the Grand*

But private reservations were smothered by public displays of patriotism, and the royal tour's effect was summed up by two men wearing Hitler and Mussolini masks who entertained the loyal crowds in Montreal: "Ach, Benito, ve haf been fooled," read the Fuhrer's placard. "Yes – and to think we believed that the Empire was crumbling," Mussolini's sign replied.

❖

King's desperate desire to avoid a choice between war and neutrality, with all its dangers for Canadian unity, led him to maintain his support for appeasement and conciliation even after Britain had effectively resigned itself to war. As late as July 1939, less than two months before the war began, he accepted an invitation to visit Germany.

In late August war in Eastern Europe became inevitable. The Soviet Union, having spent the preceding year in futile attempts to create a joint front with the British and the French to stop Hitler, signed a separate deal with Berlin. In the secret clauses, Hitler gave Stalin a free hand to re-annex most of the former territories of the Russian Empire that had been lost during the revolutionary turmoil of 1917-20 (Estonia, Latvia, Lithuania, parts of Finland and Romania, and the eastern third of Poland) in return for Soviet acquiescence in whatever Germany wished to do with the rest of Poland. The agreement neatly turned the tables on the Anglo-French ambition to embroil the Russians in a war with Germany from which they could remain aloof; now it would be Britain and France, at least for a while, that would have to stand alone against Hitler (unless they welshed on their guarantee to Poland).

But even after the Nazi-Soviet pact was signed, Mackenzie King kept the British guessing about his government's intentions if Britain declared war on Germany. The British High Commissioner in Ottawa reported that

Dr. Skelton, the Under-Secretary for External Affairs, "like the Prime Minister, felt it unwise to go to war for countries which the United Kingdom could not support effectively. His view was that Poland could be destroyed or overrun in a fortnight, and that Hitler could then sit back and profess his unwillingness to fight the Western powers." And that was exactly what happened.

For the Canadians who actually understood what was happening, especially in the Department of External Affairs, the choice was enormously difficult. They were honestly appalled at the nature of the fascist regimes, but they knew that the next great-power war would be simply a continuation of the last, and equally devoid of moral content. Most of them had once hoped that the League of Nations could change the dynamics of the international system enough to break this futile cycle of destruction, and almost all of them had now concluded that it had failed. Collective security would certainly have to be tried again eventually, for there seemed no other hope of breaking the cycle, but first there would be a terrible war.

None of them felt that it was Canada's national duty to die in the last ditch to defend the established ranking of the European great powers – nor, indeed, that Canada's military help was especially vital to Britain. The two sides in Europe seemed to be fairly evenly matched, and most people in 1939 expected the war to be a stalemate. But there was still the argument that Canada ought to participate in the war *just a little bit* in order to have a say in the design of the new international institutions whose creation would be the first task when the war ended. More importantly, there was the domestic political fact that Canada would be less divided by a cautious and limited entry into the war than by staying out entirely. Lester Pearson, still a quarter-century away from the prime ministership, combined the sensibility of the doomed fighter pilot of 1918 with the cynicism of the disillusioned junior diplomat of 1938 in his attitude to the coming war, but it can probably stand as representative of the ambivalence felt by most of his colleagues, and by most Canadians who knew what was really going on.

If [Britain] fights, it will only be in defence of her own imperial interests, defined by herself. Why should she expect any particular world support for that? . . . As a Canadian, having seen the disappearance of all post-war hopes of a new international order based on international cooperation ... largely because of England's negative ... policy, I am not going to be impressed if next year I am asked to fight because of Tanganyika or Gibraltar.

... But if I am tempted to become completely cynical and isolationist, I think of Hitler screeching into the microphone, Jewish women and children in ditches on the Polish border ... and then, whatever the British side may represent, the other does indeed stand for savagery and barbarism.

Lester Pearson to O. D. Skelton, November 1938

But it was Skelton who had the last word. One week before the war started, he wrote to Mackenzie King: "The first casualty of this war has been Canada's claim to control over her own destinies. If war comes to Poland and we take part, that war came as a consequence of commitments made by the Government of Great Britain, about which we were not in one iota consulted, and about which we were not given the slightest inkling of information in advance."

# Picture Credits

1 *The Battle of Sainte-Foy c.* 1854. Oil on canvas by Joseph Legaré (1795-1855). National Gallery of Canada, No. 18489

2 Monochrome watercolour by Thomas Davies, Capt.-Lieut. of the Royal Regiment of Artillery (1737-1812). National Gallery of Canada, No. 6270

3 Portrait miniature. Royal Ontario Museum, 78 EUR 38, 935.23.1

4 Woodcut by J. Walker. Public Archives of Canada, C-6046

5 Engraving by Edward Francis Burney (1760-1848). Public Archives of Canada, C-12124

6 Portrait miniature. Royal Ontario Museum, 78 CAN 175, 921.42.3

7 Public Archives of Canada, C-3297

8 Public Archives of Canada, C-37591

9 Public Archives of Canada

10 Public Archives of Canada

11 *Quebec Light Infantry*, 1839. Hand-coloured lithograph by Sir James Archibald Hope-Wallace (1785-1871). Public Archives of Canada, C-1680

12 *View of the Champ de Mars*, 1832, Montreal. Engraving, hand-coloured by R.A. Sproule. Public Archives of Canada, C-2640

13  Provincial Archives of British Columbia, Cat. No. 41613, Neg. No. B-7529

14  Provincial Archives of British Columbia, Cat. No. 81387, Neg. No. E-3113

15  Provincial Archives of British Columbia, Cat. No. 35260, Neg. No. G-57

16  National Library of Canada, NL 15347

17  National Library of Canada, NL 15346

18  *Canadian Illustrated News*, Vol. II, 23 July 1870, pg. 64, Public Archives of Canada, C-50336

19  National Archives of Canada, C-15282

20  Lithograph by A.H. Hider. Public Archives of Canada, C-47

21  Public Archives of Canada, C-27503

22  *World*, Toronto, 14 October 1899. National Library of Canada, L 2699

23  Public Archives of Canada, C-3477

24  Public Archives of Canada, C-24618

25  Public Archives of Canada, C-6399

26  Public Archives of Canada, C-6097

27  Public Archives of Canada, C-1868

28  Public Archives of Canada, C-22825

29  John A. Young, DND. Public Archives of Canada, PA-141315

30  City of Toronto Archives, James 816

31  City of Toronto Archives, James 724

32  Ltn. James R. Steele Collection, Memorial University of Newfoundland

33  Public Archives of St. John's

34  Ltn. James R. Steele Collection, Memorial University of Newfoundland

35  Public Archives of Canada, PA-4768

36  Public Archives of Canada, PA-24435

37  Imperial War Museum, Q-739

38  Public Archives of Canada, C-27496

39  Harry Edward Knobel. Public Archives of Canada, PA-335

40  Lizzie Caswall Smith, Gainsborough Studio. Public Archives of Canada, C-13222

41  City of Toronto Archives, James 727

42  Public Archives of Canada, PA-880

43  Public Archives of Canada, C-6859

44  *World*, Toronto, 6 June 1917, p. 6. National Library of Canada

45  National Library of Canada, C-133323

46  Public Archives of Canada, PA-2279

47  Capital Press. Public Archives of Canada, PA-110824

48  Imperial War Museum, Q-69033

**49** Department of National Defence, PMR 85 151
**50** Department of National Defence, PMR 85 149
**51** *Star*, Montreal, 25 September 1922
**52** Public Archives of Canada, C-9055

# Bibliography

All quotations in the book that are given without any bibliographical reference are taken from interviews conducted for the television series "Defence of Canada."

## Introduction

Preston, Richard A. "Two centuries in the shadow of Behemoth: The Effect on the Canadian Psyche." *International Journal*, Vol. 31, No. 3, Summer 1976.

Stacey, C.P. *The Military Problems of Canada.* Toronto: The Ryerson Press, 1940.

## Chapters One and Two

Codman, John. *Arnold's Expedition to Quebec.* New York: Macmillan and Co., 1902.

Craig, Gerald M. *The United States and Canada.* Boston: Harvard University Press, 1968.

Dearborn, Henry. *The Journal of Henry Dearborn: An Account of the War of 1775*. Cambridge: 1886.

Fergusson, C. Bruce. "The Expulsion of the Acadians." In *Canadian History before Confederation: Essays and Interpretations*. J.M. Bumstead, (ed.). Georgetown, Ontario: Irwin-Dorsey Ltd., 1979.

Hatch, Robert McConnell. *Thrust for Canada: The American Attempt on Quebec in 1775-1776*. Boston: Houghton Mifflin Co., 1979.

Lanctot, Gustave. *Le Canada et la Revolution Américaine*. Montreal: Librairie Beauchemin Ltée, 1965.

—*Les Canadiens Français et leurs voisins du sud: (Les relations du Canada avec les États-Unis)*. Montreal: Éditions Bernard Valiquette; Toronto: The Ryerson Press, 1941.

McNaught, Kenneth, and Ramsay Cook. *Canada and the United States: A Modern Study*. Toronto: Clarke, Irwin & Co., 1963.

Neatby, Hilda. *Quebec: The Revolutionary Age, 1760-1791*. Toronto: McClelland and Stewart (Canadian Centenary Series), 1966.

Rawlyk, George A. *Revolution Rejected, 1775-1776*. Scarborough, Ontario: Prentice-Hall (Canadian Historical Controversies), 1968.

Reynolds, Paul. *Guy Carleton: A Biography*. Toronto: Gage, 1980.

Smith, Justin H. *Our Struggle for the Fourteenth Colony*. Vols I and II. New York: The Knickerbocker Press, 1907.

Webster, Donald Blake, with Michael S. Cross and Irene Szylinger. *Georgian Canada: Conflict and Culture, 1745-1820*. Toronto: Royal Ontario Museum, 1984.

Wood, William. *The Father of British Canada: A Chronicle of Carleton*. Toronto: Glasgow, Brook & Co., 1920.

—*The War with the United States (Chronicles of Canada)*. Toronto: Glasgow, Brook & Co., 1920.

Wrong, George M. *Canada and the American Revolution: The Disruption of the First British Empire*. Toronto: Macmillan of Canada, 1935.

### Chapter Three

Allen, Robert S., with Bernard Pothier and Victor Suthren. *The Loyal Americans: The Military Role of the Loyalist Provincial Corps and their Settlement in British North America, 1775-1784*. Ottawa: National Museums of Canada, 1983.

Brown, Wallace, and Hereward Senior. *Victorious in Defeat: The Loyalists in Canada*. Toronto: Methuen Publications, 1984.

Craig, Gerald M. (ed.). *Early Travellers in the Canadas, 1791-1867*. Toronto: Macmillan of Canada, 1955.

Fellows, Jo-ann. *The Loyalist Myth in Canada*. The Canadian Historical Association, Historical Papers, 1971.

Moore, Christopher. *The Loyalists: Revolution, Exile, Settlement*. Toronto: Macmillan of Canada, 1984.

Skeoch, Alan. *United Empire Loyalists and the American Revolution*. Toronto: Grolier Ltd. (Focus on Canadian History Series), 1982.

Wallace, W. Stewart. *The United Empire Loyalists: A Chronicle of the Great Migration*. Toronto: Glasgow, Brook & Co., 1914.

### Chapter Four

Auchinleck, G. *A History of the War between Great Britain and the United States of America during the Years 1812, 1813, and 1814*. Toronto: Pendragon House, in association with Arms and Armour Press, 1972.

Berton, Pierre. *Flames Across the Border*. Toronto: McClelland and Stewart, 1981.

—*The Invasion of Canada, 1812-1813*. Toronto: McClelland and Stewart, 1980.

Bourne, Kenneth. *The Balance of Power in North America, 1815-1908*. Berkeley: University of California Press, 1976.

Brebner, John Bartlet. *North American Triangle: The Interplay of Canada, the United States and Great Britain*. New York: Columbia University Press, 1966.

Burt, A.L. *The United States, Great Britain and British North America: From the Revolution to the Establishment of Peace after the War of 1812*. Toronto: The Ryerson Press, 1940.

Edgar, Lady M. *General Brock: The Makers of Canada*. Toronto: G.N. Morang and Co., 1906.

Hitsman, J.M. *Sir George Prevost's Conduct of the Canadian War of 1812*. The Canadian Historical Association, Historical Papers, 1962.

—*The Incredible War of 1812: A Military History*. Toronto: University of Toronto Press, 1965.

Landon, Fred. *Western Ontario and the American Frontier*. Toronto: The Ryerson Press, 1941.

Peterson, Merrill D. *Thomas Jefferson and the New Nation*. New York: Oxford University Press, 1970.

Roy, R.H. "The Canadian Military Tradition." In *The Canadian Military*. Hector J. Massey (ed.). Toronto: Copp Clark, 1972.

Stanley, George F.G. *The War of 1812: The Land Operations*. Toronto: Macmillan of Canada, in collaboration with the National Museum of Man, 1983.

—*Canada's Soldiers: The Military History of an Unmilitary People*. Toronto: Macmillan of Canada, 1960.

Wood, William. *The War with the United States: A Chronicle of 1812*. Toronto: Glasgow, Brook & Co., 1922.

Zaslow, Morris. *The Defended Border: Upper Canada and the War of 1812.* Toronto: Macmillan of Canada, 1964.


### Chapter Five

Bergeron, Léandre. "The Metropolis Investigates." In *Canadian History before Confederation.* J.M. Bumstead (ed.). Georgetown, Ontario: Irwin-Dorsey Ltd., 1979.

Boyd, John. *Sir George-Etienne Cartier, Bart.: His Life and Times.* Toronto: Macmillan of Canada, 1914.

David, L.O. *Les Patriotes de 1837-1838.* Montreal: Jacques Frenette Éditeur Inc., 1981.

Fairley, Margaret. *The Selected Writings of William Lyon Mackenzie, 1824-1837.* Toronto: Oxford University Press, 1960.

Globensky, Maximilien. *La Rébellion de 1837 à Saint-Eustache.* Ottawa: 1883; reprinted, Ottawa: Éditions du Jour, 1974.

Groulx, Lionel. *Histoire du Canada Français, depuis la découverte.* Montreal: Ligue d'Action Nationale, 1952.

Guillet, Edwin C. *The Lives and Times of the Patriotes: An Account of the Rebellion in Upper Canada, 1837-1838.* Toronto: Thomas Nelson and Sons, 1938.

——*The Patriote Agitation in the United States, 1837-1842.* Toronto: Thomas Nelson and Sons, 1938.

——*You'll Never Die, John A.!* Toronto: Macmillan of Canada, 1967.

Lacour-Gayet, Robert. *Histoire du Canada.* Paris: Fayard, 1966.

Manning, Helen Taft. *The Revolt of French Canada, 1800-1835: A Chapter in the History of the British Commonwealth.* Toronto: Macmillan of Canada, 1962.

Moodie, Susanna. *Roughing it in the Bush.* Toronto: Bell and Cockburn, 1913; reprinted: McClelland & Stewart (New Canadian Library), 1989.

Ormsby, William. *Crisis in the Canadas, 1838-1839: The Grey Journals and Letters.* Toronto: Macmillan of Canada, 1964.

Rea, J.E. "William Lyon Mackenzie – Jacksonian?" In *Canadian History before Confederation.* J.M. Bumstead (ed.). Georgetown, Ontario: Irwin-Dorsey Ltd., 1979.

Reid, J.H. Stewart, and Kenneth McNaught. *Harry S. Crowe: A Sourcebook of Canadian History.* Toronto: Longmans, Green and Co., 1959.

Rumilly, Robert. *Histoire de Montréal*, Tome II. Montreal: Fidès, 1970.

Ryerson, Stanley B. "The Rebellion in Lower Canada, 1837: A National-Democratic Revolution." In *Canadian History before Confederation.* J.M. Bumstead (ed.). Georgetown, Ontario: Irwin-Dorsey Ltd., 1979.

Schull, Joseph. *Rebellion: The Rising in French Canada, 1837.* Toronto: Macmillan of Canada, 1971.

Senior, Elinor Kyte. *Redcoats and Patriotes: The Rebellions in Lower Canada, 1837-1838*. Stittsville: Canada's Wings Inc., with the National Museums of Canada, 1985.

Sweeny, Alistair. *George-Etienne Cartier: A Biography*. Toronto: McClelland and Stewart, 1976.

#### Chapter Six

A great deal of the research on the Pig War is from the original documents in the Public Record Office, London, which our researcher, Ian Cowan, tirelessly scoured for us.

Bourne, Kenneth. *The Balance of Power in North America, 1815-1908*. Berkeley: University of California Press, 1967.

Careless, J.M.S., and Robert Craig Brown, (eds.). *The Canadians, 1867-1967*. Toronto: Macmillan of Canada, 1968.

Craig, Gerald M. *The United States and Canada*. Cambridge, Mass.: Harvard University Press, 1968.

Creighton, Donald. *The Road to Confederation: The Emergence of Canada, 1863-1867*. Toronto: Macmillan of Canada, 1964.

Crook, D.P. *Diplomacy during the American Civil War*. New York: John Wiley & Sons, 1975.

Ganoe, William Addleman. *The History of the United States Army*. New York: D. Appleton Century Co., 1942.

Hitsman, J.M. *Safeguarding Canada, 1763-1871*. Toronto: University of Toronto Press, 1968.

Ireland, Willard E. *Pre-Confederation Defence Problems of the Pacific Colonies*. The Canadian Historical Association, Report and Papers, May 1941.

Luvaas, Jay. "General Sir Patrick MacDougall, the American Civil War and the Defence of Canada." The Canadian Historical Association, Report and Papers, 1962.

McCabe, James O. *The San Juan Water Boundary Question*. Toronto: University of Toronto Press, 1965.

Morton, W.L. *The Critical Years: The Union of British North America, 1857-1873*. Toronto: McClelland and Stewart, 1962.

Stacey, C.P. *Canada and the British Army, 1846-1871: A Study in the Practice of Responsible Government*. Toronto: University of Toronto Press, 1963.

Tunem, A. "Dispute over the San Juan Islands Water Boundary." *Washington Historical Quarterly*, 1962.

Waite, P.B. *The Life and Times of Confederation, 1864-1867: Politics, Newspapers and the Union of British North America*. Toronto: University of Toronto Press, 1962.

### Chapter Seven

Beal, Bob, and Rob McCleod. *Prairie Fire: The 1885 North-West Rebellion.*
    Edmonton: Hurtig Publishers Ltd., 1984.
De Bellefeuille, L. *Le Canada et les Zouaves Pontificaux.* Montreal, 1868.
Denison, George T. *Soldiering in Canada: Recollections and Experiences.* Toronto:
    G.N. Morang and Co., 1900.
Drolet, G.A. *Zouaviania, Étape de trente ans 1868-1898.* Montreal, 1898.
Chartier, Emile. *Zouaviania.* B.R.H., 1952.
Groulx, Lionel. *Nos Zouaves.* Action française, 1918
Morton, Desmond. *Ministers and Generals: Politics and the Canadian Militia,*
    *1868-1904.* Toronto: University of Toronto Press, 1970.
Rouleau, C.-E. *Les Zouaves Canadiens, À Rome et au Canada.* Quebec:
    Imprimerie Le Soleil, 1924.
—*Souvenirs de Voyage d'un Soldat de Pie IX.* Quebec, 1881.
Stanley, George. *The Birth of Western Canada: A History of the Riel Rebellion.*
    Toronto: McClelland and Stewart, 1985.
Woodcock, George. *Gabriel Dumont: The Métis Chief and His Lost World.*
    Edmonton: Hurtig Publishers Ltd., 1975.

### Chapter Eight

Bourassa, Henri. *Devant le tribunal de l'histoire: un plaidoyer en faveur des*
    *Canadiens qui ont condamné la guerre sud-africaine.* Montreal, 1903.
Brown, Robert Craig, and Ramsay Cook. "Canada and the New Imperialism."
    In *Canada 1896-1921: A Nation Transformed.* Toronto: McClelland and
    Stewart, 1974.
Diaries, 1899-1900, George R.D. Lyon. Public Archives of Canada (MG 30, E
    423). Corporal in "D" Company, 2nd Battalion, Royal Canadian Regiment.
Diary and Letters of John A. Perkins, 1899-1900. Public Archives of Canada
    (MG 29, E 93). Served with the 2nd Battalion, Royal Canadian Regiment.
Hopkins, J. Castell. *The Canadian Annual Review.* 1900, 1901, 1902. Toronto:
    Annual Review Publishing Co., 1901-1938. An invaluable source of
    information, it includes extracts of political speeches and quotes from
    newspapers, as well as contemporary statistics. It gives a sense of what
    people felt and thought about the time they were living in.
Kruger, Rayne. *Goodbye Dolly Gray: The Story of the Boer War.* London: Pan
    Books, 1959.
Leacock, Stephen. *Canada: The Foundations of its Future.* Montreal: House of
    Seagram (private printing), 1941.
Letters, 1899-1902, Frederick S. Lee. Public Archives of Canada (MG 30, E
    387). Lee also served with the 2nd Battalion (Special Service) of the Royal
    Canadian Regiment.

Marquis, T.G. *Canada's Sons on Kopje and Veldt: A Historical Account of the Canadian Contingents*. Toronto, Guelph, Brantford: The Canada's Sons Publishing Co., 1900.

McHarg, W.H. *From Quebec to Pretoria with the Royal Canadian Regiment*. Toronto: Briggs, 1902.

Mellish, Anne Elizabeth. *Our Boys under Fire, or Canadian Volunteers in South Africa*. Charlottetown: The Examiner Office, 1900.

Miller, Carman. "English Canadian Opposition to the South African War as Seen Through the Press." *Canadian Historical Review*, December 1974.

—*Canada and the Boer War: Canada's Visual History*. Montreal: National Film Board of Canada, with the National Museum of Man, 1976.

—*A Preliminary Analysis of the Socio-Economic Composition of Canada's South African War Contingents*. Ottawa: Carleton University Social History, 1975.

Morrison, E.W.B *With the Guns in South Africa*. Hamilton: Spectator Printing Co., 1901.

Morton, Desmond. *The Canadian General: Sir William Otter*. Toronto: Hakkert, 1974.

Penlington, Norman. *Canada and Imperialism, 1896-1899*. Toronto: University of Toronto Press, 1965.

Rumilly, Robert. *Henri Bourassa: la vie publique d'un grand Canadien*. Montreal: Éditions de l'Homme, 1953.

—*Histoire de la Province du Québec*, Tome IX. Montreal: Fidès, 1977.

—*Sir Wilfrid Laurier, Canadien*. Montreal: Fidès, 1942.

Schull, Joseph. *Laurier, the First Canadian*. Toronto: Macmillan of Canada, 1965.

Skelton, O.D. *The Life and Letters of Sir Wilfrid Laurier*. Vols. I and II. Toronto: Gundy, Oxford University Press, 1921; reprinted, McClelland and Stewart (Carleton Library Series), 1965.

Smith, Donald A. *At the Forks of the Grand*. Vol. 2. Paris, Ontario: Advance Printing, 1982.

Stacey, C.P., with Ken Bell. *One Hundred Years: The Royal Canadian Regiment, 1883-1983*. Toronto: Collier-Macmillan, 1983.

### Chapter Nine

Duncan, Sara Jeannette. *The Imperialist*. Toronto, 1904; reprinted, McClelland and Stewart (New Canadian Library Series), 1961.

Gooch, John. "Great Britain and the Defence of Canada, 1896-1914." In *The Journal of Imperial and Commonwealth History*, Vol III. May, 1975.

Harris, Stephen J. *Canadian Brass: The Making of a Professional Army, 1860-1939*. Toronto: University of Toronto Press, 1988.

Hopkins, J. Castell. *The Canadian Annual Review*. 1910, 1911, 1912, 1913. Toronto: Annual Review Publishing Co., 1901-1938.

Morton, Desmond. *A Military History of Canada*. Edmonton: Hurtig Publishers Ltd., 1985.

Phillips-Wolley, C. *The Canadian Naval Question*. Toronto, 1910.

Rumilly, Robert. *Henri Bourassa: la vie publique d'un grand Canadien*. Montreal: Éditions de l'Homme, 1953.

Tucker, G.N. *The Naval Service of Canada*. Ottawa: King's Printer, 1952.

### Chapter Ten

Bourassa, Henri. *Que devons-nous à l'Angleterre?* Montreal, 1915.

Boissonault, C.M. *Histoire politico-militaire des Canadiens-français*. Trois-Rivières: Éditions du Bien Public, 1967.

Borden, Henry. *Robert Laird Borden: His Memoirs*. Vols. 1 and 2. Toronto: Macmillan of Canada, 1938.

Brown, Robert Craig. *Robert Laird Borden: A Biography*. Vol. I, 1854-1914; Vol. 2, 1914-1937. Toronto: Macmillan of Canada, 1975.

Hopkins, J. Castell. *Canadian Annual Review*, 1914, 1915, 1916. Toronto: Annual Review Publishing Co., 1901-1938.

Wade, Mason. *The French Canadians, 1760-1967*. Toronto: Macmillan of Canada, 1968.

Much of the section on Gallipoli is based on research by Nancy Grenville of the Centre for Newfoundland Research at Memorial University, St. John's.

Cramm, Richard. *The First Five Hundred: A History of the First Newfoundland Regiment*. Albany, N.Y.: C.F. Williams and Son, 1916.

Gallishaw, John A. *Trenching at Gallipoli*. New York: A.L. Burt, 1916.

Lind, Francis Thomas. *The Letters of Mayo Lind* (to the *Daily News*). (Died 1916, Beaumont Hamel.) Memorial University Archives.

MacDonald, Ian. *W.S. Coaker and the Fisherman's Protective Union in Newfoundland Politics*. (Doctoral thesis.) London: University of London, 1971.

O'Brien, Pat. *The Newfoundland Patriotic Association and the Administration of the War Effort, 1914-1918*. (M.A. thesis.) St. John's: Memorial University, 1981.

Steele, Owen W. Diary of the Late Lieutenant Owen W. Steele of the First Newfoundland Regiment, October 3, 1914 - June 30, 1916. Memorial University Archives.

Tait, Major R.H. "With the Regiment at Gallipoli." *Veteran Magazine*, Vol. 1 (2), April 1921, 38-53.

*Their Name Liveth*. London: Commonwealth War Graves Commission, 1965.

### Chapter Eleven

Bird, William R. *And We Go On*. Toronto: Hunter-Rose Co., 1930.

—*Ghosts Have Warm Hands*. Toronto: Clarke, Irwin & Co., 1968.

Berger, Carl. "Conscription 1917." *Canadian Historical Readings*, No. 8. Toronto: University of Toronto Press.

Bishop, William A. *Winged Warfare*. Stanley M. Ulanoff, (ed.). Toronto: Totem Books, 1976.

Chaballe, Colonel Joseph. *Histoire de 22e Bataillon Canadien-Français. Tome I, 1914-1919*. Montreal: Les Éditions Chantecler Ltée., 1952.

Clint, Mabel B. *Our Bit: Memories of War Service by a Canadian Nursing Sister*. Montreal: Barwick, 1934.

Durocher, René. "Henri Bourassa, les éveques et la guerre de 1914 1918" *Communications Historiques*. La Societé Historique du Canada, 1971.

Ellis, Frank H. *Canada's Flying Heritage*. Toronto: University of Toronto Press, 1954.

English, John. *Borden: His Life and World*. Toronto: McGraw-Hill Ryerson, 1977.

Filteau, Gérard. *Le Québec, le Canada et la Guerre*. Montreal: L'Aurore, 1977.

Granatstein, J.L., and J.M. Hitsman. *Broken Promises: A History of Conscription in Canada*. Toronto: Oxford University Press, 1977.

Granatstein, J.L. "Limits of Loyalty: Enlistment in the Canadian Expeditionary Force." In *Limits of Loyalty*. Edgar Denton, (ed.). Waterloo: Wilfrid Laurier University Press, 1980.

—and R.D. Cuff (eds.). *War and Society in North America*. Toronto: Thomas Nelson and Sons, 1971.

Hamelin, Jean, and Jean Provencher. *Brève Histoire du Québec*. Montreal: Boréal Express, 1981.

McGregor, F.A. *The Fall and Rise of Mackenzie King, 1911-1919*. Toronto: Macmillan of Canada, 1962.

McKee, Alexander. *The Friendless Sky: The Story of Air Combat in World War I*. London: Souvenir Press, 1962.

Morton, Desmond. "The Limits of Loyalty: French Canadian Officers and the First World War." In *Limits of Loyalty*. Edgar Denton (ed.), Waterloo: Wilfrid Laurier University Press, 1980.

Murrow, Casey. *Henri Bourassa and French Canadian Nationalism: Opposition to Empire*. Montreal: Harvest House, 1968.

Talbot Papineau Letters. Public Archives of Canada.

Powers, Chubby. *A Party Politician: The Memoirs of Chubby Powers*. Norman Ward (ed.). Toronto: Macmillan of Canada, 1966.

Provencher, Jean. *Québec sous la loi des mesures de guerre, 1918*. Trois-Rivières: Boréal Express, 1971.

Pearson, L.B. *Mike: The Memoirs of the Right Honourable Lester B. Pearson*. Vol. I, 1897-1948. Toronto: University of Toronto Press, 1972.

Robertson, Heather. *A Terrible Beauty: The Art of Canada at War*. Toronto: James Lorimer and Co., in association with the Robert McLaughlin Gallery and the National Museums of Canada, 1971.

Sharpe, C.A. "Enlistment in the Canadian Expeditionary Force, 1914-1918: A Regional Analysis." *Journal of Canadian Studies*, No. 18, Winter 1983-84.

Skelton, O.D. *The Life and Letters of Sir Wilfrid Laurier*. Vols. 1 and II. Toronto: Gundy, Oxford University Press, 1921; reprinted, McClelland and Stewart (Carleton Library Series), 1965.

Smith, Donald A. *At the Forks of the Grand*. Vol. 2. Paris, Ontario: Advance, Printing, 1982.

Worthington, Larry. *Amid the Guns Below: The Story of the Canadian Corps, 1914-1919*. Toronto: McClelland and Stewart, 1965.

Underhill, F.H. "Canada and the Last War." In *Canada in Peace and War: Eight Studies in National Trends since 1914*. Chester Martin (ed.). Toronto: Oxford University Press, 1941.

Wilms, A.M. "Conscription 1917: A Brief for the Defence." *Canadian Historical Review*, 1956.

### Chapter Thirteen

Borden, Henry. *Robert Laird Borden: His Memoirs*. Vol. 2. Toronto: Macmillan of Canada, 1938.

Harris, Stephen J. *Canadian Brass: The Making of a Professional Army, 1860-1939*. Toronto: University of Toronto Press, 1988.

Hundevad, John. "A Saga of the North." *The Legionary*. March, April, May, July, August, September, October, 1935; and January, February, March, 1936.

Veatch, Richard. *Canada and the League of Nations*. Toronto: University of Toronto Press, 1975.

Walder, David. *The Chanak Affair*. London: Hutchison and Co., 1969.

Wise, S.F. *Canadian Airmen and the First World War: The Official History of the Royal Canadian Air Force*. Vol. I. Ottawa: University of Toronto Press, in co-operation with the Department of National Defence and the Canadian Government Publishing Centre, 1980.

Wood, Herbert Fairlie. "The Farthest North Campaign." *The Legionary*. September, 1962.

### Chapter Fourteen

Bothwell, R., and John English. *Dirty Work at the Crossroads: New Perspectives on the Riddell Incident*. Canadian Historical Association Report, 1972.

—and G.N. Hillmer. *The In-between Time: Canadian External Policy in the 1930s*. Toronto: Copp Clark, 1975.

Brown, J. Sutherland. *Defence Scheme Number One*. Sutherland Brown Papers, Douglas Library, Queen's University, Kingston.

*Confederation to 1949*. Canadian Historical Documents Series, Vol. III. Scarborough, Ontario: Prentice-Hall, 1966.

Dawson, R. MacGregor. *William Lyon Mackenzie King, 1874-1923*. Toronto: University of Toronto Press, 1958.

Eayrs, James. *In Defence of Canada: Vol. I: From the Great War to the Great Depression*. Toronto: University of Toronto Press, 1964.

—*In Defence of Canada: Vol. II: Appeasement and Rearmament*. Toronto: University of Toronto Press, 1965.

English, John, and J.O. Stubbs, (eds.). *Mackenzie King: Widening the Debate*. Toronto: Macmillan of Canada, 1978.

Granatstein, J.L., and R. Bothwell. "A Self-Evident National Duty – Canadian Foreign Policy, 1935-39." *Journal of Imperial and Commonwealth History*, 1975.

McNaught, Kenneth. *Canadian Foreign Policy and the Whig Interpretation, 1930-1936*. Canadian Historical Association Report, 1957.

Morton, Desmond. "Aid to the Civil Power: The Canadian Militia in Support of Social Order, 1867-1914." *Canadian Historical Review*, December 1970.

—"Aid to the Civil Power: Stratford, 1933." *Canadian Defence Quarterly*. Summer 1972.

Neatby, Hilda. *William Lyon Mackenzie King: Vol. II, 1924-32*. Toronto: University of Toronto Press, 1958.

—*William Lyon Mackenzie King: Vol. III, 1932-39*. Toronto: University of Toronto Press, 1963.

Norris, John. "The Vancouver Island Coal Miners, 1912-14: A Study of an Organizational Strike." *B.C. Studies*. Spring 1980.

Pariseau, Major J.J.B. *Disorder, Strikes and Disasters: Military Aid to the Civil Power in Canada, 1867-1933*. Ottawa: Directorate of History, National Defence Headquarters, 1973.

Pearson, L.B. *Mike: The Memoirs of the Right Honourable Lester B. Pearson. Vol. I, 1897-1948*. Toronto: University of Toronto Press, 1972.

Pickersgill, J.W. (ed.). *The William Lyon Mackenzie King Record. Vol. I. 1939-1944*. Toronto: University of Toronto Press, 1960.

Ritchie, Charles. *The Siren Years*. Toronto: Macmillan of Canada, 1974.

Roy, Captain Reginald H. "In Aid of Civil Power, 1877." *Canadian Army Journal*, 1953.

—"The Seaforths and the Strikers: Nanaimo, August 1913," *B.C. Studies*, 1973.

Stacey, C.P. *A Very Double Life*. Toronto: Macmillan of Canada, 1976.

Starowitz, Mark. "The Great Unfinished Task of Col. J. Sutherland Brown." In *Let Us Prey*, Robert Chodos and Rae Murphy, (eds.). Toronto: James Lorimer, 1971.

Taylor, Charles. *Six Journeys: A Canadian Pattern*. Toronto: House of Anansi, 1977.

Veatch, Richard. *Canada and the League of Nations*. Toronto: University of Toronto Press, 1975.

Acadia, 183
Acadians, 24-25, 34
Adams, Captain, 294-95
Adams, John, 26
Adams, John Quincy, 85-86
Adderley, C.B., *quoted*, 130
Africa, 115, 142, 202, 203, 326
African Light Infantry (French), 222
Ainslie, Thomas, *quoted*, 39
Air Force Act, 265
*Alabama* (raider), 125
Alaska, 85, 111, 129, 153
Alaska Boundary Dispute, 153, 159, 160-61, 173, 191
Albano, Italy, 138
Albatross D-V aircraft, 297
Alberta, 111, 211, 216, 276, 280

Alderson, Gen. Sir Edwin, 245
Algerian troops, 222
Alliances, 180-84 *passim*, 201-3, 295, 301, 304, 306-7, 325
Allison, J. Wesley, 226
Alsace region, 203
American army, 36, 38-53, 55, 74-86. *See also* United States Army
American Civil War, 124-25, 127, 131
American invasion of Canada, 315-23 *passim*
American Revolution, 23, 26-27, 29-53 *passim*, 65-66, 93, 117, 136, 139
Amiel, Barbara, *quoted*, 11, 130-31
Amiens, Battle of, 285-86

Anatolia, Turkey, 311
Ancaster, Ont., 82
Anderson, Capt. W.F., 298
Ankara, Turkey, 311
Annapolis Royal, 24
Annexation, 115-16, 120, 124, 127,
    130, 135-36, 191
Apsley, Lord Chancellor, 36
Archangel, Russia, 294, 296, 299
Archilocus, *quoted*, 310
Ardagh, Sir John, 154
Argentina, 184, 319
Arnold, Benedict, 41-52
Arnold, Hannah, 46
Arthabaska, Que., 150
Article 10, 308, 313, 325
Asia, 115, 142, 203
Asquith, Herbert, 178, 197, 252
Atholstan, Lord, 273
*At the Forks of the Grand, quoted*, 172,
    173, 209, 217-18, 221, 286
Aubrey (soldier), 286
Augsburg, Peace of, 26
Australia, 90, 108, 141, 172, 175,
    180, 197, 243, 270, 285, 290,
    302;
    Army, 228, 243
Austria, 26, 122, 233;
    Air force, 266;
    Empire, 185, 203, 204, 205-6
Austrian Succession, War of, 182,
    304

Baby, François, *quoted*, 35
Baghdad Railway, 204
Baker, Lt. J.F., 298
Banff, 206
Banks, Gen. N.P., 129
Barker, Maj. William G., 265-67
Batoche, Sask., 145
Baynes, Rear-Adm. Robert L., 120,
    122, 123
Beaujeu, Louis Liénard de, 51

Beaumont Hamel, Battle of, 228
Bédard, Pierre, 71
Belgium, 206, 233
Bell, George, 96
Belliveau, (soldier), 257
Belmont, S.A., 164
Bennett, Richard B., 254, 326, 327
Berlin, 194-95
Berlin, Ont., 248
Bermuda, 212
Bernhardi, Gen. Friedrich von,
    *quoted*, 202
Bethmann-Hollweg, Theobald von,
    207
Bethune, Rev. John, *quoted*, 81
Bierce, Ambrose, *quoted*, 180
Bird, Will, 257
Bishop, Billy, 267
Bismarck, Prince Otto von, 200
Black, Herman, 257
Black Hand society, 205
Blais, Michel, 51
Blanchet, François, 71
Boers, 158, 164, 166-69
Boer War, 141, 157-73, 175, 176,
    179, 199, 210, 219, 297
Bolsheviks, 283-84
Borden, Frederick, 176, 179, 187,
    189
Borden, Henry, *quoted*, 301
Borden, Robert, 187, 189, 191-99
    *passim*, 205, 209, 211, 213-14,
    224, 225, 229, 233, 237-38,
    240, 242, 246, 252, 257, 259,
    260, 262, 268, 269, 270, 272-79
    *passim*, 284, 285, 286-87, 296,
    298, 301-2, 303, 306, 308, 310,
    313
Boston, 30, 55, 154
Bouchette, Captain, 37
Bourassa, Henri, 140, 142, 157,
    161, 162-63, 189, 190, 198,
    199, 210, 252-58, 271, 275, 290

Bourassa, Napoléon, 140
Bourget, Bishop Ignace, 139, 140
*Boy's Own Annual*, 199
Brantford, Ont., 179
Briand, Bishop Jean-Olivier, 33-34,
    53, 63
British American Land Co., 125-26
British Columbia, 111, 113, 120-21,
    122, 130, 132, 153, 218, 239,
    316
British Empire, 13, 22, 25, 29, 67,
    89, 96, 107, 113, 114-15, 117,
    168, 177, 178, 184-85, 188,
    192, 200, 209-10, 217, 230,
    231, 261, 289, 296, 301, 310,
    311, 323, 329, 333
British Guiana, 152
British North America, 59, 65, 66,
    68, 69-70, 77-78, 86, 88, 113,
    114-18, 123, 124, 128, 130,
    136, 153
Brock, Irving, 73
Brock, Gen. Sir Isaac, 73-77
Brown, George, 126
Brown, Col. J. Sutherland "Buster,"
    315-317, 319-20, 323, 324
Brown, Maj.-Gen. Jacob, 84
Bruchési, Archbishop, 248
Brumowski, Captain, 265-66
Buchanan, James, 122, 123
Bulgaria, 233
Burgoyne, Gen. "Gentleman
    Johnny," 54
Burke, Sgt. Charles, 80
Burns, Gen. E.L.M. "Tommy," 255,
    256, 320
Business Profits Tax, 242
Butler, Benjamin F., 131
Byng, Gen. Sir Julian, 257-58

Cadet Corps, 175
Calgary, 216
California, 113

Cambodia, 26
Cambridge, Duke of, 147
Campbell, Col. Donald, 45
Campbell-Bannerman, Sir Henry,
    177
Camp Borden, Ont., 264-65
Camp Petawawa, Ont., 211
Canada:
    Air force, 263-67, 295, 298, 322,
        333
    Assembly, 126
    General Staff, 312, 317, 321
    House of Commons, 197
    Navy, 186, 187, 188, 189, 191,
        197-99, 333
    Senate, 198, 229
Canada East, 109, 126, 129. *See also*
    Lower Canada, Quebec
Canada West, 109, 115, 126, 129.
    *See also* Upper Canada, Ontario
Canadian Annual Review, *quoted*,
    239, 240
Canadian Army Medical Corps, 233
Canadian Corps, 245-47, 254-55,
    258, 268, 285;
    Heavy Artillery, 168, 267
Canadian Engineers, 294-95
Canadian Expeditionary Force
    (C.E.F), 160, 179-80, 212-13,
    225-26, 233, 235-37, 243, 244,
    250, 288, 317-18, 324, 333
Canadian Field Hospitals, 231, 234
*Canadian Military Gazette*, 160, 215
Canadian Mounted Rifles (C.M.R.),
    169
Canadian Pacific Railway, 153
Canadian Syren Party, 295
Canton, N.Y., 315
Cape Breton Island, 24, 322
Cape Colony, 158
Cape Town, 160, 164
Cardwell, Edward, 133
Cariboo gold rush, 121

Carleton, Gen. Guy, 1st Baron
    Dorchester, 27-28, 31-32, 36, 37-
    39, 42, 46, 47, 52, 54, 60, 63,
    64, 91
Caron, Abbé Ivanhoë, *quoted*, 51
Carroll, John, 223
Cartier, Georges-Étienne, 126, 127;
    *quoted*, 113-14
Cartierville, Que., 273
Casgrain, J.P.B., *quoted*, 313
Catholic Church, *see* Roman Catholic
    Church
CBC, 7, 10, 11
*Colonist* (Victoria), 277
Columbia River, 111, 125, 129
Commins, Sgt. James, *quoted*, 84
*Common Sense*, 47-48
Communist Party, 322
Concentration camps, 168
Concord, Mass., 30
Confederate Army, 125
Confederation, 125, 127, 128, 130,
    136, 137, 139, 141
Connaught, Duke of, 205, 206, 237
Conscription, 15, 236, 241-42, 260,
    262, 268-82 *passim*, 290-93, 299,
    317, 336
Conservative Party, 189, 191, 246,
    269, 276-77, 278, 310, 312,
    335-36;
    Ontario, 274
    Quebec, 272, 275
Constitutional Act (1791), 64
Continental Congress (U.S.), 30, 31,
    50, 52, 56-57
Courcelette, Battle of, 250
Coursol, C.J., 125
Covenant of the League, 307, 308,
    313, 327, 328, 331-32
Cowes, Eng., 205
Craig, Sir James, 71
Cree Indians, 144

Creelman, J.C., 246-47
Crimean Expeditionary Force, 118
Crimean War, 118
Cronje, Gen. Piet, 164, 167
Crysler's Farm, Battle of, 81-82
Cecil, Lord Robert, 306, 331
Ceylon, 227
Chabot, Mme Augustin, 35-36
Chamberlain, Joseph, 149-50, 158,
    160, 174-75, 176, 177, 188, 201
Chanak, Turkey, 311-12
Charles VI, 183
Charlottetown, 127
Château clique, 92, 93
Châteauguay, Battle of, 78-81, 87
Cheesbach, W.A., 325
Chénier, Dr. Jean-Olivier, 96-98
Chiang Kai-shek, 322
China, 322, 326
Chippawa, Ont., 84
Chlorine gas, 222
Choiseul, Duc de, 27
Cholera, 92
Churchill, Winston, 205; *quoted*,
    186, 192-93
*Citizen* (Ottawa), 168
Clark, Joe, 10
Clemenceau, Georges, 261, 287
Clint, Mabel B., *quoted*, 231, 234,
    235, 289
Cobourg Rifles, 104
Colborne, Sir John, 96-99
Cold War, 15, 186
Collective security, 306-8, 314, 325-
    32, 329-30, 331-32, 340
Collishaw, Maj. Raymond, 295, 297
*Colonial Advocate* (York), 101
Cuba, 37
Cullen, Corp. Walter, 285-86
Cullum, A.E., 223
Currie, Gen. Sir Arthur, 223-24,
    246, 258, 284

Curtis, Flight Sub-Lt. W.A., 263-64
Cutknife Hill, Battle of, 146
Cutlar, Lyman, 121, 134
Cycle Corps, 286

Dafoe, John W., 309, 330
*Daily News* (Toronto), 277
Dallas, Mr., 121
Dandurand, Raoul, 313
Dardanelles, 228, 311
Dauphin, Man., 266
Davidson, Sir Basil, 227, 228, 229-30
Davin, N.F., *quoted*, 131
Deane, Silas, *quoted*, 49
Dearborn, Capt. Henry, 43, 44
*Defence of Canada* (T.V.), 7, 8, 10
Defence Schemes, 323; Number 1, 316-17, 319-20, 323-24
De Gaulle, Charles, 183
Delaney, Mr., 144
Delaney, Mrs., 144
De la Rey's Tavern, 104
Delorme, Mr., 145
Democratic Party, 111
Denikin, General, 295
Denison, Col. T., 158-59
Deportation, 24-25, 35, 100
Derby, Lord, 117
D'Estaing, Admiral, 55
Destroyers, 192
Detroit, 74, 76, 91, 316
Devonport, Eng., 244
Devonshire, Duke of, 270
DH9 fighter aircraft, 298
Díaz, Porfirio, *quoted*, 110
Dill, Mr., 144
Dion, Wilfrid, 282
Disease, 48, 52, 92, 168, 228
Disraeli, Benjamin, *quoted*, 117
Doel's Brewery, 101
Doherty, Charles J., *quoted*, 303, 308

Dominion Police, 273-74, 281
Dorchester, Lord, *see* Carleton, Gen. Guy
Dorchester riding, 272, 277
Doric Club, 95
Douglas, Sir James, 121, 123, 125
*Dreadnought* (battleship), 187
Dreadnoughts, 188, 192-93, 205
Drummond, Gen. Sir Gordon, 83-84
Drummond-Arthabaska riding, 189
Dublin, 273
Duck Lake, Battle of, 146
Duff, Lyman, 279
Dullstroom, S.A., 168
Dumont, Gabriel, 145-46
Duncan, Sara Jeannette, *quoted*, 178-79
Dundonald, Earl of, 175
Dunlop, Dr. William "Tiger," 79
Durham, Lord, 106-8, 109, 114, 126
    Report, 107, 114
Dvina River, 294

Easter Rising (1916), 273
Eastern Front, 219, 284
Eastern Townships, Que., 60, 70, 272
Easton, Col. James, *quoted*, 39
Edmonton, 208, 215
Elba, 85
Elections:
    *1832*, 92
    *1834*, 92-93
    *1911*, 190-91
    *1917*, 276-78
    *1935*, 327, 329
Eleventh Brigade (Canadian), 29, 255, 256
Elgin, Lord, 114, 115-16, 117
Elizabeth (Queen Consort), 337-38
Elliott, Capt. William, 298
Ellis, Frank H., 264-65

*Enchantress* (yacht), 192

English Canadians, 14, 106-9, 115,
    126, 136-38, 140-43, 150-51,
    152, 170, 172, 176, 178, 179,
    185, 188, 189, 191, 196-200,
    208-11, 214, 215-16, 218, 237-
    42, 249, 254, 262, 268-69, 271,
    275, 278-79, 289-90, 291, 292,
    324, 328, 329, 334, 335, 336

Enlistment, *see* Volunteers

Entente, 202-3, 209

Esquimalt, B.C., 177, 188

Essex East riding, 332

*Essex Gazette* (Mass.), 29

Estonia, 339

Ethiopia, 326, 328, 329

Europe, 13, 68, 86, 180-81, 182,
    201, 209, 219, 290, 323-24,
    332, 339, 340

Evans, Mayor, 172

*Evening Telegram* (St. John's), *quoted*,
    230

*Everywoman's World*, 275

External Affairs, Dept. of, 178, 327,
    340


Fairchild, Alexander, 59

Falklands, 319

Family Compact, 87, 101

Fargo, N.D., 316

Fee, Maj. C.P., 298

*Fell* (ship), 39

Fenian raids, 128-29

Festubert, Battle of, 223-24

Feudalism, 28, 32

Fiala, Capt. Ritter von, 265-66

Fifth Canadian Division, 240, 243

Fiji Islands, 197

Fils de la Liberté, 95

Finland, 339

First Canadian Division, 213, 214,
    220, 223, 244, 246

First Contingent, 212, 214-15, 226

Fish, Hamilton, 131

Fisherman's Protective Union, 227

Fitzgibbon, Colonel, 105

Flanagan, Arthur, 171-72

Flanders, 270, 288, 290

Florida, 56, 122

*Florizel* (steamship), 228

Floud, Sir Francis, *quoted*, 332

Fokker D-VII fighter aircraft, 266-67

Folkestone, Eng., 215

Forbes, Sgt. R.J., 297

Forde, Colonel, 315

Fort Beauséjour, N.S., 24

Fort Garry, Man., 132

Fort Ticonderoga, N.Y., 41

Forty-ninth Parallel, 85, 111-13

47th Squadron (British), 295

Fourteenth Platoon (Canadian), 257

*Fourteen Points*, 287

Fourth Canadian Division, 240, 257

France, 22, 28, 33, 54, 55, 57, 119,
    122, 139, 142, 151, 180-86,
    201, 202, 203, 206, 209, 210,
    211, 212, 219, 220, 226, 233,
    234, 235, 236, 243, 244, 246,
    252, 253, 255, 261, 266, 268,
    270, 278, 290, 292, 305, 331,
    336, 339;
    Air force, 264;
    Army (troops), 28, 55, 63, 119,
    222, 260, 283, 284;
    Navy, 326;
    Policy, 27, 56-57, 60, 87-88,
    206-7

Franklin, Benjamin, 50, 58, 124

Franz Ferdinand (Archduke), 204,
    205

Fraser, A.D., 223

Free Trade, 114, 115, 190

French and Indian War, *see* Seven
    Years' War

French Canadians, 47, 48, 49-53, 54, 55, 59-65 *passim*, 70-72, 79, 86-87, 89-91, 106-7, 126, 135-43 *passim*, 150-52, 172, 179, 185, 190, 197, 199, 208-11, 214, 218, 249-54, 262, 268-72, 277, 290-93, 309, 311, 329, 333, 334, 336, 337
French Higher War College, 207
French Revolution, 61-62, 63, 65-66, 68, 86, 182
Frink, Mayor, *quoted*, 218
Frog Lake, Sask., 144, 145
Frost, Sarah, 60
Fuller, J.F.C., 243-44
Fur trade, 74

Gabourie, Mme, 35
Gallipoli peninsula, 228, 230-31, 234
Gallishaw, John, 228, 231-32
Galt, Alexander Tilloch, 125, 127
*Ganges* (battleship) 122
Garibaldi, Giuseppe, 139
Gas, 221-22, 223
Gatien, Lieutenant, 251
Gatling gun, 146
Gault, Capt. A. Hamilton, 219
Genêt, Edmond, *quoted*, 62
George III, 23, 29, 33, 62, 90
George V, 207, 228, 270
George VI, 336-38, 339
George family, 239
Gérard, Conrad-Alexandre, 56-57
German Canadians, 248-49
German Naval Law (1900), 186
Germany, 26, 123, 142, 182, 185, 186, 192, 194, 195, 201, 202, 203, 204-5, 206, 207, 236, 248, 261, 270, 285, 287, 325, 326, 332, 336, 339;
   Air Force, 263-64, 266-67;

   Army, 220, 222, 254, 255, 256, 284;
   Empire, 185;
   Navy, 187, 205, 261;
   Policy, 204-5, 206-7
Ghent, Treaty of, 85
Gibraltar, 183
Gilroy (soldier), 257
Girouard, Joseph, *quoted*, 99
Gladstone, William, 133
*Globe* (Toronto), 126, 160
*Globe and Mail* (Toronto), 208
Godega Aerodrome, 266
Gordon, Maj.-Gen. Charles "Chinese," 143
Gore, Colonel, 114
Goschen, Sir Edward, 207
Gosford, Lord, 93-94
Gould, Joseph, 105
Gowanlock, John, 144
Gowanlock, Theresa, 144
Graham, George, 317
Grand Pré, N.S., 24
Grand Trunk Railway, 126
Grant, Gen. Ulysses S., 131
Great Britain, 15, 57, 71, 86, 118, 119, 122, 137, 141, 142, 150, 151, 152, 182, 185, 186, 192, 201-3, 204, 207, 209, 233, 236, 241, 245, 261, 266, 272, 301, 328, 331, 339, 340;
   Admiralty, 192, 197;
   Army (troops), 31, 36, 38-39, 42, 43-45, 47, 54-55, 74-85 *passim*, 92, 96, 99-100, 118, 124-25, 128, 129, 149, 153-54, 168, 177, 207, 220, 285
   Colonial Office, 130, 160;
   Expeditionary Corps, 207;
   General Staff, 177, 178, 189, 191;
   House of Lords, 230;

Policy, 23, 24, 25, 28, 31, 33-34, 60, 70-71, 77, 90-91, 95, 114, 117-18, 122, 124-25, 127-28, 130, 137, 142-43, 149-50, 153-55, 178-79, 197, 204, 206, 207, 209, 299, 300-2, 340-41. *See also* Royal Air Force, Royal Flying Corps, Royal Navy

Great Lakes, 69, 70, 82, 85, 128-29, 153, 154

Greece, 8, 233, 311

Green, Arthur, 239

Grey, Lord Edward, 114, 117, 196

Groulx, Lionel, 252

Gueudecourt, Battle of, 228

Gulf of St. Lawrence, 152

Guyot, Yves, *quoted*, 202

Gwatkins, Gen. Sir Willoughby, 211, 235-36, 259

Habitants, 28, 32, 34, 51, 99

Haig, Sir Douglas, 257, 258

Haldimand, Frederick, 55, 60, 70

Halibut Treaty (1923), 312

Halifax, 55, 86, 133, 177, 188, 199

Hames, Clifford, 284

Hampton, Gen. Wade, 78-79, 80-81

Handfield, Marthe Houde, 337-38

Hankey, Maurice, 197

Harney, Gen. William S., 120, 121-23, 185

Harris, Mrs. John, 82-83

Havratil, Captain, 265-66

Head, Sir Francis, 102, 104

Hellyer, Paul, 321

Herbert, Gen. Ivor, 147, 149

Héroux, Omer, 337

Hey, William, 36

Hillsborough, Lord, 28

Hitler, Adolf, 331, 339, 340, 341

Hodd, Capt. R.M., 297

Hodgins, Colonel, 315

Holmes, John, *quoted*, 22

Hong Kong, 149

Hordliski, Lieutenant, 295

Hose, Comm. Walter, 321

Houde, Camillien, 337

Hubert, Bishop Charles-François, 63

Hudd, Leslie, 219, 220-21, 222, 258

Hudson Bay, 129

Hudson River, 54

Hudson's Bay Co., 111, 121, 132

Hughes, Garnet, 243

Hughes, Col. Sir Sam., 160, 199-200, 211-14, 220, 226, 242-47, 258, 268

Huguenots, 25

Hull, Gen. William, *quoted*, 72, 74, 76

Hume, Alex, 171-72

Hundevad, John, *quoted*, 295, 297, 299

Hutton, Gen. Edward, 159-60

Île-aux-Grues, 51

Île aux Noix, 52

Île d'Orléans, 35-36

Île Royale, *see* Cape Breton Island

Immigration, 88, 91, 92, 101, 110, 128, 136, 144, 172, 211, 217, 290

Imperial Conferences, 323; *1902*, 174; *1907*, 177; *1923*, 312

Imperial Council, 149

Imperial defence, 150, 176, 177-78, 186, 193-95, 197; Committee of (C.I.D.), 193-94, 195-96, 333; Conference (1909), 177-78

Imperial Federation League, 142, 150, 158

Imperial Munitions Board, 240

Imperial Reserve, 174-75
Imperial War Cabinet, 229, 238,
    260, 261, 262, 286, 301, 303
Imperial War Conferences, 238;
    *1918*, 302
India, 14, 115, 117, 238, 323
Indians, 29, 32, 69, 74, 76, 82, 144,
    145, 148
Industrial revolution, 201
Ireland, 88, 93, 128
Isolationism, 108, 309, 313, 327,
    328, 332, 334
Istanbul, 231, 311
Italy, 122, 123, 139-41, 185, 233,
    266, 305, 326, 327, 330, 331;
    Army, 283
Izard, Gen. George, 80

Jackson, Andrew, 122
Jameson, Anna, *quoted*, 118-19
Japan, 14, 150, 184, 185, 323, 326
Jefferson, John, 172, 173
Jefferson, Thomas, 69
Jellicoe, Admiral, 261
Jenkins (soldier), 257
Jews, 100
Johnson, Dr. Samuel, 29
Joint High Commission on Civil War
    claims, 133
Joint Naval and Military Committee,
    153
Jones, Judge, 104

Karelia, 295
Kemal, Mustafa (Ataturk), 311
Kerridge family, 239
Khartoum, 143
Khmer Rouge, 26
Kiel Canal, 205
King, William Lyon Mackenzie, 269,
    278, 309-11, 312, 313-14, 327,
    328, 329, 330, 332-33, 334

Kingsbridge, N.Y., 37
Kingston, Ont., 86, 132, 147
Kinmel, Wales, 317
Kipling, Rudyard, *quoted*, 151, 189,
    191
Kissinger, Henry, 310
Kitchener, Lord, 228
Kitchener, Ont., 248
Klondike gold rush, 153
Knill (soldier), 223
Knowles, Lt. J.M., 293
Kruger, Paul, 172
Kruger, Rayne, 166-67

Labelle riding, 162
Labour movement, 241
L'Acadie, *see* Nova Scotia
Lac-des-Deux-Montagnes, Que., 96
Lachine Canal, 100
Ladies Patriotic League, 218
Lafayette, Marquis de, 55, 57
La Fourche, Que., 79
Lake, Percy, 176
Lake Erie, 82, 154
Lake Michigan, 74
Lake Ontario, 60, 78, 86, 154
Lake Superior, 132
*La Liberté*, 272, 273
Lalumière, Elie, 273-74
Lang, Corporal, 256-57
Lansing, Robert, 302
*La Patrie*, 158
Lapointe, Arthur, 250, 251, 253-54,
    282-83, 291
Lapointe, Ernest, 330-31, *quoted*,
    328
Laprairie, Que., 89
*La Presse* (Montreal), 142
Larin, Napoleon, 223
Lartigue, Bishop Jean-Jacques, 95
Larue, Lt. Lucien, 165-66
Latvia, 339

Laurier, Sir Wilfrid, 145, 150, 151-52, 158, 159, 160-61, 163, 173, 175, 176, 179, 187-94 *passim*, 197, 199, 205, 209, 211, 214, 218, 269, 270-71, 273, 275, 277, 278-79, 309
Lavergne, Col. Armand, 271, 273
Law, Andrew Bonar, 237
Lawes, Captain, 44
Leach, Gen. E.P., 153-54
Leacock, Stephen, 150, 151, 335
League of Nations, 288, 302-9, 313-14, 325-26, 327, 329, 331-32, 340
Leavitt, Herb, 167
*Le Canadien, quoted*, 71
Leckie, Col. Jack, 297
*Le Devoir* (Montreal), 189, 275, 337
Lee-Enfield rifle, 220
Legge (soldier), 257
Lemnos, Greece, 231, 234-35
*Le Réveil*, 272
*Le Soleil*, 272
Lessard, Gen. F.L., 281
*Le Temps* (Paris), 208
*L'Événement* (Quebec City), 272, 281
Lewis gun, 295, 299
Lexington, Mass., 30
Liberal Party, 114, 150, 161, 191-92, 197-98, 227, 274, 276, 277, 278, 309, 321, 329;
Great Britain, 176, 177;
Ontario, 161, 162;
Quebec, 161, 191, 268-69, 271, 278, 309
Libya, 205, 206
Lithuania, 339
*Lives and Times of the Patriots, quoted*, 104, 105
Livingston, Robert R., 41
Livingston, William, *quoted*, 22

Lloyd George, David, 238, 252, 254, 258, 261, 284, 286, 302, 311, 312
London, 238
London, Ont., 106
*London Daily Mail, quoted*, 310
Long, Walter, 270
Longueuil, Que., 96
Lord Strathcona's Horse, 168, 297
Lorne (soldier), 231
Lorraine region, 203
Louis xiv, 90
Louis xv, 27
Louis xvi, 56
Louisiana Purchase, 111
Lower Canada, 60-63, 64, 70-72, 74, 90-100, 106, 107, 126;
Assembly, 71, 90, 92-94.
*See also* Quebec
Loyalists, 59-60, 61, 64, 65, 72, 87, 107
Ludendorff, Gen. Erich, 261, 285
Lundy's Lane, Battle of, 83-85
Lynn Canal, 153

Macaulay, Judge, 104
MacBrien, Gen. J.H., 321
MacDonald (soldier), 257
Macdonald, Sir John A., 100, 126, 127, 131, 133, 141, 143, 145, 147
Macdonell, Col. John, 76
Macedonia, 233
MacKenzie, Col. L.H., 298
Mackenzie, Sir William, 212
Mackenzie, William Lyon, 100-6, 114, 310
Mackenzie-Papineau Brigade, 143
MacMillan (soldier), 257
Macpherson, Capt. John, 42, 45
Madison, James, 66, 67-68

*Mail* (Toronto), 150
Maine, 82, 153, 154
Malaya, 197
Manchuria, 326
Manifest destiny, 66, 69
Manion, Dr. R.J., 335, 336
Manitoba, 15, 111, 132, 149
*Manitoba Free Press, quoted*, 141
Mann, Donald, 212
Marcle, Abraham, 82
Marsil, Tancrède, 272, 273
Martial law, 32, 282, 322-23
Martin, Paul, 331-32
Martinique, 27
Maselga, Russia, 298
Maseres, Francis, *quoted*, 34
Mason, Gen. James, 240-41
Massachusetts, 55, 154
Maus, Jairus, 220, 221, 224, 225
Mauser rifle, 166
McCrae, John, *quoted*, 288
McKenna, Reginald, 186
McLean, Judge, 104
McNaughton, Gen. Andrew, 267, 321
McPherson, Joe, 257
M'Dougall, Captain, 44
Medicine Hat, Alta., 153
Meighen, Arthur, 277, 309-10, 312
Meigs, Major, 44
Mentana, Battle of, 139
Mercier, Mr., 281
Mercier, Honoré, 142
*Mercury* (Quebec), *quoted*, 71, 95
Mesopotamia, 233
Métis, 132, 144, 145-46, 148
Mexico, 12, 110-11, 113, 297
Mexico City, 113
Michael, Sir John, 133
Michaud (soldier), 251, 253-54
Michigan, 82, 316

Michilimackinac, Mich., 74
Middleton, Sir Fred, 145
Mignault, Dr. Arthur, 214
Milan, Italy, 183
Miles, Gen. Nelson, 152
Military District No. 4 (Montreal), 320
Military Operations and Intelligence, Directorate of, 315, 319
Military Service Act, 277, 279-80, 281, 291
Military Voter's Act (1917), 276-77
Militia, 36, 42, 68, 73-74, 77-78, 87, 99-100, 102, 105, 106, 113, 119-20, 121, 123, 125, 126, 128, 133, 145, 146, 149, 151, 154, 159, 164, 166, 172, 176, 199, 200, 211-13, 243, 271, 317, 319, 321, 322;
  Act (1855), 118, 119-20;
  Active, 119, 146-49;
  American, 55, 74-76, 83;
  and National Defence, Dept. of, 246;
  French, 28, 31-32, 34, 42, 45, 49, 71, 74, 79;
  Sedentary, 119;
  Select, 79, 119
Minneapolis, 316
Minorca, 183
Minto, Lord, 158, 159, 160-61, 172-73
Mississauga Horse, 215
Mitchell, Lieutenant, 298
Modder River, S.A., 164, 165
Moltke, Gen. Helmuth von, 212; *quoted*, 206
Monk, F.D., 189, 193
Monroe Doctrine, 152, 175
Mons, France, 286
Montgomery, Janet Livingston, 37-38, 41, 45

Montgomery, Gen. Richard, 37-46
Montgomery's Tavern, York, 102, 105
Montreal, 23, 25, 36, 37, 38, 39-41, 46, 49, 51, 55, 63, 64, 70, 78, 79, 81, 86, 87, 91, 95-96, 115, 128, 140-41, 208, 215, 272, 273, 274, 277, 337, 339; Dominion Square, 337; Westmount, 277
*Montreal Gazette,* quoted, 67, 274
*Montreal Star,* quoted, 150, 215, 273, 274
Moodie, J.W.D., 102, 106
Moodie, Susannah, quoted, 102-3, 106
Morin, François, 51
Morin, Joseph, 51
Morris, Sir Edward, 227, 228-30
Morrison, Col. E.W.B., 168-70, 214-15
Morrison, Pvt. George, quoted, 38
Morton, Desmond, quoted, 283
Moscow, 68
Mount Royal Club, Montreal, 274
Mulock, William, 161, 162
Murmansk, 296, 299
Murray, Ivor, 223
Murray, Gen. James, 23-24, 25, 26, 27
Mussolini, 300, 326, 330, 331

Napanee, Ont., 200
Napierville, Que., 100
Naples, 183
Napoleon, 67-68, 85
Napoleonic Wars, 65, 68, 73, 85, 86, 182
National Film Board, 7, 11
National Defence, Dept. of, 321
*National Intelligencer,* quoted, 78
Nationalism, 16, 35, 68, 136, 150, 191, 199, 209, 333

Nationalist Party, 275
NATO, 8, 10-11
Naval Aid Bill (1912), 193-95, 197, 199, 329
Naval Crisis (1909), 186-89, 192, 205
Naval Service Act (1910), 199
Naval Service Bill, 188, 191
Nazi-Soviet pact, 339
Nelson, Adm. Horatio, 100
Nelson, Robert, 100
Netherlands, 8, 286
Neutrality, 8, 10-12, 68, 87, 96, 123, 178, 199, 206, 333, 335
Nevada, 111
New Brunswick, 60, 70, 123, 129, 130
Newcastle, Duke of, 122
Newcastle, Ont., 77
New England, 21, 60, 68, 72, 136, 316
Newfoundland, 55, 132, 183, 197, 226-30; Assembly, 229
Newfoundland Patriotic Assoc., 227-28, 229
New France, 21, 23, 28, 32, 57
New Guinea, 202
New Hampshire, 55
New Mexico, 111
New York, 54, 82
New York City, 60, 154
New Zealand, 90, 172, 180, 197, 241, 290; Army, 228
Niagara Falls, 61, 83
Niagara River, 74
Nicholas II (Russia), 205, 206, 260
Nicholson, Sir William, 196
Nielson, Erik, 11
Nile River, 143
Ninety-Two Resolutions, 92

Ninth U.S. Infantry, 121
*Niobe* (cruiser), 191
NORAD, 10
North America, 21, 23, 56, 68, 69,
  86, 96, 114, 119-20, 125, 127,
  128, 129, 136, 141, 154, 155
North Atlantic Treaty Organization,
  *see* NATO
North-West Mounted Police, 153
North-West Rebellion, *see* Riel
  rebellions
Northwest Territories, 131, 132
North York riding, 278
Norway, 8
Notre Dame Cathedral, Montreal,
  140
Nova Scotia, 24-25, 56, 58, 60, 70,
  129, 130, 131, 150
*Nova Scotia Royal Gazette, quoted,*
  67

O'Callaghan, Dr., 95
Ohio, 82
Olney, Robert, *quoted,* 152, 155
Ogdensburg, N.Y., 315
189th Battalion (Canadian), 250,
  254
Onega sector, Russia, 299
163rd Battalion (Canadian), 250
Ontario, 15, 88, 126, 130, 150, 252,
  274, 277, 279, 310, 338
Orange Free State, 158
Orangemen, 211
Oregon, 85, 111, 113, 122
Oregon Treaty, 20
Oshawa, Ont., 322
Ottawa, 86
Otter, Col. William D., 146, 164,
  166, 167
Ottoman Empire, 25
*Our Struggle for the Fourteenth
  Colony, quoted,* 52

Overseas Military Forces of Canada,
  Dept. for the, 146

Paardeberg, Battle of, 164-68
Paine, Tom, 47
Palmerston, Lord, 124, 131
Papal States, 139, 140
Papineau, Mrs., 293
Papineau, Louis-Joseph, 90, 92, 94-
  96, 99, 100, 114, 140, 161, 253
Papineau, Capt. Talbot M., 224, 252-
  53, 290, 293
Paris, 68, 208, 312
Paris, Ont., 171-72, 208-9, 217-18,
  338-39
Paris, Treaty of, 57, 183
Paris High School, Ont., 338-39
Paris Ministerial Assoc., 218
Paris Peace Conference (1919), 302
Pariseau, Maj. J.J.B., 148
Passchendaele, Battle of, 284
Patenaude, E.L., 269
Patriots, 90, 92, 94-100
Patterson, J.C., 149
Pearson, Geoffrey, 9
Pearson, Lester B. "Mike," 233-34,
  264, 284, 289, 340-41
Pelletier, Maj. Oscar, 166
Peltier, Capt. J.E., 165
Peninsular War (Spain), 85
Pentagon, 193
People's Party (Nfld.), 227, 229
Perkins, Albert, 167
Perley, Sir George, 246-47
Permanent Force (Canadian), 119,
  147-49, 177, 212, 321
*Petrel,* 134
Petrograd, 273, 296-97
Philadelphia, 130
Philip v, 183
Pickersgill, Jack, *quoted,* 334
Pig War, 121-23, 134

Pink, Col. R.C.M., 265
Pius IX, 139, 140
Plains of Abraham, 25, 90
Plattsburg, N.Y., 81
Plessis, Abbé Joseph-Octave, 63
Poil-aux-Pattes, *see* 163rd Battalion
Poincaré, Raymond, 206-7
Pointe-Lévis, Que., 51
Poland, 336, 339, 340, 341
Polk, James K., 111
Pontifical Zouaves, 138-39, 140
Population, 23, 57, 70, 91, 132,
    142, 157, 172, 215, 216, 218,
    290, 291
Port Dover, Ont., 82-83
Portland, Ore., 316
Portugal, 205
Power, Charles G. "Chubby," 281,
    309
Pratt, Art, 231-32
Près-de-Ville barricade, 45
Presquile harbour, Penn., 77
Prevost, Gen. Sir George, 71, 78
Prince Edward Island, 131, 132, 218
Princess Patricia's Canadian Light
    Infantry, 219, 318
Princip, Gavrilo, 204
Proclamation of 1763, 25-26, 27, 28
Proctor, Redfield, 153
Protestants, 26, 150
Provincial Corps of Light Infantry, 79
Puget Sound, 125

Quebec, 23, 28, 29, 31, 54, 57, 58,
    125, 126, 130, 139, 150, 153,
    164, 191, 193, 209, 214, 218,
    226, 252, 269, 271-74, 275,
    277, 278, 279, 280-82, 291;
    Act (1775), 28-30, 32-34, 63;
    Crisis (1970), 322-23
*Quebec Chronicle, quoted,* 272, 281

Quebec City, 25, 32, 34, 36, 41-47,
    48, 55, 64, 71, 78, 86, 87, 91,
    128, 129, 212, 227, 272, 273,
    281-82, 292, 324;
    Assault on, 42-47, 53;
    Lower Town, 42-43, 45, 46;
    Sault au Matelot (Sailor's Leap),
    43-44
*Quebec Gazette, quoted,* 90-91
Quebec South riding, 281
Queen Anne's War, *see* Spanish
    Succession, War of
Queenston Heights, Battle of, 74-77,
    87
Queen's University, 178, 300
Quinn, Mr., 144

Radford, Naomi, 216, 235, 247,
    248, 249, 268, 280
*Rainbow* (cruiser), 191
Rand district, S.A., 158, 159
Randolph, John, *quoted,* 69
Rasputin, 260
R.C.M.P., 273n.
Rebellions of 1837, 90-109, 114,
    126, 139
Reciprocity, 190-91;
    Agreement, 115, 125, 131.
    *See also* Free trade
Red Air Fleet, 297
Red River Expedition, 143
Red River Settlement, 132
Reformers, 100-1, 105, 126
Regina, 208
Registration, 241-42
Religion, 26, 28-33 *passim,* 52-53,
    60
Responsible government, 107-8, 114
Riall, Gen. Sir Phineas, 84
Richelieu River, 52
Richelieu Valley, 36

Riddell, Walter, 194-96, 329-31

Rideau Canal, 86, 128

Ridgeway, Ont., 129

Riel, Louis, 132, 145

Riel rebellions, 15, 143, 144-46, 164

Riots, 92, 118, 172, 277, 279, 281-82, 317

Roberts, Field Marshal Lord, 166-67, 199

Robinson, John Beverley, 76, 87, 104

Rodgers, Maj. George, 282

Rodier, Edouard, 92, 95

Roman Catholic Church, 15, 24, 25, 28-29, 30, 32-33, 52-53, 55, 62-63, 70, 95, 126, 138-39, 140, 141, 249-50, 270, 274

Roman Empire, 25

Romania, 339

Rome, 139, 140

Ross rifle, 220-21

Rouleau, Sgt. C.E., 138

Rousset, Col. François, 207

Rowell, Newton, 271

Roy, Capt. J.H., 250

Royal Air Force, 265, 295-96, 298, 333

Royal Canadian Air Force, 267, 321. *See also* Canada, Air Force

Royal Canadian Dragoons (R.C.D.), 169

Royal Canadian Navy, 321. *See also* Canada, Navy

Royal Canadian Regiment, 149, 164, 166, 167-68, 170, 172, 212, 318

Royal Colonial Institute, 192

Royal Engineers, 44

Royal Flying Corps, 264, 284

Royal Highland Emigrants, 42, 44

Royal Marines, 122

Royal Military College (Kingston, Ont.), 147

Royal Navy, 68, 70, 154, 177, 186-87, 189, 192, 195, 201, 209, 318

Royal Newfoundland Regiment, 228, 230, 231

Royal Tour (1939), 336-39

Royal 22$^{eme}$ Régiment, *see* 22nd Battalion

Rumpler observation aircraft, 266

Rupert's Land, 129, 131, 132

Rupprecht, (Prince), 257

Rush-Bagot Treaty, 85, 196

Russia, 118, 150, 185, 206, 236, 260, 283-84, 294-97, 298, 299, 300, 305;
Army, 283, 294, 295;
Policy, 206-7

Russian Revolution, 260, 273, 296, 299

Rutherford, Mabel, 210, 211


Sadler, Serres, 217

Saigon, 60

St-Anselme, Que., 277

St-Benoît, Que., 99

St. Catharines, Ont., 322

Saint-Charles, 96, 98

Saint-Denis, Que., 96, 113-14

Sainte-Foy, Que., 25

Sainte-Scholastique, Que., 99

Saint-Eustache, Que., 96-98

Saint-Jean, (St. John's), Que., 36, 38

Saint John, N.B., 60

St. John's, Nfld., 227, 228

St. John valley, 60

St. Lawrence River, 25, 42, 55, 60, 70, 79, 81, 86, 92, 129, 154, 316, 316

St. Paul, Minn., 316

St. Petersburg, 153, 296

St-Pierre-et-Miquelon, 152

Saint-Pierre de l'Île d'Orléans, 35-36
Saint-Pierre-de-Montmagny, Que., 51
Saint-Roche, Que., 46
Saint-Roche-des-Aulnaies, 51
Saint-Thomas, Que., 51
Saint-Vallier, Que., 35
Salaberry, Col. Charles-Michel de, 79-81
Salisbury, Lord, 320
Salisbury Plain, 219
Samoa, 202
San Francisco, 122
*San Jacinto* (warship), 124
San Juan Island, 120-23, 125, 129, 134, 185
Sarajevo, 204
Saratoga, N.Y., 54
Sardinia, 183
*Sardinian* (troopship), 164
Saskatchewan, 111, 129, 144-45, 276
Schools, 126, 150
Scott, Frederick George, 164
Scott, Col. Winfield, 76, 83-84, 87, 113, 122-23
Scout Bugle Band, 208
Sea Island, Georgia, 330
Seattle, Wash., 316
Second Canadian Division, 235, 244
Second Contingent, 214, 226
Second (Special Service) Battalion, 164
Segaja, Russia, 297
Seigneurs, 28, 32, 34, 51, 63, 64, 90
Selkirk, Man., 129
Senter, Dr., *quoted*, 47
Separatism, 136
Serbia, 205-6, 233
Seven Years' War, 23, 182
Sévigny, Albert, 272, 277
Sèvres, Treaty of (1918), 311
Seward, William, 124

Seychelles Islands, 227
Seymour, Horatio, 130
Shepherd, George, 172
Sherbrooke, Que., 277
Short, Major, 146
Simsbury Mines, 59
16th Canadian Infantry Battalion, 221, 297
67th Battery (Canadian), 294
Skelton, O.D., 178, 300, 327, 330, 340, 341
Sleigh, Col. B.W.A., *quoted*, 87
Smallpox, 48, 52
Smith, Donald A., *quoted*, 172, 173, 209, 217-18, 339
Smith, Goldwin, 170-71
Smith, Michael, *quoted*, 77
Smith-Dorrien, Gen. H.L., 168-69
Smuts, Gen. Jan Christiaan, 301, 304, 331
Somme, Battle of the, 245, 247, 254-56, 283, 285
Sons of Liberty, 95
Sophie (duchess of Hohenburg), 204
Sorel, Que., 38-39
Soroka, Russia, 294-95
South Africa, 13, 156, 157-59, 163, 180, 219, 323
South African War, *see* Boer War
Soviet Union, 14, 26, 326, 339. *See also* Russia
Spain, 8, 73, 86, 122, 153, 181-82, 183, 201; Republic of, 143
Spanish-American War, 153
Spanish Netherlands, 183
Spanish Succession, War of the, 23, 182, 183
Spokane, Wash., 316
Spry, Gen. Dan, 318, 322
Stevenson, (soldier), 257
Strachan, John, 105
Stratford, Ont., 322

Strathcona, Lord, 168
Strathmore, Alta., 216
Submarines, 192, 261
Sudan, 143, 203
Sulte, Benjamin, *quoted*, 80
Supreme Court of Canada, 279
Sweden, 14
Sydenham, Baron, *quoted*, 89
Syren Force (Canadian), 295, 296-97
Syria, 205

Taft, William Howard, 191
Tariffs, 191
Tarte, Israël, 158, 161, 162
Taschereau, Jean-Thomas, 71
Taxation, 77-78, 113, 241
Taylor, A.J.P., 205, 208
Texas, 111
3rd Brigade (Canadian), 223
Third Canadian Division, 240, 286
Thirteen Colonies, 26, 28, 29, 47, 54
Thirty Years' War, 181
Thomas, Gen. John, 52
Thompson, J.M., 256-57
Three Rivers, Que., 39
*Times* (London), 257; *quoted*, 128
Tintern, Ont., 144
Tobago, 58
Tokyo, 312
Toronto, 68, 149, 198-99, 215; Arena, 198; Military Institute, 158
*Toronto News*, 161
*Toronto Star*, 190
*Toronto Sun*, 150
*Toronto Telegram*, 276
Tory Party, *see* Conservative Party
Trades and Labour Congress, 242
Transvaal district, S.A., 158, 168, 272
Treaties, 183-84

*Trent* affair, 124
Trochu, Alta., 211
Trudeau, Pierre Elliott, 327
Tsaritsyn (Stalingrad), 297
Tulgas, Russia, 294
Turkey, 185, 228, 310, 311-12
Turner, George, 215-16, 254, 286
22nd Battalion (French Canadian), 214, 250, 251, 253-54, 283, 318
26th Reserve Corps (German) 222

Ukrainian Canadians 275-76
Union Party, 275, 277-78
United, States, 13, 14, 22, 26, 54, 57, 58, 59-60, 66, 67-68, 71, 86, 94, 96, 113, 115, 116, 117, 120, 124-25, 127, 129, 133, 135, 136, 142, 148, 150, 152, 153, 155, 173, 175, 180, 184, 185, 196, 209, 243, 261, 288, 289, 302, 318, 326;
  Army, 36, 121-22, 125, 130, 152, 285;
  Congress, 111, 127, 129-30, 287;
  Navy, 319;
  Policy, 82, 96, 126, 133-34, 152-53;
  Senate, 131, 309.
  *See also* Americans
Uplands Airport, Ottawa, 269
Upper Canada, 60, 64, 72-78, 82, 87-88, 90, 100-6, 126. *See also* Canada West, Ontario
Ursuline order, 25, 47
Utah, 111
Utrecht, Peace of, 183

Valcartier, Que., 212-13, 226
Valenciennes, France, 267
Vancouver, 208, 239
Vancouver Island, 120-21
Vandal, Baptiste, 145

Vansittart, Sir Robert, *quoted*, 331
Venezuela, 152, 153, 297
Vergennes, Comte de, 55-56, 57
Versailles, Treaty of, 303, 325, 326
Victoria (Queen), 149
Victoria, B.C., 121, 208, 239
*Victoria British Colonist, quoted*, 130
Victoria Cross, 267
*Victory* (man-of-war), 85
Vienna, Congress of, 183
Vimy Ridge, Battle of, 255-57, 258,
    259
Vine, John, 172
Vladivostok, 296
Voisin monoplane, 264
Volga River, 295-96
Voltaire, *quoted*, 27
Voltigeurs, *see* Provincial Corps of
    Light Infantry
Volunteers, 73-74, 96, 119, 122,
    139, 140, 160, 162, 163, 172,
    173, 211-12, 214-17, 226, 227-
    28, 236, 237, 239-41, 242-43,
    255, 259, 268, 291, 293, 297,
    312

Walpole, Sir Robert, 180
*War*, 7
Ward, Phebe, 59
War of 1812, 68, 74-88, 316
War Office (British), 153, 155, 235
Warsaw Pact, 9
Warren, Captain, 104
Wartime Elections Act (1917), 276
Washington, Gen. George, 41, 48,
    57
Washington (state), 111, 120-21
Washington, D.C., 68, 312
Washington, Treaty of, 133
Washington Naval Treaty, 318, 319
Waterloo, Que., 272
Waterloo, Battle of, 68

Watt, Ted, 210, 211
Weldie, Capt. Victor, 298
Wellington, Duke of, 73, 85
Westcott (soldier), 257
Western Front, 219-20, 228, 233-36,
    260-61, 265, 266, 284, 294, 297
West Indies, 58, 114
Westminster, Statute of (1931), 313
Westphalia, Treaty of, 183
Whig, *see* Liberal Party
Whitby, Grenville, 208-9
White Russians, 295, 296, 299
Wideman, Capt. Ludovick, 105
Wilhelm II, 286
Wilkinson, Gen. James, 79, 81
Williams, Jenkin, *quoted*, 35
Williscraft, Mr., 144
Willison, J.S., 161
Wilson, Woodrow, 287-88, 306,
    331; *quoted*, 7
Winnipeg, 208, 215, 242; General
    Strike (1919), 322
Wise, S.F., *quoted*, 298
Wolfe, Gen. James, 25
Wolseley, Gen. Garnet, 132, 143,
    154
Woman's Christian Temperance
    Union, 170-71
Women, 234, 238
Wood, William, *quoted*, 44-45
Wooster, Gen. David, 41, 47, 49
World War, First, 137, 180, 182,
    185, 208, 239, 243, 249-54,
    261, 283-88, 289, 290, 295,
    297, 300, 304, 305, 320, 325,
    335;
    Second, 137, 332
World wars, 180-85, 201, 238, 239,
    304-5, 307, 325

Yankee traders, 27
Yonge Street, 102, 105

York, 68, 78, 101, 104, 105. *See also* Toronto
York volunteers, 76
Ypres, Battle of, 220-23, 224, 245
Yugoslavia, 204

Yukon, 131, 153
Yukon Field Force, 153

Zeppelin, 38